BLACK HISTORY

MONTH
RESOURCE
BOOK

BLACK HISTORY

MONTH
RESOURCE
BOOK

MARY ELLEN SNODGRASS, EDITOR

Foreword by BERTHA CALLOWAY
–Director of the Great Plains Black Museum

 **Gale Research Inc.**

DETROIT • WASHINGTON D.C. • LONDON

Mary Ellen Snodgrass, *Editor*

Gale Research Inc. Staff

Carol DeKane Nagel, *Developmental Editor*
Jane Louise Hoehner, *Associate Developmental Editor*
Lawrence W. Baker, *Senior Developmental Editor*

Shanna P. Heilveil, *Production Assistant*
Evi Seoud, *Assistant Production Manager*
Mary Beth Trimper, *Production Director*

Terrence Glenn, *Graphic Designer*
Arthur Chartow, *Technical Design Services Manager*
Cynthia Baldwin, *Art Director*

 This book is printed on acid-free paper that meets the minimum requirements of American National Standard for Information Sciences—Permanence Paper for Printed Library Materials, ANSI Z39.48-1984.

 This book is printed on recycled paper that meets Environmental Protection Agency standards.

ISBN 0-8103-9151-1
Printed in the United States of America

Published simultaneously in the United Kingdom
by Gale Research International Limited
(An affiliated company of Gale Research Inc.)

I⟨T⟩P™

The trademark **ITP** is used under license.

To my muse, Leatrice Pearson, who has lived, taught, and reverenced black history

Contents

Foreword xiii

Preface xix

Art and Architecture

African-American Plaza...1

African-American Sculpture.......................................2

African Archaeology 2

African Art and Architecture.....................................4

African Homes 5

Black Art...6

Black Builders 7

Black Landmarks..8

A Caribbean Garden 10

Designer Mural...10

Moorish Architecture 11

Photo Map 12

Photo Tableaux of History 12

The Shotgun House 14

Arts and Crafts

African Animal Fair 15

African Cards..16

African Ornaments...17

All-Occasion Cards...18

Animal Movies..18

Batiking 19

Black History Desk Calendar 20

Bookmarks 20

Box Zoo...21

Camp Africa..22

Clasped Hands 23

Crafts Clinic 24

Crocheting a Bit of Africa..25

Crocodile Trains 25

Design America 26

Doll Displays...27

The Door to Awareness..28

Freedom Stamps 29

Gourdheads..30

Heritage Jubilee 30

Jointed Dolls...31

Maasai Pendants..32

New Games for Old..33

Origami Animals...34

Pieces of Africa 34

Puppet Show...35

Stained Glass Animals...36

Sweets to the Sweet...37

'Toon Time 38

T-shirt Factory 39

Biography

African Leaders...41

Bessie Smith 42

Bio-Flash...43

Black Autobiography and Biography 44

Black Award Winners...46

Black Hall of Fame 47

Black History Stamps..49

Frederick Douglass 49

Freedom Fighters 51
Hats Off to the Abolitionists 52
Martin Luther King, Jr. 53
Native African Biographies 55
Role-Playing History 57
Rosa Parks 58
Sally Hemings 59
Shaka, the Zulu King 60
Star of the Week 62
What's My Line? 63
William Lloyd Garrison 64
Words to Live By 65

Business and Advertising

African-American Entrepreneurs 69
African Money 71
Black Landmark Ad Campaign 71
The Black Middle Class 73
Business Incubator 74
The Economics of Slavery 75
Getting the Public's Attention 76

Cooking

African Dessert-a-thon 79
African Lentils 82
Cooking for Kwanzaa 86
Food Clinic 87
Jamaican Specialties 88
Soul Food 90

Dance

African Dance Styles 95
Black Dance Troupes 96
Caribana 97
Dance Workshop 98
Everybody Limbo! 98
Interpretive Dance 99
Jivin' to the Oldies 100
Josephine Baker 101
Sign Troupe 102

Tapping to Stardom 103
A Tribute to Judith Jamison 104

Genealogy

Alex Haley's Genealogy 107
The Family Tree 108
Photo History 109
Quilted History 110

Geography

An African Holiday 113
African Peoples 114
African Riches 115
An African Travel Guide 117
Africa's Great Rivers 118
The Atlantic Triangle 119
Bean Bag Toss 120
Black Educational Institutions 121
The Black Flavor of New Orleans 123
Caribbean Idyll 124
The Drifting Continents 126
Learning the Colors of Africa 127
Liberia 127
Life along the Nile 128
Life in a Kenyan Village 129
The Moors 130
Puzzle Me Africa 130
Safari 131
Simon Says 132
World Races 133

History

African and World Events 135
All Aboard! 136
Antislavery in England and the U.S. 137
Apartheid and the World 138
Atlanta-Bound 139
Black Heritage Trivia 140
Black History Bingo 144
Black History Calendar 145

Black History in Miniature 146
Black History Time Capsule 147
A Black History Time Line 147
Black Holidays 153
Black Indians 154
Black Military Parade 155
The Civil War 157
Colonialism 158
The Constitution and Black America 159
Courts and Racial Justice 160
Each One Teach One..........................161
The Emancipation Proclamation 162
Explorers of Africa 163
Filming Ancient Africa 164
George Washington's Will 165
Harlem: Black America's Home Town....167
The Ku Klux Klan 168
Library Scavenger Hunt 170
Matthew Henson 171
Report Writing 172
Slavery and the Caribbean................174
Slavery Diorama 175
What If?..177

Journalism

Africa in the News 179
African-Americans in the Media 180
African Heroes 180
Backing Police Efforts........................181
Black Cartoonists 182
Black History Month Newspaper 183
Black Media 183
Editorials from the Black Perspective....185
Editorials of J.C. Harris and H.W. Grady 186
Extra! Extra! 187
A Future in the Media........................188
Guest Columnist................................189
Honoring the Past 190
Lead Story Roundup 191
Race and Controversy........................192
Volunteers without Borders 193
Who's Writing News 194
You Are There....................................194

Language

Afrocentrism 197
Apartheid..198
Black English 199
Black History Glossary 200
Black Language Roundup....................202
Expatriates 205
Gullah 205
Hieroglyphics 206
Jump Rope Rhymes............................207
Kwanzaa Flash Cards..........................209
Language Pairs 210
New Names for Old 211
Sharing Words from Different Worlds....212
Translating Lyrics 214

Literature

African Authors 215
"Between the World and Me"..............216
Black Book Fair 219
Black History Book Collection............220
Black on White 220
Black Study Group..............................221
Books for Summer 224
Comparing Wisdom 225
"D.P."..226
Derek Walcott....................................227
Feminist Writers................................228
Freedom's Journal............................229
Gertrude Johnson Williams Award 231
The Latest in Books by Black Authors 231
Lyndon Johnson and the Black Panthers 232
Melville and Slavery..........................233
Militant Verse 235
Read, Read, Read 235
Reading the Black Female Writer 237
Steinbeck on American Racism..........239

Math

An African-American Profile................241

An African-American Theme Park 242
An African Museum 243
Census Comparisons 244
Counting in Swahili 245
Graphing Racial Data 246
The Migrant Scene 248
Schematic Drawings 249

Music

African Musical Instruments 251
African Music American Style 252
African Rhythm Band 254
Antiphonal Chant 255
Band Music 257
Black Music Videos 258
Choral Music 259
Dueling Pianos 260
A History of African-American Music 261
Joplin Expo 262
Motown 263
Music Workshop 265
Patois 265
Porgy and Bess 266
Rap Wrap-Up 267
Rhythm of Resistance 268
1776 269
Sing-along 270
Slavery and Negro Spirituals 271
Songs of Protest 272
We Shall Overcome 273
Work Songs 274

Religion and Ethics

Advice from Marian Wright Edelman 279
African Meditation Methods 280
"Amazing Grace" and the Slave Trade 281
Black Evangelism 282
Black Moses 283
Black Muslims 284
Quakers and the Underground Railroad 286
Religions of Africa 287

Religious Themes in Negro Spirituals 288
Things Fall Apart 289

Science

African and Caribbean Fruits and Spices 291
African Butterflies and Moths 292
African Habitats 293
African Healers 294
An African Window Garden 295
All That Glitters 296
Animal Express 297
Baobab: The Tree of Life 298
Brainstorming 300
Deadly Organisms 301
Early Humans in Africa 304
Elephant Lore 305
George Washington Carver, Inventor 306
Health Tips 308
Herbs, Tonics, Teas, and Cures 309
In the Rice Fields 311
Invent-O-Rama 312
The Palm Tree 314
Sickle Cell Anemia 315
Two-Feet, Four-Feet, Wings, Fins, Tail 317
Zoo's Who 317

Sewing and Fashion

Banner Bolster 321
Corn Rows 322
A Handful of Puppets 322
Kite Flags 323
Native Fashions 325
Proud Stitches 326

Sociology

African Culture in the Sea Islands 329
Black Excellence 330
The Black Experience 331
Black Pride Day 333
Black Social Doctrine 334

Black Towns 335
Black Women in the Third World 336
Famine in Ethiopia and Somalia 337
Human Relations Report Card 338
Maasai Seasons 339
Mr. Johnson 340
Out of Africa 341
Peoples of Africa 341
The Rights of the Child 342
Stayin' Alive 343
"Stop the Drugs" Campaign 345
Studying the Bones 346
Voting Patterns 347
Who Does the Work? 347

Speech and Drama

Action and Words 349
Africa's Liberation 351
At Home in Africa 352
Benjamin Franklin and Slavery 353
Black Philosophies 354
Black Sentiments 355
The Demands of Frederick Douglass 356
Dramatizing the Black Experience 357
Experiencing the Underground Railroad 359
First Day at School 360
Haiti Seeks Help 361
Joseph Cinque vs. the Slave Trade 361
Market Day 362
Mule Bone 363
Oral Interpretation 364
Playing the Part 365
Quoting Black Voices 366
Speaker's Bureau 367
Talk to Me 368
This Ol' Hat 369
Thomas Jefferson and Slavery 370

Sports

African-American Sports Maze 373
The Black Olympian 375
The Harlem Globetrotters 376
Hero to Hero 377
The Professional Black Athlete 378
Sports Clinic 379
Sports Debate 379
Sports on Film 380

Storytelling

An Aesop Recitation 383
African Story Swap 384
Encouraging the Storyteller 385
Griot for a Day 386
Rabbit Ears 387
Round-robin African Adventure 388
Tell-It-Yourself 389
Uncle Remus 390
Using the Storyboard 390

Writing

Black History Essay Contest 393
Black Mystery 394
Campaign Push 394
The *Clothilde* 395
Denouncing Slavery 396
Emblems of Africa 397
A Friend in Africa 398
A Letter of Application 399
Letter-Writing Campaign 399
Poetry Workshop 400
Slave Days 401
Words and Snapshots 402
Writing Epitaphs 403
Writing Genre 403

Appendix 405
◆ Books 405
◆ Articles 408
◆ Publishers 408
◆ Films and Videos 409
◆ Video Distributors 409
◆ Music Distributors 409
◆ Dance Ensembles 410
◆ Theater Companies 410

◆ Contents

◆ Software Packagers 410
◆ Computer Networks....................................411
◆ Supplies 411
◆ Resource Centers...412

Entry Index 413
Age/Grade Level Index................................419
Budget Index 427

Avenues to Excellence

By Bertha Calloway
Director of the Great Plains Black Museum, Omaha, Nebraska

 Changing oneself; playing many roles.

As a child I spent several years in west Denver, Colorado. Here was a community that included Russian Jews, Mexican Americans, and Italian Americans. Cultural diversity was a living, breathing reality of everyday life. But that cultural diversity stopped at the schoolhouse door. Inside the classroom there was scarcely a word about my African-American heritage or the ethnic heritages of my classmates. Of course it was impossible for the texts and teachers to completely ignore the existence of racial slavery in the United States, but we learned nothing about the life experiences of African Americans under slavery or of the positive achievements of African Americans. As an adult I have been able to do my part in correcting this shameful condition, but it has taken a great collective, cooperative effort of scholars, educators, activists, artists, and concerned parents to make an honest history of America's multicultural history a necessary element in the curriculum. That work is not finished; really it is not a job *to* finish but a timeless responsibility. The volume you have before you is designed to help us all meet that responsibility more effectively.

In 1946 I married and moved to Omaha, Nebraska. As my children progressed through the Omaha school system, I discovered that they were learning no more of their African-American heritage than I had learned as a youngster in Denver. With the help of Eugene Skinner, the first African American principal in the Omaha public school system, I developed programs to present in the schools to observe Negro History Week, the annual event initiated in 1925 by Carter G. Woodson that has evolved into Black History Month. The success of these programs motivated me to join a handful of other concerned community members to found in 1963 the Negro Historical Society of Omaha. For more than a decade we struggled to obtain funding, develop a collection, and procure a site for a museum. As a result of a successful grant application to the Bicentennial Commission, we were able in 1976 to move in to our current facility and open to the public as the Great Plains Historical Museum. Maintaining and developing our collection, preparing new exhibits, and providing programs for schools and community groups are our constant missions.

Our museum is an unimposing physical structure. It is an old red brick building that has gone through many changes and at one point even sat unoccupied since it was built early in this century. There are no marble arches, no courtyards with fountains and palm trees. What we do have, and what we must have to survive, is a direct, vital connection to the life of the African-American community in Omaha. We are, and must be, a community center, for it is our mission not only to preserve but to celebrate, teach, and contribute our little bit to the African-American heritage, which is a living, evolving stream of activity.

"Heritage" has always been a more appealing word to me than "history." A heritage is something you possess, something of value, something personal for which you are responsible. "History" can sound so remote and lifeless, finished and impersonal. Our mission is to put our energy and intellect to use to transform our "history" as African Americans into our "heritage."

If this history-as-heritage is a living presence built over generations by the struggle and achievement of countless persons famous as well as unrecorded, a living presence we add to and change as well as preserve, then it must be shared. It must be shared with African American boys and girls, who deserve to know of, and need to know of, the achievements and the hard-won victories of African Americans past and present. The accomplishments of Frederick Douglass, W.E.B. DuBois, and Ida B. Wells-Barnett can seem remote to young persons; we need to begin with things close and familiar—family history, the history of a neighborhood, local history. The materials in *Black History Month Resource Book* can help us all build that base of familiar history young people need.

Young people benefit if we concentrate on a heritage in which they participate. Youngsters should act, build, relive, narrate, orate, sing, dance. Here the ancient African proverb "Changing oneself; playing many roles" expresses a fundamental truth.

Michael Jackson and Michael Jordan are icons of the modern age, and a list of eminent African Americans in sports and entertainment would fill pages. But we should be wary of concentrating on the fame—and incomes—of these figures to the neglect of the breadth and diversity of African-American achievement. Opera is certainly an acquired taste, yet those of us who never develop that taste should be able and knowledgeable enough to honor African American opera stars. Marian Anderson led the way; Leontyne Price, Shirley Venett, Jessye Norman, and Kathleen Battle now thrill audiences across Europe and America. Their stories should be known. "Changing oneself; playing many roles."

The literary achievement of African Americans is common knowledge. Think of autobiographies, *Invisible Man, The Color Purple,* Langston Hughes. But the sheer volume of talent is amazing! Think of Toni Morrison, Gloria Naylor, Gwendolyn Brooks, Terry McMillan, Maya Angelou, Ann Petry, Zora Neale Hurston, Jamaica Kincaid. Think of Charles Johnson's *Middle Passage,* which won a National Book Award for fiction in 1990. Think of the new anthologies such as *Bearing Witness: Selections from African-American Autobiography in the Twentieth Century,* edited by Henry Louis Gates, Jr.

The line of eminent African American social scientists begins with DuBois. The facts of his life would amaze any student, and with selections of his works available in paperback and in libraries across America, there is no reason students should not be introduced to his works as well as his life. The dominant figure in the second generation of African American social scientists was E. Franklin Frazier, who studied the role of the black family in society. Kenneth Clark's studies on the psychological effects of racism contributed to the Supreme Court decision in *Brown* v. *Board of Education of Topeka* to desegregate schools, and his *Dark Ghetto* was one of the most thoughtful books of the 1960s. Today the works of William Julius Williams continue the tradition of commitment, scholarship, and independent thinking.

Cast your gaze where you will in the intellectual and cultural life of the nation, and there you will find African Americans of repute making their own contributions and building upon the foundations laid by their trailblazing predecessors. Students should know there are many avenues to excellence. "Changing oneself; playing many roles" applies again.

If the African American heritage is as dramatic, lively, and available as I believe, then it must also be shared with persons of every ethnic background. But in sharing our heritage we cannot be defensive or exclusive, for exclusion—"it's a black thing, you wouldn't understand"—runs counter to any understanding of how complicated any culture or heritage is. Members of every culture have their individual differences, and their personal likes and dislikes. Not every African American will have black-eyed peas on New Year's Day, and to draw a distinction between those who do and those who do not would be unfair. And there are also regional variations. Differences in climate, geography, and economy bring differences in diet and dress. Though this statement is undeniable, it bears repeating since perhaps we do not remember it often enough.

And, we know cultures change over time. Grandparents regret how many of the old ways have been forgotten or ignored; grandchildren resent how many of the old ways have been preserved. Sometimes cultural history can play tricks too. The banjo was invented in Africa and brought to the United States by slaves, but today scarcely any African Americans play the instrument; banjo-playing is now characteristic of white cultures. If we truly recognize individual differences, regional variations, and evolutionary changes, then exclusion—drawing barriers—should be beyond our powers as well as inconsistent with a genuine pride in our achievements.

Let us remember too that other people, whether the most recent immigrants or the most direct descendants of the Mayflower Pilgrims, need to know African-American history, need to know how much of contemporary American culture is the creation of African Americans. The history and heritage of African Americans is a fundamental element in the history of the United States. The plight of African Americans is intertwined with the issue of how the American ideal of equality has translated into reality, demonstrated in the evolution from slavery through legal segregation to discrimination. The moral meaning and the usefulness of history also depends upon the existence of heroic figures, examples of excellence, in the nation's history. The courage, the thirst for justice, the determination, the passion and eloquence of Douglass, Wells–Barnett, and Martin Luther King, Jr.—to name only three—set standards to which everyone should aspire. To deny any student the chance to know about them and to have the chance to aspire to achievements such as theirs is to morally impoverish American students—and history—beyond excuse.

The history and heritage of African Americans is not only a possession to share with others, it is a fundamental element in the history of the United States. I repeat, American history without the history of African Americans just isn't America's history. Examples of this truth are legion. Forty years ago the standard histories of the abolitionist movement said next to nothing of the black abolitionists; today such an approach is inconceivable. The American Revolution was once a military and political history dominated by the figures of George Washington, Thomas Jefferson, and John Adams and narrated with scarcely a mention of either the issue of slavery or the conduct of bondsmen in the Southern states. Now the body of contemporary scholarship, beginning with the publication in 1961 of Benjamin Quarles's *The Negro in the American Revolution,* makes this neglect impossible and forces responsible historians to view the Revolution in the South as a complicated three-sided conflict among Patriots, loyalists and British regulars, and bondsmen. In a similar fashion the history of the Western frontier has been transformed by the discovery of the black cowboys and buffalo soldiers. Even the history of the Civil War and Reconstruction has been transformed by the disclosure of the active part African Americans played in these decisive years. The contribution of African Americans to the Union army has gone beyond the history books and has touched the public in films such as *Glory*. And now we recognize the degree to which the destruction of slavery was the work of the slaves themselves.

In case after case the deeper, truer understanding of American history has depended on discovering the role of African Americans. Ask yourself this question: If forced to choose between a standard American history textbook written before the explosion of works in African American history, say for example Commager and Nevins, versus John Hope Franklin's *From Slavery to Freedom* as your source for understanding the true significance of America's past, which would you choose? I would pick *From Slavery to Freedom*. It is a paradox that proves my point: American history has been written that excludes African Americans, but the history of African Americans cannot exclude the history of America. Anyone who understands this will understand that the question of whether there should or should not be multicultural education is irrelevant. The history of the United States is inherently, inescapably multicultural.

Today multicultural education ignites passionate controversy. Of course, something can be done badly or done well, but if it is the principle that is at stake, then the conclusion is inevitable: the real history of the United States is multicultural. This means that a multicultural focus in February to meet the requirements of Black History Month is useful but not sufficient. The whole history curriculum has to be transformed. It is slightly ironic that where we used to hear that there weren't enough primary sources available to teach black history, now there is so much scholarship on African Americans it will crowd fundamental things out of the curriculum!

It is valuable to remember that it is less important what the textbooks say than what the students learn. Certainly texts must be accurate and balanced. Even then they comprise only a part of what is to be learned. The activities suggested in *Black History Month Resource Book* are another part of education, and an essential part. Let us not become fixated on the text, and ignore the education.

The image of the rainbow popularized by Jesse Jackson with the Rainbow Coalition appeals to me as a valuable image to express my sense of America's history. A rainbow has to have several colors; lacking that, there just isn't a rainbow. There may be rain drops, sunlight, refraction, but no rainbow. American history is multicultural; lacking that, there are names, dates, places, but no history. But even the image of the rainbow misses something, the necessary element of interaction. History is made by interaction—conflict (all too often) or cooperation. Individuals have to live with the consequences of what they have done and what has been done to them, but history is jointly made.

The heritage of African Americans—our collective and individual achievement—is an inescapable feature of any profound history of this nation. And the best way to introduce students to the African American heritage is by activity, by action. Open *Black History Month Resource Book* and read how to dramatize the pivotal episodes in the lives of eminent African Americans. Make Maasai pendants from dried beans and seeds and aquarium gravel. Have students research their family trees.

This volume is the work of many hands. It is in itself testimony to the revolution in Black studies that began in the 1960s that is today a rich and massive body of scholarship devoted to the history and culture of African Americans. Every day it grows; every day it finds more readers. *Black History Month Resource Book* will contribute to that continuing process. And as you—teacher, concerned parent, student—make use of that tremendous body of scholarship selected and employed by the contributors to this volume, stop to remember and celebrate this achievement.

Preface

If I were assigning typing exercises in celebration of Black History Month, I would choose two models:

The quick brown fox jumped over the incomplete textbook.
and
Now is the time for all good people to come to the aid of black history.

As I assembled ideas for this study and acknowledgment of Black History Month, too often from all over the country at every level of education and community outreach I heard the same reply: "Oh, we just invite a guest speaker or have our kids study the 'I Have a Dream Speech.'" This offhand dismissal of Black History Month as a passing holiday worthy of a short recitation and a few moments of interest in Martin Luther King, Jr., discounts the vast wealth of areas that could enrich and ennoble public education. If children—and adults—were learning the history of Africa, about Caribbean cuisine, art, and music, and the life stories of black inventors, military leaders, writers, and innovators, they would defeat the racism that divides Americans as surely as democracy smashed the Berlin Wall.

To hurry along the process of educating all races in the study of what black people have meant to history and their continuing contributions to the quality of human life, I sought ideas for *Black History Month Resource Book.* These suggestions, derived from books, plays, poems, sheet music, periodicals such as *Ebony, Emerge,* and *Jet,* compendia such as *Notable Black American Women, Encyclopedia of Southern Culture,* and *The African-American Almanac,* and a network of friends, colleagues, librarians, and strangers, have poured in—many in response to requests at library conferences and teacher conventions and printed in *Mensa Bulletin* and *Instructor* magazine—filling my in-box with enough material for many more volumes. The result is an accessible, useful work meant to be shared and discussed by educators, docents, museum directors, city officials, scout leaders, church school teachers, retirement home program leaders, music and historical societies, book clubs—in short, any group that attempts to improve humanistic knowledge, awareness, understanding, and appreciation.

Content

Black History Month Resource Book contains 333 entries organized into 22 chapters covering a variety of interests: art and architecture, arts and crafts, biography, business and advertising, cooking, dance, genealogy, geography, history, journalism, language, literature, math, music, religion and ethics, science, sewing and fashion, sociology, speech and drama, sports, storytelling, and writing. Under these headings appear suggestions for games, displays, contests, bulletin boards, programs, and individualized study and enjoyment. Each entry contains a descriptive heading and the name of the originator if the item came from an outside source. The entries list specific age/grade levels or audiences, such as classes, clubs, or gatherings that might benefit most from the activities. A general description of each topic is followed by a detailed procedure, budget, and sources. To suit the material to specific needs, I have included alternative applications for maximum benefit to organizers.

To assist the reader in locating items most appropriate to a particular group, *Black History Month Resource Book* includes three indexes: the first listing entries in alphabetical order, with separate headings for bulletin boards, contests, displays, and games; the second organized by age/grade level; and the third arranged by budget, with costs ranging from under $25 to more than $100. Appended to the text is a list of resources, including the books, periodicals, articles, films and videos, musical recordings, software packages, and organizations I found most helpful in compiling this work.

Acknowledgments

When the manuscript for *Black History Month Resource Book* was complete, it left my computer and passed into the capable hands of Carol Nagel, the Gale Research editor who whipped it into shape in record time. I thank Carol, acquisitions editor Amy Marcaccio, associate editor Jane Hoehner, copy editor Paulette Petrimoulx, proof reader Fran Locher Freiman, page and cover designer Terrence Glenn, and typesetter Marco Di Vita. Bert Calloway topped off the final copy with her splendid, inspiring introduction. Just as books take the cooperative effort of many people, race relations require some muscle and grunt work. I commend the efforts that have put *Black History Month Resource Book* on paper and into the hands of teachers, librarians, community leaders, and club program chairs who will finish the job—who will teach us all the importance of black heritage.

The editor and Gale Research Inc. welcome comments and suggestions for this and future editions of *Black History Month Resource Book*. Please contact:

Editor, *Black History Month Resource Book*
Gale Research Inc.
835 Penobscot Bldg.
Detroit, MI 48226
Telephone: (313)961-2242
Toll-free: (800)347-GALE
Fax: (313)961-6741

M.E.S.
May 3, 1993

Art and Architecture

African-American Plaza

Age/Grade Level or Audience: Civic groups.

Description: Plan an African-American commemorative plaza.

Procedure: Locate community planners, architects, sculptors, landscapers, and artists who can coordinate plans for a local plaza, garden, sign, mural, or boulevard dedicated to the accomplishments of African Americans.

Budget: $$$$$

Sources:

A field trip to centers of African-American pride, such as New Orleans, Louisiana; Harlem, New York; Atlanta, Georgia; Louisville, Kentucky; Africatown in Montgomery, Alabama; or other Afrocentric areas that might stimulate ideas for a local tribute to black contributions.

Cantor, George, *Historic Landmarks of Black America,* Gale, 1991.

Alternative Applications: Set aside a section of a local museum or civic hall to honor black citizens. Consider the following suggestions:

- ◆ Collect local paintings, photographs, sculpture, and framed awards to arrange in a display.
- ◆ Offer videotapes of singing groups, theatrical organizations, and other performances.
- ◆ Display handicrafts, for example, stained glass, ironwork, basketry, needlework, doll-making, carving, taxidermy, and publications, such as recipe collections and poetry albums.
- ◆ Provide plaques to explain how each citizen contributed to community life.
- ◆ Honor black veterans of all wars by listing names and awards.

◆ Stress the accomplishment of youth groups, for instance, junior police, Big Brothers and Big Sisters, scouts, and 4-H clubs.

 ## African-American Sculpture

Age/Grade Level or Audience: Middle school, high school, and college art classes; civic center and museum displays; art leagues.

Description: Study the work of Ed Hamilton, Cincinnati-born sculptor.

Procedure: Present the artistic works of Ed Hamilton on slides, magazine pictures, photographs, or posters. Discuss his most famous works: *Joe Louis, Booker T. Washington, Bush Warrior, Sun Goddess, Juju Man, Confinement Emerging, In Memory of Joseph Cinque,* and *Nile Mother.* Invite volunteers to present historical background in the form of handouts, brochures, oral commentary, or overhead projection.

Budget: $$

Sources:
Naylor, Colin, ed., *Contemporary Artists,* 3rd ed., St. James Press, 1989.
Estell, Kenneth, ed., *The African-American Almanac,* 6th ed., Gale, 1993.
Willis, Judy Marie, "Ed Hamilton: Molding History," *Upscale,* June/July 1992, pp. 54-55.

Alternative Applications: Invite art students to emulate Hamilton's search for an understanding of African influences by molding models of significant figures from black history or designs for memorials, monuments, or plaques. Encourage the inclusion of people of both sexes, such as Shaka Khan, Sheba, Mae Jemison, Charles Drew, Mari Evans, York, Pearl Bailey, Toussaint L'Ouverture, Lionel Hampton, or Judith Jamison.

 ## African Archaeology

Age/Grade Level or Audience: Middle school and high school history classes.

Description: Research early African civilizations and create a time line of great world events that place ancient African cultures in perspective.

Procedure: Have groups of students gather facts about African achievements and civilizations as these:

Great Zimbabwe	Axumites	Abu Simbel
Berbers	Bachwezi	Carthage
Nok	Kilwa	Changamire
Kongo	Songhay	Benin
Monomotapa	Kanem-Bornu	Kush
Darfur	Wadai	Oyo
Luba	Lunda	Lozi
Mali	Sheba	Library of Alexandria
Cheops' pyramid	Sphinx of Gizeh	Ewe

Place their findings chronologically alongside these artistic and architectural accomplishments:

Great Wall of China	Rosetta Stone	Chichen Itza
Taj Mahal	Stonehenge	Indian burial mounds
Suez Canal	Code of Hammurabi	Washington Monument
Easter Island	Leptis Magna	Roman Colosseum
Palace of Knossos	ancient Troy	Parthenon
Notre Dame Cathedral	Temple at Jerusalem	Great Buddha
Angkor Wat	Sancta Sophia	Tintagel Abbey
Colossus of Rhodes	Caernarvon	Camelot
Point Hope, Alaska	Olduvai Gorge	Mount Rushmore
Appian Way	Nintoku mounds	Anasazi pueblos
Eiffel Tower	Hadrian's Wall	Hanging Gardens of Babylon

Budget: $

Sources:

Brooks, Lester, *Great Civilizations of Ancient Africa,* Four Winds Press, 1971.

Chu, Daniel, and Elliott Skinner, *A Glorious Age in Africa: The Story of Three Great African Empires,* Doubleday, 1965.

Dobler, Lavinia, and William A. Brown, *Great Rulers of the African Past*, Doubleday, 1965.

Grun, Bernard, *The Timetables of History: A Horizontal Linkage of People and Events,* Simon & Schuster, 1991.

Joseph, Joan, *Black African Empires,* Watts, 1974.

Murphy, E. Jefferson, *Understanding Africa,* Crowell, 1978.

Murray, Jocelyn, ed., *Cultural Atlas of Africa,* Facts on File, 1989.

Trager, James, *The People's Chronology,* Henry Holt, 1992.

Alternative Applications: Have students create a hall display by placing dated information on a long horizontal scroll illustrating the development of various architectural structures such as these: post and lintel, ziggurat, pyramid, fortress temple, mosque, cone-topped buildings, and beehive style.

African Art and Architecture

Age/Grade Level or Audience: Middle school, high school, and college art classes; museums; art leagues.

Description: Study uniquely African art forms.

Procedure: Present a multimedia showing of African art forms, emphasizing these:

- Sub-Saharan sculpture, panels, screens, and woodcarvings
- Nok terra-cotta masks
- Ashanti brass castings
- Yoruba funereal art and shrine objects
- Nigerian stone carvings
- Poro masks and headdresses
- Ibo beadwork
- Zimbabwean stone buildings
- Congolese bronze work
- Sudanese jewelry

Also include utilitarian objects, for instance, baskets, wooden utensils and trays, woven fiber rugs and mats, ivory carvings, mud architecture, fetishes, pottery, ornamental swords, combs, mirrors, pipes, staffs, ornate musical instruments, leather goods, ironwork, and pyroengravings.

Budget: $$

Sources:
"Africa Adorned," *National Geographic,* November 1984.

Bassini, E., *Africa and the Renaissance: Art in Ivory,* Center for African Art, 1988.

Bomani, Asake, and Belvie Rooks, *African and Caribbean Artists in Paris,* Q.E.D. Press, 1992.

Bomani and Rooks, *Paris Connections: African American Artists in Paris,* Q.E.D. Press, 1992.

Decker, Andrew, "New York: Protecting Africa's Heritage," *ART News,* April 1991, pp. 63-65.

Leuzinger, Elsy, *The Art of Black Africa,* Rizzoli, 1977.

Murray, Jocelyn, ed., *Cultural Atlas of Africa,* Facts on File, 1989.

"Oasis of Art in the Sahara," *National Geographic,* August 1987.

"Stone Age Art of Tanzania," *National Geographic,* August 1983.

Willett, Frank, *African Art: An Introduction,* Thames & Hudson, 1971.

Alternative Applications: Invite an art expert to present a lecture, workshop, or slide program illustrating the connection between African art and

European artists Henri Matisse, Georges Braque, Amadeo Modigliani, and Pablo Picasso, each of whom was influenced by African styles and techniques.

African Homes

Age/Grade Level or Audience: Kindergarten and elementary school art classes; church and school groups; 4-H clubs; scout troops.

Description: Create a gallery of African homes.

Procedure: Have students work in groups to sketch various types of African houses, particularly these:

- ◆ Bemileke cluster houses with tall cone roofs made of grass
- ◆ Mousgoum mud cone houses molded of mud and stones and marked with vertical lines to channel the rain
- ◆ Malian village compounds, including round-top houses for the extended family, granaries, and walls
- ◆ Nuba linked houses, which feature red clay walls, pointed cone roofs, and pig and goat houses
- ◆ Asante steep thatched wood-frame houses joined in a circle and linked by mud walls
- ◆ Somolo multistory mud roofs and central granary and grinding room
- ◆ Zulu semispherical framework houses covered with grass mats and arranged in a ring protected by a woven twig fence
- ◆ Yoruba courtyard houses with carved posts, thatched roofs around the outer rooms, and open central court
- ◆ Caribbean balcony houses with an African flair

Have students draw people in the houses. Encourage the use of crayons, washable paints, and markers available in multicultural skin tones of sepia, burnt sienna, mahogany, tan, peach, olive, bronze, terra cotta, tawny, and beige.

Budget: $$

Sources:
"Colors of the Caribbean," *House Beautiful,* December 1985, pp. 74-79.
Morris, Jan, "Island Vernacular," *House and Garden,* November 1985, pp. 206-211.
Murray, Jocelyn, ed., *Cultural Atlas of Africa,* Fact on File, 1989.
Saitoti, Tepilit Ole, *Maasai,* Abradale Press, 1980.

Alternative Applications: Have volunteers imagine a day in the life of the residents of these homes. Decide who performs what chores, including tending animals; collecting firewood; cooking; preserving food; gathering herbs, fruits, and berries; gardening; protecting the family; washing clothes; baby-sitting; teaching young children; making clothes, baskets, and utensils; and hunting for fresh meat. Ask volunteers to describe how idle time is spent, such as in singing, drumming, or playing a flute; weaving; making pottery and jewelry; and storytelling.

Black Art

Originator: Charles L. Blockson.

Age/Grade Level or Audience: Middle school and high school art and humanities classes; civic clubs.

Description: Analyze and discuss works by major black artists from all parts of the world, particularly Africa and the Caribbean.

Procedure: Display slides, books, prints, and films of black art and architecture, featuring the work of these:

- architects Paul R. Williams, Vertner Woodson Tandy, John Anderson Lankfor, and Norma Merrick Sklarek
- art satirists Palmer Hayden and Archibald Motley
- collagist Romare Bearden
- illustrator Brian Pinkney
- landscape artists Adele Chilton Gaillard and Lois Mailou Jones
- lithographers Ugo Mochi, Elizabeth Catlett, Grafton T. Brown, Camille Billops, and James Wells
- muralists Jacob Lawrence, Robert S. Duncanson, and Charles Alston
- painters William E. Scott, Charles White, Alma Woodsey Thomas, Emilio Cruz, Malvin Gray Johnson, Phoebe Beasley, Georg Olden, Sam Gilliam, Claude Clark, Charles Searles, Cheri Zamba, David Butler, Minnie Evans, Clementine Hunter, Tshibumba Kanda-Matulu, Gwendolyn Knight, Alma Thomas, Allan Rohan Crite, Edward Mitchell Bannister, Elazier Corter, William Henry Johnson, Frederick Brown, Bob Thompson, and Henry Ossawa Tanner
- photographers Gordon Parks, James VanDerZee, Lorna Simpson, and John W. Mosley
- portrait artists Thomas Blackshear, Higgins Bond, Jerry Pinkney, Hyppolite, Philomé Obin, Rigaud Benoit, Joshua Johnston, and Castera Brazile
- sculptors Geraldine McCullough, Meta Warrick Fuller, Richard Barthé, Sokari Douglas Camp, S. J. Akpan, Kane Kwei, Selma Hortense Burke, Eddie Dixon, Marion Perkins, Elizabeth Catlett, Barbara Chase-Riboud, Mae Howard Jackson, Elizabeth Prophet, and Richard Hunt

Consider highlighting the works of a few notable black artists, particularly:

- ◆ Augusta Savage, New York sculptor whose *Lift Every Voice and Sing* was exhibited at the 1939 New York World's Fair
- ◆ Jacob Lawrence, creator of series of paintings on Frederick Douglass and Harriet Tubman
- ◆ Henry Ossawa Tanner's *Raising of Lazarus*
- ◆ vigorous primitive paintings of William H. Johnson, a Paris expatriate who gained fame two decades after his death
- ◆ Edmonia Lewis's *Death of Cleopatra* and a bust of Henry Wadsworth Longfellow, which stands in the Harvard University Library

Determine themes and techniques that separate black art from works by other races, as is evident in Savage's use of the Negro National Anthem for a title.

Budget: $$$

Sources:

Bomani, Asake, and Belvie Rooks, *African and Caribbean Artists in Paris,* Q.E.D. Press, 1992.

Bomani and Rooks, *Paris Connections: African American Artists in Paris,* Q.E.D. Press, 1992.

Brown, Christie, "Look at the Eyes! They Evoke a Serpent," *Forbes,* September 14, 1992, pp. 512-524.

Estell, Kenneth, ed., *The African-American Almanac,* 6th ed., Gale, 1993.

Hughes, Robert, "Return from Alienation," *Time,* August 31, 1992, pp. 65-66.

Naylor, Colin, ed., *Contemporary Artists,* 3rd ed., St. James Press, 1989.

Wilson, Charles Reagan, and William Ferris, eds., *Encyclopedia of Southern Culture,* University of North Carolina Press, 1989.

Alternative Applications: Set up a children's workshop to encourage imitation of black art styles and media. Consider the following outlets for youth art: a sidewalk chalk drawing contest; a group mural; experiments in mosaic made from paper, colored sand, or aquarium rock; papier mâché masks; weaving and macramé workshops; and clay reproductions of ceremonial pottery.

Black Builders

Originator: Marjorie Roberts, teacher, Scottsdale, Arizona.

Age/Grade Level or Audience: Elementary and middle school history classes.

Description: Explore the role black Americans had in building America's historic monuments.

Procedure: Present drawings, pamphlets, travel guides, and other examples of historic residences, gardens, orchards, wells, piers, barns, granaries, businesses, churches, graveyards, and monuments which were built by slave labor. Include these:

- ◆ Thomas Jefferson's Monticello, Charlottesville, Virginia
- ◆ Farmington Mansion, Louisville, Kentucky
- ◆ Slave Market, Charleston, South Carolina
- ◆ Tryon's Palace, Tryon, North Carolina
- ◆ George Washington's Mount Vernon in Virginia
- ◆ historic sections of the levee along the Mississippi River
- ◆ the antebellum mansions of Louisiana, Mississippi, Georgia, and South Carolina, such as Drayton Hall, Boone Plantation, Kinsley Plantation, and Fairvue Farm.
- ◆ Caribbean mansions and sugar mills, including Sweet Bottom, Sally's Fancy, Bonne Esperance, and Parasol on St. Croix

Budget: $$

Sources:

Travel guides from the Automobile Association of America (AAA) or state travel bureaus, such as "A Closer Look: Louisville's African American Historic and Cultural Guide" from the Louisville Convention and Visitors Bureau.

Cantor, George, *Historic Landmarks of Black America,* Gale, 1991.

Estell, Kenneth, ed., *The African-American Almanac,* 6th ed., Gale, 1993.

Alternative Applications: Discuss the labor-intensive job of brick-making, which was done by hand by African slaves, including women, the elderly, and children. Ask a volunteer to describe the process and note the demands this job placed on workers as they paved whole cities, courtyards, and harbors. Present variations in the process that resulted from using the raw materials of a given area, such as red clay of the Southern Piedmont and gray clay and clam and mussel shells along the eastern U.S. shore. Note that slave-made bricks and cobbles are now collectors' items.

 ## Black Landmarks

Age/Grade Level or Audience: Middle school, high school, and college art, architecture, and African-American studies classes; travel clubs; museums.

Description: Organize a display featuring buildings and monuments significant to black history in the United States.

Procedure: Using posters, postcards, art prints, drawings, photographs, and other media, create a display of architectural sites that highlight black history, such as these:

◆ Slave Market, Middleton Plantation, Drayton Hall, and Catfish Row, Charleston, South Carolina
◆ Black regimental headquarters, Fort Huachuca, Arizona
◆ Home of Frederick Douglass, Cedar Hill, Washington, D.C.
◆ Dexter Avenue Baptist Church, Montgomery, Alabama
◆ Reconstructed plantation, Stone Mountain, Georgia
◆ Home of Louis Armstrong, Long Island, New York
◆ Charles L. Blockson Afro-American Collection, Temple University, Philadelphia, Pennsylvania
◆ Levi Coffin House, an Underground Railroad station, Fountain City, Indiana
◆ African Meeting House, Boston, Massachusetts
◆ Home of Scott Joplin, St. Louis, Missouri
◆ Boley Historic District, Boley, Oklahoma
◆ Fairvue-Isaac Franklin Plantation, Sumner County, Tennessee
◆ Tallman House, an Underground Railroad station, Janesville, Wisconsin
◆ Jackson Square, New Orleans, Louisiana
◆ Cotton Club, Harlem, New York
◆ Gettysburg National Cemetery, Gettysburg, Pennsylvania
◆ Ford Theater, Washington, D.C.
◆ Jamestown, Williamsburg, and Harpers Ferry, Virginia
◆ Appomattox Courthouse, Appomattox, Virginia
◆ Underground Railroad Museum, Nebraska City, Nebraska
◆ Africatown, Mobile, Alabama
◆ Afro-American Historical and Cultural Museum, Philadelphia, Pennsylvania
◆ National Museum of African Art, Smithsonian Institution, Washington, D.C.
◆ Museum of National Center for Afro-American Artists, Roxbury, Massachusetts
◆ Schomburg Center for Research in Black Culture, New York Public Library, New York, New York

Budget: $$$

Sources:
Reference works, including encyclopedias, art histories, and travel guides.
Cantor, George, *Historic Landmarks of Black America,* Gale, 1991.
Gebhard, David, and Robert A. Winter, *A Guide to Architecture in Los Angeles and Southern California,* Peregrine Smith, 1977.
Walker Art Center (Minneapolis), *Naives and Visionaries,* Dutton, 1974.

Alternative Applications:
Using slides, posters, postcards, art books, and other media, demonstrate the purpose and meaning of the Watts Towers to the black community in Los Angeles. Explain how Simon Rodia (1875-1965) built its spires from crushed glass, rock, and other found materials. Lead a discussion on the significance of art created by ordinary people. List artistic components, particularly bits of quartz, aluminum cans, driftwood, wrought iron, and other recycled construc-

tion materials, suitable for cementing into a wall, corner marker, monument, or welcome sign. Present suggestions for a community beautification project similar to the Watts Towers to a civic or garden club, chamber of commerce, or city council.

 A Caribbean Garden

Age/Grade Level or Audience: Kindergarten and elementary art classes.

Description: Design and draw a Caribbean garden.

Procedure: Have students study pictures of native Caribbean plants, such as frangipani, breadfruit, passion fruit, banana and lime trees, lilies, bougainvillea, oleander, hibiscus, bamboo, royal palms, guava, ginger, orchids, tuberose, dusty miller, jade vine, mahogany and casuarina trees, whitewood, sea grape, anthurium, vanilla, allspice, flamingo flower, pineapple, and bay trees. Have one group of students draw a scene from a park depicting the colors and shapes of Caribbean flora. Have another group sketch in colorful native birds, particularly pelicans, herons, parrots, and parakeets.

Budget: $

Sources:
Dodge, Bertha, *Quests for Spices and New Worlds,* Anchor Books, 1988.
Isles of the Caribbean, National Geographic Society, 1980.
Rosengarten, Frederick, *The Book of Spices,* Livingston Publishing, 1969.

Alternative Applications: Bring to class some of the most fragrant substances harvested in the Caribbean. Blindfold volunteers and have them identify the aromas of coffee, bay leaf, banana, vanilla, cinnamon, ginger, lime, allspice, and pineapple.

 Designer Mural

Age/Grade Level or Audience: Civic, church, community, and school groups; 4-H clubs; scout troops; garden clubs; neighborhood beautification committees.

Description: Create a designer mural to brighten a neighborhood.

Procedure: Have volunteers lay out a design featuring accomplishments of

African-Americans from the arrival of the first slave to the present. Arrange scenarios in chronological order, for example, beginning with the arrival of the first slaves at Jamestown and advancing through the Emancipation Proclamation to the civil rights sit-ins and marches of the 1950s and 1960s up to the present day. Use bright colors to emphasize diversity and creativity.

Budget: $$$

Sources:

Estell, Kenneth, ed., *The African-American Almanac,* 6th ed., Gale, 1993.

Grun, Bernard, *The Timetables of History: A Horizontal Linkage of People and Events,* Simon & Schuster, 1991.

Hornsby, Alton, Jr., *Chronology of African-American History: Significant Events and People from 1619 to the Present,* Gale, 1991.

Alternative Applications: Select a volunteer per day to draw in a segment of the mural until it is completed. Suggest that each volunteer pick one person or event that portrays a particular aspect of black history, such as these: women's rights; the Harlem Renaissance; black Olympic medalists or popular athletes; the founding of influential black colleges or universities; achievements in film, television, literature, dance, and stage; and the struggle to secure voting rights.

Moorish Architecture

Age/Grade Level or Audience: College art and architecture classes; adult travel clubs.

Description: Present an overview of the world's most famous Moorish architecture.

Procedure: Organize a slide show, series of drawings, photographs, or other depictions of Moorish art and architecture, which spread throughout southern Europe from 711 to 1400 A.D. Point out details that set it apart from other styles. Feature buildings such as the Alhambra in Spain and palaces in Venice.

Budget: $$$

Sources:

Kunjufu, Jawanza, *Lessons from History: A Celebration of Blackness,* African American Images, 1987.

Lane-Poole, Stanley, *Moors in Spain,* Khayats, 1967.

Alternative Applications: Have students draft details from Moorish architecture alongside the delineations of other styles, such as Egyptian, Celtic, Mayan, Aztec, Greek, Ionic, Doric, Corinthian, Gothic, Romanesque, and modern.

 ## Photo Map

Age/Grade Level or Audience: All ages.

Description: Organize a photo history of African-American life in a city, county, or state.

Procedure: Highlight an oversized map with detailed views of architectural or historical landmarks significant to African-American history. Have volunteers provide pictures that document community growth, such as homes, churches, factories, historical streets, auditoriums, cemeteries, monuments, theaters, sports centers or teams, singing groups, dancers, sculptors, artists, inventors, civil rights leaders, schools, and other memorable people and places.

Budget: $$$

Sources:
Local historical societies, public libraries, travel bureaus, and chambers of commerce.
Cantor, George, *Historic Landmarks of Black America,* Gale, 1991.
Ki-Zerbo, Joseph, "Oral Tradition as a Historical Source," *UNESCO Courier,* April 1990, pp. 43-46.

Alternative Applications: Videotape a tour of an area, detailing the achievements of African-Americans. Photograph still shots, processions, religious celebrations, holidays, and other significant events. Provide voice-over and background music to complete the montage. Display at museums, street fairs, libraries, schools, or public meetings. Offer the videos for sale. Collect similar creative efforts from other areas.

 ## Photo Tableaux of History

Age/Grade Level or Audience: Photography classes and clubs; drama classes; civic gatherings; church and school ethnic fairs; Black History Month celebrations.

Description: Reenact significant historical events to photograph or videotape.

Procedure: Recreate scenes from African-American history using a variety of participants, settings, costumes, and props. Photograph the tableaux as a lasting record of the group's effort. Place finished photos in an album alongside explanations of the events. Consider these important historical moments:

◆ The arrival of twenty black slaves on an unnamed ship in Jamestown, Virginia.

◆ In November 1786, black worshippers led by Richard Allen and Absalom Jones boycotted St. George's Methodist Episcopal Church in Philadelphia, Pennsylvania, rather than be segregated in a separate gallery.

◆ On August 21, 1831, Nat Turner led seventy confederates on a rampage that terrified slave owners with the dangers of a general revolt of all slaves.

◆ The summer of 1865 brought Jubilee, the freeing of the slaves, which spread gradually across the United States.

◆ Booker T. Washington delivered his "Atlanta Compromise" speech in Atlanta, Georgia, on September 18, 1895, to encourage social accommodation of free blacks.

◆ In 1906, W. E. B. Du Bois organized the Niagara Movement at Harpers Ferry, Virginia, a drive that evolved into the National Association for the Advancement of Colored People (NAACP).

◆ The black migrations from southern plantations to northern industry, beginning in 1910 and continuing into the 1940s.

◆ On May 17, 1954, Chief Justice of the Supreme Court Earl Warren announced to Thurgood Marshall, adviser to the NAACP, and all of America that the court voted unanimously to end the policy of "separate but equal" in public schools.

◆ From the courage of one dissenting seamstress, Rosa Parks, on December 1, 1955, black bus patrons in Montgomery, Alabama, launched a 381-day boycott, giving rise to a new leader, Martin Luther King, Jr.

◆ On September 25, 1957, one thousand troops entered Little Rock, Arkansas, to enforce the federal order to integrate schools by escorting nine black teenagers into Central High School.

◆ On April 4, 1968, the nation mourned the assassination of Martin Luther King, Jr., at the Lorraine Motel in Memphis, Tennessee. Five days later, two hundred thousand mourners accompanied a mule-drawn wagon bearing the coffin through Atlanta to King's grave.

Budget: $$$$

Sources:

Bennett, Lerone, "Ten Most Dramatic Events in African-American History," *Ebony*, February 1992, pp. 107-116.

Hornsby, Alton, Jr., *Chronology of African-American History: Significant Events and People from 1619 to the Present*, Gale, 1991.

Trager, James, *The People's Chronology*, Henry Holt, 1992.

Alternative Applications: Collect candid shots of farmers, migrant

workers, vendors, street workers, carpenters, cooks, fishers, iron workers, weavers, seamstresses, performers, doctors, lawyers, educators, ministers, families, mothers and babies, worshippers, and funerals, weddings, graduations, and festivals. Use photos or videotape in a gallery display or as studies for sculptors, muralists, painters, or commercial artists.

 ## The Shotgun House

Age/Grade Level or Audience: All ages.

Description: Present a floor plan and description of the shotgun house.

Procedure: Using drawings, posters, or overhead projection, detail the architectural style of the shotgun house, symbolic of black southern lifestyle. Depict the typical arrangement of three rooms in a row, a door at each end, and the gable end facing the street. Discuss the expedience of its arrangement, especially as it applies to heating and cooling. Explain why these buildings are common to the Caribbean, New Orleans, Louisiana, and Charleston, South Carolina.

Budget: $$

Sources:

Vlach, John Michael, *The Afro-American Tradition in Decorative Arts,* University of Georgia Press, 1990.

Wilson, Charles Reagan, and William Ferris, eds., *Encyclopedia of Southern Culture,* University of North Carolina Press, 1989.

Alternative Applications: Using the shotgun floor plan, create a mural, triptych, or cartoon of black family life on a tobacco or truck farm, indigo, rice, or sugar plantation, or fishing village. Indicate daily activities, especially cooking, dining, relaxation, play, handicrafts, gardening, and sleep.

Arts and Crafts

African Animal Fair

Age/Grade Level or Audience: Kindergarten and elementary craft classes; religious schools; classes for handicapped children.

Description: Organize a clay animal fair.

Procedure: Have students use commercial clay or a homemade recipe made from one of the following recipes:

Simple Dough

4 c. flour
1 c. salt
1½ c. cold water
vegetable dye

Combine ingredients in a bowl and work into a dough. Shape into figures. The dough will harden in 2 to 3 hours.

Cooked Clay

¾ c. salt
½ c. plain or shaker flour
2 tsp. alum
¾ c. water
2 tbs. oil
vegetable dye or paint

Stir first four ingredients in a pot over medium heat until thickened. Blend in oil. Cool; then color with drops of food coloring or tempera paint if desired.

Demonstrate how to roll, knead, and shape the clay into African animals, such as the giraffe, crocodile, gnu, gorilla, lion, tiger, dik-dik, rhinoceros, gazelle, emu, cobra, or wildebeest. Paint figures and then bake on a cookie sheet for one hour at 350˚.

Or use clay to make oversized animal heads. Emphasize the variety of pelts and skins by painting black and white stripes for the zebra, brown with buff spots for the giraffe, and a hairy brown ruff for the lion. Attach a clay arrow to the finished heads. Bake, then use heads as pot pets by securing the arrow in the soil of a potted plant.

Budget: $$$

Sources:

Brown, Leslie, *Africa: A Natural History,* Random House, 1965.

Ellis, Veronica Freeman, *Afro-Bets First Book about Africa: An Introduction for Young Readers,* Just Us Books, 1989.

"Etosha Park," *National Geographic,* March 1983.

Greene, Peggy R., *Things to Make,* Random House, 1978.

Isadora, Rachel, *Over the Green Hills,* Greenwillow Books, 1992.

"Journey up the Nile," *National Geographic,* May 1985.

Kasza, Keiko, *A Mother for Choco,* Putnam, 1992.

Kingdon, Jonathan, *Island Africa: The Evolution of Africa's Rare Animals and Plants,* Princeton University Press, 1992.

Lester, Julian, *How Many Spots Does a Leopard Have? And Other Tales,* Scholastic, Inc., 1989.

MacClintock, Dorcas, *African Images,* Scribner, 1984.

Sattler, Helen Roney, *Recipes for Art and Craft Materials,* Lothrop, Lee & Shepard, 1987.

"Serengeti," *National Geographic,* May 1986.

Alternative Applications: As an alternate method of shaping animals, use papier mâché:

Papier Mâché

> wet paper strips
> glue
> wire

Form with wire a simple animal shape of head, backbone, legs, and tail. Soak paper in water. Squeeze dry. Shape mass around wire structure. Complete with a coating of glue and a layer of dry paper strips. Dry and paint. Decorate with yarn, felt, cloth, or fake fur.

 ## African Cards

Age/Grade Level or Audience: Elementary and middle school art classes.

Description: Redesign a deck of playing cards based on African or African-American themes.

Procedure: Discuss with students the medieval European history of ordinary playing cards. Have them work in groups to replace the joker, ace, king, queen, jack, spade, heart, diamond, club, and numbers with African motifs found on Maasai, Egyptian, Zulu, Berber, Moorish, or Ethiopian pottery, jewelry, architecture, and costumes. Select another group to redesign the back of the deck. Suggest a map, musical instrument, profile, or flag as a unifying motif. Use the colors of Africa: red, green, yellow, black, and white.

Budget: $

Sources:
Brooks, Lester, *Great Civilizations of Ancient Africa,* Four Winds Press, 1971.
Dacey, Donna, "Crafts of Many Cultures: Three Seasonal Art Projects with Global Appeal," *Instructor,* November-December 1991, pp. 30-33.
Estell, Kenneth, ed., *The African-American Almanac,* 6th ed., Gale, 1993.
Saitoti, Tepilit Ole, *Maasai,* Abradale Press, 1980.

Alternative Applications: Have students extend their project to a redesign of Tarot or I Ching cards, family crests, the Bayeux Tapestry, royal coats of arms, and other cultural symbols arising from sources other than Africa. Designs should feature important moments in black history, such as the arrival of the first slave ship to New World shores, the Emancipation Proclamation, or the creation of the Freedman's Bureau.

African Ornaments

Age/Grade Level or Audience: Kindergarten and elementary crafts classes; religious schools; classes for the handicapped.

Description: Create African ornaments for decorating trees, windows, doorways, wreaths, and packages.

Procedure: Have handicrafters cross two thin 6-inch dowels or bamboo garden sticks and secure in place with a pipe cleaner. Using red, green, yellow, and black yarn, wind a single thread around each rod and on to the next rod. Alternate colors to create variations in the pattern. For an unusual effect, twine two colored strands at a time, such as green and red or yellow and black. Tie the last thread into a knot. Complete the ends of the ornament with yarn pompons, paper stars, or foil streamers.

Budget: $$$

Sources:
Greene, Peggy R., *Things to Make,* Random House, 1978.
MacClintok, Dorcas, *African Images,* Scribner, 1984.

Alternative Applications: Make oversized ornaments to serve as Kwanzaa door or mailbox decorations. Hang several models from ceilings or paddle fans. Use the ends of the dowels as spokes on which to hang smaller ornaments.

 ## All-Occasion Cards

Age/Grade Level or Audience: All ages.

Description: Create a mass-produced card factory.

Procedure: Assemble tools and art supplies to create a selection of all-occasion cards for birthdays, anniversaries, Bar Mitzvahs, graduations, sympathy, get well wishes, and holidays such as Easter, Thanksgiving, Kwanzaa, Christmas, Hanukkah, New Year's, Ramadan, and Valentine's Day. Select the best designs for each occasion and make multiple copies of each using desktop publishing, photocopies, tracings, or block prints. Collate the finished cards into stacks, match with colored or white envelopes, and assemble in boxes. Take orders or sell the card selections in a hospital or museum gift shop, retirement home, street fair, or door to door.

Budget: $$$

Sources:

Christian Children's Fund, P.O. Box 96005, Washington, DC 20090-6005; telephone: (800)776-6767.

Thurgood Marshall Scholarship Fund, P.O. Box 44251, Atlanta, GA 30336-1251; telephone: (800)444-4483.

UNICEF, 1 Children's Blvd., P.O. Box 182233, Chattanooga, TN 37422; telephone: (800)553-1200.

MacDonald, Margaret Read, *Folklore of World Holidays,* Gale, 1992.

Alternative Applications: Create a postcard series featuring landmarks in Africa, the Caribbean, or black America, such as scenes of the Limpopo River, Mount Kilimanjaro, and Lake Chad in Africa; Ocho Rios in Jamaica; the marketplace of Antigua, Jamaica; the island of St. Kitts in the West Indies; Catfish Row in Charleston, South Carolina; the Apollo Theater in Harlem, New York; and Motown in Detroit, Michigan.

 ## Animal Movies

Age/Grade Level or Audience: Elementary and middle school art classes; religious schools; scout troops; 4-H clubs; classes for the handicapped.

Description: Organize a filmmaking workshop.

Procedure: Have participants follow these suggestions:

- ◆ Study the movements and habits of an African animal, such as the swift gazelle, the awkward, lumbering hippopotamus, the flapping flamingo, or the bounding leopard.
- ◆ Select an animal to draw on twenty index cards.
- ◆ Depict the animal moving from one side to another or from ground into the air through twenty small increments.
- ◆ Arrange the twenty pictures in time order.
- ◆ Fasten the left edge of the card stack with staples or brads.
- ◆ Flip the right edge rapidly or slowly to make the animal move.

Budget: $$

Sources:

Kingdon, Jonathan, *Island Africa: The Evolution of Africa's Rare Animals and Plants,* Princeton University Press, 1992.

Simons, Robin, *Recyclopedia: Games, Science Equipment, and Crafts from Recycled Materials,* Houghton Mifflin, 1976.

Alternative Applications: Create similar index card movies featuring one of the following scenes: Caribbean limbo line, steel drum band, Zulu dancer, or practicing shaman or native healer.

Batiking

Age/Grade Level or Audience: Kindergarten and elementary art classes; religious schools; scout troops; 4-H clubs.

Description: Organize a batiking workshop.

Procedure: Have students decorate handkerchiefs, T-shirts, or pillowcases with crayon drawings of African or Caribbean designs. Have them cover their work with newspaper or brown wrapping paper and iron lightly. After repeated ironings, the wax crayon will soak into the paper, leaving the color in the fabric.

Budget: $$$

Sources:

Robin Simons, *Recyclopedia: Games, Science Equipment, and Crafts from Recycled Materials,* Houghton Mifflin, 1976.

Alternative Applications: For older handicrafters, have participants paint fabric with melted paraffin, then dip into dye. Conclude by ironing fabric between layers of newspaper or brown wrapping paper until wax is absorbed.

Black History Desk Calendar

Age/Grade Level or Audience: Middle school and high school art classes.

Description: Provide artwork for a twelve-month calendar.

Procedure: Encourage twelve students to create contrasting, thought-provoking artwork to accompany a twelve-month calendar. Stress events that fall within a particular month, such as these:

- ◆ Martin Luther King, Jr.'s birthday and the Emancipation Proclamation in January
- ◆ Black History Month in February
- ◆ Malcolm X Day and African Liberation Day in May
- ◆ Juneteenth in June
- ◆ Marcus Garvey's birthday in August
- ◆ Umoja Karamu in November
- ◆ Kwanzaa in December

Use photography, collage, or other media to highlight calendars. Reproduce in black and white and distribute as gifts or sell as a sorority, art, or civic club project.

Budget: $$

Sources:
Grun, Bernard, T*he Timetables of History: A Horizontal Linkage of People and Events,* Simon & Schuster, 1991.
Hornsby, Alton, Jr., *Chronology of African-American History: Significant Events and People from 1619 to the Present,* Gale, 1991.
MacDonald, Margaret Read, *Folklore of World Holidays,* Gale, 1992.
Trager, James, *The People's Chronology,* Henry Holt, 1992.

Alternative Applications: Post a monthly calendar board in a school, museum, library, post office, mall, or civic building. Hang colored markers, crayons, and pencils on strings and encourage participants to enter important dates in black history.

Bookmarks

Originator: Gary Carey, teacher, editor, and writer, Lincoln, Nebraska.

Age/Grade Level or Audience: Elementary school students.

Description: Create a variety of hand-lettered bookmarks featuring quotations by Martin Luther King, Jr., Maya Angelou, Jesse Jackson, Barbara Jordan, Sammy Davis, Jr., Fannie Lou Hamer, Faye Wattleton, Booker T. Washington, Frederick Douglass, Sojourner Truth, and other black notables.

Procedure: Have students use yardsticks to mark large sheets of tagboard or construction paper in 1" x 5" rectangles and inscribe short, memorable quotations on each. Suggested lines include these by Martin Luther King, Jr.:

- ◆ Injustice anywhere is a threat to justice everywhere.
- ◆ I believe that unarmed truth and unconditional love will have the final word in reality.
- ◆ Nonviolence is the answer to the crucial political and moral questions of our time.
- ◆ He who accepts evil without protesting against it is really cooperating with it.
- ◆ Our destiny is tied up with the destiny of America.
- ◆ Now is the time to make real the promises of democracy.

After decorating with drawings, stickers, or pictures cut from magazines, have students coat the tagboard with sheets of clear stick-on plastic or laminate by machine. Cut the final page with scissors or paper cutter. Use bookmarks as banquet favors, rewards for reading or class attendance, and gifts to handicapped children and retirement home dwellers.

Budget: $$

Sources:
Bell, Janet Cheatham, *Famous Black Quotations and Some Not So Famous,* Sabayt Publications, 1986.
King, Anita, ed., *Quotations in Black,* Greenwood Press, 1981.

Alternative Applications: Paperclip bookmark on a classroom clothesline made of twine. Or attach tassels to markers through a hole punched in one end and distribute as tray markers in hospitals, cafeterias, or restaurants.

Box Zoo

Age/Grade Level or Audience: Kindergarten and elementary crafts classes; religious schools; scout troops; 4-H clubs; classes for the handicapped.

Description: Create an African zoo.

Procedure: Have students collect grocery boxes and cartons and spray paint them with a neutral color. Have students use colored pencils, chalk, crayons, colored markers, or tempera paint to depict a different African animal on each box, for instance, the gorilla, rhinoceros, emu, hippopotamus, ostrich, elephant, giraffe, lion, tiger, gnu, wildebeest, dik-dik, orangutang, crocodile, mamba, and cobra. Arrange the finished boxes in a window display or create a pyramid or wall for a hall display.

Budget: $$$

Sources:

Brown, Leslie, *Africa: A Natural History,* Random House, 1965.

Ellis, Veronica Freeman, *Afro-Bets First Book about Africa: An Introduction for Young Readers,* Just Us Books, 1989.

"Etosha Park," *National Geographic,* March 1983.

Greene, Peggy R., *Things to Make,* Random House, 1978.

Isadora, Rachel, *Over the Green Hills,* Greenwillow Books, 1992.

"Journey up the Nile," *National Geographic,* May 1985.

Kasza, Keiko, *A Mother for Choco,* Putnam, 1992.

Kingdon, Jonathan, *Island Africa: The Evolution of Africa's Rare Animals and Plants,* Princeton University Press, 1989.

Lester, Julian, *How Many Spots Does a Leopard Have? And Other Tales,* Scholastic, Inc., 1985.

MacClintock, Dorcas, *African Images,* Scribner, 1984.

"Serengeti," *National Geographic,* May 1986.

Alternative Applications: Use a box zoo as a stage setting for a PTA program on African wildlife or endangered species. Have each participant carry a box to center stage and explain the pictured animal's habits, diet, colors, shape, and natural enemies. For an added treat, have students put their words into poems or songs.

 | **Camp Africa** |

Originator: Kim Jolly, Director, International House, Charlotte, North Carolina.

Age/Grade Level or Audience: Elementary and middle school students.

Description: Create an in-house camp.

Procedure: On successive Saturdays, after school, or in the evenings, introduce campers to a different African culture at each session by telling stories, playing native music, organizing map drawing, introducing students to Kwanzaa rituals, showing videotapes such as Sarafina, Sounder, The Learning Tree, and The Power of One, or developing craft tables where young artisans can choose among cloth or mask painting, cooking, jewelry making, calligraphy, puppetry, rock painting, or flag and banner making. A useful craft focus is the creation of a Kwanzaa table setting:

◆ Have students saw 1" x 12" boards into one foot platter lengths and sand the ends smooth.

◆ Organize a grass, vine, rushes, or straw weaving shop to create covered baskets to hold bread and fruit or decorations, such as native flowers, ferns, or feathers.

◆ Include mat weaving to provide the table with a single runner, place mats, or mats for seating. Weave typical African patterns using geometric designs in red, green, black, and yellow.

◆ Form bowls, serving spoons, and ladles out of gourds and clay. Paint them with nontoxic materials to match mats.

◆ Create decorative jewelry out of different pasta shapes strung on elastic thread. Paint the finished pieces in the colors of Africa.

◆ Use acrylic paints or colored markers to decorate smooth stones to resemble African frogs, toads, locusts, butterflies, fish, birds, snakes, or alligators.

◆ Make spice balls from 12-inch circles of cheesecloth filled with whole spices and tied with raffia, yarn, or ribbon.

Conclude Camp Africa with a public display of student work alongside candid shots of participants at work, dancing, or listening to stories.

Budget: $$$

Sources:

Bohannan, Paul, *Africa and Africans,* Waveland Press, 1988.

Dacey, Donna, "Crafts of Many Cultures: Three Seasonal Art Projects with Global Appeal," *Instructor,* November-December 1991, pp. 30-33.

Dede, Alice, *Ghanaian Favorite Dishes,* Anowuo Educational Publications, 1969.

Greene, Peggy R., *Things to Make,* Random House, 1978.

Merson, Annette, *African Cookery: A Black Heritage,* Winston-Derek Publishers, 1987.

Saitoti, Tepilit Ole, *Maasai,* Abradale Press, 1980.

Alternative Applications: Create a similar day camp for handicapped or elderly people. Distribute Afrocentric workshop ideas and methods to day-care workers, educators, 4-H and scout troop leaders, PTA committees, settlement workers, and religious leaders for application to other settings, such as church school, camporees, classrooms, and community fairs.

Clasped Hands

Originator: Susan E. Koricki, elementary school teacher, Germantown, Maryland.

Age/Grade Level or Audience: Elementary, middle school, and high school art classes; church schools; scout troops; 4-H clubs; retirement homes.

Description: Create a sign-in board celebrating Black History Month.

Procedure: Have a volunteer create two model hands, one dark and one light. Place hands at the center of a bulletin board that features a quotation urging racial harmony, such as Rodney King's plea, "Can't we just get along?" Suspend a pencil by a long string so that students, parents, staff, and visitors can make personal replies to the quotation.

Budget: $$

Sources:

King, Anita, ed., *Quotations in Black,* Greenwood Press, 1981.
Lanker, Brian, *I Dream a World: Portraits of Black Women Who Changed America,* Stewart, Tabori, and Chang, 1989.

Alternative Applications: Distribute dark and light paper so that students can draw two hands and interlock them. Have students inscribe their opinions of how racial harmony can be achieved. Post hands on walls of schools, malls, restaurants, museums, libraries, retirement homes, and hospitals. Center the display with a caption, such as "Give Fellowship a Hand."

Crafts Clinic

Originator: Obakunle and Tejuola Akinlana, storytellers, teachers, and artisans.

Age/Grade Level or Audience: All ages.

Description: Locate artisans to staff a crafts workshop.

Procedure: Invite black artists and crafts specialists to demonstrate the fundamentals of weaving, batiking, sand sculpture, basketry, carpentry, pottery, carving, tanning and leathercraft, jewelry and mask making, stained glass, ironwork, and other crafts. For instance, offer a class in gourd decoration. Demonstrate how to weave twine and beads over a globular gourd to create a shekere, a musical instrument common to the Yoruba. Provide the workshop free or at reduced cost to indigent community members. Include craft demonstrations as part of a street or craft fair, museum display, or community Pan-African festival. Invite participants to sell their wares.

Budget: $$$

Sources:
For information about the shekere, contact Obakunle and Tejuola Akinlana, Midland, NC; telephone: (704)888-6302.

Dacey, Donna, "Crafts of Many Cultures: Three Seasonal Art Projects with Global Appeal," *Instructor,* November-December 1991, pp. 30-33.

Estell, Kenneth, ed., *The African-American Almanac,* 6th ed., Gale, 1993.

Greene, Peggy R., *Things to Make,* Random House, 1978.

Alternative Applications: Create a database of craft ideas, such as making a shekere or other African musical instrument or producing jewelry, batiking, pottery, and other handicrafts of Africa or the Caribbean. Share your information on IRIS, Prodigy, or other computer networks.

Crocheting a Bit of Africa

Age/Grade Level or Audience: Elementary, middle school, and high school art classes; church schools; scout troops; 4-H clubs; classes for the handicapped; shelter workshops; retirement homes.

Description: Incorporate the colors of Africa into crocheted items.

Procedure: Teach a small group to crochet simple chain stitches in a straight line or circle. Use mixed yarns in Africa's traditional colors—red, green, yellow, and black. Have students shape their work into table mats, runners, afghans, couch throws, and lap robes. For more advanced handicrafters, suggest patterns for round caps, mittens, and vests.

Budget: $$$

Sources:
Bonando, Wanda, *Stitches, Patterns, and Projects for Crocheting,* Harper & Row, 1984.

Alternative Applications: Organize a similar workshop to teach knitting. Concentrate on the garter stitch, which is a simple knit stitch. Repeat to create shawls, afghans, baby blankets, and other items in the colors of Africa.

Crocodile Trains

Age/Grade Level or Audience: Kindergarten and elementary craft classes; religious schools; classes for handicapped children.

Description: Create crocodile train pull toys.

Procedure: Have students tie together two egg cartons, bottom sides up, with strings or pipe cleaners. Attach a whole carton, top side up, to the front for a head, and half a bottom portion, split lengthwise, for a tail. Paint the entire train green to resemble a crocodile; on the front portion paint eyes and a red mouth, and glue cardboard teeth to the inside of the mouth. Attach cardboard or plastic wheels to the outer edges with brads. Tie a pull string to the front.

Budget: $$

Sources:
Brown, Leslie, *Africa: A Natural History,* Random House, 1965.
Greene, Peggy R., *Things to Make,* Random House, 1978.

Alternative Applications: Create a living crocodile train. Using burlap or muslin bags painted green, cut out arm and neck holes and place a bag on each child. Have participants hold to the waist of the child ahead in line and move in wobbly crocodile movements around the room. Provide music, such as "See You Later Alligator," "Never Smile at a Crocodile," "I Went to the Animal Fair," or "The Hokey-Pokey," for the crocodile to dance to.

Design America

Age/Grade Level or Audience: All ages.

Description: Hold a black history design contest.

Procedure: Have entrants redesign a common American symbol to include the contributions of nonwhite people. For example, redesign one of these:

- ◆ American flag
- ◆ national seal
- ◆ paper currency or a coin
- ◆ White House or Capitol
- ◆ U.S. Marine insignia
- ◆ Tomb of the Unknown Soldier
- ◆ Air Force One
- ◆ Arlington Cemetery
- ◆ Justice Department statue
- ◆ Statue of Liberty
- ◆ Washington Monument, Lincoln Memorial, Jefferson Memorial
- ◆ Smithsonian Institution

Publish results in a local newspaper or arts newsletter or feature them on a television interview program or traveling show.

Budget: $$$

Sources:
Grun, Bernard, *The Timetables of History: A Horizontal Linkage of People and Events,* Simon & Schuster, 1991.
MacClintock, Dorcas, *African Images,* Scribner, 1984.

Alternative Applications: Propose the creation of a new insignia, building, monument, or other commemoration of American multiculturalism. Have a group choose a purpose, place, style, and inscription for the memorial, such as a permanent Smithsonian exhibit honoring all Olympic athletes, a bas-relief on the U.S. Capitol featuring the diversity of races and their contributions to America, a tribute to victims of slavery or civil rights demonstrations, or a national children's theme park honoring all races.

Doll Displays

Originator: Leatrice Pearson, teacher, Lenoir, North Carolina.

Age/Grade Level or Audience: All ages.

Description: Dress dolls in period costumes and arrange them in scenarios to represent events in black history.

Procedure: Invite local civic clubs, literary guilds, sororities, fraternities, and other public-spirited organizations to dramatize a significant moment in African-American history by dressing small plastic dolls and placing them in shadow-box settings or displays. Feature events such as the bravery of couriers for the Underground Railroad, the exploits of Buffalo Soldiers, the Montgomery bus boycotts organized by Martin Luther King, Jr., the first black fighter pilots in the United States military, or the activism of Sojourner Truth, Fannie Lou Hamer, Faye Wattleton, and other abolitionists and women's rights leaders. Accompany each entry with a short summary of the event, its date, and the outcome. For example, a depiction of the Underground Railroad might tell how and where it was started, its duration, and the approximate number of people who used it to escape slavery. Plastic dolls can be found in handicraft supply stores. For inexpensive substitutes, use wooden clothes pins or dowels with styrofoam or papier mâché heads.

Budget: $$

Sources:

Sanders, Marlita, "Dollmaking: The Celebration of a Culture," *School Arts,* January 1992, p. 27.

Alternative Applications: Organize an annual competition, especially in areas where there are numerous clubs. Include a multiracial panel drawn from newspaper staffs, school and college faculty, libraries, city and county offices, and art councils.

The Door to Awareness

Age/Grade Level or Audience: Elementary, middle school, and high school classes; shopping malls; office buildings; civic centers; hospitals.

Description: Sponsor a door decorating contest.

Procedure: Have participants use found objects, collage, watercolor, pencil sketches, or African designs as decorations for doors. Give prizes for the most original, the most artistic, or the most historically accurate. Emphasize the following motifs:

- ◆ African animals in their natural settings
- ◆ Kwanzaa table settings
- ◆ natural foodstuffs from Africa and the Caribbean
- ◆ African hairstyles, jewelry, and headdresses
- ◆ maps
- ◆ symbols and flags

Budget: $$

Sources:

Magazines such as *Ebony, Essence, Jet,* and *Emerge.*

Brown, Leslie, *Africa: A Natural History,* Random House, 1965.

Ellis, Veronica Freeman, *Afro-Bets First Book about Africa: An Introduction for Young Readers,* Just Us Books, 1989.

Estell, Kenneth, ed., *The African-American Almanac,* 6th ed., Gale, 1993.

Alternative Applications: Have students decorate a series of cardboard or wooden panels with African or Caribbean scenes, such as market day, a fishing expedition, gardening and harvesting, a native festival or religious rite, and family scenes. Locate the panels in an auditorium or mall and have visitors vote for the winners in each category.

Freedom Stamps

Age/Grade Level or Audience: Elementary, middle school, and high school art classes; church schools; scout troops; 4-H clubs; retirement homes.

Description: Design stamps for the United States, Caribbean, or African postal systems.

Procedure: Instruct students to use oils, pastels, water colors, acrylics, charcoal, or pen and ink to create designs commemorating important people and events in black history. Consider these as models:

- ◆ Shaka's rise to the throne
- ◆ Phillis Wheatley's poems
- ◆ Matthew Henson's arrival at the North Pole
- ◆ Sojourner Truth's feminist speeches
- ◆ Duke Ellington's performance at Carnegie Hall
- ◆ Salem Poor's role in the Revolutionary War
- ◆ Faye Wattleton's leadership of Planned Parenthood
- ◆ Alex Haley's creation of a family tree
- ◆ emancipation of Haitian slaves
- ◆ Solomon's introduction to the Queen of Sheba
- ◆ Ossie Davis's contributions to entertainment
- ◆ Mae Jemison's first space flight
- ◆ Spike Lee's depiction of young black Americans in movies

Budget: $$

Sources:

Bennett, Lerone, "Ten Most Dramatic Events in African-American History," *Ebony,*
  February 1992, pp. 107-16.
"Champ Stamp," *Jet,* October 5, 1992, p. 4.
"I Have a Dream: A Collection of Black Americans on U.S. Postage Stamps,"
  Philatelic and Retail Services Department, U.S. Postal Service, 475 L'Enfant Plaza
  S.W., Washington, DC 20260-9998.

Alternative Applications: Design other advertising media, particularly billboards, television and magazine ads, book jackets, packaging, as well as commercial products aimed at young consumers, such as milk cartons, cereal boxes, sportswear, and snack foods. Determine concepts that deserve emphasis, such as family unity, education, good health practices, and active participation in government.

Gourdheads

Age/Grade Level or Audience: Elementary, middle school, and high school art classes; church schools; scout troops; 4-H clubs; retirement homes.

Description: Create a gourd painting workshop.

Procedure: Have students depict famous black people in gourd paintings. Supply acrylic paints and dried gourds that resemble heads. Glue on hair, ears, noses, and other features cut from styrofoam, cardboard egg cartons, clay, or papier mâché. Fill a gallery with a particular group of famous gourdheads, such as athletes, inventors, civil rights and feminist leaders, and military heroes.

Budget: $$$

Sources:
Estell, Kenneth, ed., *The African-American Almanac,* 6th ed., Gale, 1993.
Low, W. Augustus, and Virgil A. Clift, eds., *Encyclopedia of Black America,* McGraw Hill, 1981.
Smith, Jessie Carney, ed., *Notable Black American Women,* Gale, 1992.

Alternative Applications: Make gourdheads of a variety of racial groups. Decorate with hats, mustaches, glasses, elaborate wig styles, pipes, cigarette holders, and earrings. Feature famous musical groups, such as the Supremes, Harlem Boy's Choir, Platters, Inkspots, Pointer Sisters, and the Jackson Five. Assemble and mark with a banner or caption their greatest achievements, such as platinum albums, movies, or public appearances.

 Heritage Jubilee

Age/Grade Level or Audience: All ages.

Description: Organize a heritage jubilee, a fair featuring crafts and talent of all types, from cooking to poetry, posters to dance.

Procedure: Have participants send in a written proposal of craft or talent to be displayed at a local community center, church, library, museum, or school. Arrange booths to accommodate crafts such as these:

- ◆ sweet grass basketry
- ◆ painting, posters, and photography

- carvings, statues, and masks
- batiking and weaving
- jewelry
- fashions

Provide a stage for dancing, singing, recitation, and skits. Include a children's section for face painting, storytelling, puppetry, and cornrowing, as well as a kitchen area for the sampling of foods.

Budget: $$$

Sources:

Dacey, Donna, "Crafts of Many Cultures: Three Seasonal Art Projects with Global Appeal," *Instructor,* November-December 1991, pp. 30-33.

Estell, Kenneth, ed., *The African-American Almanac,* 6th ed., Gale, 1993.

Wilson, Charles Reagan, and William Ferris, eds., *Encyclopedia of Southern Culture,* University of North Carolina Press, 1989.

Alternative Applications: Introduce youngsters to African instruments, such as the water drum, thumb piano, shekere, or panpipes. Have them perform in ensembles at the Jubilee.

Jointed Dolls

Age/Grade Level or Audience: Middle school and high school classes; scout troops; church schools; 4-H clubs.

Description: Assemble oversized paper dolls with jointed limbs and dress them in the style of a particular tribe, such as the Maasai, Ibo, Berber, Zulu, Kikuyu, or Yoruba.

Procedure: Using themselves as models, have students do the following:

- Lie down on heavy wrapping paper or cardboard while another student traces around body.
- Cut the shape into pieces to make moveable upper arms, lower arms, hands, thighs, lower legs, feet, and head.
- After connecting the pieces with brads or cord, have students tack their models to the wall.
- Using cloth scraps, yarn, and other found materials, color or dress each model in the style of a particular African tribe.

Budget: $$

Sources:

Ellis, Veronica Freeman, *Afro-Bets First Book about Africa: An Introduction for Young Readers,* Just Us Books, 1989.

Saitoti, Tepilit Ole, *Maasai,* Abradale Press, 1980.

Sanders, Marlita, "Dollmaking: The Celebration of a Culture," *School Arts,* January 92, p. 27.

Simons, Robin, Recyclopedia: *Games, Science Equipment, and Crafts from Recycled Materials,* Houghton Mifflin, 1976.

Alternative Applications: Have students group paper dolls into families that include children, infants, and older adults. Show family members involved in normal activities, such as planting and harvesting; worshipping or celebrating a military victory or national holiday; cooking, preserving food, and eating; entertaining guests from other tribes or nations; playing games; dancing and singing; and carrying out important ceremonies or rituals such as coming of age, marriage, burials, or hunting parties.

To increase doll motion, have students attach twine or wire to the upper edge of the arms or legs. By pulling downward on the cords, the puppeteer can make the doll move.

 Maasai Pendants

Age/Grade Level or Audience: Kindergarten through elementary school students; scout troops; classes for the handicapped; religious schools.

Description: Create an individualized pendant from found materials or common kitchen items.

Procedure: Have students cut a 5-inch circle from cardboard, punch a hole through the edge, then insert a 30-inch cord or lanyard through the hole. Supply dried beans or peas, aquarium gravel, bits of colored tile, acorns, seeds, popcorn, and other small particles to be arranged in concentric circles and glued into place. Apply a layer of hairspray or polyurethane spray to strengthen each design.

Budget: $$

Sources:

Ellis, Veronica Freeman, *Afro-Bets First Book about Africa: An Introduction for Young Readers,* Just Us Books, 1989.

MacClintok, Dorcas, *African Images,* Scribner, 1984.

Saitoti, Tepilit Ole, *Maasai,* Abradale Press, 1980.

Alternative Applications: Have students complete a wardrobe of jewelry and clothing, including upper-arm bands, earrings, torques, waist chains, anklets, head wraps, sarongs, and toe and finger rings, or have them work as a team to dress a single mannequin, papier-mâché model, or small doll.

New Games for Old

Age/Grade Level or Audience: Kindergarten, elementary, middle school, and high school students.

Description: Redesign familiar games from a black perspective.

Procedure: Have students select a game to redesign, such as Monopoly, Clue, Scrabble, darts, or Pin the Tail on the Donkey. Replace old gameboard and game paraphernalia with information gleaned from black history and experience. For example, try these alterations:

- ◆ For Monopoly, replace Park Place with Bourbon Street and the Reading Railroad with the Underground Railroad. Use play money copied from African currency.
- ◆ For Clue, exchange Colonel Mustard with Bill Pickett. Substitute a lasso for the candlestick.
- ◆ For Scrabble, make a special list of words that count for extra points, such as Zulu, Yoruba, gnu, emu, ostrich, Zaire, Benin, Egypt, Congo, Niger, or Limpopo.
- ◆ For Pin the Tail on the Donkey, create large color pictures of African animals, such as a giraffe, elephant, gnu, wildebeest, gorilla, dik-dik, gazelle, baboon, hyena, or water buffalo. Offer a variety of tails to suit the animals. Have blindfolded students pin the appropriate tail on the animal it belongs to.
- ◆ Make paper javelins or dart guns from soda straws. Post a large map of Africa and vary the targets, for instance the Niger River, Lake Chad, Victoria Falls, or the Seychelles Islands. Assign values to each goal, depending on size (e.g., a single point for the Sahara Desert, three points for South Africa or Algeria, or five points for the Ivory Coast or Mount Kilimanjaro).

Budget: $$

Sources:

Cantor, George, *Historic Landmarks of Black America,* Gale, 1991.
Simons, Robin, *Recyclepedia: Games, Science Equipment, and Crafts from Recycled Materials,* Houghton Mifflin, 1976.

Alternative Applications: Create a new board game by having students draw a large map of Africa and develop rules for a safari.

◆ Make game pieces representing various ways of traveling, such as canoe, raft, camel, donkey, elephant, bicycle, ox cart, bush plane, ferry, rail, or all-terrain vehicle.

◆ Turn natural and social barriers into lost turns, such as poachers in Kenya, Victoria Falls, a termite hill, the Sahara Desert, the Nile River, animal stampedes, grass fires on the savannah, dry water holes in Somalia, sandstorms in Tunisia, passport check south of the Aswan Dam, rebel juntas, or apartheid laws.

◆ Have players advance on the roll of the dice, the selection of a card from a deck, or the spin of the arrow toward a number.

◆ Give extra turns to players who roll doubles, land on a capital city, or pass two borders in one turn.

◆ Reward the player who completes the circuit.

 ## Origami Animals

Age/Grade Level or Audience: Elementary, middle school, and high school art classes; church schools; scout troops; 4-H clubs; retirement homes.

Description: Fashion African animals in origami.

Procedure: Distribute tissue, typing paper, onion skin, or rice paper along with patterns for making African animals out of folded paper. Have groups create a menagerie of African animals, including gorillas, lions, elephants, crocodiles, emus, rhinoceroses, gazelles, flamingos, cobras, and others. Group animals into a shelf display.

Budget: $$

Sources:
Brown, Leslie, *Africa: A Natural History,* Random House, 1965.
Isadora, Rachel, *Over the Green Hills,* Greenwillow Books, 1992.
Montroll, John, *African Animals in Origami,* Dover Publications, 1991.

Alternative Applications: Suspend origami animals on strings or create mobiles by tying finished figures to crossed dowels or a series of interconnected bamboo sticks. Vary colors and shapes.

 ## Pieces of Africa

Age/Grade Level or Audience: Elementary, middle school, and high school art classes; church schools; scout troops; 4-H clubs; retirement homes.

Description: Organize a mosaic workshop in honor of Black History Month.

Procedure: Demonstrate how mosaics are made with the following steps:

◆ Have mosaic makers select an African theme to recreate, such as a colorful animal (e.g., giraffe, lizard, butterfly, moth), or a famous landmark (e.g., Mount Kilimanjaro, Lake Chad, River Nile, Victoria Falls).
◆ Draw a simple outline on cardboard, glass, or wood.
◆ Assemble colored bits of construction paper, shredded magazine pages, broken pottery, aquarium rock, glass beads, sand, or found objects, such as pasta, dried peas, or seeds.
◆ Match strength of glue with weight of pieces.
◆ Fill in one color section with glue.
◆ Sprinkle on pieces in that color.
◆ Continue gluing and filling in one color at a time.
◆ Spray the finished work with polyurethane fixative or hair spray.

Budget: $$$

Sources:
Asante, Molefi K., *Historical and Cultural Atlas of African Americans,* Macmillan, 1991.
Dacey, Donna, "Crafts of Many Cultures: Three Seasonal Art Projects with Global Appeal," *Instructor,* November-December 1991, pp. 30-33.
Isadora, Rachel, *Over the Green Hills,* Greenwillow Books, 1992.

Alternative Applications: Have advanced mosaic makers embellish and texturize their drawings with larger pieces, for instance, twigs, leaves, grass, and other found objects. Suggest that some mosaics may be pressed into clay ashtrays, pots, dishes, trays, wall hangings, or hot pads. Display horizontally on tables rather than vertically on walls to protect mosaics from disintegration.

Puppet Show

Age/Grade Level or Audience: Kindergarten and elementary school students; scout troops; 4-H clubs.

Description: Organize a puppet show on black heroes of the old West.

Procedure: Have participants make brown paper bag or thin cardboard puppets attached to wooden spoons, dowels, or paint stirrers to act out the lives of Nat Love, Bill "Bull-Dogger" Pickett, Britton Johnson, Arthur L. Walker, Jessie Stahl, Matthew Bones Hooks, Jim Taylor, "Stagecoach Mary" Fields, Charlie Glass, George Mourse, William Robinson, and other famous black cowboys, stagecoach drivers, broncobusters, pony express riders, and rodeo stars. Present the finished show for a banquet, camporee, parents' night, PTA function, shopping mall or retirement home demonstration, program for handicapped children, county fair exhibit, or civic presentation.

After research is completed, divide participants into small groups. Have one group write the words of the rodeo announcer, sheriff, or trail boss, who will tell the backgrounds of the main characters and announce their ranch, stage driving, and rodeo feats. Have a second group use colored pencils or markers, crayons, chalk, or watercolors to draw the characters on the backs of brown paper, cardboard, or cartons. Cut out the figures and attach to wooden spoons, dowels, paint stirrers, or clothespins. To make the puppets more realistic, attach moveable paper arms and legs with brads and glue on felt, cloth, or string for hair, eyebrows, jeans, boots, hats, and western shirts. Have the last group follow a similar procedure to create additional items, such as horses, steer, and stagecoaches.

Present the puppet show behind a draped table, counter, or puppet theater with curtain and puppeteers' bench. Have the narrator stand at the side and read the script as other group members manipulate the puppets.

Budget: $$

Sources:

Champlin, Connie, and Nancy Renfro, *Storytelling with Puppets*, American Library Association, 1985.

Estell, Kenneth, ed., *The African-American Almanac*, 6th ed., Gale, 1993.

Katz, William Loren, *Black Indians: A Hidden Heritage*, Atheneum, 1986.

Sierra, Judy, *Fantastic Theater: Puppets and Plays for Young Performers and Young Audiences*, H.W. Wilson, 1991.

Simons, Robin, *Recyclepedia: Games, Science Equipment, and Crafts from Recycled Materials*, Houghton Mifflin, 1976.

Stewart, Paul W., and Wallace Y. Ponce, *Black Cowboys*, Phillips Publishers, 1986.

Alternative Applications: Organize a traveling Wild West show for visits to some groups neighborhoods, schools, churches, clubs, or libraries. Use the black western puppet show for other groups as well, such as church school studies, neighborhood and police clubs, and library summer reading groups. If there are large numbers of participants involved, have some groups make posters announcing the show or create scenery, such as fencing, trees, ranch buildings, audiences, passengers, or arenas.

 ## Stained Glass Animals

Age/Grade Level or Audience: Elementary, middle school, and high school art classes; church schools; scout troops; 4-H clubs; retirement homes.

Description: Create a window display of stained glass animals.

Procedure: Have students color African animals on translucent paper. Have groups create a window display of African animals, including the hippopotamus, rhinoceros, African elephant, gorilla, tiger, zebra, camel, and others. Make a lighted display by placing stained glass animals on a lightboard or sheet in front of a spot light. Use the backdrop as part of a skit or presentation on African wildlife or endangered species.

Budget: $$

Sources:
Butterfly Stained Glass Coloring Book, Dover.
Cymerman, John Emil, *Zoo Animals Punch-Out* Stencils, Dover.
Exotic Birds Stained Glass Coloring Book, Dover.
Green, John, *Wild Animals Coloring Book,* Dover.
Wild Animals Stained Glass Coloring Book, Dover.

Alternative Applications: Stencil animal shapes onto banners, poster paper, T-shirts, tablecloths, and other blank surfaces or color wild animals and display the finished pages on a bulletin board. Contrast African animals with animals from other countries, such as the buffalo, llama, koala, yak, dingo, and kangaroo.

Sweets to the Sweet

Age/Grade Level or Audience: Kindergarten and elementary art classes; church schools; scout troops; 4-H clubs; classes for the handicapped; retirement homes.

Description: Create valentines acknowledging the contributions of great black Americans.

Procedure: Have students cut out large valentines and decorate each with a name and symbol of that person's contribution. For example:

- ◆ Matthew Henson—dogsled
- ◆ Judith Jamison—ballet slippers
- ◆ Frederick Douglass—liberty bell
- ◆ Mae Jemison—spaceship
- ◆ Louis Armstrong—trumpet
- ◆ Scott Joplin—piano
- ◆ Maggie Lena Walker—penny
- ◆ Nat Love—lasso

- ◆ Whoopi Goldberg—purple flower
- ◆ Thurgood Marshall—gavel
- ◆ Hattie McDaniel—Oscar
- ◆ Alex Haley—map of Africa
- ◆ Michael Jackson—glove
- ◆ Harry Belafonte—bongo drums
- ◆ Diana Ross—microphone
- ◆ Gregory Hines—tap shoes
- ◆ Faye Wattleton—family
- ◆ Jackie Robinson—baseball bat
- ◆ Maya Angelou—caged bird
- ◆ Arthur Ashe—tennis racket
- ◆ Madame C. J. Walker—curling iron
- ◆ Jean Du Sable—map of Chicago

Post valentines on a bulletin board, lunchroom banner, hallway, door, or ceiling. Send a bundle of valentine mementos to a local library, museum, civic center, retirement home, legislator, or school for handicapped children. Vary the shapes of the cutouts to represent the symbols of each person's contribution. Hang the cutouts on a tree or bare branch, from a mobile or railing, or tape to window panes. Use the colors of Africa: green for nature, yellow for the sun, black for black people, and red for the blood of all humankind, which had its beginnings on the continent of Africa.

Budget: $$

Sources:

Asante, Molefi K., *Historical and Cultural Atlas of African Americans*, Macmillan, 1991.

Hornsby, Alton, Jr., *Chronology of African-American History: Significant Events and People from 1619 to the Present*, Gale, 1991.

Lanker, Brian, *I Dream a World: Portraits of Black Women Who Changed America*, Stewart, Tabori & Chang, 1989.

Smith, Jessie Carney, ed., *Notable Black American Women*, Gale, 1992.

Alternative Applications: Share biographical valentines with other classes on computer networks, such as IRIS or Prodigy. For more information, consult Sandra Oehring's "Teaching with Technology," *Instructor*, November-December, 1992, p. 60.

 ## 'Toon Time

Age/Grade Level or Audience: All ages.

Description: Hold a cartooning contest.

Procedure: Help the Friends of the Library, a local newspaper, journalism class, civic club, or arts league organize a contest featuring political or humorous cartoons illustrating a moment in black history. Develop guidelines such as these:

◆ One entry per person
◆ Drawings must be on white 11" X 14" paper
◆ Drawings must be done in black ink, charcoal, or pencil
◆ Captions must be produced in 10 or 12 point type

Divide the contest by age. Award prizes for children, teens, and adult divisions. Post entries in a store window, mall, civic center, art museum, sidewalk display, or other centralized location. Have visitors to the exhibit vote on the best work in each category. Reproduce the best efforts for sale or distribution or print a brochure featuring the top cartoons.

Budget: $$$

Sources:

Asante, Molefi K., *Historical and Cultural Atlas of African Americans,* Macmillan, 1991.
Snodgrass, Mary Ellen, *Contests for Students,* Gale, 1991.

Alternative Applications: Use black themes, events, or heroes in a cartooning workshop. Clip examples by noted cartoonists, especially Elmer Simms Campbell's cartoons from *Esquire,* Ray Billingsley's "Curtis," Robin Harris and Bruce Smith's animated "Bebe's Kids," and "Where I'm Coming From," drawn by Barbara Brandon. Also examine the humor of Walt Carr and Gerald Dyes in *Ebony* and the political cartoons of Ron Bryant in *Emerge.* Have participants isolate unique elements in each, such as profiles, caricatures, dialect, and satire.

T-shirt Factory

Age/Grade Level or Audience: All ages.

Description: Organize a T-shirt factory to celebrate Black History Month.

Procedure: Have participants applique, embroider, paint, or stencil appropriate symbols, words, messages, patterns, or figures on T-shirts to be worn during Black History Month. Suggest the following decorations:

◆ messages of peace and healing
◆ tributes to civil rights leaders, particularly Martin Luther King, Jr., Sojourner Truth, Abraham Lincoln, Rosa Parks, Fannie Lou Hamer, and Nelson Mandela
◆ symbols of African pride, such as flags, family scenes, or portrait busts of leaders

◆ abstract designs surrounding single words, such as "Peace," "Unity," or "Brotherhood"
◆ short African aphorisms, such as these:
    ◆ He who learns, teaches.
    ◆ Poverty is slavery.
    ◆ A brother is like one's shoulder.
    ◆ The teeth are smiling, but is the heart?
    ◆ Love is like a baby: it needs to be treated tenderly.
    ◆ There is no medicine to cure hatred.
    ◆ To try and to fail is not laziness.
◆ quotations from white leaders, such as Abraham Lincoln's famous comments:
    ◆ As I would not be a slave, so I would not be a master.
    ◆ A house divided against itself cannot stand.
    ◆ Might makes right.
    ◆ A just and lasting peace among ourselves.
    ◆ With malice toward none, with charity for all.

Budget: $$$

Sources:

Estell, Kenneth, ed., *The African-American Almanac,* 6th ed., Gale, 1993.
King, Anita, ed., *Quotations in Black,* Greenwood Press, 1981.
Leslau, Charlotte, and Wolf Leslau, *African Proverbs,* P. Pauper Press, 1982.

Alternative Applications:

Sell stenciled or screen printed T-shirts, tote bags, posters, calendars, placemats and napkins, note paper, caps, and other items at museums, street fairs, or civic celebrations. Set a community goal and use the money to build a day-care center; shelter for the homeless or AIDS victims; halfway house for alcoholics, mental patients, or the mentally handicapped; or a road marker or other monument to black pride.

Biography

African Leaders

Age/Grade Level or Audience: Elementary, middle school, and high school history classes; historical societies; civic clubs.

Description: Narrate capsule biographies of great African leaders.

Procedure: Describe in short biographies the contributions of Africa's founders, philosophers, rulers, and freedom fighters. Include these:

Shaka	Mansa Musa	King Ezana
Usman Dan Fodio	Ahmadu	Ibn Battuta
Osai Tutu Kwamina	King Menelik II	Jomo Kenyatta Kwame
Nkrumah	Imhotep	Akhenaton
Tarik	Nelson Mandela	Hannibal
King Tut	Queen N'Zinga	Mobutu
Ramses	Joseph Cinque	Nefertiti
Akhenaten	Julius Nyerere	the Mahdi
Chief Khama	Sir Seretse Khama	Quett Masire
Michel Micombero	Amilcar Cabral	Mayotte
Barthelemy Boganda	Felix Eboué	Ngouabi
Felix Houphouet-Boigny	Macias Nguema	Theodore
Haile Selassie	Sekou Touré	Moshesh
Queen Ranavalona III	Hastings Kamuzu Banda	Modibo Keita
Leopold Senghor	Sobhuza I	King Mswati
Frederick Mutesa II	Milton Obote	King Lobengula
Cleopatra	Jugurtha	Gudit
Affonso I	Osei Tutu	Menelik II

Budget: $

Sources:

The films *Zulu* (1964), *Khartoum* (1966), and *Mandela* (1987).

Chancellor, William, *Destruction of Black Civilization: Great Issues of a Race from 4500 B.C. to 2000 A.D.*, Third World Press, 1974.

Dobler, Lavinia, and William A. Brown, *Great Rulers of the African Past*, Doubleday, 1965.

Green, Richard L., *A Salute to Historic African Kings and Queens*, Empak Enterprises, 1988.

Stanley, Diane, and Peter Vennema, *Shaka: King of the Zulus*, Morrow Junior Books, 1988.

Welsing, Frances Cress, *The Isis Papers*, Third World Press, 1991.

Alternative Applications: Have students make an illustrated time line of great African leaders. Key major items a map that places individuals in their home-lands or kingdoms, such as Ashanti, Axum, Basuto, Congo, Edo, Ethiopia, Ewe, Ngola, Shoa, Songhay, Somalia, and Zulu.

 ## Bessie Smith

Age/Grade Level or Audience: School music groups; music clubs; civic groups.

Description: Present a profile of a black person who overcame prejudice.

Procedure: Highlight the life of Bessie Smith, a singer who refused to allow discrimination to eclipse her career. Create a bulletin board, handout sheet, or oral report including these details:

- born into poverty on September 26, 1894, in Chattanooga, Tennessee
- discovered by Gertrude Rainey at age thirteen
- joined a minstrel show
- discovered by the head of Columbia Records at age seventeen
- recorded "Down Hearted Blues" in 1923
- became the highest paid black entertainer of her time
- achieved fame for "Nobody Knows You When You're Down and Out"
- died in Mississippi in 1937 as the result of a car accident

Budget: $

Sources:

LaBlanc, Michael L., *Contemporary Musicians*, Volume 3, Gale, 1990.

Smith, Jessie Carney, ed., *Notable Black American Women*, Gale, 1992.

"This Week in Black History," *Jet*, September 28, 1992, p. 29.

Alternative Applications: Create a bulletin board honor roll featuring other prominent people who overcame prejudice, for example Marian Anderson, Wilma Rudolph, Josephine Baker, Jackie Robinson, Joe Louis, Arthur Ashe, and Charles Drew. Award each a symbolic ribbon, medal, or title.

Bio-Flash

Originator: Leatrice Pearson, teacher, Lenoir, North Carolina.

Age/Grade Level or Audience: Elementary and middle school history and language classes.

Description: Generate a series of biographical flashcards to teach students about the accomplishments of black people.

Procedure: Inscribe the front of a 4" X 12" card with a few details about a famous person's life, for example:

- ◆ co-discoverer of the North Pole
- ◆ playwright in ancient Rome
- ◆ first black female astronaut in space
- ◆ Greek slave who wrote animal fables
- ◆ singer invited by Eleanor Roosevelt to perform in Washington, D.C.
- ◆ author of *The Count of Monte Cristo*
- ◆ founder of Chicago, Illinois
- ◆ comedienne and actress who starred in *The Color Purple* and *Sarafina*

On the back, print the answers in large block letters: Matthew Henson, Terence, Mae Jemison, Aesop, Marian Anderson, Alexandre Dumas, Jean Baptiste Pointe Du Sable, and Whoopi Goldberg. Drill students on the names until the class is familiar with at least twenty-five famous blacks.

Budget: $

Sources:

Bigelow, Barbara Carlisle, ed., *Contemporary Black Biography,* Gale, various years.
Cantor, George, *Historic Landmarks of Black America,* Gale, 1991.
Haskin, Jim, *One More River to Cross: The Stories of Twelve Black Americans,* 1992.
Katz, William Loren, *The Black West,* 3rd ed., Open Hand Publishers, 1987.
Low, W. Augustus, and Virgil A. Clift, eds., *Encyclopedia of Black America,* McGraw Hill, 1981.
Skow, John, "The Joy of Being Whoopi," *Time,* September 21, 1992, pp. 58-60.

Alternative Applications: Play this game in reverse, with students identifying names by mentioning details of famous lives. For example:

- ◆ Eddie Robinson, football coach for Grambling State University
- ◆ Shirley Chisholm, first black woman to run for U.S. President
- ◆ William Lloyd Garrison, editor of the abolitionist newspaper *The Liberator*
- ◆ William H. Johnson, painter

Follow up with student-made search-and-find puzzles, rebuses, cloze activities, and other word games that require the students to match names with accomplishments. Distribute word games via desktop publishing, databases, or computer networks, such as IRIS or Prodigy. Share students' work with other classes or sister schools.

Black Autobiography and Biography

Originator: Leatrice Pearson, retired English teacher, Lenoir, North Carolina.

Age/Grade Level or Audience: High school and college language, history, and African-American studies classes; adult book clubs; literary societies.

Description: Organize a roundtable to read and discuss black biography and autobiography, major contributions to literature from African-American writers.

Procedure: Introduce readers to a variety of black narratives, particularly these:

- ◆ Wally Amos's *The Famous Amos Story*
- ◆ Pearl Bailey's *Raw Pearl*
- ◆ Linda Brent's *Incidents in the Life of a Slave Girl*
- ◆ Claude Brown's *Manchild in the Promised Land*
- ◆ Eldridge Cleaver's *Soul on Ice*
- ◆ Sammy Davis, Jr.'s *Yes I Can*
- ◆ Frederick Douglass's *Narratives of the Life of Frederick Douglass*
- ◆ Dick Gregory's *Nigger*
- ◆ Lorraine Hansberry's *To Be Young, Gifted and Black*
- ◆ Chester Himes's *The Quality of Hurt and My Life as Absurdity*
- ◆ Langston Hughes's *I Wonder as I Wander*
- ◆ Charlayne Hunter-Gault's *In My Place*
- ◆ Malcolm X and Alex Haley's *The Autobiography of Malcolm X*
- ◆ Billie Holiday's *Lady Sings the Blues*
- ◆ Winnie Mandela's *Part of My Heart Went with Him*
- ◆ Melton A. McLaurin's *Celia: A Slave*
- ◆ Anne Moody's *Coming of Age in Mississippi*
- ◆ James W. C. Pennington's *The Fugitive Blacksmith*
- ◆ Nina Simone's *I Put a Spell on You*

◆ Thordis Simonsen's *You May Plow Here: The Narrative of Sara Brooks*
◆ Darryl Strawberry's *Darryl*
◆ Susie King Taylor's *A Black Woman's Civil War Memoirs*
◆ Mary C. Terrell's *A Colored Woman in a White World*
◆ Tina Turner's *I, Tina*
◆ Ethel Water's *His Eye Is on the Sparrow*
◆ Richard Wright's *Black Boy*

Include the life stories of Muhammed Ali, Marian Anderson, Kathleen Battle, Steven Biko, Marva Collins, Bill Cosby, Josiah Henson, Zora Neale Hurston, Michael Jordan, Florence Griffith Joyner, Jackie Joyner Kersee, Huddie "Leadbelly" Ledbetter, Thurgood Marshall, Robert Mugabe, Jessye Norman, Rosa Parks, Adam Clayton Powell, Leontyne Price, Prince, Paul Robeson, Jackie Robinson, Wilma Rudolph, Haile Selassie, Bessie Smith, Tituba, and Harriet Tubman. Invite participants to read aloud from significant passages and discuss personal strengths that made these people overcome racism and despair.

Budget: $$

Sources:
Black Writers, Gale, 1989.
Edwards, Barbara Audrey, and Dr. Craig K. Polite, *Children of the Dream: The Psychology of Black Success*, Doubleday, 1990.
Farmer, James, *Lay Bare the Heart: An Autobiography of the Civil Rights Movement*, Arbor House, 1985.
Gates, Henry Louis, *Classic Slave Narratives*, New American Library, 1987.
King, Martin Luther, Jr., *Why We Can't Wait*, Harper, 1964, reprinted, New American Library, 1987.
Lanker, Brian, *I Dream a World: Portraits of Black Women Who Changed America*, Stewart, Tabori, and Chang, 1989.
Smith, Jessie Carney, ed., *Notable Black American Women*, Gale, 1992.
Terry, Wallace, *Bloods: An Oral History of the Vietnam War by Black Veterans*, Random House, 1984.

Alternative Applications: Using Maya Angelou's skillful approach as a model, discuss autobiography as a multicultural art form. Contrast her personal narratives, especially *I Know Why the Caged Bird Sings* or *The Heart of a Woman*, with these works:

◆ Joy Adamson's *Born Free*
◆ *Black Elk Speaks*
◆ Jung Chang's *Wild Swans: Three Daughters of China*
◆ Anne Frank's *The Diary of Anne Frank*
◆ James Joyce's *Portrait of the Artist as a Young Man*
◆ Maxine Hong Kingston's *Woman Warrior*
◆ Scott Momaday's *The Way to Rainy Mountain*

- George Orwell's "Shooting an Elephant"
- Amy Tan's *The Joy Luck Club* or *The Kitchen God's Wife*
- Mark Twain's *Life on the Mississippi*
- Elie Wiesel's *Night*
- Corrie ten Boom's *The Hiding Place*

Black Award Winners

Age/Grade Level or Audience: Middle school and high school history and journalism classes; civic groups; museums; libraries.

Description: Name prestigious awards given to black people.

Procedure: Make a bulletin board display listing important honors and awards given to black achievers such as these:

- Susan Taylor's recognition by the Women in Communications Matrix Award
- Ralph Ellison's receipt of the Harold Washington Award
- Gwendolyn Brooks's Guggenheim Fellowship
- Ernie Davis's receipt of the Heisman Trophy
- Lorna Simpson's solo photographic exhibition at New York's Museum of Modern Art
- Henry Johnson's and Needham Roberts's receipt of Croix de Guerre awards during World War I
- Hattie McDaniel's Academy Award for best supporting actress in *Gone with the Wind*
- Bill Cosby's election to the Television Hall of Fame
- Gwendolyn Brooks's appointment as Illinois's poet laureate
- Martin Luther King, Jr.'s, Desmond Tutu's, and Ralph Bunche's receipt of Nobel Peace Prizes
- Alice Childress's and Leontyne Price's Coretta Scott King Awards for young adult literature
- Al Jarreau's Grammy for pop-jazz music
- Katherine Dunham's receipt of the Albert Schweitzer Music Award
- Alain Locke's acceptance as a Rhodes Scholar
- Lorraine Hansberry's, Lena Horne's, and Ruth Brown's Tony awards
- Vanessa Williams's and Suzette Charles's Miss America titles
- Receipt of Jim Thorpe Awards by football star Gale Sayers, tennis player Arthur Ashe, baseball player Ernie Banks, basketball stars Michael Jordan and Kareem Abdul-Jabbar, and boxers Floyd Patterson, Michael Spinks, Muhammad Ali, Kenny Norris, and Archie Moore
- Chanda Rubin's and Althea Gibson's tennis championships at Wimbledon
- Alice Coachman's, Florence Griffith Joyner's, and Wilma Rudolph's Olympic gold medals

- ◆ Paul Robeson's Donaldson Award for his 1944 performance in Shakespeare's *Othello*
- ◆ Phyllis Tucker Vinson's National Association for the Advancement of Colored People (NAACP) Medgar Evers Community Service Award
- ◆ Clara Hale's Truman Award
- ◆ Duke Ellington's and Marian Anderson's Presidential Medals of Freedom
- ◆ Maya Angelou's and Judith Jamison's Candace Awards
- ◆ Charles Gordone's, Scott Joplin's, Toni Morrison's, and Maya Angelou's receipt of Pulitzer Prizes
- ◆ Maya Angelou's being asked to write a poem to recite at President Bill Clinton's inauguration
- ◆ Augusta Savage's commission for a sculpture for the 1939 New York World's Fair
- ◆ Gwendolyn Brooks's, Toni Morrison's, and W. E. B. DuBois's admittance to the National Institute of Arts and Letters
- ◆ Architect Paul R. Williams's receipt of the Beaux Arts Medal
- ◆ Clarice D. Reid's receipt of the Public Health Service Superior Service Award
- ◆ Cicely Tyson's, Oprah Winfrey's, and Suzanne de Passe's NAACP Image Awards
- ◆ The Spingarn Medal, awarded to Marian Anderson, George Washington Carver, Jackie Robinson, Ernest E. Just, Louis T. Wright, Gordon Parks, James Weldon Johnson, Daisy Bates, Charles Young, Carl Murphy, Mary Bethune, Charles W. Chestnutt, Rosa Parks, and Martin Luther King, Jr.
- ◆ Aretha Franklin's twenty-one gold records

Budget: $

Sources:

Infotrac, Newsbank, and other on-line databases and microfilm reference sources.
Bigelow, Barbara Carlisle, ed., *Contemporary Black Biography,* Gale, various volumes.
Brelin, Christa, ed., *Who's Who among Black Americans,* 7th ed., Gale, 1993.
Current Biography, H.W. Wilson, various years.
Furtaw, Julia C., ed., *Black American Information Directory,* Gale, 1992.
Smith, Jessie Carney, ed., *Notable Black American Women,* Gale, 1992.
Terry, Ted, *American Black History: Reference Manual,* Myles Publishing, 1991.

Alternative Applications: Have history classes propose black leaders for awards, particularly for people who may have been passed over, such as heroes of the Persian Gulf War, spokespersons for AIDS research and prevention, peacekeepers, religious leaders, architects, philanthropists, or noteworthy volunteers.

Black Hall of Fame

Originator: Lela Coley and Gail Freeman, middle school teachers, Deerfield Beach, Florida.

Age/Grade Level or Audience: Elementary, middle school, and high school speech, drama, civics, and language classes.

Description: Hold a contest among local schools in which students present five-minute speeches nominating contemporary black people to a Hall of Fame.

Procedure: Have speakers focus on living people, such as entertainers, educators, military and political leaders, artists and filmmakers, writers and journalists, news and business leaders, and civil rights activists. Some likely candidates include:

Maya Angelou	Toni Morrison	Kathleen Battle
Ed Bradley	Tom Bradley	Ron Brown
Katherine Dunham	Nikki Giovanni	Clara Hale
Anita Hill	Mae Jemison	Quincy Jones
Coretta Scott King	Spike Lee	Bill Cosby
Jessye Norman	Rosa Parks	Colin Powell
Richard Pryor	Bernard Shaw	Alice Walker
Faye Wattleton	Andrew Young	Marian Wright Edelman

Offer prizes for different age groups. Encourage students to mail copies of their speeches to their chosen nominees. Addresses can be located in *Who's Who*.

Budget: $$

Sources:
Current copies of *Time, Newsweek, U.S. News and World Report, Jet, Essence, Ebony,* and *Emerge;* Infotrac, Newsbank, Africa Watch, and other on-line and microfilm indexes.
Brelin, Christa, ed., *Who's Who Among Black Americans,* 7th ed., Gale, 1993.
Current Biography, H. W. Wilson, various years.
Smith, Jessie Carney, ed., *Notable Black American Women,* Gale, 1992.

Alternative Applications: Have participants make a list of qualities and experiences that tend to propel a person into a position of influence and notoriety. For example:

- ◆ character and high ideals
- ◆ strong family ties
- ◆ a sense of place in a community
- ◆ a desire for education
- ◆ a willingness to try new challenges and to risk failure
- ◆ a sense of humor
- ◆ a desire to serve others

Black History Stamps

Age/Grade Level or Audience: All ages.

Description: Arrange a display of postal stamps from the United States, Africa, and the Caribbean.

Procedure: Select stamps that feature famous blacks, such as Marian Anderson, Nelson Mandela, Booker T. Washington, Toussaint-L'Ouverture, Charles Drew, Sarah Walker, and Martin Luther King, Jr. Place stamps on cards that detail the event or achievement featured on the stamp. Display where visitors can use a magnifying glass to examine stamps. Have art students enlarge drawings on stamps featuring famous black people. Place the enlargements on a bulletin board or feature them in a weekly newspaper column.

Budget: $$

Sources:
"Champ Stamp," *Jet,* October 5, 1992, p. 4.
"I Have a Dream: A Collection of Black Americans on U.S. Postage Stamps," Philatelic and Retail Services Department, U.S. Postal Service, 475 L'Enfant Plaza S.W., Washington, DC 20260-9998.

Alternative Applications: Have students propose a series of commemorative stamps. Organize groups to sketch individual plates featuring famous people and events, for instance, Matthew Henson's arrival at the North Pole, Garret Morgan's invention of the gas mask, the formation of the Buffalo Soldiers, or Mae Jemison's space flight.

Frederick Douglass

Age/Grade Level or Audience: Middle school, high school, and college history, literature, and journalism classes.

Description: Present the essence of Frederick Douglass's philosophy.

Procedure: Use quotations from Frederick Douglass's speeches and writings to illustrate his importance to the cause of black liberation. Present the following passages from *The North Star* as springboards to discussion. Pay particular attention to the italicized diction:

◆ We solemnly dedicate the *North Star* to the cause of our long *oppressed* and *plundered* fellow countrymen.

◆ While it shall boldly advocate emancipation for our enslaved brethren, it will omit no opportunity to gain for the *nominally free*, complete *enfranchisement*.

◆ While advocating your rights, the *North Star* will strive to throw light on your *duties*; while it will not fail to make known your virtues, it will not *shun* to discover your faults. To be faithful to our foes it must be *faithful to ourselves*, in all things.

◆ Remember that *we are one*, that our cause is one, and that we must help each other if we would succeed.

◆ We have drunk to the dregs the *bitter cup of slavery*; we have worn the heavy *yoke*; we have sighed beneath our bonds, and writhed beneath the bloody lash—*cruel mementoes* of our oneness are *indelibly marked* in our flesh.

◆ When you suffer, we *suffer*; what you endure, we *endure*.

Also, present for debate Frederick Douglass's insistence that the Fourth of July is meaningless to slaves by discussing his core argument made in 1852, thirteen years before the end of the Civil War:

What to the American slave is your Fourth of July? I answer, a day that reveals to him more than all other days of the year the gross injustice and cruelty to which he is the constant victim. To him your celebration is a sham; your boasted liberty an unholy license; your national greatness, swelling vanity; your sounds of rejoicing are empty and heartless; your denunciation of tyrants, brass-fronted impudence; your shouts of liberty and equality, hollow mockery; your prayers and hymns, your sermons and thanksgivings, with all your religious parade and solemnity, are to him mere bombast, fraud, deception, impiety, and hypocrisy—a thin veil to cover up crimes which would disgrace a nation of savages. There is not a nation of the earth guilty of practices more shocking and bloody than are the people of these United States at this very hour.

Go where you may, search where you will, roam through all the monarchies and despotisms of the Old World, travel through South America, search out every abuse and when you have found the last, lay your facts by the side of the everyday practices of this nation, and you will say with me that, for revolting barbarity and shameless hypocrisy, America reigns without a rival.

Budget: $

Sources:

Estell, Kenneth, ed., *The African-American Almanac,* 6th ed., Gale, 1993.
Ravitch, Diane, *The American Reader: Words That Moved a Nation,* HarperCollins, 1990.

Alternative Applications: Consider the years of service that Douglass

put into abolitionism and rights for black people. Compose a theme justifying a national memorial to his work by commenting on this statement:

We shall be the advocates of learning, from the very want of it, and shall most readily yield the deference due to men of education among us; but shall always bear in mind to accord most merit to those who have labored hardest, and overcome most, in the praiseworthy pursuit of knowledge, remembering "that the whole need not a physician, but they that are sick," and that "the strong ought to bear the infirmities of the weak."... Shall this gift be blest to our good, or shall it result in our injury? It is for you to say. With your aid, cooperation and assistance, our enterprise will be entirely successful. We pledge ourselves that no effort on our part shall be wanting.

Freedom Fighters

Age/Grade Level or Audience: Elementary, middle school, and high school history classes; historical societies; civic clubs.

Description: Generate capsule biographies of great African-American leaders.

Procedure: Have pairs of students pose as interviewers and great civil rights leaders, such as these:

Ralph Abernathy	Medgar Evers	James Meredith
Martin Luther King, Jr.	Mary C. Terrell	Elijah Muhammad
Marcus Garvey	Martin Delany	Paul Cuffe
Nat Turner	Daisy Bates	Whitney Young
Fannie Lou Hamer	Stokely Carmichael	H. Rap Brown
Constance Baker Motley	Thurgood Marshall	Adam Clayton Powell
Roy Wilkins	Angela Davis	Jesse Jackson
Coretta Scott King	James Foreman	James Farmer
Malcolm X	Louis Farrakhan	Josiah Henson
Charlayne Hunter-Gault	Rosa Parks	Faye Wattleton

Compose question-and-answer sessions between pairs of participants. Concentrate on the theme of progress and liberation for black people.

Budget: $

Sources:
Films such as *An Amazing Grace* (1974), *Eyes on the Prize* (1986), *Malcolm X* (1992), and *Do the Right Thing* (1989).
"Civil Rights Heroes Who Were Killed in Fight to Help Blacks Gain Right to Vote," *Jet*, October 26, 1992, pp. 10-11, 16.
Hunter-Gault, Charlayne, *In My Place*, Farrar, Straus & Giroux, 1992.

Lanker, Brian, *I Dream a World: Portraits of Black Women Who Changed America,* Stewart, Tabori, and Chang, 1989.

Meriwether, Louise, *Don't Ride the Bus on Monday: The Rosa Parks Story,* Prentice-Hall, 1973.

Alternative Applications: Create a newspaper, creative writing magazine, or daily public address program featuring information about African-American freedom fighters. Over individual strength and power, emphasize the importance of education, beliefs, courage, determination, religious faith, cooperation, and nonviolent collective action, as demonstrated by Malcolm X, Faye Wattleton, Adam Clayton Powell, Rosa Parks, and Martin Luther King, Jr.

Hats Off to the Abolitionists

Age/Grade Level or Audience: Elementary and middle school history classes; libraries and museums; religious schools.

Description: Create a wall display honoring famous abolitionists.

Procedure: On an oversized wall map, display the names, home states, and accomplishments of noted abolitionists. Record information on hat-shaped cutouts. Include these examples:

- ◆ Richard Allen, founder of Philadelphia's Free African Society
- ◆ Samuel Cornish, organizer of Philadelphia's first black Presbyterian Church
- ◆ Alexander Crummell, Philadelphia abolitionist writer
- ◆ Martin Delany, Philadelphia writer for *Freedom's Journal* who tried to help blacks resettle in Africa
- ◆ Frederick Douglass, runaway slave from Maryland who fueled New England's abolitionist movement
- ◆ Hosea Eaton, Boston abolitionist pamphleteer
- ◆ James Forten, Philadelphia sailor who employed blacks in his sail-making business
- ◆ Henry Highland Garnet, Washington, D.C., minister and speaker
- ◆ William Lloyd Garrison, Bennington, Vermont, abolitionist publisher and organizer
- ◆ Frances Ellen Watkins Harper, Philadelphia abolitionist and women's rights activist
- ◆ Absalom Jones, a founder of the Free African Society
- ◆ Toussaint L'Ouverture, Haitian revolutionary
- ◆ James W. C. Pennington, Maryland blacksmith and brick mason who became an abolitionist orator and writer
- ◆ Robert Purvis, South Carolina landowner who founded antislavery societies

- ◆ Charles Lenox Redmond, official spokesman for the Massachusetts Antislavery Society
- ◆ David Ruggles, New York City writer for abolitionist papers
- ◆ John Russworm, Philadelphia founder of Freedom's Journal, the first black newspaper
- ◆ James McCune Smith, Philadelphia physician and abolitionist columnist
- ◆ Thaddeus Stevens, Lancaster, Pennsylvania, civil rights activist
- ◆ Harriet Beecher Stowe, Cincinnati antislavery novelist
- ◆ Sojourner Truth, Hurley, New York, orator and organizer
- ◆ Harriet Tubman, Auburn, New York, conductor for the Underground Railroad
- ◆ Richard Worrell, Germantown, Pennsylvania, Mennonite activist
- ◆ Theodore S. Wright, Rhode Island minister and conductor for the Underground Railroad

Budget: $$

Sources:

Cantor, George, *Historic Landmarks of Black America,* Gale, 1991.

Estell, Kenneth, ed., *The African-American Almanac,* 6th ed., Gale, 1993.

Hornsby, Alton, Jr., *Chronology of African-American History: Significant Events and People from 1619 to the Present,* Gale, 1991.

Metcalf, Doris Hunter, *African Americans: Their Impact on U.S. History,* Good Apple, 1992.

Alternative Applications: Create a time line of the abolition movement as it reached other parts of the world. Include these dates:

1771—England	1851—Russia	1888—Brazil
1779—France	1852—Colombia	1898—Cuba
1803—Haiti and Jamaica	1854—Venezuela	1923—Afghanistan
1807—British colonies	1856—Portugal	1924—Iraq
1827—British Guyana	1860—Peru	1924—Iran
1829—Mexico	1862—Paraguay	1926—Nepal and Kalat
1831—Bolivia	1865—United States	1929—Joran and Persia
1842—West Indies	1872—Spain	1937—Bahrain
1842—Uruguay	1873—Puerto Rico	1942—Ethiopia

Martin Luther King, Jr.

Originator: Richard Kruglak and Robert DiAndreth, teachers, Linton Middle School, Pittsburgh, Pennsylvania.

Age/Grade Level or Audience: Middle school, high school, and college history and English classes; civic clubs; scout troops.

Description: Present the life and writings of Martin Luther King, Jr.

Procedure: Using handouts, present a brief biography of King. Include these points:

- ◆ King, whose father was a Baptist minister and his mother a teacher, was born in 1929 in Atlanta, Georgia.
- ◆ The son and grandson of minister/activists, King absorbed the difficulty of the black struggle for freedom.
- ◆ A bright student at Booker T. Washington High School, he enrolled at Morehouse College at age fifteen and studied sociology.
- ◆ He was ordained into the ministry in 1947.
- ◆ In 1948, King enrolled at Crozer Theological Seminary.
- ◆ He served as president of his class and won an award for leadership.
- ◆ While attending Boston University on a fellowship, King married voice major Coretta Scott.
- ◆ In 1954, he became pastor of Montgomery's Dexter Avenue Baptist Church.
- ◆ King was influenced by the writings of Gandhi and Henry David Thoreau to adopt a philosophy of nonviolent civil disobedience.
- ◆ He helped organize the Montgomery bus boycott in December 1955.
- ◆ King delivered his "Give Us the Ballot" speech before the Lincoln Memorial in Washington, D.C., on May 17, 1957.
- ◆ In 1959, King joined his father at Atlanta's Ebenezer Baptist Church and began a series of national and international travels and speaking engagements.
- ◆ He launched a desegregation movement in Albany, Georgia, in December 1961.
- ◆ Two years later, he delivered his most famous sermon, the "I Have a Dream" speech.
- ◆ In 1964, he won the Nobel Peace Prize.
- ◆ After denouncing the Vietnam war, he led the Poor People's March on Washington, D.C., in March 1968.
- ◆ On April 4, James Earl Ray assassinated King at the Lorraine Motel in Memphis, Tennessee.

Complete the study of King's impact on civil rights and black unity by studying his "Letter from Birmingham Jail." Consider this passage:

The question is not whether we will be extremists but what kind of extremist will we be. Will we be extremists for hate or will we be extremists for love? Will we be extremists for the cause of justice? In that dramatic scene on Calvary's hill, three men were crucified for the same crime—the crime of extremism. Two were extremists for immorality, and thus fell below their environment. The other, Jesus Christ, was an extremist for love, truth, and goodness, and thereby rose above his environment. So, after all, maybe the South, the nation and the world are in dire need of creative extremists.

Budget: $$

Sources:

Contact Coretta Scott King care of the Martin Luther King, Jr., Center for Nonviolent Social Change, Inc., 449 Auburn Ave. N.E., Atlanta, GA 30312; telephone: (404)524-1956.

Estell, Kenneth, ed., *The African-American Almanac*, 6th ed., Gale, 1993.

Garrow, David J., *Bearing the Cross: Martin Luther King, Jr., and the Southern Christian Leadership Conference*, Morrow, 1986.

King, Coretta Scott, *My Life with Martin Luther King, Jr.*, Holt, 1969.

Witherspoon, William Roger, *Martin Luther King, Jr.: To the Mountaintop*, Doubleday, 1985.

Alternative Applications: Have students analyze King's rhetorical style in the conclusion to his "Letter from Birmingham Jail," which ends with an historical overview:

Before the Pilgrims landed at Plymouth, we were here. Before the pen of Jefferson etched across the pages of history the majestic words of the Declaration of Independence, we were here. For more than two centuries, our foreparents labored in this country without wages; they made cotton "king," and they built the homes of their masters in the midst of brutal injustice and shameful humiliation—and yet out of bottomless vitality, they continued to thrive and develop. If the inexpressible cruelties of slavery could not stop us, the opposition we now face will surely fail. We will win our freedom because the sacred heritage of our nation and the eternal will of God are embodied in our echoing demands.

Native African Biographies

Age/Grade Level or Audience: Elementary and middle school students.

Description: Read aloud the biography of a native African.

Procedure: As you begin a story, point out on a map the location of the protagonist's tribe. Then develop incidents that shaped the life of the character. For instance, here are details about the life of Nana, an Itsekiri native of Benin:

- ◆ Nana was born in 1852 in Jakpa, Benin, and lived in Ebrohimi.
- ◆ He learned to speak English as well as the native languages of Ijo and Urhobo.

◆ He helped paddle his father's war canoe and served as his bodyguard.

◆ In 1876, after Nana's father was falsely accused of mistreating prisoners, Nana appeared in his father's behalf before the British consul.

◆ After Nana's father died in 1883, Nana became head of the household, which included ninety-two children, and grew to be a wealthy man.

◆ As an important chief, Nana served as governor of the Benin River from 1851 to 1883 and negotiated with emissaries of Queen Victoria.

◆ Disagreements with the British led to a war on August 3, 1894.

◆ Before the British cannon destroyed Ebrohimi, Nana escaped by a secret canal and fled to Lagos.

◆ The British captured and tried Nana in 1894; his punishment was exile to the Gold Coast and confiscation of most of his wealth.

◆ In 1906, Nana's son Johnson attended school in Accra.

◆ From 1898 to 1905, Nana petitioned the British consulate for pardon.

◆ In 1906, Nana was allowed to return home, where his people honored him.

◆ In his last years he built a palace, which featured an open courtyard for ceremonies and dancing.

◆ In 1907, Nana promised to help spread the Christian faith.

◆ From 1914 to 1916, Nana was too ill to work. He died July 3, 1916.

Budget: $

Sources:

"African Historical Biographies" series, Heinemann Educational Books (48 Charles Street, London WIX 8AH, England). Biographies include:

Alagoa, E. J., *King Boy of Brass*, Heinemann Educational, 1975.

Bhebe, Ngwabi, *Lobengula of Zimbabwe*, Heinemann Educational, 1977.

Daaku, K. Yeboa, *Osei Tutu of Asante*, Heinemann Educational, 1976.

Dachs, Anthony J., *Khama of Botswana*, Heinemann Educational, 1971.

Darkwah, R. H. Kofi, *Menelik of Ethiopia*, Heinemann Educational, 1972.

Igbafe, Philip Aigbona, *Obaseki of Benin*, Heinemann Educational, 1972.

Ijagbemi, Adeleye, *Naimbana of Sierra Leone*, Heinemann Educational, 1976.

Ikime, Obaro, *Nana of the Niger Delta*, Heinemann Educational, 1972.

Ikime, *Chief Dogho of Warri*, Heinemann Educational, 1976.

Rasmussen, R. Kent, *Mzilikazi of the Ndebele*, Heinemann Educational, 1977.

Tamuno, Tekena N., *Herbert Macaulay, Nigerian Patriot*, Heinemann Educational, 1976.

Unomah, A. C., *Mirambo of Tanzania*, Heinemann Educational, 1977.

Alternative Applications:

Create a flow chart of world events that were occurring during Nana's life, such as the death of Queen Victoria in 1901 and the accession of her son Edward. Place a star beside items that would have affected English-African relations, particularly the invention of the steam engine and the beginning of World War I.

Role-Playing History

Age/Grade Level or Audience: Elementary, middle school, and high school history classes; historical societies; civic clubs.

Description: Organize mock replays of famous African-Americans and the events with which they are associated.

Procedure: Have students pose as great black pioneers, such as these:

Sojourner Truth	Harriet Tubman	Frederick Douglass
Rosa Parks	Fayc Wattlcton	Ralph Abernethy
Medgar Evers	Anne Moody	Adam Clayton Powell
Jessye Norman	Marian Anderson	James Meredith
Martin Luther King, Jr.	Thurgood Marshall	Spike Lee
Ossie Davis	Sara Lou Harris	Charlayne Hunter-Gault
Dionne Warwick	Melba Moore	Marian Wright Edelman
Alex Haley	Nancy Wilson	Lloyd Richards
Wilt Chamberlain	David Dinkins	Andrew Young
Donald McHenry	Mal Goode	Elizabeth Keckley
Maxine Waters	Donald Payne	Jesse Jackson
Mae Jemison	Josiah Henson	Miriam Makeba

Capture their greatness at particular moments in history, such as these:

◆ Marian Wright Edelman's creation of Child Watch
◆ Jean Baptiste Point du Sable's founding of the city of Chicago, Illinois
◆ Elizabeth Keckley's creation of Mary Todd Lincoln's inaugural gown
◆ Jessye Norman's first operatic role
◆ Lawrence Winters's debut in Rigoletto as the first black performer in a leading operatic role
◆ Susie King Taylor's efforts as a volunteer army nurse during the Civil War
◆ Martin Luther King, Jr.'s march through Selma, Alabama
◆ Dorothea Towles's modeling career with top Paris designers
◆ Nella Larsen's receipt of a Guggenheim fellowship
◆ Edward Perkin's ambassadorship to South Africa
◆ Constance B. Motley's appointment as a federal judge
◆ Arsenio Hall's debut as a late-night television talk show host
◆ Rosa Parks's refusal to sit at the back of the bus
◆ Harriet Tubman's assistance of passengers on the Underground Railroad
◆ James Meredith's enrollment at the University of Mississippi
◆ Anne Moody's participation at the Greensboro lunch counter sit-ins
◆ Marian Anderson's performance with the Metropolitan Opera
◆ Medgar Evers's defiance of bigotry
◆ Amy Kleinhans's receipt of the Miss South Africa title

- ◆ Mother Clara Hale's ministering to AIDS and crack babies
- ◆ Naylor Fitzhugh's receipt of an MBA from Harvard
- ◆ Pilot Willa Brown Chappell's training flyers for service in World War II
- ◆ John Murphy's founding of the *Baltimore Afro-American*
- ◆ A. Philip Randolph's organization of the Brotherhood of Sleeping Car Porters
- ◆ Mary Eliza Mahoney's entry into registered nursing
- ◆ W. C. Handy's publication of "The St. Louis Blues"
- ◆ Anita Hill's testimony against Supreme Court nominee Clarence Thomas
- ◆ Josiah Henson's escape to Ontario and founding of a trade school
- ◆ Charlayne Hunter-Gault's enrollment at the University of Georgia School of Journalism
- ◆ Florence B. Price's receipt of the Wanamaker Award for composing Symphony in E Minor

Videotape these minidramas and present them for an assembly, open house, or museum display.

Budget: $

Sources:

Films such as *An Amazing Grace* (1974), *Roots* (1977), *The Josephine Baker Story* (1990), and *Malcolm X* (1992).

Asante, Molefi K., *Historical and Cultural Atlas of African Americans*, Macmillan, 1991.

Grun, Bernard, *The Timetables of History: A Horizontal Linkage of People and Events*, Simon & Schuster, 1991.

Hunter-Gault, Charlayne, *In My Place*, Farrar, Straus & Giroux, 1992.

Lanker, Brian, *I Dream a World: Portraits of Black Women Who Changed America*, Stewart, Tabori, and Chang, 1989.

Alternative Applications: Create a database of great figures from African-American history. Fill in the following information on each entry: name, birth and death dates, parents and birthplace, contributions and achievements, repercussions, awards and honors, and sources.

Rosa Parks

Originator: Michael McSweeney, teacher, Auburn, Washington; Ellen Auten, teacher, Sandwich, Illinois.

Age/Grade Level or Audience: Middle school or high school history, literature, and black studies classes.

Description: Conduct an in-depth study of Rosa Parks.

Procedure: Organize a variety of methods to study the example set by Rosa Lee McCauley Parks, the woman who on December 1, 1955, refused to move to the back of a Montgomery city bus. For example:

- ◆ Read aloud "I Am Only One Person," an anonymous poem from *Ms.,* August 1974.

- ◆ Lead a discussion of the psychological impact of one person's rejection of racism.

- ◆ Have students speak extemporaneously on the statement Parks made about racism: "Why can't we be treated like ordinary human beings? It's not me so much as the others—the ones the police hit over the head for no reason, the ones who won't have a lawyer to represent them in court. It's just the whole unbearable Jim Crow living week after week, year after year. If it will do any good, I'll just stay here in jail."

- ◆ Have students work as a team to design an appropriate monument to the quiet heroism of Rosa Parks. Select a small group to create an inscription honoring her achievement, and choose an appropriate spot for the monument, such as the place where Parks boarded the bus, her birthplace, or a state museum, government center, or library.

- ◆ Have a volunteer write to Parks to express the group's reaction to her heroism. Address letters care of Rep. John Conyers, 669 Federal Building, Detroit, MI 48226.

Budget: $

Sources:

Lanker, Brian, *I Dream a World: Portraits of Black Women Who Changed America,* Stewart, Tabori, and Chang, 1989.

Meriwether, Louise, *Don't Ride the Bus on Monday: The Rosa Parks Story,* Prentice-Hall, 1973.

Metcalfe, George R., *Black Profiles,* McGraw Hill, 1971.

"Rosa Parks," *Ms.,* August 1974.

Smith, Jessie Carney, ed., *Notable Black American Women,* Gale, 1992.

Sterne, Emma Gelders, *I Have a Dream,* Knopf, 1965.

Alternative Applications: Play "Sister Rosa," a song on the Neville Brothers' album *Yellow Moon.* Discuss with students the influence of Martin Luther King, Jr.'s philosophy on Parks. Have students make individual statements about the value of one person's example.

Sally Hemings

Age/Grade Level or Audience: High school and college American history classes.

Description: Study the influence of Sally Hemings on the life of Thomas Jefferson.

Procedure: Assign a report on the life of Sally Hemings, slave and common-law wife of Thomas Jefferson. Present these data:

- ◆ born in Virginia in 1773 to Elizabeth Hemings, a mulatto slave, and John Wayles, a white man
- ◆ was the half sister of Jefferson's wife, Martha Wayles Jefferson, who died in 1782
- ◆ granddaughter of a white ship captain and an African slave
- ◆ lived and worked at Monticello, Jefferson's Virginia estate
- ◆ accompanied Jefferson to Paris in 1788 and is reputed to have been fluent in French
- ◆ is believed to have been the mother of seven children by Jefferson, her owner
- ◆ was sensationalized as Jefferson's mistress by Thomson Callender on September 1, 1802
- ◆ died in 1836
- ◆ was memorialized by her sixth child, Madison Hemings, a carpenter
- ◆ was the subject of scurrilous racist attacks on Jefferson's ownership of slaves

Note the circumstances under which Hemings entered Jefferson's life. Discuss the ambivalence of Jefferson and other planters toward slave ownership and their desire to write into the United States Constitution a clause forbidding further slave trade.

Budget: $

Sources:
Brodie, Fawn, *Thomas Jefferson,* Norton, 1974.
Chase-Riboud, Barbara, *Sally Hemings,* Avon, 1979.
Smith, Jessie Carney, ed., *Notable Black American Women,* Gale, 1992.

Alternative Applications: Lead a "What if" discussion based on these scenarios:

- ◆ Thomas Jefferson acknowledges his relationship with a common-law slave wife.
- ◆ Jefferson publicly admits fathering children born to Sally Hemings.
- ◆ Hemings persuades Jefferson to abolish slavery during the founding of the nation.

 ## Shaka, the Zulu King

Age/Grade Level or Audience: Kindergarten and elementary classes.

Description: Tell the story of Shaka, the Zulu king.

Procedure: Have volunteers use hand gestures, mimicry, and pantomime to tell the story of Shaka. Emphasize these facts:

- ◆ Shaka was born in 1787 and learned by age six to tend goats, sheep, and cows.
- ◆ One day a dog killed one of Shaka's sheep.
- ◆ Because Shaka's mother defended the child, Shaka's father drove her out of their village.
- ◆ Shaka and his mother lived with her parents.
- ◆ Other children made fun of Shaka.
- ◆ When a famine struck, Shaka and his mother moved on.
- ◆ While they lived with another clan, Shaka learned to be a warrior.
- ◆ He designed better weapons for his people to use against enemies and wild animals.
- ◆ After Shaka's father died, Shaka returned to take charge of the Zulus.
- ◆ An evil spy stabbed Shaka.
- ◆ A doctor visiting from England saved Shaka from death.
- ◆ After Shaka's mother died, he grieved for her.
- ◆ Shaka's enemies finally succeeded in killing him.
- ◆ Shaka's people honored him after his death because he was a great leader.

Budget: $

Sources:
Stanley, Diane, and Peter Vennema, *Shaka, King of the Zulus,* Morrow Junior Books, 1988.
"This Week in Black History," *Jet,* November 2, 1992, p. 29.

Alternative Applications: Ask listeners to answer questions about Shaka and other leaders:

- ◆ Why did Shaka grow to be a great man?
- ◆ What other great leaders have suffered before rising to power?
- ◆ How did Shaka's mother help him?
- ◆ How did Shaka help his tribe?
- ◆ Why would enemies want to kill someone who made their nation strong?
- ◆ How might the Zulus have honored their dead king?
- ◆ What could modern leaders learn from Shaka?

Provide information on a more current leader to compare with Shaka such as Haile Selassie, the Ethiopian emperor who was enthroned in 1930 and who created the nation's first written constitution, which outlawed slavery.

Star of the Week

Age/Grade Level or Audience: Middle school, high school, and college language, history, mass media, and African-American studies classes.

Description: During Black History Month, focus on one famous movie actor or actress per week.

Procedure: Post photos, biographies, movie reviews, stills, and dialogue from films starring famous black actors and actresses. Note the contribution of the performer to the entertainment world and list the honors they received, such as Academy Awards. Stress a diverse selection of performers, such as Hattie McDaniel, Ethel Waters, Morgan Freeman, Lou Gossett, LaVar Burton, Paul Winfield, Sidney Poitier, Dorothy Dandridge, Yvonne de Carlo, Whoopi Goldberg, Bill Cosby, Billy Dee Williams, Butterfly McQueen, Stepin Fetchit, Cicely Tyson, Kevin Hooks, Danny Glover, Diahann Carroll, the Wayan brothers, Ice Cube, Diana Ross, Esther Rolle, and Denzel Washington.

Budget: $

Sources:

Magazines such as *Jet, Emerge,* and *Ebony.*

Brelin, Christa, ed., *Who's Who among Black Americans,* 7th ed., Gale, 1993.

Connors, Martin, and Julia C. Furtaw, *Videohound's Golden Movie Retriever 1993,* Visible Ink Press, 1992.

Halliwell, Leslie, ed., *Halliwell's Film Guide,* 7th ed., Harper & Row, 1989.

Monaco, James, *The Encyclopedia of Film,* Perigee Books, 1991.

Alternative Applications: Hold a marathon movie month at the public library featuring a variety of dramas and comedies. Features films such as these:

Field of Dreams	*Ragtime*	*Glory*
Diggstown	*Jungle Fever*	*To Kill a Mockingbird*
White Nights	*Mo' Money*	*Member of the Wedding*
Cotton Comes to Harlem	*Beverly Hills Cop*	*An Officer and a Gentleman*
Malcolm X	*To Sir With Love*	*Guess Who's Coming to Dinner*
The Color Purple	*Ghost*	*Sounder*
Birth of a Nation	*In the Heat of the Night*	*Boyz 'n the Hood*
The Little General	*Lilies of the Field*	*A Patch of Blue*
Song of the South	*Places in the Heart*	*Gone With the Wind*
Clara's Heart	*Native Son*	*Mahogany*
Daughters of the Dust	*Sarafina*	*Autobiography of Miss Jane Pittman*

Offer a different movie or video each evening. Hold an election to select the area's favorite living black cinema performer. Encourage fans to write to their favorites to express their opinions and thanks for good performances.

What's My Line?

Originator: Thea Sinclair, high school science teacher and writer, Hickory, North Carolina.

Age/Grade Level or Audience: Middle school and high school science classes.

Description: Play a version of the television game show *What's My Line?*

Procedure: Have one student pose as a noted African-American scientist, engineer, doctor, or inventor, such as Benjamin Banneker, Sarah Walker, Elijah McCoy, Ben Carson, James Walker, Ulysses Grant Dailey, Daniel Hale Williams, Garrett A. Morgan, Donald Cotton, Ernest Coleman, Mae Jemison, or Charles Drew, and have a panel guess the nature of the person's work.

Budget: $

Sources:

The video "Tracing the Path," available from the American Chemical Society, 1155 Sixteenth St. N.W., Washington, DC 20036.

Asante, Molefi K., *Historical and Cultural Atlas of African Americans*, Macmillan, 1991.

Haber, Louis, *Black Pioneers of Science and Invention*, Harcourt Brace Jovanovich, 1970, reprinted, 1991.

James, Portia P., *The Real McCoy: African-American Invention and Innovation, 1619-1930*, Smithsonian Institution Press, 1989.

Klein, Aaron E., and Cynthia L. Klein, *The Better Mousetrap: A Miscellany of Gadgets, Labor-saving Devices, and Inventions that Intrigue*, Beaufort Books, 1982.

Terry, Ted, *American Black History: Reference Manual*, Myles Publishing, 1991.

Alternative Applications: Extend the game to include other important figures, such as these:

- ◆ television stars Esther Rolle and Bill Cosby
- ◆ editors Marcia Gillespie and Stephanie Stokes Oliver
- ◆ columnist William Raspberry
- ◆ cartoonist Barbara Brandon
- ◆ politician and teacher Barbara Jordan
- ◆ authors Lorraine Hansberry and Richard Wright

- ◆ poets Mari Evans and Langston Hughes
- ◆ dancers Bill Robinson, Katherine Dunham, Gregory Hines, Judith Jamison, and Josephine Baker
- ◆ actors Cicely Tyson, Lou Gossett, Jr., Danny Glover, and Hattie McDaniel
- ◆ athletes Tony Dorsett, Sugar Ray Leonard, Wilma Rudolph, and William "Refrigerator" Perry
- ◆ astronauts Guion Bluford and Mae Jemison
- ◆ sportscaster Greg Gumbel
- ◆ television personality Bryant Gumbel
- ◆ newscasters Bernard Shaw and Ed Bradley

William Lloyd Garrison

Age/Grade Level or Audience: Middle school and high school history and language classes; religious schools.

Description: Study William Lloyd Garrison's reasons for fighting slavery.

Procedure: Present segments of William Lloyd Garrison's *The Liberator*, which he published weekly in Boston from 1831 to 1865. Have volunteers explain why he made certain bold assertions such as these:

- ◆ I have a system to destroy, and I have no time to waste.
- ◆ I determined, at every hazard, to live up to the standard of emancipation in the eyes of the nation, within sight of Bunker Hill and in the birthplace of liberty.
- ◆ That standard is now unfurled; and long may it float, unhurt by the spoliations of time or the missiles of a desperate force—yea, till every chain be broken, and every bondman set free!
- ◆ Let Southern oppressors tremble—let their secret abettors tremble—let their Northern apologists tremble—let all the enemies of the persecuted blacks tremble.
- ◆ I am aware that many object to the severity of my language; but is there not cause for severity?
- ◆ I will be as harsh as truth and as uncompromising as justice.
- ◆ On this subject I do not wish to think, or speak, or write with moderation. No! No!
- ◆ Tell a man whose house is on fire, to give a moderate alarm, tell him to moderately rescue his wife from the hands of the ravisher, tell the mother to gradually extricate her babe from the fire into which it has fallen—but urge me not to use moderation in a cause like the present.
- ◆ I am in earnest—I will not equivocate—I will not excuse—I will not retreat a single inch—AND I WILL BE HEARD.

Budget: $

Sources:
Concise Dictionary of American Literary Biography, Volume 1: *Colonization to the American Renaissance, 1640-1865*, Gale, 1988.
Estell, Kenneth, ed., *The African-American Almanac*, 6th ed., Gale, 1993.

Alternative Applications: Discuss why modern writers adopt a similar tone and approach when discussing current atrocities against black people, particularly famine in Ethiopia and Somalia, apartheid in South Africa, and unemployment, workplace discrimination, drug use, suppression, and poverty. Have students gather examples of letters to the editor, editorials, poetry, and songs that parallel William Lloyd Garrison's style of writing. Some likely comparisons are these:

- ◆ Richard Wright's *Black Boy*
- ◆ Maya Angelou's *I Know Why the Caged Bird Sings*
- ◆ Martin Luther King's "Letter from Birmingham Jail"
- ◆ speeches by Nelson Mandela and Jesse Jackson
- ◆ Toni Morrison's *The Bluest Eye* and *Beloved*
- ◆ James Baldwin's *The Fire Next Time*
- ◆ rap lyrics

Words to Live By

Originator: Leatrice Pearson, retired English teacher, Lenoir, North Carolina.

Age/Grade Level or Audience: All ages.

Description: Highlight the advice of famous black American women.

Procedure: Utilize quotations from notable black women as chalkboard slogans, banners, program focuses, bulletin and newsletter features, and topics for discussion, debate, and writing. Select from the following memorable lines:

- ◆ I don't like the idea of the black race being diluted out of existence. I like the idea of all of us being here. (Gwendolyn Brooks, poet)
- ◆ The black woman has deep wells of spiritual strength. She doesn't know how she's going to feed her family in the morning, but she prays and in the morning, out of thin air, she makes breakfast. (Margaret Walker, novelist)
- ◆ In knowing how to overcome little things, a centimeter at a time, gradually when bigger things come, you're prepared. (Katherine Dunham, dancer)
- ◆ I will die for my right to be human—just human. (Cicely Tyson, actress)
- ◆ The only way I was going to make a difference for myself or any other black person is to say the hurdles were there and do what I had to do. (Wyomia Tyus, Olympic runner)

◆ We don't have nothin', so we ain't losing nothin' and our life don't mean nothin' if we continue this way with no freedom. (Unita Blackwell, former mayor of Mayersville, Mississippi)

◆ It is the linkage of humanity which has to solve the problem. (Barbara Jordan, former U.S. Senator)

◆ What you were born to do, you don't stop to think, should I? could I? would I? I only think will I? And, I shall. (Eva Jessye, choral director)

◆ White people have suffered as much as we have. They just don't know it. (Anna Arnold Hedgeman, activist)

◆ Most women that have to fight for survival get a special strength sooner or later. (Elizabeth Catlett, sculptor and lithographer)

◆ I don't hate white people. I hate the idea that someone, black or white, condescends or looks down on me, on anyone. (Autherine Lucy, activist)

◆ I weep a lot. I thank God I laugh a lot, too. The main thing in one's own private world is to try to laugh as much as you cry. (Maya Angelou, writer)

◆ I am grateful and blessed because those women whose names made the history books, and a lot who did not, are all bridges that I've crossed over to get to this side. (Oprah Winfrey, entertainer)

◆ The struggle is to share the planet, rather than to divide it. (Alice Walker, novelist)

Budget: $

Sources:

Bell, Janet Cheatham, *Famous Black Quotations and Some Not So Famous,* Sabayt Publications, 1986.

King, Anita, ed., *Quotations in Black,* Greenwood Press, 1981.

Lanker, Brian, *I Dream a World: Portraits of Black Women Who Changed America,* Stewart, Tabori, and Chang, 1989.

Smith, Jessie Carney, ed., *Notable Black American Women,* Gale, 1992.

Alternative Applications: Select a famous quotation to illustrate with a political cartoon, woodcut, pen-and-ink drawing, watercolor, collage, sculpture, or other art form. Choose from these:

◆ I have no choice but to keep on. (Rosa Parks, activist)

◆ It's a bitter experience when the assumption is that it's for all of us, and then you find out it's for some of us. (Johnnetta Betsch Cole, Spelman College president)

◆ What I do concerns me, not what people think. (Marva Nettles Collins, educator)

◆ Our proclamations and resolutions are great. We have yet to live them out. (Bishop Leontine Kelly)

◆ We balance on each others' shoulders and even if you stand on my head it's okay, if it will hold you up. (Rachel Robinson, psychiatric nurse)

- You can focus on the obstacles, or you can go on and decide what you do about it. (Gloria Scott, president of Bennett College)
- God is good, that's what I'll say. (Sarah Vaughan, singer)
- Racism just blinds us to the real problems that face us all. (Ruby Dee, actress)
- The challenge is still there. (Wilma Rudolph, athlete)
- This country couldn't call us Africans because if it had, we would have understood some things about ourselves. (Sonia Sanchez, poet)
- The racism will continue. The coping will improve. (Carrie Saxon Perry, former mayor of Hartford, Connecticut)
- I have great belief in the fact that whenever there is chaos, it creates wonderful thinking. I consider chaos a gift. (Septima Clark, activist)
- The time has come for a perception of compassion in this world. (Beah Richards, actress)
- We're good people and we try. (Clara McBride Hale, activist)
- [Happiness] comes from within. It was there all the time. (Ernestine Anderson, jazz singer)

Business and Advertising

FIVE

African-American Entrepreneurs

Age/Grade Level or Audience: Middle school, high school, and college math, business, and history classes.

Description: Organize a study of America's most successful African-American entrepreneurs.

Procedure: Have students study books, reference sources, newspapers, and magazines for information about successful black business people, for example:

- Madame C. J. Walker (inventor of the "hot" comb), Cornell McBride (M & M), Susan Taylor (Nequai), and Comer J. Cottrell (Pro-Line), cosmetics and hair care
- John H. Johnson, publishing and broadcasting
- Raymond V. Haysbert (Parks Sausage Co.)
- David Lloyd (Bay City Marine), ship building and repair
- Reginald L. Lewis (Beatrice International), food processing and distribution
- Carl A. Brown (Mandex), telecommunications
- Al Watiker, highway and bridge construction
- Leamon M. McCoy (True Transport), transportation
- Edward Lewis (Essence Communications), magazine and television production
- Biddy Mason, real estate investment
- Wally Amos (Famous Amos cookies), bakery goods
- John Cornelius Asbury, burial services
- Thomy Lafon, H.C. Haynes, and John Jones, merchandising
- David Bing (Bing Steel)
- Spike Lee (40 Acres and a Mule), merchandising
- Herman J. Russell, construction and communications
- John Merrick and A. M. Moore (North Carolina Mutual Life Insurance)

◆ Susan dePasse (Gordy/dePasse Productions)
◆ Joshua Smith (Maxima) and Gale Sayers (Crest Computer Supplies), computers
◆ Naylor Fitzhugh (Small Business Center)
◆ Paxton K. Baker (PKB Arts and Entertainment Productions)
◆ Robert J. Hurst (president of Michigan Bell Telephone)
◆ Bill Cosby and Oprah Winfrey, television production
◆ Robert Johnson (head of Black Entertainment Television)
◆ Meredith Gourdine (Gourdine Industries), manufacturing of electro-gas dynamics equipment
◆ Larry A. Huggins (Ritway Construction)
◆ Maggie Lena Walker (St. Luke Penny Savings Bank)
◆ Bernard Beal (M. R. Beal Investments)
◆ Richard R. Wright (Citizens and Southern Bank and Trust Co.)
◆ Earl G. Graves, publications
◆ Robert S. Browns, technical development
◆ Leroy Callender, engineering
◆ Berry Gordy (Motown Industries)
◆ Ronald Brockett (Dover Graphics), advertising

Conclude with general questions, such as these:

◆ What areas of business have produced the most success for black entrepreneurs?
◆ What avenues of advertising have produced the greatest response?
◆ How can schools promote similar entrepreneurial goals in future generations of black children?
◆ How can society assure equal success for black women?

Budget: $

Sources:

Black Enterprise, October 1992.

Buy, Pat, "Magazines Seek Minorities," *USA Today*, October 22, 1992, p. 4B.

Estell, Kenneth, ed., *The African-American Almanac*, 6th ed., Gale, 1993.

"JPC Publisher Succeeds against Odds," *Jet*, November 9, 1992, p. 6.

Randall, Eric D., "Black Financiers Gaining: Good Education Adds Up," *USA Today*, September 22, 1992, p. 8B.

Smith, Jessie Carney, ed., *Notable Black American Women*, Gale, 1992.

Alternative Applications: Have groups of students examine current markets and suggest new areas in which black business people would be successful.

African Money

Age/Grade Level or Audience: Middle school and high school business or economics class.

Description: Assemble an international money chart explaining the types of currency used in African countries.

Procedure: Assign students to work in pairs to create a money chart for Africa listing country, names of greater and lesser forms of currency, and their international symbols. Obtain samples of the currencies from banks to affix to the chart. For instance:

Country	Currency	Symbol
Ethiopia	birr, cents	E$ or EB
Benin	franc, centimes	Fr or F
Lesotho	lot, licente	—
Malawi	kwacha, tambala	K
South Africa	riyal, qursh, halala	R or SR
Zaire	zaire, makuta	Z

Have students extend the chart to include other countries where the population is largely black, especially Haiti and Jamaica. Explain why travelers to these places will want to know the exchange rate before they leave the United States.

Budget: $

Sources:
Full service banks, foreign embassies, books on currency or international banking. *Webster's Ninth New Collegiate Dictionary,* Merriam-Webster, Inc., 1991.

Alternative Applications: Have students create a flexible, applicable Afro-centric monetary system for an evolving black nation. Include sketches of paper currency and coins, denominations, metals, and weight. Decorate with drawings of notables and famous events connected with the history of the country. Stress prominent female figures.

Black Landmark Ad Campaign

Age/Grade Level or Audience: Middle school and high school business, journalism, art, and writing classes.

Description: Compose attractive magazine ads featuring African-American historical or cultural tourist attractions.

Procedure: Select some places tourists or school groups might enjoy visiting in order to learn more about black history. Highlight the area with a carefully planned ad campaign, including slogans, maps, drawings, descriptions, and other enticements. Consider spots such as:

- Detroit's famed 24-foot-long sculpture "The Fist," which symbolizes the black power movement and commemorates Joe Louis, a championship boxer from Detroit. Also in Detroit is the Motown Museum, which contains a collection of memorabilia from some of the most successful black music stars.
- the Buffalo Soldier Monument in Fort Leavenworth, Kansas.
- Scott Joplin's home in St. Louis, Missouri, which has been restored with accurate details from the early twentieth century.
- Mobile's Africa Town, where slaves brought illegally to the United States aboard the *Clothilde* in 1859 settled and maintained their African culture. Feature the statue of Cudjoe Lewis, the last surviving African passenger.
- the Lorraine Motel in Memphis, where Martin Luther King, Jr., was assassinated. Currently in use as a civil rights museum, the building houses displays about the civil rights movement, including a bus commemorating the 1955 Mobile transportation strike.
- the historical part in Jamestown, Virginia, where the first black slaves were settled and where the first black child was born in New World territory.
- the Afro-American Museum of Chattanooga, Tennessee, where Bessie Smith and other black notables are honored.
- the Robert Smalls Memorial at the Baptist Tabernacle Church in Beaufort, South Carolina, which captures the spirit of a slave who captained the *Planter*, a navy steamer, during the Civil War.
- Hollywood, California's Mann's Chinese Theatre, where Sidney Poitier became the first black actor immortalized with his footprints in cement.
- Omaha, Nebraska's Great Plains Black Museum, which honors Mary Fields, manager of a stagecoach station in Cascade, Montana.
- Louisville, Kentucky's Knights of Pythias Hall, dating to 1915 and housing the first African-American fraternal group.
- New York's Apollo Theatre, site where many of the pioneers of black music entertained integrated audiences in the 1920s and 1930s.

Budget: $$

Sources:

Brochures, maps, and travel guides from area chambers of commerce and the Automobile Association of America (AAA).

Asante, Molefi K., *Historical and Cultural Atlas of African Americans,* Macmillan, 1991.

Cantor, George, *Historic Landmarks of Black America,* Gale, 1991.

Estell, Kenneth, ed., *The African-American Almanac,* 6th ed., Gale, 1993.

"General Colin Powell Dedicates a Monument to the Buffalo Soldiers: Unsung Black Heroes," *Jet,* September 7, 1992.

Naylor, Colin, ed., *Contemporary Artists,* 3rd ed., St. James Press, 1989.

Alternative Applications: Organize a field trip or walking tour to interesting black monuments in your area. Have a group work together to create a schematic drawing or map of the tour. Supply the following information:

- ◆ locations of museums, churches, libraries, schools, or homes of famous people
- ◆ times that buildings are open
- ◆ admission fees
- ◆ locations of gift shops or book stores featuring African-American lore
- ◆ suggestions for photographic opportunities, particularly sculpture, plaques, historic architectural styles, or reenactments of scenes from black history. Write up the day's excursion in journal or letter form.

The Black Middle Class

Age/Grade Level or Audience: College economics classes; adult civic groups, such as the Business and Professional Women's League and Rotary Club.

Description: Discuss the social burdens borne by the rising black middle class.

Procedure: Invite a business or economics expert to address an adult college, business, or civic group on the difficulties faced by the black bourgeoisie.

- ◆ the emergence of a class within a class
- ◆ a cultural gap between wealthy and poor blacks
- ◆ psychological problems, such as guilt and self-doubt
- ◆ response to Affirmative Action quotas and the "glass ceiling"
- ◆ ambivalence toward success
- ◆ accepting social and moral responsibility to the black race and the nation as a whole

Budget: $

Sources:

Du Bois, W. E. B., "Talented Tenth" speech, *Forbes,* September 14, 1992, p.132-138.

Estell, Kenneth, ed., *The African-American Almanac,* 6th ed., Gale, 1993.

Gates, Henry Louis, "Two Nations ... Both Black," *Forbes,* September 14, 1992, p. 132-138.

Alternative Applications: Hold a round robin exploring the problems of the black bourgeoisie and present your findings in a local newspaper. Discuss ways to overcome prejudices among people of differing financial and educational standings.

Business Incubator

Age/Grade Level or Audience: Adult civic groups.

Description: Organize a consortium to create methods of encouraging black enterprise.

Procedure: Invite participants to brainstorm methods of encouraging young people to establish their own businesses. Consider some of the following methods:

◆ Create an ongoing business referral service.
◆ Open money markets to high-risk entrepreneurs.
◆ Offer reduced-rate advertising for minority businesses.
◆ Organize think tanks for high school and college students interested in business ventures.
◆ Revitalize dying city areas by offering young entrepreneurs storefront space at reduced rates in exchange for refurbishment.
◆ Meet with successful minority entrepreneurs from surrounding areas to share ideas and promote networking.
◆ Set up computer workshops to help young business leaders stay up to date on software.
◆ Challenge problems before they become too big to handle, such as unemployment, market shifts, insurance problems, and tight money.

Budget: $$$

Sources:

The Federal Small Business Administration; philanthropic societies, volunteer agencies, and civic groups such as the Business and Professional Women's League; contact Dr. Stewart E. Perry, Institute for New Enterprise Development, 25 Highland Ave., Cambridge, MA 02233-1021; telephone: (617)491-0203.

Kunjufu, Jawanza, *Black Economics: Solutions for Economics and Community Empowerment*, Highsmith, 1992.

Alternative Applications: Present ideas, campaigns, and suggestions in a regular newspaper column slanted toward beginners in the marketplace. Invite write-in questions. Establish a hotline staffed by volunteer bankers, political leaders, and business and industrial managers.

The Economics of Slavery

Age/Grade Level or Audience: High school and college business, history, and economics classes; civic groups.

Description: Organize a panel to discuss how economics favored the institution of slavery in the Western Hemisphere.

Procedure: Present the following facts for discussion:

- ◆ Southern and Caribbean plantations depended on free slave labor to manage labor-intensive crops such as cotton, sugar cane, spices, rice, and tobacco.
- ◆ Plantation owners encouraged polygamy to increase the slave population, then sold offspring like livestock to supplement agricultural income.
- ◆ Elite Southern and Caribbean lifestyles, based on European notions of gentility and refinement, required substantial incomes, support staff, and leisure time.
- ◆ Southerners and Caribbean plantation owners feared a wholesale freeing of slaves or a general uprising.
- ◆ If Southern states had elected to end slavery, they would have faced the problem of housing, feeding, and educating blacks to become self-sufficient.
- ◆ Most of the churches and abolitionist societies that opposed slavery were in Pennsylvania and New England, far from the reality of the slave economy.
- ◆ Caribbean slave owners began emancipation proceedings decades before Southern planters.

Conclude with a discussion of the division of North and South and the ensuing war. Discuss the role of Caribbean privateers, who served successfully as blockade runners during the war.

Budget: $

Sources:

Fodor's Caribbean: A Complete Guide to 27 Island Destinations, Fodor's Travel Guides, 1993.

Kunjufu, Jawanza, *Lessons from History: A Celebration of Blackness,* African American Images, 1987.

Low, W. Augustus, and Virgil A. Clift, eds., *Encyclopedia of Black America,* McGraw Hill, 1981.

Parish, Peter, *Slavery: History and Historians,* Harper & Row, 1989.

Wilson, Charles Reagan, and William Ferris, eds., *Encyclopedia of Southern Culture,* University of North Carolina Press, 1989.

Alternative Applications: Extend the discussion of the economics of slavery to the collapse of the Southern economy during the Civil War and reasons why recovery has taken so long. Consider the following details in your examination of economic trends:

- General William Tecumseh Sherman's destruction of Atlanta
- disruption of rail service
- loss of managers, technicians, and business leaders during the war
- dislocation of the labor force
- malaise among leaders who looked to a restoration of the past economy
- collapse of the Confederate monetary system
- the burden of wounded veterans, amputees, and victims of tuberculosis and other diseases brought on by hunger, exposure, stress, and cold
- the inability of the federal government to decide on a workable plan of economic recovery
- confusion and dismay among free blacks who were deceived by promises of "forty acres and a mule"
- restrictive legislation such as Black Codes, the Grandfather Clause, and Jim Crow Laws
- the rise of sharecropping and tenant farming, which mimicked slavery in their control of black lives
- the rise of opportunity during the world wars
- black migration to Northern industrial centers
- cultural support systems, particularly the extended family, schools, and churches

Getting the Public's Attention

Age/Grade Level or Audience: All ages.

Description: Increase a public awareness of Black History Month through advertisement.

Procedure: Suggest that local business groups, visitors bureaus, and the chamber of commerce launch an advertising campaign to stimulate black history awareness. Use banners, media announcements, shopping bags, yard markers, billboards, hats, paper napkins, cups, toys, and giveaways, such as yo-yos, kites, key chains, luggage tags, posters, calendars, lapel pins, and bumper stickers. Have school art, history, and English classes provide drawings, maps, slogans, and quotations to serve as the basis of the campaign, which should continue throughout February. Offer a prize for the most creative display suggestion, drawing, or slogan. Display runners-up at a civic center or museum.

Budget: $$$

Sources:

Survey the advertising market and adapt ideas from catalogs, displays, promotions, and other sources to focus on black history.

Dacey, Donna. "Crafts of Many Cultures: Three Seasonal Art Projects with Global Appeal," *Instructor,* November-December 1991, pp. 30-33.

Estell, Kenneth, ed., *The African-American Almanac,* 6th ed., Gale, 1993.

Alternative Applications:
Organize a local contest to create a city seal, flag, banner, plaque, plaza, signboard, mural, slogan, or other symbol of community pride. Feature all racial groups involved in acts depicting good citizenship through racial harmony.

Cooking

African Dessert-a-thon

Originator: Gary Carey, teacher, writer, and editor, Lincoln, Nebraska.

Age/Grade Level or Audience: All ages.

Description: Organize a tasting booth of African desserts.

Procedure: For a street fair or other get-together in celebration of Black History Month, present a variety of African desserts for sampling and comparison. Use recipes such as these for food demonstrations at county fairs, appliance shows, and home economics projects:

Angolan Coconut Pudding

In a 5-quart saucepan, combine the following:
>   2 c. sugar
>   6 c. water
>   4 whole cloves

Boil until mixture reaches 230°. Discard cloves. Add 4 cups grated coconut. Cook 10 minutes, stirring constantly. Remove from heat. Whisk 12 egg yolks and blend into the hot mixture. Cook 10 minutes. Pour into dessert cups, sprinkle with ground cinnamon, and refrigerate until firm.

Banana Sweeties

Slice bananas lengthwise. Coat inside with peanut butter and press halves together. Top with the following mixture:
>   2 tbs. molasses
>   1 c. sugar
>   1 tsp. cinnamon
>   1 c. whipped evaporated milk

Mozambique Papaya Pudding

Whirl the following ingredients in a blender:

      1 ripe papaya, seeded and chopped

      ¼ c. lime or lemon juice

      ¼ c. water

Place in a small saucepan and add these ingredients:

      2 c. sugar

      1 stick cinnamon

      4 cloves

Cook, stirring constantly, until mix reaches 230°. Remove cinnamon and cloves and cool. Whisk 5 egg yolks until thick. Add the hot mixture in a thin stream and beat until smooth. Pour into dessert dishes and refrigerate.

South African Crullers

Prepare a syrup from the following ingredients:

      4 c. sugar

      2 c. water

      3 sticks cinnamon

      2 tbs. lemon or lime juice

      peel of 1 lemon

      ¼ tsp. cream of tartar mixed with 2 tsp. water

      ⅛ tsp. salt

Cook mixture until sugar melts. Cool immediately in container of ice.

Combine dry ingredients:

      4 c. flour

      4 tsp. baking powder

      ½ tsp. each cinnamon, nutmeg, and salt

Knead in 2 tablespoons each butter and lard. Roll balls of dough into rectangles. Cut into three vertical strips and braid. Fry in 3-inch hot peanut oil. Drain and dip into syrup.

South African Figure Eight Cookies

Sift together the following:

      1½ c. flour

      1 tsp. baking powder

      1 tsp. cinnamon

      ⅛ tsp. salt

In a separate bowl, cream 7 tablespoons butter with ½ cup sugar. Beat in an egg; add the mixture to the dry ingredients. Knead dough into a ball. Roll out ¼-inch thick, cut into strips, and roll into cylinders. Shape into figure eights and place on cookie sheet. Spread with a mixture of lightly beaten egg white. Sprinkle with ½ cup slivered almonds and ¼ cup sugar. Chill for ½ hour, then bake 12 minutes at 400°.

South African Rice with Raisins

Melt 2 tablespoons butter in a skillet and brown 1 cup white rice. Add these ingredients:

2 c. boiling water
1 stick cinnamon
½ tsp. turmeric
⅛ tsp. saffron
1 tsp. salt
¾ c. sugar

Cover and simmer 20 minutes. Remove cinnamon stick. Add 1 cup raisins. Serve with cream.

South African Stewed Sweet Potatoes

Peel and slice 2 pounds sweet potatoes into ½-inch rounds. On the bottom of a 4-quart saucepan, alternate slices and sprinkle with the following mixture:

1 tsp. salt
1 tbs. flour
¼ c. brown sugar
1 tbs. butter

Slide 3 1-inch sticks of cinnamon under the potatoes. Pour in ½ cup water. Cook 45 minutes.

Tanzanian Fruit Whip

To 2 cups mashed banana add 3 whipped egg whites, ½ teaspoon vanilla, and 1 tablespoon sugar. Serve over mixed fruit slices, rice, or pudding.

West African Banana Fritters

Whisk together the following ingredients:

1½ c. flour
6 tbs. sugar
3 eggs

Puree 5 bananas and blend with the mixture. Heat 3 inches of peanut or corn oil in a heavy dutch oven and drop in dollops of the banana mixture. When they are brown on all sides, drain on brown paper and sprinkle with confectioner's sugar.

Budget: $$$

Sources:

Longacres, Doris Janzen, *More-with-Less Cookbook,* Herald Press, 1976.
Nabwire, Constance, and Bertha Vining Montgomery, *Cooking the African Way,*
  Lerner Publications, 1988.
van der Post, Laurens, *African Cooking,* Time-Life Books, 1970.

Alternative Applications: Demonstrate African desserts and comment on common ingredients, particularly cream, rice, yogurt, fresh bananas, papayas, yams, coconut, peanuts, cinnamon, cloves, and coriander. Hold a workshop in which participants experiment with original recipes made from typical African ingredients. Maintain a database of original recipes. Publish the results of the workshop in a handout or booklet.

▤ African Lentils

Originator: Gary Carey, teacher, writer, and editor, Lincoln, Nebraska.

Age/Grade Level or Audience: All ages.

Description: Hold a neighborhood dinner or Africa Night PTA supper to celebrate Black History Month.

Procedure: Select volunteers to cook and service an Egyptian or Zambian one-dish meal. Consider recipes such as these:

Kusherie

Heat 2 tablespoons peanut oil in a saucepan or covered skillet. Add 1¼ cup lentils. Brown for 5 minutes, stirring constantly. Blend in 3 cups boiling water or chicken stock, salt and pepper. Cook 10 minutes at a slow boil. Add 1½ cups brown rice and one cup boiling water or chicken stock. Simmer 30 minutes.

While the main ingredients are cooking, heat these ingredients for the sauce:

> ¾ c. tomato paste
> 3 c. tomato juice, puree, or sauce
> 1 green, yellow, or red pepper, chopped
> 1 c. chopped celery leaves and heart
> 1 tbs. sugar
> ½ tbs. salt
> 1 tbs. cumin
> ¼ tbs. cayenne pepper or crushed chilis

Simmer sauce 30 minutes.

Heat 3 sliced onions and 4 minced garlic cloves in 2 tablespoons oil. Serve rice and lentils with sauce and onion topping. Leftover rice and lentil mix can be eaten with plain yogurt or sour cream. Serves 6-8.

For other ways of cooking lentils, consider these variations:

Lentils Deluxe

Simmer for ½ hour the following:

> 1 c. lentils
> 2½ c. water
> 2 beef, chicken, or vegetable bouillon cubes
> 1 bay leaf
> the tops of one bunch of celery
> 1 tbs. each salt and pepper

Cover with Lentil Curry topping:

Lentil Curry

Sauté 1 chopped onion and 1 garlic clove in ¼ cup oil or margarine. Add 1 tablespoon salt and 2 tablespoons curry powder. Remove from heat, and blend with chopped parsley and 2 tablespoons lemon or lime juice.

Lentil Salad

Season ½ pound cooked lentils with the following ingredients:

> 3 tbs. wine vinegar
> 2 tbs. peanut or vegetable oil
> 1 tsp. salt
> 1 tsp. pepper
> 8 shallot cloves, peeled and halved
> 2 hot chilies stemmed, seeded, and cut into thin strips

Marinate salad for ½ hour, stirring gently. Serve with crackers or fresh vegetables.

Lentil Soup

Cook 1 cup lentils in 4 cups water seasoned with ½ tablespoon cumin. Meanwhile sauté a chopped onion and garlic clove in 1 tablespoon peanut or olive oil. Blend in 1 tablespoon flour. Add mixture to cooked lentils and bring to a boil. Top off the soup with salt, pepper, and lemon or lime juice.

Lentil Stew

To cooked lentils add the following:

> ½ lb. diced ham, browned ground or string beef, or sausage
> ¾ c. tomato paste
> 2 c. water
> ¼ tbs. oregano
> 1 tbs. salt
> 1 chopped onion
> 2 stalks celery, chopped
> 1 minced garlic clove

Bring ingredients to a boil, and simmer until vegetables are tender. Serve over rice, couscous, or pita rounds.

Sweet and Sour Lentils

Cook lentils in 2 cups water. When lentils are cooked, add these ingredients:

> ¼ c. apple or pineapple juice
> ¼ c. cider vinegar
> ¼ c. brown sugar
> 1 crushed garlic clove
> ⅛ tbs. ground cloves
> sautéed onion

If you prefer a green accompaniment, serve a Zambian side dish of chopped beet tops or leaves from beans, pumpkin vines, cauliflower, or broccoli. Boil greens with salt and chopped peanuts. Other alternatives include these:

Kenyan Cucumber or Onion Salad

Thinly slice 3 cups cucumber or onion and dress with these ingredients:

2 tbs. dill weed

2 tbs. sour cream, yogurt, or mayonnaise

1 tbs. vinegar

2 tbs. olive, peanut, or corn oil

salt, pepper, chopped chilies, and paprika to taste

Serve chilled.

South African Beet and Onion Salad

Cut the leafy tops from 1 pound of small fresh beets. Drop beets into boiling water and simmer ½ hour. Drain and skin beets and slice into strips. Marinate for a ½ hour in the following dressing:

¼ c. wine vinegar

1 tsp. salt

½ tsp. sugar

¾ c. thinly sliced onion rings

Budget: $$

Sources:

Longacres, Doris Janzen, *More-with-Less Cookbook*, Herald Press, 1976.

Merson, Annette, *African Cookery: A Black Heritage*, Winston-Derek, 1987.

van der Post, Laurens, *African Cooking*, Time-Life Books, 1970.

Alternative Applications: Feature eggplant or other vegetables instead of lentils in any of the following dishes:

Eggplant Supreme

Peel and slice a large eggplant into ¼-inch pieces. Heat in a large skillet with 1 tablespoon peanut or corn oil or margarine, onion, and chopped or slivered green pepper. Sprinkle with chili powder and salt. As eggplant cooks, whip five eggs and stir in two large tomatoes, chopped. Pour over softened vegetables. When egg is cooked on one side, flip and brown the other side. Serve like crepes, frittatas, or pancakes.

Egyptian Tabikh

Cook 6 cups green beans or zucchini in 2 cup tomato juice. Add 2 tablespoons tomato paste, sauteed onion, and bits of ham or chicken. Cook 20 minutes. Serve over rice, orzo, or couscous.

South African Cabbage Rolls

Boil 1 large head of cabbage for 10 minutes. Remove cabbage from liquid and peel off thick outside leaves. Spread leaves and cut out the tough ribs. Fill each leaf with a patty made from ⅓ cup of the following ingredients:

2 c. cooked ground lamb

½ c. bread crumbs

½ c. chopped onion

2 eggs

¼ tsp. nutmeg

1 tsp. coriander

2 tsp. salt

1 tsp. pepper

¼ c. peanut, corn, or vegetable oil

1 c. beef stock

1 tbs. flour

1 tbs. cold water

Wrap leaves around patties and tie with cotton cord. Place seam side down in a dutch oven. Cover with 2 cups beef or vegetable stock and simmer for 1 hour. Remove to platter. Whisk 2 tablespoons flour with ½ cup water and add to stock. Cook sauce until thickened and pour over cabbage rolls.

West African Chicken and Peanut Stew

Cut a 6-pound chicken into pieces and rub with 1 tablespoon each salt and ground ginger. Brown in a lightly oiled dutch oven along with 1 cup chopped onions. Add the following ingredients:

5 pureed tomatoes

¼ c. tomato paste

½ c. dried ground shrimp

1 finely chopped garlic clove

¼ tsp. grated ginger

½ tsp. each white and hot red pepper or paprika

Simmer five minutes. Add these ingredients:

6 c. boiling water

¼ c. dried small fish

2 hot chilies

Coat chicken in the mixture and cook 15 minutes. Make a paste of 1 cup peanut butter and 1 cup water. Add paste and 12 stemmed okra pods and cook 1 hour. Add 6 hard-boiled eggs and simmer 5 minutes. Serve stew along with a choice of garnishes, such as chopped onion, pineapple chunks, roasted peanuts, diced tomatoes, spiced okra, avocado chunks, plantain or papaya cubes, or fufu (mashed yams).

Zambian One-Dish Pumpkin

In a large dutch oven combine these ingredients:

2 lbs. chopped potato

1 lb. cooked pumpkin or 2 lbs. chopped carrot or turnip

2 chopped onions

2 stalks of celery, chopped

3 tbs. fresh parsley, chopped

2 minced garlic cloves

salt and pepper

water or broth to moisten vegetables

¼ c. peanut or corn oil or margarine

When vegetables are tender, add 1 tablespoon bouillon powder dissolved in ¼ cup water and ½ cup ground peanuts.

Cooking for Kwanzaa

Originator: Roberta Brown, teacher, Fort Bragg, North Carolina.

Age/Grade Level or Audience: Kindergarten and elementary school students; church schools.

Description: Help students make simple foods to celebrate Kwanzaa.

Procedure: Help students prepare simple recipes. For instance:

Coconut Sudi

Blend the meat and milk of a fresh coconut with one teaspoon each vanilla, nutmeg, and cinnamon.

Add an American touch. Explain to students how George Washington Carver helped change the South's economy by teaching people to rely on peanut butter to enrich their diet with protein. Then have students make their own peanut butter.

Peanut Butter

Shell enough roasted peanuts to fill 1 cup. Put the nuts along with ½ teaspoon salt and 3 tablespoons corn or vegetable oil in a blender and process for 1 minute. Serve on small crackers.

Expand this lesson by introducing students to sweet potato recipes, including fufu dumplings and sweet potato souffle.

Fufu Dumplings

Mash baked sweet potatoes and form paste into balls 2 inches in diameter. Drop into soup stock, stew, or broth.

Sweet Potato Souffle

Blend a 1-pound can of sweet potatoes with the juice of 1 lemon and 6 egg yolks. Whip 6 egg whites separately and blend in 1 cup sugar. Fold first mixture into sweetened whites. Bake in buttered casserole 30 minutes at 375°.

Budget: $$

Sources:

Karenga, Maulana, *The African-American Holiday of Kwanzaa: A Celebration of Family, Country, and Culture,* University of Sandore Press, 1988.

McClester, Cedric, *Kwanzaa,* Gumbs & Thomas, 1985.

My First Kwanzaa, Scholastic, Inc., 1992.

Alternative Applications: Encourage students to publish their Kwanzaa recipes by these methods:

- ◆ Using hole punchers and shoelaces or cord, fasten large pieces of tagboard into a Kwanzaa Big Book. Share with a sister school.
- ◆ Use desktop publishing to create individual recipe handout sheets. Illustrate with drawings of Kwanzaa symbols. Distribute at a multicultural fair, PTA function, or open house.
- ◆ Reproduce ideas on computer networks, such as IRIS or Prodigy.
- ◆ Videotape cooking sessions for other classes to view. File a copy in the school library.
- ◆ Keep a classroom database of recipes. Have students type in new recipes throughout the year.
- ◆ Submit Kwanzaa recipes for publication in children's magazines, such as *Cricket, Cobblestone,* or *Hopscotch.*

Food Clinic

Age/Grade Level or Audience: All ages.

Description: Invite black cooks to staff a foods clinic.

Procedure: Invite black cooks to teach the fundamentals of cooking typical Caribbean, African, or African-American menus. Provide the workshop free to assist indigent community members in improving their skills. Emphasize good health habits with these strategies:

- ◆ Trim fat from meats and substitute vegetable oil for animal fats.
- ◆ Replace cream, whole milk, sour cream, and cream cheese with skim milk, yogurt, and reduced-calorie cheese.
- ◆ Emphasize spices over salt and sugar.
- ◆ Replace sugar with aspartame, fruit juice or pulp, honey, dried dates, raisins, or molasses.
- ◆ Encourage the addition of roughage, such as shredded green vegetables, unpeeled potatoes, corn, coconut, raisins, and nuts.
- ◆ Introduce uses for less familiar ingredients, such as couscous, lentils, curry, sun-dried tomatoes, yellow rice, saffron, coconut milk, banana liqueur, papaya, mango, currants, and fenugreek.
- ◆ Offer handouts featuring nutritional tips and recipes designed to meet a variety of needs, including those of small children, the elderly, and people with dental, metabolic, and other health problems.

Budget: $$$

Sources:

Consult local college and university home economics departments, home demonstration clubs, or county extension agencies for suggested personnel to staff food clinics.

Alternative Applications: Distribute information from the food clinic through various media:

- ◆ Videotape food demonstrations for later use.
- ◆ Coordinate handouts or a booklet featuring ideas from the food workshop.
- ◆ Offer a collection of recipes to the food section of a newspaper, newsletter, or journal.
- ◆ Share food ideas with other communities through computer networks, such as IRIS or Prodigy.

Plan regular updates with new recipes and health advice.

 ## Jamaican Specialties

Age/Grade Level or Audience: All ages.

Description: Invite friends to a Jamaican food tasting.

Procedure: Prepare a group of Jamaican foods, including baked sweet potatoes, red beans and rice, and cole slaw spiced with a touch of horseradish. Serve as accompaniments to Jamaican specialty dishes from the following authentic recipes:

Fruit Compote

Cut mangos, oranges, papayas, pineapple, and bananas into bite-sized pieces. Sprinkle with the juice of 1 lime and 1 cup freshly grated coconut. Serve chilled.

Fruit Punch

Blend 1 papaya, 1 mango, and 2 cups each orange and pineapple juice. Mix in 1 cup each sugar and guava juice, 12 ounces club soda, and the juice of 2 limes. Serve over crushed ice with banana bread or fresh coconut cake.

Hushpuppies

Mix the following dry ingredients:

       1 c. each plain flour and yellow corn meal
       2 tsp. sugar
       ½ tsp. each salt and vanilla
       ¼ tsp. each nutmeg and baking soda

Stir in ½ cup milk to make a thick batter. Drop by teaspoonfuls into deep fat. When batter browns, drain on brown paper.

Marinated Chicken

Blend the following ingredients in a food processor:

1½ c. chopped onion or scallions

2 tsp. thyme

1 tsp. salt

2 tsp. sugar

1 tsp. allspice

½ tsp. each nutmeg and cinnamon

1 tsp. each black pepper and hot pepper or pepper sauce

1 tbs. vegetable or peanut oil

1 tbs. vinegar

Place 7 pounds chicken strips or pieces in a plastic bag. Pour in marinade. Refrigerate 4 hours Grill, basting with leftover marinade.

Plaintain Strips

Peel and slice 2 pounds of plantains into 1-inch cylinders. Fry in vegetable or peanut oil until brown. Drain on brown paper.

Pork Roast

Marinate 4 pounds pork roast with a tropical seasoning of the these ingredients:

1 chopped garlic clove

1 tbs. hot pepper sauce

½ tsp. each thyme and allspice

Bake at 375° for 1½ hours, basting frequently with leftover juice. Cool, then slice roast into ½-inch rounds and allow to soak up drippings.

Pumpkin Soup

Heat 1½ pounds beef cubes or pickled pigtails in 2 quarts water. When meat is tender, add 2 pounds pumpkin cubes, 1 garlic clove, 2 whole scallions, and 1 chopped green, yellow, or red pepper. Boil until vegetables dissolve. Season with sprigs of thyme and parsley.

Salmagundi

Soak 2 pounds pickled shad and ½ pounds each pickled herring and mackerel for 4 hours. Drain and cover with fresh water. Bring to a boil, then let stand 5 minutes. Drain and skin fish. Shred into small pieces. Arrange on a serving platter and top with a mixture of ⅓ cup oil, 1½ cup chopped onion, and 1 teaspoon each red, white, and black pepper. Heat a sauce of 1 cup vinegar and 1 tablespoon pimento seeds and drizzle over fish. Cover and leave unrefrigerated overnight. Serve with toast rounds, crackers, or wafers.

Decorate tables with Jamaican flags, palm leaves, and fresh coconuts and bananas. Play reggae or calypso music. Finish the meal with hot Jamaican coffee topped with whipped cream and a sprinkle of nutmeg.

Budget: $$$

Sources:

Brandon, Leila, *A Merry-Go-Round of Recipes from Independent Jamaica*, Color Graphic Printers, 1963.

Willinsky, Helen, *Jerk: Barbecue from Jamaica*, Crossing Press, 1990.

Alternative Applications: Share the work by having a progressive dinner, with fruit punch and fruit kabob appetizers at one house, chicken at the next, and continuing down the menu at different residences. Conclude with an evening of reggae music and dancing.

 Soul Food

Age/Grade Level or Audience: High school home economics classes; gourmet and home demonstration clubs; civic displays; street fairs.

Description: Organize a cook-off or buffet of soul food for sale and/or sampling.

Procedure: Examine the importance of food as a unifying and bonding agent in black family and community life. Comment on Sunday dinners, holiday meals, church reunions, and gifts of food to shut-ins, bereaved families, catastrophe victims, and the elderly and homeless. Stress the importance of barbecues, fish fries, cookouts, and picnics, particularly when these gatherings are linked to a single patriarch.

Using local cooks, create a colorful spread of traditional African-American dishes for people to buy and/or sample, such as spoonbread, pork rinds, chitlins, turnip and mustard greens, corn fritters, hoppin' john, cracklins', pinto beans with chowchow, corn pudding, baked sweet potatoes, pralines, and pecan pie. To create a homey atmosphere, blend a variety of crockery, china, tinware, and wooden platters on a checkered cloth and decorate with a simple vase of wildflowers. Consider the following recipes:

Candied Yams

Boil 6 yams in 6 cups water. Drain, cool, and peel. Cut yams into quarters or one-inch slices. Coat with the following mixture:

> 3 c. sugar
> 4 tbs. melted butter
> 1½ tsp. cinnamon
> ½ tsp. each nutmeg and cloves
> 1 c. pecan pieces (optional)
> 1 c. miniature marshmallows (optional)

Bake in a medium oven 1½ hours. Serves 4-6. An alternate method of candying yams is to replace sugar and marshmallows with a can of crushed pineapple or pineapple tidbits.

Chow-Chow

Chop the following ingredients:

 2 pts. each sweet red and green peppers

 2 qts. cabbage

 2 pts. onions

 4 hot peppers

Sprinkle vegetables with 10 tablespoons canning (noniodized) salt. Marinate for 8 hours, then drain, pour into a kettle, and mix well with these flavorings:

 8 tbs. mustard seed

 4 tbs. celery seed

 2 tbs. dill weed

 1 c. sugar

 2 qts. vinegar

Cook 15 minutes. Pack into sterilized jars and process for 10 minutes. Cool and store. Serve with bland foods, such as pinto beans, field peas, hominy, or creamed corn.

Cornbread

Mix the following ingredients:

 2 c. white or yellow cornmeal

 2 eggs

 1 tbs. sugar (optional)

 2 tsp. baking powder

 2 tbs. vegetable or peanut oil or bacon drippings

 2½ c. buttermilk

For added texture, add a cup of corn kernels or creamed corn. Bake in greased casserole for 25 minutes at 450°.

Corn Pudding

Shave kernels from 10 ears of corn. Make a paste of 3 tablespoons melted butter and 2 tablespoons plain flour. Stir in kernels plus these ingredients:

 1 pt. cream or half-and-half

 3 beaten egg yolks

 1 tsp. salt

 ½ tsp. vanilla

 3 tbs. sugar (optional)

Whip 3 egg whites into stiff peaks and fold into mixture. Bake in greased casserole at 350° for 45 minutes. Serve immediately.

Ham Hocks and Collard Greens

Cut stalks from leaves of 9 pounds of collard greens. Soak leaves in salted cold water. Rinse, then slice or chop leaves into 1-inch pieces and soak for another hour. Place 6 ham hocks and greens in 3 quarts of water. Add red pepper to taste, cover, and cook for 2½ hours, stirring occasionally.

Ribs

Cook 3-4 pounds of spareribs in a shallow pan at 325° for an hour. Baste every quarter hour with a mixture of 4 tablespoons vinegar in two cups water. Cover with barbecue sauce and roast an additional half hour.

Smithfield Ham

Soak a whole ham overnight in cold water, changing the water every few hours. Boil in fresh water along with these ingredients:

> 1 tbs. peppercorns
> 3 bay leaves
> 1 tbs. hot sauce
> 1 cinnamon stick
> 1 tbs. lemon rind
> 1 c. cider or apple juice
> 1 c. chopped celery or 1 tbs. celery seed

Cool and skin the ham. Mix the following:

> ½ c. ham drippings
> 3 egg yolks
> 2 tbs. brown sugar
> 1 tbs. hot sauce
> 1 tsp. dry mustard
> 1 c. crushed cracker or bread crumbs

Coat the ham with mixture and bake at 450° until the crust browns. Serve thinly sliced in fresh split biscuits or Parker House rolls. Accompany with a variety of mustards.

Sweet Potato Pie

Mix the following ingredients:

> ⅔ c. sugar
> 1 tsp. of cinnamon
> ½ tsp. each ginger and cloves
> 2 eggs
> 1½ c. milk
> ½ c. molasses or maple syrup
> 1½ c. cooked or canned pumpkin
> 1 tsp. lemon juice.
> 1 tsp. grated lemon rind

Pour into unbaked pie shell. Bake 10 minutes at 450°. Lower temperature to 350° and bake 40 minutes more. Serve with whipped cream.

Budget: $$$

Sources:

Hultman, Tami, *The Africa News Cookbook: African Cooking for Western Kitchens,* Penguin, 1986.

John, Yvonne, *Guyanese Sea of Soul: How to Prepare West Indian Foods,* R & M Publishing, 1980.

John, *Guyanese Seed of Vegetables, Seafood, and Desserts: The Vegetarians' and Food*

Lovers' Paradise, R & M Publishing, 1985.

O'Neill, Molly, "Southern Thanksgiving," *New York Times Magazine,* November 22, 1992, pp. 75-76.

van der Post, Laurens, *African Cooking,* Time-Life Books, 1970.

"What's Cooking," *USA Today,* September 23, 1992, p. 6D.

Alternative Applications: Organize a progressive dinner, with each participant preparing a part of the soul food meal. Conclude with pie and espresso coffee blended with a few drops of vanilla, curaçao, brandy, or kahlua. Supply each participant with recipes or publish a booklet featuring recipes of the entire meal. Offer recipe booklet as a table favor for a club or civic convention, distribute through the state visitors bureau or city chamber of commerce, or sell at street fairs and book stores.

Dance

African Dance Styles

Age/Grade Level or Audience: Kindergarten, elementary, and middle school dance and physical education classes; dance schools and troupes; gymnastics classes.

Description: Invent dances based on African rhythmic movements and dance steps.

Procedure: Explain to students how African dance steps influenced the conga, samba, rhumba, and mambo. Invite an expert to demonstrate standard African rhythmic movements and steps, such as the Cameroon makossa, Haitian soca, Nigerian afrobeat and juju, Senaglese mbalax, South African mbaqanga and mbube, Zaireian soukous, and Zimbabwean chimurenga and jit-jive, and native steps from the Seychelles, including the sega, moutia, tinge, and komtale. Have students create their own dances, incorporating these basic events:

- leaping
- dancing on stilts
- imitation of insects, birds, fish, reptiles, or other animals
- marching or imitating the python in single file formation
- kneeling and sweeping arms and head sideways and back and forth
- standing shoulder-to-shoulder in a circle dance and sliding counterclockwise
- syncopation of the Juba or Jumba
- the Muslim ring-shout, which dancers perform while holding lighted candles or pine knots
- the dignified and formalized movements of chalk-line walks or cakewalk
- solo and duo dances
- block formation accompanied by humming, clapping, body slapping, and kazoos
- ritual prayer dance

Accompany new combinations with authentic African music.

Budget: $$

Sources:
Films about Africa such as *Zulu* (1964), *Mister Johnson* (1991), and *The Power of One*. Professional dance films from Indiana University Audio-Visual Center, Bloomington, IN 47405; telephone: (812)855-8087; University of California, Los Angeles, Instructional Media Library, Powell Library, Room 46, Los Angeles, CA 90024; telephone: (213)825-0755; and Filmmakers Library, 124 East 40th St., New York, NY 10016; telephone: (212)808-4980.
Considine, J. D., "Dancing to a Different Beat," *Baltimore Sun*, 1989.
Haskins, James, *Black Dance in America: A History through Its People,* Harper Trophy, 1990.
Nketia, J. H. Kwabena, *The Music of Africa,* Gollancz, 1975.

Alternative Applications: Contrast African dance movements with Native American ritual dances, such as those by the Hopi, Cherokee, Navajo, Sioux, and Ojibwa. Draw conclusions about what types of rhythms, steps, gestures, and movements seem to be universal, especially those that relate to mourning, elation, victory, patriotism, romance and courtship, nature, childhood, and coming of age.

 Black Dance Troupes

Originator: Louis Nunnery, ballet instructor, Hickory, North Carolina.

Age/Grade Level or Audience: Elementary, middle school, high school, and adult cultural arts groups; dance classes.

Description: Present the background and accomplishments of Alvin Ailey's Dance Company or Arthur Mitchell's Dance Theatre of Harlem.

Procedure: Illustrate the talent, discipline, and expression of the Alvin Ailey Dance Company, which was organized in 1958, by showing videotapes of the group's performances, such as *District Storyville, Hidden Rites, Blues Suites, North Star, Forgotten Time Cry, Revelations, Strange Fruit,* or *Creole Giselle,* performed by the Dance Theatre of Harlem.

Budget: $

Sources:
Video rental stores.
"Creative Woman," *Ebony*, August 1977, p. 135.

Haskins, James, *Black Dance in America: A History through Its People,* Harper
  Trophy, 1990.
Sherman, Ellen, "Bringing Dance Home Again," *Essence,* February 1975, p. 34.
Tobias, Tobi, "Rites of Passage," *New York,* January 7, 1991, pp. 55-56.

Alternative Applications: Have a panel contrast the exuberance and
energy of Alvin Ailey's choreographic style with the more controlled, formalized
movements of more traditional troupes, such as the Bolshoi, Saddler's Wells, Kirov,
Joffrey, Dance Theatre of Canada, or San Francisco Ballet. Discuss with dance students the difference in training and choreography between more expressive dance
groups and the rigorously synchronized *corps de ballet* of traditional dance. Include
these items of interest: partnering, soloing, character portrayal, individualized interpretation, and full company choreography.

Caribana

Age/Grade Level or Audience: All ages.

Description: Organize a Trinidadian carnival.

Procedure: Invite participants to create fantasy costumes and celebrate the
ten-day native West Indian carnival. Choose from the following events:

- ◆ a procession or parade with marching bands
- ◆ masked ball
- ◆ costume competition
- ◆ crafts and talent display
- ◆ West Indian food fest

Budget: $$$

Sources:
Doyle-Marshall, William, "Caribana Rocks Toronto with Music and Masquerade,"
  Emerge, August 1992, p. 54.
Slater, Les, "Twenty-fifth Anniversary of West Indian-American Day Carnival," *Class,*
  July-August 1992, pp. 57-58.

Alternative Applications: Invite a dance teacher to instruct small
groups in the native dances of Caribana, which are often featured in American festi-
vals, such as Spoleto in Charleston, South Carolina, and Mardi Gras in New Orleans,
Louisiana. Have students sketch and color costumes topped by fantastic headdresses
featuring fruit, feathers, woven straw, beads, lace, ribbons, and sequins. Emphasize
island colors: citrus yellow, orange, and lime, sunset red, sea blue, and palm green.

Have a group work together on a cardboard or chalkboard backdrop depicting tropical trees, flowers, vines, sand, surf, and native huts.

 | **Dance Workshop** |

Age/Grade Level or Audience: All ages.

Description: Locate black dancers to staff a dance workshop.

Procedure: Invite black dancers to instruct students in the fundamentals of ballroom, tap, ballet, acrobatic, jazz, rock and roll, and other forms of dance. Include an overview of the history of black dance, for example:

- ◆ early syncopated forms of celebration, such as buck, pigeon wing, jig, cakewalk, ring dances, buzzard lope, and juba
- ◆ the New Orleans coonjine, chica, babouille, cata, voudou, and congo
- ◆ T. D. Rice's loose-limbed blackface caricatures of Jim Crow
- ◆ the emergence of more serious dancers, particularly William Henry Lane, Billy Kersands, and Ernest Hogan

Have participants imitate shuffling, jigging, and strutting. Introduce more complex dance steps, such as the Charleston, black bottom, shimmy, ballin' the jack, mooche, lindy hop, jitterbug, shag, camel walk, moon walk, hip-hop, and truckin'. Provide the workshop free to assist indigent community members in improving their skills and to provide exercise for children, the handicapped, and the elderly.

Budget: $$$

Sources:
Consult local college and university dance departments and private studios for suggested personnel to staff dance workshops.

Alternative Applications: Videotape dance demonstrations, and place the videos in local libraries, schools, and recreation centers.

 | **Everybody Limbo** |

Age/Grade Level or Audience: Kindergarten and elementary classes.

Description: Teach a class to limbo.

Procedure: Organize a line dance and teach participants how to limbo. Have them follow the leader as the limbo pole moves lower with each pass under it. Invite the other students to clap and sing calypso tunes such as "Mary Ann" or "The Banana Boat Song" as they wait their turn.

Budget: $$

Sources:
Calypso albums by the Beach Boys and Harry Belafonte.

Alternative Applications: Have groups of students make up verses to limbo songs. Suggest birds, flowers, and Caribbean scenery as illustrations. Use the following prompts for starters:

Bright Stars
Caribbean sky, bright with many stars
Shine on me ...

Calypso Lou
Gotta friend, name-a Lou,
Calypso is his beat ...

Limber Limbo
Sing a limber tune,
Follow in a line ...

String of Shells
I caught the clam in my net
I opened it up to see ...

Interpretive Dance

Originator: Louis Nunnery, ballet teacher, Hickory, North Carolina

Age/Grade Level or Audience: All ages.

Description: Present a religious interpretive dance.

Procedure: As part of a black history festival, worship service, or demonstration, organize a group of dancers to interpret Pablo Casals's *Nigra Sum*, a choral work expressing the concerns of a slave at the court of Solomon. Use costumes evocative of slave days.

Budget: $$

Sources:

Ladji Camara African Music Dance Ensemble, 1706 Davidson Ave., Suite 513, Bronx, New York 10453; telephone: (212)716-4711.

Harlem Cultural Council, 215 West 125 St., New York, NY 10027; telephone: (212)316-6277.

Charles Moore Dance Theater, 1043 President St., Brooklyn, New York 11225; telephone: (718)467-7127.

Alternative Applications: Apply this suggestion to other music, such as "Listen to the Lambs," "Nobody Knows the Trouble I See," "Poor Wayfarin' Stranger," "On That Great Gettin' Up Morning," "Good News," "Didn't It Rain," "Mary Had a Baby," "Joshua Fought the Battle of Jericho," "Standin' in the Need of Prayer," "I'm Just a Wanderer," or other spirituals, anthems, and hymns.

Jivin' to the Oldies

Age/Grade Level or Audience: All ages.

Description: Hold a neighborhood sock hop.

Procedure: Revive the oldies and introduce young participants to the dances and great names of early rock by holding a sock hop. Use tapes or disc recordings. Invite a local deejay to announce the songs and give background about periods, instrumentalists, dances, and singers. For example, stress these:

- ◆ Chubby Checkers's creation of the twist craze
- ◆ beach music and the shag
- ◆ Motown's early hits by Diana Ross and the Supremes, Smokey Robinson and the Miracles, and others
- ◆ the jitterbug of World War II
- ◆ Michael Jackson and the moon walk
- ◆ breakdancing
- ◆ disco

Offer prizes for the best line dancers and dancers of the funky chicken, Charleston, disco, or stroll. Select a few volunteers to teach children the steps and hand motions of significant dances from the era.

Budget: $$$

Sources:

Films such as *The Glenn Miller Story* (1954), *The Cotton Club* (1984), *For the Boys* (1991), and *Malcolm X* (1992).

Alternative Applications: Have art students draw panels or a mural to typify the fashion, gestures, and background of dance crazes, such as the cloche hat, flapper chemise, fringe, bugle beads, and rolled hose of the 1920s; zoot suits and long watch chains of the late 1930s; and elegant tuxedos, long dresses, and corsages of the big band era, which led into World War II and influenced USO troupes. Use the art as a backdrop for a neighborhood or club dance.

Josephine Baker

Age/Grade Level or Audience: Civic groups; music and dance clubs.

Description: Present an overview of the career of dancer Josephine Baker.

Procedure: Assign a committee to report on Josephine Baker's contributions to entertainment and to the emancipation of black women. Stress these facts:

- born in St. Louis, Missouri, on June 3, 1906
- began domestic work at age eight
- ran away from home in her early teens to escape an unsuitable marriage to Willie Wells
- danced with the Dixie Fliers
- performed in Chocolate Dandies in 1924 and the next year at the Plantation Club
- appeared in the Revue Nègre and the Folies Bergère in Paris
- opened the Chez Joséphine in Paris in 1926
- published an autobiography, *Les Mémoires de Joséphine Baker,* the next year
- began a world tour in 1928
- returned to her Paris home and danced in La Joie de Paris
- danced in Offenbach's La Créole in 1934, the same year she appeared in the movie *Zouzou*
- accepted work with the Ziegfeld Follies two years later
- served as a spy for the French Resistance during World War II
- suffered life-threatening illness following a hysterectomy in 1942
- was named the National Association for the Advancement of Colored People (NAACP) woman of the year for her demand for integrated audiences in the 1950s
- filled her French country house with twelve adopted children of a variety of ethnic backgrounds
- after two heart attacks, made a comeback in Monte Carlo at the age of sixty-eight
- died of cerebral hemorrhage April 14, 1975
- was honored by the French with a state funeral and buried in Monaco

Budget: $

Sources:

The films *The Josephine Baker Story* (1990) and *Chasing a Rainbow: The Life of Josephine Baker.*

Haney, Lynn, *Naked at the Feast: A Biography of Josephine Baker,* Dodd, Mead, 1981.

Papich, Stephen, *Remembering Josephine Baker,* Bobbs, Merrill, 1976.

Rose, Phyllis, *Jazz Cleopatra: Josephine Baker in Her Time,* Vintage Books, 1991.

Smith, Jessie Carney, ed., *Notable Black American Women,* Gale, 1992.

Alternative Applications: Have a panel present information on the lives of a variety of female performers, including Pearl Bailey, Sarah Vaughan, Ella Fitzgerald, Mahalia Jackson, Natalie Cole, Gladys Knight, Diana Ross, Bessie Smith, Ethel Waters, Tina Turner, Marian Anderson, Kathleen Battle, Jessye Norman, or Aretha Franklin. Contrast the struggles of each with those of Josephine Baker, who found receptive audiences in Europe when Americans ignored or exploited her.

Sign Troupe

Age/Grade Level or Audience: All ages.

Description: Organize a sign troupe to perform for a mixed audience of hearing and hearing impaired.

Procedure: Invite a sign troupe to perform memorable dance, tableau, mime, and signed history lessons for the deaf. Consider the following events as suitable material for representation:

- ◆ the voyage of the *Clothilde*
- ◆ Martin Luther King, Jr.'s "I Have A Dream" speech
- ◆ Frederick Douglass's work as an abolitionist
- ◆ James Weldon Johnson's The Creation
- ◆ Harriet Tubman's journeys on the Underground Railroad
- ◆ Sojourner Truth's "Ain't I a Woman" speech
- ◆ Maya Angelou's *Now Sheba Sings the Song*
- ◆ Robert Shaw's all-black regiment during the Civil War
- ◆ Alex Haley's search for his African roots
- ◆ Mae Jemison's role as the first black female astronaut

Budget: $$$

Sources:

Consult local school administrators and state bureaus of the handicapped; Deaf-REACH, 3722 12th St. N.E., Washington, DC 20017; telephone: (202)832-6681;

National Theatre of the Deaf, David Hays, Artistic Director, P.O. Box 659, Chester, CT 06412; telephone: (203)526-4971, FAX: 203-526-9732; TDD: 203-526-4974.

Alternative Applications: Present a choreographed or mime overview of black history narrated for the hearing and interpreted for the deaf. Mix media by using slides, film clips, readers, dancers, actors, and instrumentalists. Emphasize black experiences in the United States, Caribbean, Africa, and Europe, particularly during the two world wars. Conclude with a glimpse of the future of race relations in the United States and the world.

Tapping to Stardom

Originator: Charles L. Blockson, editor, Temple University, Philadelphia, Pennsylvania.

Age/Grade Level or Audience: Music societies; civic groups.

Description: Present an overview of America's great tap dancers.

Procedure: Assign a committee to report on famous African-American tap dancers, particularly Stepin Fetchit, Billy Kersands, Sandman Sims, Chuck Green, Bunny Buggs, Leon Collins, Four Step Brothers, Charles "Honi" Coles, Cholly Atkins, Florence Mills, Ernest Hogan, Bill "Bo Jangles" Robinson, Clayton "Peg-Leg" Bates, John W. Bubbles, Harold and Fayard Nicholas, Lynn Whitfield, and Gregory Hines. Present a video showcase of black tap dancers by showing clips of films, such as *Stand Up and Cheer, Tap, The Josephine Baker Story, Malcolm X, The Cotton Club, Breakdance, Showboat,* and *White Nights.*

Budget: $$

Sources:
Films such as *No Maps on My Taps* (1979), *Tapdancin'* (1982), *In a Jazz Way: A Portrait of Mura Dehn* (1986), *Call of the Jitterbug* (1988), *Songs Unwritten: A Tap Dancer Remembered, Black Dance America.*
Dance Magazine, May 1984, March 1985.
Emery, Lynne F., *Black Dance in the United States from 1619 to 1970,* National Press Books, 1972.
Haskins, James, *Black Dance in America; A History through Its People,* Harper Trophy, 1990.

Alternative Applications: Invite an expert to demonstrate variations of African-American dance steps, particularly the buck, pigeon wing, jig, cake-walk, juba, black bottom, shimmy, mooche, suzi-q, camel walk, moon walk, truckin', breakdancing, lindy hop, jitterbug, shag, ballin' the jack, Charleston, big apple, hip-hop, and funky chicken. Have participants describe the emotions, naturalistic attitudes, mimicry, and posturing illustrated by each step.

 ## A Tribute to Judith Jamison

Originator: Louis Nunnery, ballet instructor, Hickory, North Carolina.

Age/Grade Level or Audience: Civic and school groups; dance classes.

Description: Present an overview of the career of Judith Jamison, African-American prima ballerina.

Procedure: Comment on significant roles in Jamison's career, particularly her work with Alvin Ailey. Note these facts:

- ◆ born May 10, 1944, in Philadelphia, Pennsylvania
- ◆ began dancing at age six
- ◆ attended Fisk University on an athletic scholarship and studied psychology
- ◆ dropped out in her sophomore year to enroll in the Philadelphia Dance Academy
- ◆ debuted in *Giselle*
- ◆ was mentored by Agnes de Mille at age twenty
- ◆ joined Alvin Ailey in November 1965 in Congo Tango Palace
- ◆ toured Europe and danced in Senegal the following year
- ◆ suffered an ankle injury in 1967 while dancing with the Harkness Ballet
- ◆ achieved stardom in Europe with the Hamburg Ballet, England's Royal Ballet, and the ballet company of the Vienna State Opera
- ◆ received an award from *Dance* magazine, presented by Katherine Dunham in 1972
- ◆ served on the board of the National Endowment for the Arts
- ◆ partnered with Mikhail Baryshnikov in *Pas de Duke*
- ◆ danced on Broadway in Duke Ellington's *Sophisticated Ladies* in 1980
- ◆ presented *Divining,* an original choreography, in 1984
- ◆ organized her own company, the Jamison Project, in 1988
- ◆ replaced Alvin Ailey as head of his company after his death in 1989

Budget: $

Sources:
Tapes from video rental services.
Allen, Zita, "Majesty in Motion: Judith Jamison," *Encore,* December 22, 1974, pp. 27-28.

Harris, Jessica, "Judith Jamison," *Essence,* May 1978, pp. 62, 64.

Haskins, James, *Black Dance in America: A History through Its People,* Harper Trophy, 1990.

"Judith Jamison: Extending the Alvin Ailey Dance Legacy," *Ebony,* December 1990, pp. 132-136.

Smith, Jessie Carney, ed., *Notable Black American Women,* Gale, 1992.

Tobias, Tobi, "Standing Tall," *New York,* December 1990, p. 106.

Alternative Applications: Invite a local ballet teacher or dance historian to speak on the techniques that have set Judith Jamison apart from other black dance stars, particularly Pearl Primus, Geoffrey Holder, Carmen DeLavallade, Alvin Ailey, James Truitt, Lynn Whitfield, Gregory Hines, Miriam Makeba, Albert Evans, Rhonda Burke Spero, and Janet Collins. Emphasize African rhythms, symbolic body language, and feminist themes, especially in Jamison's signature work, *Cry.*

Genealogy

Alex Haley's Genealogy

Originator: Leatrice Pearson, teacher, Lenoir, North Carolina.

Age/Grade Level or Audience: High school or college literature classes; literary societies.

Description: Diagram Alex Haley's family tree from a group reading of *Roots*.

Procedure: Have volunteers read segments of Alex Haley's *Roots* and plot his family tree, noting particularly family members who contribute significantly to family pride, such as Chicken George, Kizzy, and Kunta Kinte.

Budget: $$

Sources:
The miniseries *Roots* (1977).
Haley, Alex, *Roots: The Saga of an American Family,* Doubleday, 1976.
"Haley's Malcolm X Manuscript Is Auctioned for $100,000," *Jet,* October 19, 1992, pp. 14-15.
Ki-Zerbo, Joseph, "Oral Tradition as a Historical Source," *UNESCO Courier,* April 1990, pp. 43-46.

Alternative Applications: Create a wall hanging, banner, cushion, or quilt from the information learned from the genealogy. Display the finished product in a traveling show to school groups who are also reading Alex Haley's book. Have participants conclude the activity with a discussion of Marcus Garvey's statement, "A people without a sense of their history is like a tree without roots."

The Family Tree

Originator: Leatrice Pearson, teacher, Lenoir, North Carolina.

Age/Grade Level or Audience: Middle school history and language classes.

Description: Collect information for a family scrapbook. Include details such as family surnames, traditional first and middle names, traditions, lore, participation in historical events, reunions, recipes, military and birth records, deeds, family trees, slave lists and bills of sale, wills, tax records, letters, diaries, plantation daybooks, Bibles, ledgers, photographs, and albums.

Procedure: Have students create a uniform questionnaire featuring a set of questions to jog the memories of family members. For example:

- Describe the schooling, courtship, and marriage of your parents and grandparents. Supply dates and places for graduations and weddings.
- List names and nicknames that recur in your family, such as Big Arthur and Little Art, Mama Lucille and Big-Mama Lucille. Comment on alternate spellings or shortened versions.
- Name major events in which your family has taken part, such as wars, political movements, and community development.
- Describe family reunions. List locations, branches of the family included in the gathering, numbers of attendees, and favorite foods. Supply traditional recipes, particularly for holiday foods.
- Summarize information from family albums, written histories, newspaper clippings, home movies and videos, military uniforms and medals, diplomas, awards, trophies, and other memorabilia.
- Detail geographical locations of major branches of your family and shifts to new locations. Explain situations and events that caused a major migration, such as the Depression, new factories, or periods of prosperity.
- Sketch a family burial plot, noting locations of graves, birth and death dates, and characteristics of markers, headstones, and epitaphs.
- Characterize your family's celebration of birthdays, holidays, and other joyous occasions. Add information about how they note a death, catastrophe, or loss (e.g., car accidents, tornado or flood damage).
- Enumerate anecdotes and humorous stories that grow and change with passing time. Stress details that have been added or altered. Be sensitive to information that might embarrass or shock a family member.
- List questions about your background that you would like to have answered, even if there is not a current source of information for you to consult. For example, inquire about a person who left home and never reunited with family members.

◆ Consult genealogical centers, especially the Family History Library in Salt Lake City, Utah, the world's largest collection of family information.

◆ Consult local sources, for example, family papers, church records, county tax lists, jury pools, voter registration, fraternal memberships, graduation records, and inscriptions on tombstones.

◆ Note any informal adoptions in which a family raised an abandoned or orphaned child or merged with a segment of the family that had been dispossessed by fire or loss of supportive family members.

◆ Describe colorful, eccentric characters from your family's past, for instance, whistlers, taxidermists, hubcap collectors, and whittlers.

For advanced groups, this material could be included in an annotated family tree, complete with quotations and photographs.

Budget: $$

Sources:

"Our Family, Our Town: Essays on Family and Local History Sources in the National Archives," available through the National Archives and Records Administration, Washington, DC 20408. For more detailed information about genealogy, consult *Family Folklore*, available through Folklife Programs, Smithsonian Institution, L'Enfant 2100, Washington, DC 10560.

Doane, Gilbert H., and James B. Bell, *Searching for Your Ancestors: The How and Why of Genealogy*, University of Minnesota Press, 1992.

Helmbold, F. Wilbur, *Tracing Your Ancestry: A Step-by-Step Guide to Researching Your Family History*, Oxmoor House, 1976.

Ki-Zerbo, Joseph, "Oral Tradition as a Historical Source," *UNESCO Courier*, April 1990, pp. 43-46.

U.S. Department of Commerce, Bureau of the Census, "Family Folklore: Interviewing Guide and Questionnaire," U.S. Government Printing Office, 1990.

Alternative Applications: Have students compose vignettes of family activities, including holidays, birthdays, church homecomings, school and cultural events, reunions, weddings, and births. Share these written vignettes with other classes on databases or computer networks, such as IRIS or Prodigy. For more information, consult Sandra Oehring, "Teaching with Technology," *Instructor*, November/December, 1992, p. 60.

Photo History

Originator: Leatrice Pearson, teacher, Lenoir, North Carolina.

Age/Grade Level or Audience: All ages.

Description: Assemble a community album from donated photographs.

Procedure: Locate a single sponsor, such as a historical society, newspaper, library, or college, to create a community album celebrating blacks and their contributions to the area. Arrange the album in chronological order. Feature these items:

- ◆ graduations
- ◆ gatherings at depots and airports
- ◆ new homes
- ◆ business openings
- ◆ anniversary parties
- ◆ family reunions
- ◆ church socials
- ◆ street fairs
- ◆ political campaigns
- ◆ recreation and sports, such as swimming meets or wrestling tournaments

Augment still photos with videos of family reunions, graduations, weddings, parades, block parties, and other memorable occasions. Keep a written record of names, dates, and places for later reference.

Budget: $$$

Sources:

Collect photographs from local black families, churches, schools, museums, businesses, newspapers, and county archives. Consult Kevin Leman's *Keeping Your Family Together When the World Is Falling Apart*, or the following brochures from the U.S. Consumer Information Center: "Using Records in the National Archives for Genealogical Research," "Where to Write for Vital Records," and "Your Right to Federal Records."

Alternative Applications: Blend a photo gallery with a display of vintage clothing, books, school desks, radios, victrolas, medicine bottles, hair curlers, tools, crafts, farm machinery, automobiles, and other memorabilia. Have volunteers collect memoirs or interviews on audio or video tape from elderly community residents. For a model, follow "Aunt Airie" from Eliot Wigginton's *Foxfire*.

LIVE | **Quilted History**

Age/Grade Level or Audience: All ages.

Description: Make a family quilt.

Procedure: Organize workers to create a family quilt. Select important events to fill separate blocks, such as the opening of a family business, the awarding of an advanced degree or appointment, or the building of a local church ar recreation center. Embroider or paint information clearly on the block. Connect blocks into quilt form. Finish edge with symbolic colors or edging. Display at the family home-place, a local museum or library, or in the lobby of a family business.

Budget: $$$$

Sources:

Benberry, Cuesta, *Always There: The African-American Presence in American Quilts*, The Museum of History and Science, 1992.

Christmas, Rachel Jackson, "Gathering the Clan," *Essence*, August 1992, pp. 86-94.

Doane, Gilbert H., and James B. Bell, *Searching for Your Ancestors: The How and Why of Genealogy*, University of Minnesota Press, 1992.

Knight, Kimberley, "Preserving Family Heirlooms," *Essence*, August 1992.

Alternative Applications: Create individual segments of needlework to honor family traditions, beliefs, background, or accomplishments, such as a visit to an African country symbolized by a national flag. Display finished products in a variety of ways, including framing the works to hang in a prominent place, using them as upholstery on chair backs and seats, forming them into pillows or footstools, entering them in a county fair or craft exhibits, and photographing them and sharing prints of the design.

Geography

An African Holiday

Age/Grade Level or Audience: Elementary, middle school, and high school geography classes.

Description: Create a four-week itinerary for a tour of Africa.

Procedure: Assign students to groups to work out the following details of an extended African vacation:

- itinerary
- overseas airline schedule
- currencies and traveler's checks
- visas and passports
- vaccinations
- alternate forms of land transportation
- hotels, inns, and bed and breakfasts
- campgrounds
- overseas telephone, fax, and mail services
- travel and luggage restrictions
- water and food advisories
- clothing advisory

Budget: $

Sources:
Travel agencies; video travel guides from Rand McNally or local dealers.
Fodor's Kenya Tanzania Seychelles, Fodor's Travel Guides, 1993.
"Ivory Coast," *National Geographic,* July 1982.
"Journey up the Nile," *National Geographic,* May 1985.
"Malawi," *National Geographic,* September 1989.

"Mali," *National Geographic,* October 1990.

Musgrove, Margaret, *Ashanti to Zulu: African Traditions,* Dial Press, 1976.

"Serengeti," *National Geographic,* May 1986.

Alternative Applications: Create a travel guide to Africa, denoting the differing customs and problems of each country, including hunting restrictions, common foods, and local diseases, such as malaria, cholera, schistosomiasis, and AIDS.

African Peoples

Originator: Leatrice Pearson, teacher, Lenoir, North Carolina.

Age/Grade Level or Audience: Elementary and middle school history and geography classes.

Description: Draw a large map of Africa and locate the most prominent tribes.

Procedure: Provide students with the names of African tribes, particularly these:

Afrikaners	Akan	Amhara	Angola
Ashanti	Azanda	Banum	Baule
Berbers	Bini	Bushmen	Chagga
Congo	Dogon	Edo	Ekoi
Ewe	Fali	Fanti	Fon
Fulbe	Ga	Grebo	Hausa
Hottentot	Ibo	Ikoma	Isoko
Jabo	Jie	Kikuyu	Kom
!Kung	Lozi	Mandinka	Mangbetu
Maasai	Mbunder	Moor	Namib
Ndaka	Nuer	Nyanga	Osei
Ouadai	Pondo	Pygmie	Quimbande
Rendille	Serere	Shangaan	Shilluk
Soninke	Sotho	Tsonga	Tuaregs
Tutu	Twa	Uge	Vai
Wagenia	Watutsis	Wolof	Xhosa
Yedseram	Yombe	Yoruba	Zande
Zulu			

Have students put placards in the areas inhabited by these African peoples.

Budget: $$

Sources:

Asante, Molefi K., *Historical and Cultural Atlas of African Americans,* Macmillan, 1991.

Bentsen, Cheryl, *Maasai Days,* Anchor Books, 1991.

"Botswana," *National Geographic,* December 1990.

Chandler, Edna Walker, *Will You Carry Me?,* A. Whitman, 1965.

Demko, George J., *Why in the World: Adventures in Geography,* Anchor Books, 1992.

"Ivory Coast," *National Geographic,* July 1982.

"Malawi," *National Geographic,* September 1989.

"Mali," *National Geographic,* October 1990.

Murray, Jocelyn, ed., *Cultural Atlas of Africa,* Facts on File, 1989.

Musgrove, Margaret, *Ashanti to Zulu: African Traditions,* Dial Press, 1976.

Oliver, Roland, *The African Experience,* IconEditions, 1992.

Saitoti, Tepilit Ole, *The Worlds of a Maasai Warrior,* Abradale Press, 1980.

"Senegambia," *National Geographic,* August 1985.

"Serengeti," *National Geographic,* May 1986.

Smith, H. S., *Ancient Centres of Egyptian Civilization,* Kensal Press, 1983.

"Zaire," *National Geographic,* November 1991.

Alternative Applications: Have each student focus on a tribe and fill in the following data by creating a booklet or database on each group:

- ◆ styles of government, flag, and relations with the United States
- ◆ food and cooking styles
- ◆ music, dancing, and ceremonies
- ◆ storytelling, lore, and educational opportunities
- ◆ weapons, tools, and common utensils
- ◆ languages
- ◆ religion
- ◆ hairstyles, jewelry, headdresses
- ◆ housing, gardens, and domesticated animals

Assemble the booklets for a library, school, civic, or museum display or share databases on IRIS, Prodigy, or other computer networks.

African Riches

Age/Grade Level or Audience: Elementary school and church school students; scout troops; 4-H clubs.

Description: Study reference books about Africa to find its most important products and place symbols of these products on a map.

Procedure: Assemble reference books, films, filmstrips, and videos about Africa. Have students work in groups to organize a list of African products, such as the following:

- *timber, fruit, and vegetables:* palm oil, sisal, pyrethrum, yams, rice, vanilla, peanuts, millet, cocoa, barley, wheat, corn, sugar cane, cotton, tea, dates, bananas, figs, coffee, tobacco, grapes, olives, papyrus
- *minerals:* bauxite, phosphates, mica, copper, petroleum, lead, platinum, tin, zinc, tungsten, cobalt, vanadium, sulphur, uranium, graphite, chromium, silver, titanium, asbestos, diamonds
- *refined or manufactured materials and goods:* rubber, cork, paper, building materials, jewelry, dyes, hydroelectric power
- *woven goods:* clothing, linen and cotton textiles, rugs, baskets, wall hangings
- *livestock and animal byproducts:* sheep, cattle, camels, goats, ivory, hides, wool, dairy products

Create symbols to represent each. Assign a few volunteers to place the symbols in the areas where they are most common, such as diamonds from South Africa, goats in Kenya, and hydroelectric power in Egypt.

Budget: $$

Sources:

African Geography, a computer program from KnowMaster; "Math of Africa," a poster from Dale Seymour.

Clarendon Press Cartographic Department Staff, *The Oxford Economic Atlas of the World,* Oxford University Press, 1972.

Martin, Phyllis M., and Patrick O'Meara, *Africa,* Indiana University Press, 1986.

Murray, Jocelyn, ed., *Cultural Atlas of Africa,* Facts on File, 1989.

Pritchard, J. M., *A Geography of East Africa,* J. M. Dent, 1971.

Alternative Applications: Have students contrast exports common to the United States and other nations with those of Africa. For example, note these exports:

- British Isles, France, and Italy: wine, cheese, tea, paper products, books, films, records and tapes, perfume
- Germany and eastern Europe: electronics, laboratory equipment, leather goods
- Sweden, Denmark, Finland, and Norway: fish, cheese, hides, films, books
- Japan, Singapore, Hong Kong, and Korea: seafood, automobiles, electronic equipment
- India: teak, jewelry, spices, madras, other cotton clothing
- Caribbean Islands and Central and South America: carvings and other wood products, oil, coffee, beef, spices, bauxite, fruit, music
- Australia and New Zealand: wool, beef, fruit

Encourage students to realize that all nations share in world trade by supplying what others lack.

An African Travel Guide

Age/Grade Level or Audience: Elementary and middle school geography and history classes.

Description: Compile an organized travel guide to Africa.

Procedure: Suggest that students begin at a particular spot, such as Agra or Cairo, then move in a clockwise direction around the continent, providing distances between points and suggesting methods of travel, such as camel or horse, train or car, plane or boat. Focus on important tourist attractions such as these:

- ◆ Mt. Kilimanjaro, Kenya, Table Mountain, Aberdare, Ahaggar, Muchinga, Virunga, Cameroon, Tibesti, Drakesberg, Atlas, Futa Jallon, Ruwenzori Meru, and the Ethiopian Highlands
- ◆ Qattara Depression, Ngorongoro Crater, Zambezi Basin
- ◆ Watumu Beach
- ◆ Cape Verde, Cape Agulhas, Cape of Good Hope, Cape Blanc
- ◆ Ras Hafun, Ras Beni Sako
- ◆ Victoria Falls, Kebrabassa Falls, Stanley Falls, Stanley Pool
- ◆ the Serengeti Plains
- ◆ the Ituri Rain Forest
- ◆ the Nile Delta, Gulf of Guinea, Strait of Gibraltar, Suez Canal
- ◆ the Red Sea, Indian Ocean, Mediterranean Sea, Atlantic Ocean
- ◆ the cities of Freetown, Abidjan, Durban, Mombasa, Casablanca, Khartoum, Cairo, Accra, Cape Town, Conakry, Addis Ababa, Lagos, Johannesburg, Kampala, Kinshasa, Port Elizabeth, Marrakesh, Pretoria, Brazzaville, Timbuktu, Alexandria, Tripoli, Tunis, Djibouti, Alwa, Nairobi, Dar-es-Salaam, Monrovia, and Dakar
- ◆ Marsabit Nature Reserve, Sabi Sabi, Rungwa, Ugalla River, Maswa, Losai, South Turkana, and Kora game reserves; and Kruger, Amboseli, Serengeti, Masai Mara, Tsavo, and Kafue national parks
- ◆ Cabora Bassa, Aswan, Asokombo Main, Ayame, Jos, Kainji, Kariba, and Inga dams
- ◆ the islands of Zanzibar, Madagascar, Mauritius, Seychelles, Saint Helena, Réunion, Comoros, Saint Helena, Ascension, São Tomé, Principe, Annobón, Bioko, Canaries, Madeiras, and Pemba
- ◆ the gold mines of Ghana
- ◆ Snake Park, Koobi Fora, and Nairobi museums
- ◆ lakes Leopold, Assal, Victoria, Chad, Kivu, Tana, Tanganyika, Malawi, Mweru, Kariba, Kioga, Rudolf, Manyara, Baringo, Turkana, Natron, Bangweulu, Albert, and Edward
- ◆ the Kalahari, Sahara, Libyan, and Nubian deserts
- ◆ the Great Rift Valley and Olduvai Gorge
- ◆ the pyramids of Cheops and Khafre in Giza

Budget: $

Sources:

"Facing Mount Kenya and Kilimanjaro, Too: The Thrill of a Safari—By Land or By Air," *Black Enterprise,* April 1987, pp. 66-67.

McBee, Susanna, "Safaris to Where the Wild Things Are," *U.S. News and World Report,* July 7, 1986, p. 61.

Mercier, Pat, "The Voyage of the Sand Ship Discovery," *Off Road,* August 1990, pp. 72-77.

Riley, Elfriede, and Frank Riley, "Cheetahs in the Mist: Africa on Your Own, from Kenya to Kilimanjaro, from Morocco to Cleopatra's Nile," *Los Angeles Magazine,* June 1989, pp. 160-165.

Alternative Applications: Have travel planners survey catalogs of safari clothing and footwear, tents, equipment, cameras, and other gear so they can make useful suggestions about pretravel purchases. Give advice about innoculations, drinking water, swimming, and protection from heat, insects, and poisonous snakes.

 | **Africa's Great Rivers**

Originator: Paula Montgomery, editor, Baltimore, Maryland.

Age/Grade Level or Audience: Kindergarten, elementary, and middle school geography classes.

Description: On a large map, name and explore Africa's rivers.

Procedure: Post large topographical maps of Africa and have students name the Niger, Congo, Aruwimi, Lualaba, Ubangi, Shire, Zambezi, Volta, Vaal, Kasai, Juba, Gambia, Lwango, Kwando, Benue, Atbara, Ogooué, Orange, Senegal, Limpopo, Lualaba, and Nile rivers. Then have them trace by hand the main channel and branches. Lead a discussion of how each river influences the lifestyle of local tribes. Include commentary on the types of plants and animals that thrive on African river banks, particularly the hippopotamus, crocodile, flamingos, fish, and water hyacinths and lilies.

Budget: $

Sources:

Computer software such as Data Disc International's *World Data* or MECC's *World Geography*

"Botswana," *National Geographic,* December 1990.

Clarendon Press Cartographic Department Staff, *The Oxford Economic Atlas of the World,* Oxford University Press, 1972.

"Ivory Coast," *National Geographic,* July 1982.

"Malawi," *National Geographic,* September 1989.

"Mali," *National Geographic,* October 1990.

"Senegambia," *National Geographic,* August 1985.

"Serengeti," *National Geographic,* May 1986.

"Zaire," *National Geographic,* November 1991.

Alternative Applications: Supply smaller maps to groups of two or three children and have them letter the names of the Congo, Niger, Nile, and other important waterways. Complete the assignment by writing in names of major cities that depend on the rivers for trade, recreation, irrigation, transportation, and water power.

The Atlantic Triangle

Age/Grade Level or Audience: Elementary and middle school history or geography classes.

Description: Create a bulletin board outlining the trade arrangement known as the Atlantic Triangle.

Procedure: Post a map of the area bounded by Bristol, England, Africa's west coast, and the West Indies. Label each point of the triangle with its trade goods: cloth and trinkets from Bristol, slaves from Africa, and sugar and tobacco from the West Indies. Estimate the distances on each segment of the triangle and the time it took clipper ships to cover each leg of the route.

Budget: $

Sources:

Asante, Molefi K., *Historical and Cultural Atlas of African Americans,* Macmillan, 1991.

McCrum, Robert, *The Story of English,* Penguin Books, 1993.

Murray, Jocelyn, ed., *Cultural Atlas of Africa,* Facts on File, 1989.

Alternative Applications: Have students prepare a time line of slavery, noting when it was protested and ultimately outlawed in different parts of the Atlantic Triangle. Include the importance of William Lloyd Garrison, John Newton, Mennonites and Quakers, Sojourner Truth, Frederick Douglass, Harriet Beecher Stowe, Abraham Lincoln, Toussaint L'Ouverture, and William Wilberforce.

Bean Bag Toss

Age/Grade Level or Audience: Kindergarten and elementary school geography classes.

Description: Play bean bag toss on an oversized map of Africa.

Procedure: Outline a map of Africa approximately eight feet long on an asphalt or concrete playground. Color code the countries with chalk or paint. To protect the map from rain damage, spray with a fixative, such as polyurethane or water seal. This game could also be drawn on a tarp or piece of canvas rolled up for storage, then played in a gymnasium, hallway, community center, church activities room, or neighborhood street festival.

Vary rules with each use. Have students toss bean bags onto the map or play variations of hopscotch. For example:

- ◆ Only the bags that land on a particular country, such as Benin or Cameroon, earn points. The smaller the country, the greater the number of points.
- ◆ Have students name the country they are aiming for before tossing bean bags. If they are successful, they win points.
- ◆ Have students continue tossing as long as they hit the countries they name beforehand. When the bean bag lands on another country, the turn passes to another player.
- ◆ Have students hop on one foot onto a series of countries without touching borders. In order to win points, they must call out the name of the country they land on.
- ◆ Have students name the capital of the nation they land on. The capitals include the following:

Algeria—Algiers	Madagascar—Antananarivo
Angola—Luanda	Malawi—Lilongwe
Benin—Porto-Novo	Mali—Bamako
Botswana—Gaborone	Mauritania—Nouakchott
Burkina—Ouagadougou	Mauritius—Port Louis
Burundi—Bujumbura	Morocco—Rabat
Cameroon—Yaoundé	Mozambique—Maputo
Cape Verde—Praia	Namibia—Windhoek
Central African Republic—Bangul	Niger—Niamey
Chad—N'Djamena	Nigeria—Lagos
Comoros—Moroni	Rwanda—Kigali
Congo—Brazzaville	São Tomé and Principe—São Tomé
Djibouti—Djibouti	Senegal—Dakar
Egypt—Cairo	Seychelles—Victoria
Equatorial Guinea—Malabo	Sierra Leone—Freetown

Ethiopia—Addis Ababa	Somalia—Mogadishu
Gabon—Libreville	South Africa—Pretoria
Gambia—Banjul	Sudan—Khartoum
Ghana—Accra	Swaziland—Mbabane
Guinea—Conakry	Tanzania—Dar es Salaam
Guinea-Bissau—Bissau	Togo—Lomé
Ivory Coast—Abidjan	Tunisia—Tunis
Kenya—Nairobi	Uganda—Kampala
Lesotho—Maseru	Zaire—Kinshasa
Liberia—Monrovia	Zambia—Lusaka
Libya—Tripoli	Zimbabwe—Harare

Budget: $$$

Sources:

Brown, Leslie, *Africa: A Natural History,* Random House, 1965.

Clarendon Press Cartographic Department Staff, *The Oxford Economic Atlas of the World,* Oxford University Press, 1972.

Murray, Jocelyn, ed., *Cultural Atlas of Africa,* Facts on File, 1989.

Alternative Applications:

Extend the use of the oversized African map with a whole world map covering an entire asphalt or concrete playground. Organize a PTA committee or other volunteers to lay out continents and color code countries. Lead students in comparative studies of Africa with other nations. For example:

◆ Use small steps to measure the Nile, Niger, Limpopo, or Congo rivers. Compare the length with that of the Amazon, Yalu, or Missouri.

◆ Walk the distance from Africa west to Brazil and east to India. Contrast the difference.

◆ Name the countries directly north of Africa and the languages spoken in each, such as French in France, Greek in Greece, and Spanish in Spain.

◆ Play follow-the-leader by pretending to fly over the whole world. Name countries in each continent where you intend to land.

Black Educational Institutions

Age/Grade Level or Audience: High school juniors and seniors; vocational classes; guidance offices.

Description: Create a map locating the nation's black colleges and universities.

Procedure: Establish a bulletin board where students, parents, guidance counselors, and teachers can locate black educational institutions or schools which maintain strong black studies departments. Mark with a push pin the location of each. For example:

- ◆ Alabama A & M University, Normal, Alabama
- ◆ Alabama State University, Montgomery, Alabama
- ◆ Albany State College, Albany, Georgia
- ◆ Alcorn State University, Lorman, Mississippi
- ◆ Atlanta Metropolitan College, Atlanta, Georgia
- ◆ Bethune-Cookman College, Daytona Beach, Florida
- ◆ Bowie State University, Bowie, Maryland
- ◆ Central State University, Wilberforce, Ohio
- ◆ Chicago State University, Chicago, Illinois
- ◆ Clark Atlanta University, Atlanta, Georgia
- ◆ Delaware State College, Dover, Delaware
- ◆ Dillard University, New Orleans, Louisiana
- ◆ Fisk University, Nashville, Tennessee
- ◆ Grambling State University, Grambling, Louisiana
- ◆ Hampton University, Hampton, Virginia
- ◆ Howard University, Washington, D.C.
- ◆ Johnson C. Smith University, Charlotte, North Carolina
- ◆ Langston University, Langston, Oklahoma
- ◆ Lincoln University, Jefferson City, Missouri
- ◆ Medgar Evers College of City University of New York, Brooklyn, New York
- ◆ Morehouse College, Atlanta, Georgia
- ◆ Morgan State University, Baltimore, Maryland
- ◆ Norfolk State University, Norfolk, Virginia
- ◆ North Carolina A & T, Greensboro, North Carolina
- ◆ Prairie View A & M University, Prairie View, Texas
- ◆ Roxbury Community College, Roxbury Crossing, Massachusetts
- ◆ Savannah State College, Savannah, Georgia
- ◆ Shaw University, Raleigh, North Carolina
- ◆ South Carolina State College, Orangeburg, South Carolina
- ◆ Southern University, Baton Rouge, Louisiana
- ◆ Tennessee State University, Nashville, Tennessee
- ◆ Texas Southern University, Houston, Texas
- ◆ Tuskegee Institute, Tuskegee, Alabama
- ◆ University of Arkansas, Pine Bluff, Arkansas
- ◆ University of the District of Columbia, Washington, D.C.
- ◆ Virginia State University, Petersburg, Virginia
- ◆ West Virginia State College, Institute, West Virginia
- ◆ Winston-Salem State University, Winston-Salem, North Carolina
- ◆ Xavier University of Louisiana, New Orleans, Louisiana

Attach a string from the pin to an index card listing essential information, such as size, range of majors, specialty courses (e.g., women's studies or urban planning), extracurricular activities, scholarship and work-study programs, tuition, required tests, and addresses of student aid officers and admissions directors.

Budget: $

Sources:

A free pamphlet, "Choosing to Succeed," P.O. Box 23345, Kankakee, IL 60902. Also, contact The Opportunity Line, a service of the National Urban League, by calling 1-800-NUL-FUND.

Bowman, J. Wilson, *America's Black Colleges,* Sandcastle Publishing, 1992.

Furtaw, Julia C., ed., *Black American Information Directory*, 2nd ed., Gale, 1992.

Alternative Applications: To encourage interest in higher education, invite graduates of black educational institutions to address students. Display slides, posters, and charts of pertinent data, and provide a table for handouts, brochures, college catalogs, and student aid forms.

The Black Flavor of New Orleans

Age/Grade Level or Audience: All ages.

Description: Hold a New Orleans festival as a community celebration of Black History Month.

Procedure: Recreate the atmosphere of New Orleans, Louisiana, in architecture, fashion, song, food, instrumental music, dance, pageantry, and drama. Label festival booths "Preservation Hall," "The Quarter," "Cafe du Monde," "Jackson Square," "Bourbon Street," "Storyville," "The Levee," "St. Charles Avenue," and "Satchmo." Serve local foods such as muffalettas, red beans and rice, crawfish etouffée, gumbo, beignets, and coffee with chicory. Play music that originated in New Orleans, particularly Dixieland jazz, Cajun and Creole folk music, and zydeco. Stress the success with which African people have blended with Indians, French, Spanish, Portuguese, Irish, Acadian, and English settlers.

Budget: $$$

Sources:

The films *The Big Easy* (1987), *American Patchwork: Jazz Parades* (1990), *American Patchwork: The Land Where Blues Began* (1990), and *Feet Don't Fail Me Now;* Automobile Association of America (AAA) guidebooks to New Orleans, Louisiana.

Cantor, George, *Historic Landmarks of Black America,* Gale, 1991.

Fodor's New Orleans, Fodor's Travel Guides, 1993.

Wilson, Charles Reagan, and William Ferris, eds., *Encyclopedia of Southern Culture,* University of North Carolina Press, 1989.

Alternative Applications: Launch a study of black influence on Harlem, Memphis, St. Louis, Atlanta, Charleston, Chicago, Mobile, Louisville, Philadelphia, Boston, Indianapolis, or the Mississippi Delta. Highlight African-American contributions to each area, such as Memphis's Beale Street, Mobile's Africatown, Atlanta's Underground, or Harlem's Cotton Club.

Caribbean Idyll

Age/Grade Level or Audience: Elementary, middle school, and high school students; travel clubs.

Description: Create a Caribbean oasis with a display or bulletin board featuring the area's most famous historical spots, products, and tourist attractions.

Procedure: Have volunteers draw an oversized map of the Caribbean islands, particularly tourist favorites such as Jamaica, Puerto Rico, Curaçao, Aruba, St. Martin, St. Bart, Guadaloupe, St. Thomas, St. Lucia, Haiti, St. Kitts, Nevis, Antigua, Martinique, Santo Domingo, and the Bahamas. Apply these activities to class study:

- ◆ Use colored markers and string to add posters and placards explaining the historical features, such as ruins of Indian villages, sugar and indigo plantations, slave markets, fishing ports, and the birthplace of Toussaint L'Ouverture.
- ◆ Use a system of symbols to indicate leading exports, particularly rum, perfume, oil, bauxite, fruit, fish, and vanilla.
- ◆ Indicate landmarks and tourist attractions, particularly lighthouses, underwater parks, caves, lagoons, ghost sightings, and the homes of famous freedom fighters.
- ◆ Read aloud from the writings of famous Caribbean authors, particularly James Berry, Jamaica Kincaid, and Derek Walcott, winner of the 1992 Nobel Prize for Literature.

Budget: $

Sources:

Clarendon Press Cartographic Department Staff, *The Oxford Economic Atlas of the World,* Oxford University Press, 1972.

"Endless Caribbean," *Traveler,* 1991 Special Edition, pp. 81-117.

Fodor's Caribbean: A Complete Guide to 27 Island Destinations, Fodor's Travel Guides, 1993.

Page, Clarence, and Lisa Page, "St. Lucia: Family Vacationing in the Caribbean," *Emerge,* December 1992, pp. 62-63.

Send for information from these tourist boards:

Antigua and Barbuda Tourist Office
121 Southeast First St., Suite 1001
Miami, FL 33131
(305)381-6762

Aruba Tourism Authority
2344 Salzedo St.
Miami, FL 33134-5033
(800)862-7822

Bahamas Tourist Office
4801 E. Independence Blvd., Suite 1000
Charlotte, NC 28212
(704)532-1290

Bonaire Tourist Information Office
201½ East 29th St.
New York, NY 10016
(800)826-6247

British Virgin Islands
360 Lexington Ave., Suite 416
New York, NY 10017
(800)835-8530

Cayman Islands Department of Tourism
6100 Blue Lagoon Dr., Suite 150
Miami, FL 33126
(305)266-2300

Curaçao Tourist Board
330 Biscayne Blvd., Suite 808
Miami, FL 33132
(800)445-8266

Dominican Republic Tourist Office
2355 Salzedo St.
Coral Gables, FL 33134
(305)444-4592

French West Indies Tourist Board
(Guadeloupe, Martinique, St. Bart, St. Martin)
610 Fifth Ave.
New York, NY 10020

Grenada Tourist Board
820 Second Ave., Suite 9-D
New York, NY 10017
(800)927-9554

Jamaica Tourist Board
1320 South Dixie Hwy., Suite 1100
Coral Gables, FL
(305)664-0557

Puerto Rico Tourism Company
575 Fifth Ave., 23rd Floor
New York, NY
(800)223-6530

Saba and Sint Eustatius
271 Main St.
Northport, NY 11768
(800)344-4606

Sint Maarten (St. Martin)
Netherlands Antilles Windward
    Islands Rep.
275 Seventh Ave.
New York, NY 10001-6788
(212)989-0000

St. Lucia Tourist Board
830 Second Ave., 9th Floor
New York, NY 10017
(800)456-3984

Trinidad and Tobago Islands
25 West 43rd St., Suite 1508
New York, NY 10036
(800)232-0082

Turks and Caicos Islands
331 Madison Ave.
New York, NY
(800)441-4419

U.S. Virgin Islands
2655 Le Jeune Rd., Suite 907
Coral Gables, FL 33134
(305)442-7200

Alternative Applications: Feature an island each week during Black History Month. Explain through posters and time lines how Africans came to populate the area and dominate its growth, particularly in Jamaica, Haiti, Santo Domingo, and Antigua. Mention other settlers in the area, especially French, Dutch, Portuguese, and English colonists. Note each area's struggle for civil rights.

 ## The Drifting Continents

Age/Grade Level or Audience: Elementary, middle school, and high school geography and earth science classes.

Description: Study the shifting continents of the globe.

Procedure: Have students make contrasting maps of the world before and after continental drift. Point out the following facts:

- ◆ During the Mesozoic era before continental drift, Africa was the center of a cluster of lands.
- ◆ This African cluster is referred to as Pangaea, which is Greek for "all lands."
- ◆ The first to separate during the Cretaceous era was South America, followed by Asia.
- ◆ The drifting continents formed North and South America, Europe, Asia, Australia, and Antarctica.
- ◆ Studies of fossil plants and animals prove when this separation was completed.
- ◆ Fluctuations in the earth's crust have produced the Great Rift Valley, Lake Tanganyika, the Luangwa Valley of Zambia, and the Ethiopian Highlands.
- ◆ Louis, Mary, and Richard Leakey located the earliest human remains in the Olduvai Gorge, Kenya.

Budget: $

Sources:
Brown, Leslie, *Africa: A Natural History,* Random House, 1965.
Kingdon, Jonathan, *Island Africa: The Evolution of Africa's Rare Animals and Plants,* Princeton University Press, 1992.
Murray, Jocelyn, ed., *Cultural Atlas of Africa,* Facts on File, 1989.

Alternative Applications: Have students cite geological and climatic reasons for the creation of the Sahara Desert, Zambezi Basin, Kalahari Desert, Namib Desert, Olifants Gorge, Batoka Gorge, Mount Kilimanjaro, and Okavango Swamps. Give evidence that the surface of Africa is continually shifting and changing, for instance, in the newly arid areas of Somalia and Ethiopia, where famine endangers farmers and herders. Discuss how the Canary Islands, the Seychelles, and Madagascar formed offshore.

Learning the Colors of Africa

Age/Grade Level or Audience: Preschool and kindergarten children.

Description: Study colors that represent Africa.

Procedure: Teach the four colors of Africa by having children color and display black, red, yellow, and green objects that represent Africa.

- ◆ black: black-skinned children, hippopotamus, coal
- ◆ red: wildflowers, fruit, smiles
- ◆ yellow: sunlight, grain, birds
- ◆ green: grasslands, palm branches, grasshoppers

Budget: $$

Sources:

Ellis, Veronica Freeman, *Afro-Bets First Book about Africa: An Introduction for Young Readers,* Just Us Books, 1989.

Gray, Nigel, *A Country Far Away,* Orchard Books, 1989.

Greenfield, Eloise, *Africa Dream,* HarperCollins, 1989.

Porter, A. P., *Kwanzaa,* Carolrhoda Books, 1991.

Stock, Catherine, *Armien's Fishing Trip,* Morrow Junior Books, 1990.

Alternative Applications: Present big books, posters, color prints, and fabrics. Have children point out objects or shapes by color. Discuss how the colors of Africa—black, red, yellow, and green—differ from the traditional American red, white, and blue. Explain why Africans stress colors from nature.

Liberia

Age/Grade Level or Audience: Elementary and middle school geography and history classes.

Description: Lead a study of Liberia.

Procedure: Using lecture, film, filmstrips, posters, videos, and other materials, explain to students how freed American slaves founded the nation of Liberia. Discuss the following data:

- ◆ significance of the country's name
- ◆ arrival of Americo-Liberians in 1821

◆ emptying of slave ships
◆ Liberia's independence in 1847
◆ opening of the Firestone rubber plantation in 1927
◆ presidency of William Tubman
◆ establishment of republican government in 1945
◆ extension of voting rights in 1947
◆ becoming a charter member of the United Nations
◆ the violent end of William Tolbert's corrupt government in 1980

Budget: $$

Sources:

Humphrey, Sally, *A Family in Liberia,* Lerner Publications, 1987.
Murray, Jocelyn, ed., *Cultural Atlas of Africa,* Facts on File, 1989.
Sullivan, Jo Mary, *Liberia in Pictures,* Lerner Publications, 1988.

Alternative Applications: Have students celebrate Liberia's uniqueness by doing the following:

◆ dressing in Liberian costume
◆ cooking Liberian foods
◆ listening to Liberian music
◆ reading stories or poems by Liberian authors
◆ identifying plants and animals common to Liberia
◆ drawing a map illustrating the diversity of the brewing, chemical, farming, mining, timber, rubber, and palm industries
◆ trying some native recipes featuring rice, cassava, and cocoa

Life along the Nile

Age/Grade Level or Audience: Elementary and middle school geography and history classes.

Description: Study the extensive history of the Nile.

Procedure: Assist students in preparing a database history, scroll, or time line of the Nile River. Include mention of earliest inhabitants, the builders of the pyramids and sphinx; colonial explorations; the removal of Abu Simbel to accommodate the building of the Aswan Dam; and more recent developments, such as the earthquake of October 1992, which destroyed much of Cairo. Have groups of students contribute segments to the overall study of the Nile, then bind the finished reports into a single scrapbook about the river's rich history.

Budget: $$

Sources:
Brown, Leslie, *Africa: A Natural History,* Random House, 1965.
"Journey up the Nile," *National Geographic,* May 1985.
Murphy, E. Jefferson, *Understanding Africa,* Crowell, 1978.
Murray, Jocelyn, ed., *Cultural Atlas of Africa,* Facts on File, 1989.

Alternative Applications: Discuss how Western fiction and nonfiction writers celebrate the Nile in their works, including William Shakespeare in *Antony and Cleopatra* and the explorer Richard Francis Burton in *Goa, and the Blue Mountains and First Footsteps in East Africa.*

Life in a Kenyan Village

Age/Grade Level or Audience: Kindergarten and elementary school geography and crafts classes.

Description: Organize the building of a miniature Kenyan Village.

Procedure: Have students examine books about life in Kenya. Have them use clay, wooden dowels or clothespins, twigs, cardboard, and found objects to create a miniature Kenyan village. Stress the following details:

- ◆ fields of tea, coffee, sugar cane, hemp, wheat, and rice
- ◆ pastures grazed by cattle, sheep, oxen, and goats
- ◆ palm trees
- ◆ Kikuku and Luo people
- ◆ the port of Mombasa
- ◆ open-air markets

Budget: $$

Sources:
Griffin, Michael, *A Family in Kenya,* Lerner Publications, 1988.
Lerner Geography Department Staff, *Kenya in Pictures,* Lerner Publications, 1988.
Murphy, E. Jefferson, *Understanding Africa,* Crowell, 1978.
Murray, Jocelyn, ed., *Cultural Atlas of Africa,* Facts on File, 1989.

Alternative Applications: Have students build two villages to illustrate life in contrasting parts of Africa, such as Ethiopia and Nigeria, Ivory Coast and Algeria, Morocco and South Africa, Niger and Swaziland, Angola and Mozambique, and Egypt and Madagascar.

The Moors

Age/Grade Level or Audience: Elementary, middle school, high school, and college geography and history classes.

Description: Describe the Moorish people, lands where they settled, and their influence on civilization.

Procedure: Have students work in groups to research and present oral reports on Moorish civilization and its influence. For example:

- ◆ the origin of the term "Moor"
- ◆ Moorish migration to Iberia
- ◆ eleventh-century expulsion of Moors from Europe
- ◆ Moorish architecture around the Mediterranean
- ◆ Moorish mosques
- ◆ Moors and the Spanish Inquisition
- ◆ Moorish pottery, textiles, and metalwork
- ◆ Shakespeare's use of Othello, a Moorish general from Venice, as protagonist of a major English drama
- ◆ conversion of North African Berbers and blacks to Islam

Budget: $$

Sources:

Lane-Poole, Stanley, *Moors in Spain,* Khayats, 1967.

Michell, George, *Architecture of the Islamic World: Its History and Social Meaning,* Thames & Hudson, 1984.

"Moors," *National Geographic,* July 1988.

Oliver, Roland, *The African Experience,* IconEditions, 1992.

Shakespeare, William, *Othello,* Bantam Books, 1988.

Stewart, Judy, *A Family in Morocco,* Lerner Publications, 1986.

Alternative Applications: Have participants sketch a series of posters illustrating Moorish styling in jewelry, metalwork, mosaic flooring, wall hangings, and architecture. Have a group write a round-robin short story about the arrival of Moors in Spain and their experiences among people of a vastly different culture.

Puzzle Me Africa

Age/Grade Level or Audience: Elementary and middle school geography classes; religious schools; Brownie and Cub Scouts.

Description: Put together an African map puzzle.

Procedure: Draw a map of Africa on tagboard, canvas, or wrapping paper. After individual countries are colored with markers, chalk, crayon, or paint, laminate the finished map, then cut apart along border lines. Have students work in teams to reassemble the map. The team that finishes in the shortest time wins.

Budget: $

Sources:

Clarendon Press Cartographic Department Staff, *The Oxford Economic Atlas of the World,* Oxford University Press, 1972.

Demko, George J., *Why in the World: Adventures in Geography,* Anchor Books, 1992.

Murray, Jocelyn, ed., *Cultural Atlas of Africa,* Facts on File, 1989.

Alternative Applications: Have an individual hold up a single puzzle piece and report to the class on the products, people, culture, languages, religions, and landmarks of that country. As speakers finish, have them place their puzzle parts in correct order among the other map pieces. The finished map could serve as the focal point of a Black History Month open house, PTA program, civic display, foyer mural, or library or museum bulletin board.

Safari

Age/Grade Level or Audience: Kindergarten, elementary, and middle school geography and history classes; scout troops; 4-H clubs.

Description: Organize a game of "I Spy" with an African touch.

Procedure: Select a leader to say, "I spy something that begins with an M." The first player to name an African place, object, people, or language, such as Mozambique, Morocco, Maasai, mat, or mask becomes the leader. Leaders should vary the letters of the alphabet from A to Z.

Budget: $

Sources:

Alexander, Lloyd, *The Fortune-Tellers,* Dutton, 1992.

Haskins, Jim, *Count Your Way through Africa,* Carolrhoda Books, 1989.

Hathaway, Jim, *Cameroon in Pictures,* Lerner Publications, 1989.

Lewin, Hugh, *Jafta: The Town,* Carolrhoda Books, 1984.

McKenna, Nancy Durrel, *A Zulu Family,* Lerner Publications, 1986.

Schultz, John, *Nigeria in Pictures,* Lerner Publications, 1988.
Watson, R. L., *South Africa in Pictures,* Lerner Publications, 1988.

Alternative Applications: Assign students only one letter to find on their safari, such as C. Then reward the person who names the most words, such as Chad, Cameroon, crocodile, cork, cotton, corn, chimpanzee, and Cairo.

Simon Says

Age/Grade Level or Audience: Kindergarten and elementary classes; religious schools; day-care centers.

Description: Play an African version of Simon Says.

Procedure: Have students act out a game of Simon Says from an African point of view. For example, give these commands:

- ◆ Growl like the lion.
- ◆ Swim like the crocodile.
- ◆ Stretch like the giraffe.
- ◆ Giggle like the monkey.
- ◆ Trumpet like the elephant.
- ◆ Trot like the hyena.
- ◆ Wallow like the hippopotamus.
- ◆ Climb like the gorilla.
- ◆ Wiggle like the cobra.
- ◆ Snort like the rhinoceros.
- ◆ Flap like the emu.
- ◆ Build like the termite.
- ◆ Scurry like the ant.

Budget: $

Sources:
Alexander, Lloyd, *The Fortune-Tellers,* Dutton, 1992.
Ellis, Veronica Freeman, *Afro-Bets First Book About Africa: An Introduction for Young Readers,* Just Us Books, 1989.
Jones, Bessie, and Bess Lomax Hawes, *Step It Down: Games, Plays, Songs, and Stories from the Afro-American Heritage,* Harper & Row, 1972, reprinted, University of Georgia Press, 1987.

Alternative Applications: Have students make up African games suited to life in particular climates and surroundings, such as steamy jungles of Zaire, plains of

Kenya, riverbanks of the Nile, fortune-tellers' tents in the Cameroons, sandy beaches of the Seychelles, thatched villages of Nigeria, and oases of the Sahara Desert. Suggest guessing games and listening and speaking activities for keeping cool, watching animals, playing in sand or surf, picking bananas and coconuts, sipping coconut milk, making mud houses, digging for diamonds, playing drums and flutes, stringing beads, braiding hair, taking photos, and drawing animal pictures.

World Races

Age/Grade Level or Audience: Elementary and middle school history and geography classes.

Description: Create a map illustrating the locations of major concentrations of black people.

Procedure: Have students research information about the locations of black people on the globe. Divide the class into six groups, one for each continent. Have students draw the continents and islands and indicate with a bar graph the distribution of black people among other races.

Budget: $

Sources:
Clarendon Press Cartographic Department Staff, *The Oxford Economic Atlas of the World*, Oxford University Press, 1972.
Demko, George J., *Why in the World: Adventures in Geography*, Anchor Books, 1991.
Statistical Abstract of the United States, U.S. Department of Commerce, Bureau of the Census, 1992.
"You Get the Drift? Turns Out We Did," *Discover*, September 1985, p. 8.

Alternative Applications: Have students apply this assignment to a study of all races by state throughout the United States and the rest of North America. Note in particular the most cosmopolitan world cities, particularly New York, Seattle, Los Angeles, San Diego, Miami, Toronto, and Mexico City. Have students draw conclusions about how diversity in large cities affects the following traits:

- ◆ fashion, hairstyles, music, and dining
- ◆ government
- ◆ religion and holidays
- ◆ community attitudes
- ◆ education
- ◆ literature and lore

History

African and World Events

Age/Grade Level or Audience: All ages.

Description: Create a wall chart pairing African events with happenings in other parts of the globe.

Procedure: Create a time line of significant events. Tie them to other areas of human development. Stress these important happenings:

- ◆ **4000-3000 B.C.** As Mesopotamian civilization was beginning in the Tigris-Euphrates Valley, Middle Easterners were migrating to Africa across the Sinai Peninsula.
- ◆ **2000 B.C.** As Ethiopia flourished, Indian civilization was beginning in the Indus Valley.
- ◆ **2000-1000 B.C.** Hammurabi was ruling Babylon and farmers were tilling Central American fields during the Egyptian invasion of Nubia.
- ◆ **1200 B.C.** Jews were exiting Egypt about the time of the Trojan War and the beginning of Peruvian culture.
- ◆ **814 B.C.** Greek city-states were flourishing while the Phoenicians were founding Carthage in North Africa, half a century before Rome was founded on the Tiber River.
- ◆ **500 B.C.** Hanno, a Carthaginian explorer, sailed the coast of Africa while Greece enjoyed its Golden Age.
- ◆ **100 B.C.** Shortly after the building of the Great Wall of China, North Africa came under Roman domination.
- ◆ **700 A.D.** Arabs converted North Africa and Spain to Islam at the same time.
- ◆ **1250** Shortly after the Magna Carta was signed, the nation of Ghana was established on the African west coast.
- ◆ **1488** Bartholomeu Dias sailed around the Cape of Good Hope while the Aztec and Incan empires were reaching their heights.

◆ **1607** While aboriginal peoples populated arid regions of Australia, the slave trade began in the United States and Caribbean Islands.

◆ **1800** In the years before and after the completion of the Suez Canal, colonizers from Britain, Belgium, France, Germany, and Italy staked out claims in Africa.

◆ **1950s** A decade after the end of World War II and the creation of a free Jewish state in Israel, twenty-seven African republics won their independence from colonialism.

◆ **1990s** At the same time that the United States launched an exploration of Mars, South Africa continued its struggle against racist oppression.

Budget: $

Sources:

Estell, Kenneth, ed., *The African-American Almanac,* 6th ed., Gale, 1993.

Grun, Bernard, *The Timetables of History: A Horizontal Linkage of People and Events,* Simon & Schuster, 1991.

Trager, James, *The People's Chronology,* Henry Holt, 1992.

Turnbull, Colin M., *The Peoples of Africa,* World Publishing, 1962.

Alternative Applications: For a more detailed version of "African and World Events," divide a display into five segments, each representing the five continents. Synchronize histories of each continent, giving detailed information about time, place, participants, and events. Emphasize each area's struggles against oppression, exploitation, and tyranny, for example the French and Russian revolutions in Europe, the Spanish conquest of Mexico, Captain Cook's arrival in Australia, and Japan's attack on China during World War II.

 **All Aboard!**

Age/Grade Level or Audience: All ages.

Description: Organize a black history cavalcade.

Procedure: Offer the public a special city bus tour or motorcade to local black history centers, landmarks, and points of interest, particularly black colleges, historic churches, recreation centers, and family homes. Connect local history with the greater picture by pointing out how area figures participated in abolitionism, the Underground Railroad, sit-ins, or civil rights marches. For example, consider the following points of interest in Louisville, Kentucky:

◆ the fall Corn Island Storytelling Festival
◆ riverfront "Gateway to Freedom"

- ◆ Portland Museum's collection of photos and artifacts
- ◆ Hillerich and Bradsby's "Louisville Slugger," the bat used by Hank Aaron
- ◆ J. B. Speed Art Museum African art collection
- ◆ Quinn Chapel, named for Bishop Paul Quinn
- ◆ Muhammad Ali's home on Grand Avenue
- ◆ Kentucky Derby Museum's displays featuring Isaac B. Murphy, three-time winner of the Kentucky Derby
- ◆ Louisville Free Public Library, the first established for black patrons
- ◆ Mammoth Life and Accident Insurance Company, established by black owners in 1915
- ◆ Russell Historic Neighborhood, featuring homes built by black contractor Samuel Plato
- ◆ Frank Stanley's *Louisville Defender,* the state's first black newspaper

Budget: $$$

Sources:
Enlist the mayor and city council or county commission in offering this tour to citizens and visitors; local guidebooks.
Cantor, George, *Historic Landmarks of Black America,* Gale, 1991.

Alternative Applications: Print a walking tour, including map and markers or plaques indicating historic events and noteworthy districts. Leave free copies at convention centers, the chamber of commerce, public libraries and museums, school administration offices, media centers, shopping malls, and visitors' bureaus.

Antislavery in England and the U.S.

Age/Grade Level or Audience: Middle school, high school, and college history classes.

Description: Compose a double time line paralleling the U.S. abolitionist movement with England's antislavery movement.

Procedure: Have students work in pairs to locate data for a double time line. On the English side, emphasize the work of John Newton, whose hymn "Amazing Grace" influenced William Wilberforce to spearhead the antislavery movement in England. On the American side, stress similar work by Frederick Douglass, Quakers, Mennonites, Harriet Beecher Stowe, Harriet Tubman, Sojourner Truth, and other abolitionist leaders.

Budget: $

Sources:

Evitts, William J., *Captive Bodies, Free Spirits: The Story of Southern Slavery,* Messner, 1985.

Low, W. Augustus, and Virgil A. Clift, eds., *Encyclopedia of Black America,* McGraw-Hill, 1981, reprinted, Da Capo Press, 1984.

Walvin, James, *Slavery and the Slave Trade: A Short Illustrated History,* University Press of Mississippi, 1983.

Alternative Applications: Have students report facts about slavery's growth and abolishment in Caribbean islands. Note the influence of places such as Jamaica, Haiti, the Dominican Republic, Aruba, St. Martin, Tortola, Cuba, Bermuda, Antigua, Martinique, and Nassau. Comment on the effects of home rule as colonial governments collapsed, were voted out, or abandoned each island.

Apartheid and the World

Age/Grade Level or Audience: Middle school, high school, and college history classes.

Description: Conduct a thorough study of apartheid and its effect on world trade and international relations.

Procedure: Provide a selection of resource material about apartheid, including novels, biographies, newspaper and magazine studies, and reference books. Have students complete the following activities:

- ◆ Compose an extended definition of apartheid, with its origins and ramifications in local and global relations.
- ◆ Contribute information and draw inferences about the nature of severe systems of racial segregation.
- ◆ Stress the irony of the South African flag, which features small insets of the Dutch, British, and Orange Free State flags in the center.
- ◆ Explain the role of Nelson Mandela, Winnie Mandela, and Steven Biko as national heroes.
- ◆ Discuss the future of colonialism in Africa.

Budget: $

Sources:

Debroey, Steven, *South Africa to the Sources of Apartheid,* University Press of America, 1989.

Moss, Joyce, and George Wilson, *Peoples of the World: Africans South of the Sahara,* Gale, 1991.

Mostert, Noël, *Frontiers: The Epic of South Africa's Creation and the Tragedy of the Xhosa People,* Knopf, 1992.
Murphy, E. Jefferson, *Understanding Africa,* Crowell, 1978.
Woods, Donald, *Apartheid: A Graphic Guide,* Henry Holt, 1988.

Alternative Applications: Have students present a school assembly program on apartheid. Include posters, overhead transparencies, handouts, maps, and mock interviews with significant figures, particularly the president of the United Nations, human rights leaders, the Pope, Nelson Mandela, Winnie Mandela, Steven Biko, Ian Smith, F. W. de Klerk, and former and current secretaries of state and presidents of the United States. Stress forensic studies that prove that freedom fighters were beaten and abused while in custody.

Atlanta-Bound

Age/Grade Level or Audience: All ages.

Description: Organize a trip to Atlanta's Freedom Walk.

Procedure: Organize a bus trip to Atlanta, Georgia. Focus on the life and accomplishments of Martin Luther King, Jr., by beginning the group's tour at the King Center for Nonviolent Social Change. Include on your itinerary the Joel Chandler Harris Museum, office of the Atlanta *Constitution,* and Underground Atlanta. Highlight the role of Atlanta in important segments of African-American history, such as the civil rights movement, Sherman's siege, and the slave trade.

Budget: $$$$

Sources:
Atlanta chamber of commerce and Automobile Association of America (AAA) brochures, maps, and travel guides.
Cantor, George, *Historic Landmarks of Black America,* Gale, 1991.
King, Coretta Scott, *My Life with Martin Luther King, Jr.,* Henry Holt, 1992.

Alternative Applications: Present a historical overview of Atlanta through brochures, photos, maps, diagrams, film clips of *Gone with the Wind,* and media articles. Create a bulletin board featuring a map of Atlanta and memorabilia from each area, such as programs from the diorama, a schematic drawing of Underground Atlanta, and literature from museums.

Black Heritage Trivia

Originator: Leatrice Pearson, teacher, Lenoir, North Carolina.

Age/Grade Level or Audience: All ages.

Description: Organize a group into teams to play Black Heritage Trivia.

Procedure: Provide a list from which players may select answers to the following questions:

History

◆ Who was the first black born in the English colonies? (William Tucker)
◆ What was the first Negro newspaper? (*Freedom's Journal*)
◆ What female agent helped form the Underground Railroad? (Harriet Tubman)
◆ In what city was the National Association for the Advancement of Colored People (NAACP) created? (New York)
◆ Who founded the National Council of Negro Women? (Mary McLeod Bethune)
◆ In what year was the Civil Rights Act passed? (1964)
◆ Who was the U.S. President that year? (Lyndon B. Johnson)
◆ Who was the first black general of the U.S. Army? (Benjamin Davis)
◆ What is the title of Martin Luther King, Jr.'s most famous speech? ("I Have a Dream")
◆ What does SCLC stand for? (Southern Christian Leadership Conference)
◆ Which constitutional amendment abolished slavery? (Thirteenth)
◆ Who was the first black to be pictured on a postage stamp? (Booker T. Washington)
◆ To what state were the first slaves brought? (Virginia)
◆ What school did Booker T. Washington establish? (Tuskegee Institute)
◆ What black man was the first to die at the Boston Massacre? (Crispus Attucks)
◆ For what is Iman famous? (fashion modeling)
◆ Which African-American won the Nobel Peace Prize in 1964? (Martin Luther King, Jr.)
◆ Who was the first black to win a Nobel Peace Prize? (Ralphe Bunche)
◆ In what city did Jesse Owens win four gold Olympic medals? (Berlin)
◆ Who led a bloody slave revolt in Virginia in 1831? (Nat Turner)
◆ What was Harriet Tubman's code name? (Moses)
◆ Whose fashion label was "Williwear"? (designer Willi Smith)
◆ Who spearheaded the Back to Africa movement? (Marcus Garvey)
◆ What famous regiment did Robert Gould Shaw command during the Civil War? (the only black regiment)
◆ In what field was Maggie Lena Walker a first? (female bank president)
◆ What crime did journalist Ida B. Wells-Barnett fight? (lynching)

Music

◆ What is the title of the song that begins, "Lift every voice and sing"? (Negro National Anthem)

◆ Which film featured Scott Joplin's music as its score? (*The Sting*)

◆ What singer dubbed her voice onto recordings made by her father? (Natalie Cole)

◆ Who is called the "Queen of Soul"? (Aretha Franklin)

◆ What dance did Chubby Checker popularize? (the Twist)

◆ What is Steveland Morris's stage name? (Stevie Wonder)

◆ Who was the first black star of the Metropolitan Opera? (Marian Anderson)

◆ What prominent organization humiliated Marian Anderson? (Daughters of the American Revolution)

◆ What prominent D.A.R. member resigned because of the humiliation of Marian Anderson? (Eleanor Roosevelt)

◆ In what Southern city did black students stage sit-ins at a Woolworth's lunch counter? (Greensboro, North Carolina)

◆ In what field was Bessie Coleman first? (female pilot)

◆ From what university did a group of famous World War II airmen come? (Tuskegee)

Literature

◆ Who wrote *To Be Young, Gifted, and Black?* (Lorraine Hansberry)

◆ Who was the first black to receive a Pulitzer Prize? (Gwendolyn Brooks)

◆ For what novel did Toni Morrison win a Pulitzer Prize? (*Beloved*)

◆ What novel won Ralph Ellison a National Book Award in 1952? (*Invisible Man*)

◆ What play title is taken from Langston Hughes's "A Dream Deferred"? (*A Raisin in the Sun*)

◆ What was Malcolm X's real surname? (Little)

◆ What black journalist is featured on "60 Minutes"? (Ed Bradley)

◆ Who was "The Brown Bomber"? (Joe Louis)

◆ What black Georgia state legislator is also a poet? (Julian Bond)

◆ What literary movement started in New York City in the 1930s? (Harlem Renaissance)

◆ What black writer shocked readers by publishing a novel about female circumcision? (Alice Walker)

◆ Where is Ann Petry's book *Tituba* set? (Salem, Massachusetts)

◆ What writer described himself as the "manchild in the promised land"? (Claude Brown)

◆ What American novelist and author of *The Fire Next Time* felt more at home in Paris? (James Baldwin)

Television and Film

◆ Who portrayed Gale Sayers in Brian's Song? (Billy Dee Williams)

◆ What black singer starred in *Stormy Weather* and *Cabin in the Sky*? (Lena Horne)

◆ Who portrayed Mother Younger in the film *A Raisin in the Sun*? (Ruby Dee)

◆ What actor was the first black All-American football player? (Paul Robeson)
◆ What football star played a role in the film *The Dirty Dozen?* (Jim Brown)
◆ Who was the first black woman to win an Oscar? (Hattie McDaniel)
◆ For what film did she win the award? (*Gone with the Wind*)
◆ In what film did Sammy Davis, Jr., play Sportin' Life? (*Porgy and Bess*)
◆ What black actor starred in *The Defiant Ones, To Sir with Love, Guess Who's Coming to Dinner,* and *In the Heat of the Night?* (Sidney Poitier)
◆ Who won an Oscar for his supporting role in *An Officer and a Gentleman?* (Lou Gossett, Jr.)
◆ What black television star appeared on a televised special about AIDS and announced the death of his son from the disease? (Robert Guillaume)
◆ Who played the train conductor in *Silver Streak?* (Scatman Carruthers)
◆ What comedian created a character called Geraldine? (Flip Wilson)
◆ Who was the first black female to have her own television series? (Diahann Carroll)
◆ Who were the first black male and female television stars to host talk shows? (Arsenio Hall and Oprah Winfrey)
◆ What black actor won an Academy award for his role in *Glory?* (Denzel Washington)

Sports

◆ In what sport was Cheryl White the first black female participant? (horse racing)
◆ What black comedian started out as a track star? (Dick Gregory)
◆ Who was the first black coach of a major league team? (Bill Russell)
◆ Who broke Babe Ruth's batting record? (Hank Aaron)
◆ What black male tennis star was the first to win at Wimbledon? (Arthur Ashe)
◆ Which major league baseball team was the first to hire a black athlete? (Brooklyn Dodgers)
◆ Who was the first black major league baseball player? (Jackie Robinson)
◆ Who was the first black golfer admitted to the Professional Golf Association? (Charlie Sifford)
◆ What National Basketball Association star is nicknamed "Air"? (Michael Jordan)
◆ What National Football League star is nicknamed "Sweetness?" (Walter Payton)
◆ What athlete was nicknamed "The World's Fastest Human"? (Bob Hayes)
◆ What athlete dropped the name Cassius Clay? (Muhammad Ali)
◆ What black tennis star announced he contracted AIDS from a blood transfusion? (Arthur Ashe)
◆ Who was the first black heavyweight champion? (Jack Johnson)
◆ What black athlete did Adolf Hitler snub? (Jesse Owens)
◆ What black athlete is nicknamed "Mr. October"? (Reggie Jackson)
◆ What team did Magic Johnson twice retire from? (Los Angeles Lakers)

Politics and National Events

◆ What disease did the U.S. government study through injections to black human experimental subjects? (syphilis)

◆ Who was the first black U.S. senator? (Hiram Revels of Mississippi)

◆ In what year did black voters first cast their ballots in a presidential election? (1868)

◆ Who was the first black cabinet member? (Robert C. Weaver, Housing and Urban Development, under Franklin Roosevelt in 1941)

◆ Who was the first black justice of the Supreme Court? (Thurgood Marshall)

◆ What state did Senator Edward Brooke represent? (Massachusetts)

◆ What U.S. president retired to build low-interest houses for poor blacks? (Jimmy Carter)

◆ What controversial New York congressman published the *People's Voice?* (Adam Clayton Powell)

◆ What was the name of the black regiment formed to fight Indians? (Buffalo Soldiers)

◆ Who was the first black woman elected to Congress? (Shirley Chisholm)

◆ What does the acronym PUSH stand for? (People United to Save Humanity)

◆ Who organized PUSH? (Jesse Jackson)

◆ What do the letters NAACP stand for? (National Association for the Advancement of Colored People)

◆ What state did Congresswoman Barbara Jordan represent? (Texas)

◆ What do the letters SNCC stand for? (Student Nonviolent Coordinating Committee)

◆ Who founded SNCC? (Andrew Young)

◆ What United Nations post did Andrew Young hold? (U.S. Ambassador to the United Nations)

◆ What black Atlanta mayor has served two terms? (Maynard Jackson)

◆ In what state did black militants protest the jailing of the Wilmington Nine? (North Carolina)

Budget: $$

Sources:
Trivia Game about Black Americans, available through The Ali Group, P.O. Box 13093, Columbus, OH 43213; telephone: (614)866-7215.

Asante, Molefi K., *Historical and Cultural Atlas of African Americans,* Macmillan, 1991.

Estell, Kenneth, ed., *The African-American Almanac,* 6th ed., Gale, 1993.

Low, W. Augustus, and Virgil A. Clift, eds., *Encyclopedia of Black America,* McGraw Hill, 1981.

Alternative Applications:
Provide students a variety of resource materials about black history, such as *Africa Watch, Ebony, Jet, Emerge, Black Business, Current Biography, Statistical Abstract of Black America, Who's Who, The Times Atlas,* Infotrac, and Newsbank. Assign subject headings, such as art, dance, architecture, sculpture, medicine, religion, education, women's rights, U.S.-Africa relations, geography, the Caribbean, and international news, and have groups create their own set of trivia questions.

Black History Bingo

Originator: Michele Spence, teacher, editor, and writer, Lincoln, Nebraska.

Age/Grade Level or Audience: All ages.

Description: Organize a game of bingo to determine how well students understand a study of black history.

Procedure: Have students prepare a blank gameboard similar to a bingo card containing a central free space and marked with a random arrangement of any twenty-four numbers from one to seventy-five in the remaining blanks.

7	25	68	11	9
42	10	36	59	23
21	51	FREE	74	67
32	5	59	70	45
19	39	22	53	67

Prepare seventy-five questions, each on a separate slip of paper, then draw a slip and read aloud the number and question. Players locate the number on their cards and write the answer in the space. The first person to get a straight line of correct answers, either across, down, or diagonally, wins the game.

Budget: $

Sources:
Alexander, Lloyd, *The Fortune-Teller*, Dutton, 1992.
Cantor, George, *Historic Landmarks of Black America*, Gale, 1991.
Low, W. Augustus, and Virgil A. Clift, eds., *Encyclopedia of Black America*, McGraw Hill, 1981.

Simons, Robin, *Recyclopedia: Games, Science Equipment, and Crafts from Recycled Materials,* Houghton Mifflin, 1976.

Alternative Applications: Make this game more interesting by playing T, L, U, X, postage stamp, picture frame, and cover the card.

- ◆ T credits only the answers that fill the top horizontal row and the center vertical row.
- ◆ L credits answers down the left vertical row and across the bottom.
- ◆ U is the same as L plus the right vertical row.
- ◆ X requires players to complete the diagonal rows passing through the free space or the horizontal and vertical rows passing through the free space.
- ◆ Postage stamp requires winners to fill any block of four.
- ◆ Picture frame requires the player to fill the outer rim or the inner rim surrounding the free square.
- ◆ Covering the card requires that the player fill the board with correct answers.

Black History Calendar

Age/Grade Level or Audience: Middle school history classes; 4-H clubs; scout groups; youth clubs.

Description: Create a wall mural featuring an oversized calendar.

Procedure: Assign students a specific area to research, such as politics, world events, sports, entertainment, science and technology, medicine, dance, or architecture. Using biographical dictionaries, clip files, biographies, or other source material, have participants contribute significant entries to the calendar and fill blocks with important dates from black history, such as these:

- ◆ the Emancipation Proclamation
- ◆ Frederick Douglass's first abolitionist speech
- ◆ Jackie Robinson's entrance into major league baseball
- ◆ lunch counter sit-ins in Greensboro, North Carolina
- ◆ Thurgood Marshall's nomination to the Supreme Court
- ◆ the first patent obtained by a black inventor
- ◆ the first African-American to run for president of the United States
- ◆ the first African-American to earn an Academy Award
- ◆ the first African-American to serve as an astronaut

Budget: $$

Sources:
February issues of school and library journals, particularly *Instructor* and *Learning,* as well as *Jet* and *Ebony.*

Estell, Kenneth, ed., *The African-American Almanac,* 6th ed., Gale, 1993.

Hornsby, Alton, Jr., *Chronology of African-American History: Significant Events and People from 1619 to the Present,* Gale, 1991.

Terry, Ted, *American Black History: Reference Manual,* Myles Publishing, 1991.

Alternative Applications: Begin this project for Black History Month, then continue it as an ongoing compendium of facts. Carry over the group's work to the following February so that the next celebration of Black History Month adds details to the original calendar. Place months on individual sheets and bind into resource booklets or preserve on a database. Place copies, illustrated with original drawings, in libraries, display cases, public meetings halls, museums, malls, and civic centers.

Black History in Miniature

Originator: Lela Coley and Gail Freeman, middle school teachers, Deerfield Beach, Florida.

Age/Grade Level or Audience: All ages.

Description: Create a miniature black history museum.

Procedure: Organize volunteers to collect and display crafts and objects related to black history. Consider these items:

- ◆ tobacco can, corncob pipe, drawstring bag of loose tobacco, rolling papers
- ◆ washboard and tub, bluing, cast-iron wash pot, and bars of lye soap
- ◆ quilts, quilting frame, and quilt rack
- ◆ curling iron and straightening comb
- ◆ kerosene lamp and lighter stick
- ◆ bonnets, high-button shoes, gaiters, spats, suspenders, bowler hats
- ◆ spider, churn, coffee mill, grater, potato masher, eggbeater, waffle iron, and other kitchen utensils
- ◆ early crystal set or radio
- ◆ Victrola and cylinders, jukebox, or 78 recordings of black artists
- ◆ lace tablecloth and napkins
- ◆ old baby bottles
- ◆ paper fans with Bible pictures and inscriptions

Provide posters or audiotaped guides to explain how each display relates to black history.

Budget: $$$

Sources:

Encourage participants to check attics, used clothing stores, yard sales, and Salvation Army and Goodwill stores.

Asante, Molefi K., *Historical and Cultural Atlas of African Americans,* Macmillan, 1991.

Low, W. Augustus, and Virgil A. Clift, eds., *Encyclopedia of Black America*, McGraw Hill, 1981.

Alternative Applications: For a minimuseum in a hurry, have students create cardboard copies of items or draw three-dimensional settings of kitchens, porches, sitting rooms, classrooms, church choir lofts, factories, sawmills, blacksmith forges, tanneries, woodworking shops, sugar mills, barns, granaries, and other locations connected with black history.

Black History Time Capsule

Age/Grade Level or Audience: All ages.

Description: Create a display of items to enter a black history time capsule.

Procedure: Collect items that epitomize the emancipation of the black race. Include a chain, drawing of a slave ship, Abraham Lincoln's Emancipation Proclamation, amendments to the Constitution giving black citizens the right to vote, the "Negro National Anthem," Alex Haley's *Roots* or Margaret Walker's *Jubilee,* covers of popular magazines featuring entertainers such as Cicely Tyson, Lou Gossett, Jr., Sammy Davis, Jr., Natalie Cole, Morgan Freeman, and Bill Cosby, judgments of Thurgood Marshall, compact discs of Scott Joplin's music, photos of Mae Jamison's space flight, and other appropriate memorabilia.

Budget: $$$

Sources:

Drawings, photos, and clippings from the popular press.

Ravitch, Diane, *The American Reader: Words That Moved a Nation,* HarperCollins, 1990.

Alternative Applications: Hold an assembly in which you explain why each item to be placed in the time capsule deserves recognition by future generations. Open the last portion of the meeting for suggestions from the audience.

A Black History Time Line

Age/Grade Level or Audience: Middle school, high school, and college social studies class.

Description: Prepare a detailed time line of African-American history.

Procedure: Organize students into groups to cover African-American history from the beginning of European colonization of the United States to current times. Present findings through mixed media, including handmade filmstrips, transparencies, databases, friezes or scrolls, photographs, and taped speeches and songs. Begin with the following framework and enhance it with vivid details, such as locations, cause and effect, and interesting circumstances:

Thirteenth Century

- ◆ Skeletal evidence from a cemetery in the Virgin Islands suggests that Africans were present in the New World by 1250.

Fourteenth Century

- ◆ A Malinese oral history describes the Atlantic voyage of a Mandingo king in 1312.

Fifteenth Century

- ◆ In 1492, a black Spaniard, Pedro Alonzo Niño, accompanied Columbus on his voyage to the New World.
- ◆ Columbus's son Ferdinand reported seeing blacks in Honduras.

Sixteenth Century

- ◆ In 1501, black explorers and seamen arrived in the New World.
- ◆ In 1502, Portugal transported black slaves to the New World.
- ◆ On September 25, 1513, a black, Nufo de Olano, accompanied Balboa's expedition to the Pacific Ocean.
- ◆ In 1526, black slaves fled a South Carolina settlement and took up residence with Indians.
- ◆ In 1538, Estebanico, a black explorer, entered Arizona and New Mexico.
- ◆ In 1562, British slaver John Hawkins sold blacks to Spanish planters.

Seventeenth Century

- ◆ In 1619, the first slaves—Antony, Pedro, and Isabella—were brought to Jamestown, Virginia, aboard a Dutch vessel.
- ◆ In 1624, William Tucker was the first black child born in the United States.
- ◆ In 1630, Massachusetts enacted laws to protect slaves from cruel masters.
- ◆ In 1639, slaver William Pierce exchanged Indian slaves for African in the West Indies.
- ◆ By 1640, the slave population of Barbados reached 6,000.
- ◆ In 1651, black planter Anthony Johnson attempted to establish a black village in North Hampton, Virginia.
- ◆ In 1672, a bounty was set on maroons, fugitive slaves who were declared outlaws.
- ◆ On February 18, 1688, Quakers led the first abolitionist protest.
- ◆ In 1693, Quaker George Keith published the first abolitionist pamphlet.

Eighteenth Century

◆ By 1700, the colonial slave population was 5,000 in New England and 23,000 in the southern colonies.

◆ In 1712, a slave rebellion in New York City resulted in public execution of blacks by hanging or burning alive.

◆ In 1763, Gershom Prince and other blacks defended colonists during the French and Indian War.

◆ In 1770, Philadelphia Quakers opened a school for blacks.

◆ On March 5, 1770, Crispus Attucks was killed in the Boston Massacre.

◆ In 1774, Lemuel Haynes served with minutemen at the Battle of Lexington.

◆ In 1775, Peter Salem and Salem Poor fought with a company of black soldiers at the Battle of Bunker Hill.

◆ On February 2, 1776, George Washington answered a letter from black poet Phillis Wheatley.

◆ In 1777, Prince Hall petitioned the Massachusetts legislature to end slavery.

◆ In 1779, Pompey Lamb served the army as a spy.

◆ In 1780, in Torrington, Connecticut, Lemuel Haynes became the first black minister of a white congregation.

◆ In 1791, Benjamin Banneker published an almanac.

◆ In 1793, Eli Whitney made slavery more profitable by inventing the cotton gin. Also, Richard Allen established the Mother Bethel African Methodist Episcopal Church in Philadelphia, and Canada passed an antislavery law.

◆ In 1794, Andrew Bryan builds the first black Baptist church.

◆ In 1796, Toussaint L'Ouverture commanded the French at Santo Domingo.

◆ In 1797, a slave named Doctor practiced medicine in Charleston, South Carolina.

Nineteenth Century

◆ In 1800, Philadelphia's free blacks influenced Congress to end slavery.

◆ On August 30, 1800, Gabriel Prosser led an assault on the arsenal in Richmond, Virginia.

◆ In 1803, American colonies double in size after the Louisiana Purchase.

◆ In 1807, laws end the slave trade in the United States and Great Britain.

◆ In 1811, Paul Cuffe and his thirty-eight black passengers sailed the *Traveller* from Massachusetts to Sierra Leone.

◆ In 1815, Napoleon banned the slave trade in France and French possessions.

◆ In 1819, the slave trade thrived through an underground market system.

◆ By 1820, Congress enacted the Missouri Compromise to balance free and slave states.

◆ By 1820, abolitionists aired their protests in letters, speeches, and pamphlets.

◆ In 1821, the African Methodist Episcopal Zion Church was established.

◆ In July 1822, Denmark Vesey, a free black carpenter, was executed for launching a slave revolt in Charleston, South Carolina.

◆ In 1826, Edward Jones and John Russwurm became the first black college graduates.

◆ In 1827, the first black newspaper, *Freedom's Journal,* went to press.

◆ In 1831, New Englanders formed an Anti-Slavery Society and William Lloyd Garrison founded *The Liberator,* an abolitionist newspaper, in Boston.

◆ On August 21, 1831, Nat Turner led a slave revolt that terrorized Virginia.

◆ By 1840, thousands of slaves escaped servitude and fled to Canada.

◆ In 1841, slaves who were forced aboard the *Amistad* gained their freedom by Supreme Court decree.

◆ In 1843, Henry Highland Garnett led a slave revolt.

◆ In 1844, the Dominican Republic was established.

◆ In 1847, Frederick Douglass launched the *North Star,* an abolitionist newspaper. Also, Green Flake was one of the first Mormons to settle Salt Lake City.

◆ In 1850, pressure from the Fugitive Slave Act led William Still to organize the Underground Railroad.

◆ In 1851, delegates of the Women's Rights Convention welcomed Sojourner Truth as guest speaker.

◆ In 1852, Harriet Beecher Stowe's *Uncle Tom's Cabin* promoted antislavery sentiments.

◆ In 1854, Lincoln University, the first black college, opened its doors to students in Chester County, Pennsylvania.

◆ In 1857, the Supreme Court declared Dred Scott the property of his owner.

◆ On December 2, 1859, John Brown, a white abolitionist, was martyred after leading an abortive slave revolt at Harper's Ferry, Virginia.

◆ In 1861, Mary Peake began teaching former slaves under Emancipation Oak in Hampton, Virginia.

◆ On April 12, 1861, civil war broke out at Fort Sumter, South Carolina.

◆ On January 1, 1863, Lincoln ended slavery by issuing the Emancipation Proclamation.

◆ On February 1, 1865, John S. Rock, a Massachusetts lawyer and physician, became the first black to plead a case before the Supreme Court.

◆ In 1870, the Fifteenth Amendment to the Constitution guaranteed the right to vote to males of all races.

◆ On February 25, 1870, Hiram Revels became the first black elected to the U.S. Senate.

◆ In 1873, Henry O. Flipper became the first black to graduate from West Point.

◆ On March 23, 1873, slavery was abolished in Puerto Rico.

◆ In 1878, Caroline Virginia Anderson became the first black woman to earn a medical degree.

◆ In 1879, Mary Eliza Mahoney became the first black graduate nurse in the United States.

◆ In 1881, Booker T. Washington founded Tuskegee Institute.

◆ In 1883, Frederick Douglass made heavy demands on white society in a speech delivered in Washington, D.C.

◆ In 1886, Lucy Craft Laney opened Haines Normal Institute in Macon, Georgia.

◆ In 1888, the Capitol Savings Bank, the first U.S. bank operated by blacks, opened in Washington, D.C.

◆ In 1893, Daniel Hale Williams performed the first open heart surgery.

◆ In 1896, the National Association of Colored Women was founded.

◆ In 1898, North Carolina Mutual Life, the first black insurance company, was founded.

Twentieth Century

◆ In 1903, Maggie Lena Walker became the first woman to establish a financial institution, the Saint Luke Penny Savings Bank.

◆ On April 6, 1909, Matthew Henson reached the North Pole.

◆ In 1910, the National Association for the Advancement of Colored People (NAACP) was begun to organize black political efforts.

◆ In 1917, the first black officers training camp was established at Fort Des Moines.

◆ On January 17, 1917, the United States purchased the Virgin Islands.

◆ The Harlem Renaissance reached its height from 1922 to 1929.

◆ In 1926, Carter G. Woodson inaugurated Negro History Week.

◆ In 1938, Pennsylvania's Crystal Bird Fauset was the first black woman elected to the a U.S. state legislature.

◆ In 1939, Eleanor Roosevelt withdrew from the Daughters of the American Revolution because it refused Marian Anderson's bid to sing in Washington, D.C.

◆ In 1940, Booker T. Washington became the first black pictured on a U.S. postage stamp and Hattie McDaniel the first black to win an Academy award.

◆ On December 7, 1941, in Pearl Harbor, Hawaii, messman Dorie Miller took over an anti-aircraft gun to ward off strikes on the *Arizona* by Japanese planes.

◆ In 1942, three black regiments helped construct the 1,400-mile Alcan Highway to protect Alaska from Japanese attack.

◆ In 1943, the first platoon of black paratroopers formed at Fort Benning, Georgia.

◆ In 1944, the United Negro College Fund was established.

◆ On April 11, 1947, Jackie Robinson became the first black professional baseball player.

◆ In 1948, Harry Truman integrated the armed services.

◆ In 1950, Gwendolyn Brooks won a Pulitzer Prize.

◆ In 1950, Ralph Bunche, U.N. peacekeeper and mediator, won a Nobel Peace Prize.

◆ On May 17, 1954, segregated schools were outlawed.

◆ On December 2, 1955, Rosa Parks refused to give up her seat on a bus in Montgomery, Alabama, and Martin Luther King, Jr., an Atlanta minister, organized the Montgomery bus boycott.

◆ In 1957, Congress passed the Civil Rights Act.

◆ On February 15, 1957, the Southern Christian Leadership Conference was organized.

◆ In 1959, Lorraine Hansberry's *A Raisin in the Sun* opened on Broadway.

◆ On February 2, 1960, students from North Carolina A & T led sit-ins at a Woolworth's lunch counter in Greensboro, North Carolina, to draw attention to segregation of public facilities.

◆ On August 28, 1963, Martin Luther King, Jr., led a march on Washington, D.C., and delivered his "I Have a Dream" speech.

◆ In 1964, the Nobel committee conferred its peace prize on King. Also, Bill Cosby became the first black actor to star in a dramatic television series, *I Spy.*

◆ In 1965, Elizabeth Duncan Koontz became the first black to head the National Education Association.

◆ On February 21, 1965, Muslim leader Malcolm X was assassinated.

◆ In 1967, Thurgood Marshall became the first black Supreme Court justice.

◆ On April 4, 1968, Martin Luther King, Jr., was assassinated.

◆ On October 18, 1968, Olympic track stars John Carlos and Tommy Smith were suspended for giving the black power salute at an awards ceremony in Mexico City.

◆ In 1972, Barbara Jordan of Texas became the first black woman to preside over a state legislature.

◆ In 1974, Hank Aaron set a homerun record.

◆ In 1983, Lt. Col. Guion S. Bluford, Jr., became the first black U.S. astronaut.

◆ In 1986, January 15 was officially established as a legal holiday honoring Martin Luther King, Jr.

◆ In October 1991, construction workers unearthed an eighteenth-century black burial site in lower Manhattan containing 20,000 skeletons.

◆ In September 1992, astronaut Mae Jemison gave up her Los Angeles medical practice to become the first black woman in space.

◆ In January 1993, poet Maya Angelou was asked to speak at the Inauguration ceremony for 42nd President William Jefferson Clinton.

Budget: $$

Sources:

Refer to "Black Studies: A Select Catalog of National Archives Microfilm Publications" from the National Archives, P.O. Box 100793, Atlanta, GA 30384.

Brailsford, Karen, "Sacred Ground: Dry Bones Speak," *Emerge,* October 1992, p. 73.

Cairnes, John Elliott, *Slave Power: Its Character, Career, and Probable Designs,* Negro University Press, 1969.

Dennis, Denise, *Black History for Beginners,* Highsmith, 1992.

Grun, Bernard, *The Timetables of History: A Horizontal Linkage of People and Events,* Simon & Schuster, 1991.

Hampton, Henry, and Steve Fayer, *Voices of Freedom: An Oral History of the Civil Rights Movement from the 1950s through the 1980s,* Bantam Books, 1990.

Hornsby, Alton, Jr., *Chronology of African-American History: Significant Events and People from 1619 to the Present,* Gale, 1991.

Linton, Calvin Darling, *The Bicentennial Almanac: 200 Years of America, 1776-1976,* T. Nelson, 1975.

Miller, Elizabeth W., and Mary L. Fisher, *The Negro in America,* Harvard University Press, 1970.

Trager, James, *The People's Chronology,* Henry Holt, 1992.

Alternative Applications: Divide students into small groups to complete a similar time line of African and/or Caribbean history. Record information on a database. Throughout the school year, add data and retrieve information as students have need for it.

 | **Black Holidays** |

Age/Grade Level or Audience: All ages.

Description: Present an overview of major black holidays.

Procedure: Make a bulletin board, brochure, display, or database of holiday information. Beside each holiday, give the date, purpose, and customs. Include these occasions:

- ◆ **Martin Luther King's Birthday** (third Monday in January). This holiday honors Nobel Peace Prize winner Martin Luther King, Jr., minister and freedom fighter who organized nonviolent boycotts and marches, the most memorable being the Montgomery bus strike and the Selma freedom riders. The occasion is a federal holiday celebrated with speeches, community gatherings, and serious consideration of the advancement of civil rights.
- ◆ **Black History Month** (February). This celebration, begun in 1926 by Carter G. Woodson, the father of black history, seeks to promote truth about the Negro's place in history. Observances feature plays, special business and recreational programs, civic assemblies, church meetings, and coverage in the media. The month can be divided into segments: the first week honoring African heritage; the second week honoring people who died in slavery, lynchings, and riots; the third week honoring distinguished individuals; and the last week commemorating rites of passage as young people pledge to accept cultural, family, and religious values.
- ◆ **Malcolm X Day** (May 19). Since his assassination on February 21, 1965, Malcolm X has been honored for furthering the Black Muslim movement and for symbolizing hope to the lowest levels of society. Celebrants offer assistance to the homeless, imprisoned, and the poor, elderly, and unemployed.
- ◆ **African Liberation Day** (May 25). Selected by the Organization of African Unity in 1963, the day commemorates the liberation of African nations from colonial rule. Festivities feature parades, processions, conferences, and rallies to honor freedom fighters and to remind black people that South Africans are still struggling for their rights. Symbolized by the red, black, and green flag designed by Marcus Garvey, the holiday supports unity among black people everywhere.
- ◆ **Juneteenth** (June 19). African-American Emancipation Day, June 19, 1865, brought the message to Texas blacks that slavery had ended as of January 1.

The occasion, first celebrated officially in 1972, honors the Thirteenth Amendment to the Constitution and recalls the exuberance of the slaves as they danced, sang, and feasted in celebration of their new freedom. Starting with food and story telling on the evening before, Juneteenth celebrations often feature parades, music, speeches, games, fairs, feasts, exhibits, and the drinking of strawberry soda, a traditional holiday drink.

◆ **Marcus Garvey's Birthday** (August 17). A reminder to followers of black history of the "Back to Africa" movement. The holiday is celebrated with newsletters and articles written about Pan-Africanism, a political, social, and economic movement that unites black people worldwide.

◆ **Umoja Karamu** (fourth Sunday in November). The unity feast, first celebrated in 1971, acknowledges the importance of the black family. Groups gather for feasts of black-eyed peas, rice, tomatoes, greens, and sweet potatoes or corn. Decorations are done in the five food colors: black, white, red, green, and yellow. Candles and incense are burned, creating a spiritual atmosphere that is enhanced by prayer and readings.

◆ **Kwanzaa** (December 26-January 1). Begun by Maulana Karenga in 1966, this harvest celebration reminds black people of their strengths through unity, sharing, responsibility, faith, talents, determination, and generosity.

Budget: $$

Sources:

Anyike, James C., *African American Holidays: A Historical Research and Resource Guide to Cultural Celebrations,* Popular Truth, Inc., 1991.

Cohen, Hennig, and Tristram Potter Coffin, *Folklore of American Holidays,* 2nd ed., Gale, 1991.

Hatch, Jane M., *The American Book of Days,* 3rd ed., H. W. Wilson, 1978.

Kunjufu, Jawanza, *Lessons from History: A Celebration of Blackness,* African American Images, 1987.

MacDonald, Margaret Read, *Folklore of World Holidays,* Gale, 1992.

Porter, A. P., *Kwanzaa,* Carolrhoda Books, 1991.

Alternative Applications: Insert these holidays into a study of the full spectrum of America's religious, patriotic, and secular festivals, including Easter, Hanukkah, Christmas, Rosh Hashanah, Halloween, Flag Day, Arbor Day, St. Patrick's Day, Yom Kippur, Ramadan, and New Year's Day. Arrange a group of symbols or drawings of celebrations, such as a shamrock, Star of David, pumpkin, menorah, Koran, bells, ram's horn, American flag, Kwanzaa table runner, and a map of the world denoting the largest populations of black people.

Black Indians

Originator: Roberta Brown, teacher, Fort Bragg, North Carolina.

Age/Grade Level or Audience: Elementary, middle school, high school, and college social studies classes; civic presentations; multicultural festivals.

Description: Make a group presentation concerning runaway slaves and the Indian tribes that gave them a home.

Procedure: Collect data about persons of mixed native American and African-American blood, for instance:

◆ rodeo star Bill Pickett, a black Cherokee
◆ pioneering black Kiowa, Diana Fletcher, and Biddy Johnson Arnold, a black Apache
◆ singer Roland Hayes
◆ black Sioux Isaiah Dorman, army scout at the Battle of Little Big Horn
◆ black Seminole Chief John Horse, who defeated American troops at the Battle of Cheechebee in 1837 and helped negotiate the tribe's removal to Fort Dixon and Fort Duncan
◆ fifty black Seminole army scouts, including John Ward, Isaac Payne, and Pompey Factor
◆ Crispus Attucks, a black Natick, who, on March 5, 1770, became the first person to die during the Boston Massacre, a prelude to the American Revolution
◆ black Chippewa sculptor Edmonia Lewis, who is best known for *Forever Free*

Budget: $

Sources:
Banbury, Horace A., "Music Pouring out of His Body," *Class,* July/August 1992, p. 59.
Katz, William Loren, *The Black West,* 3rd ed., Open Hand Publishers, 1987.
Low, W. Augustus, and Virgil A. Clift, eds., *Encyclopedia of Black America,* McGraw Hill, 1981.

Alternative Applications: Comment on the fate of black Indians, particularly those who married and bore children of mixed ancestry, after the government forced tribes west to Oklahoma reservations. Consult census figures to learn the size of the mixed African-Native American population.

Black Military Parade

Originator: Leatrice Pearson, teacher, Lenoir, North Carolina; Roberta Brown, teacher, Fort Bragg, North Carolina; R. M. Browning, Jr., U.S. Coast Guard Headquarters, History and Museums Division, U.S. Marine Corps.

Age/Grade Level or Audience: Elementary, middle school, and high school history classes.

Description: Select an honor roll of black military leaders.

Procedure: Have students comb sources for names of black military leaders who have distinguished themselves both in peacetime and in war. Post the names on a bulletin board or prepare a scroll of names along with the branch of service each represents. For example:

◆ Air Force

Otis B. Young	Guion S. Bluford	Daniel James, Jr.
Edward J. Dwight	George S. Robert	Joseph D. Alsberry
Benjamin O. Davis, Jr.		

◆ Army

Colin Powell	Milton L. Olive III	Nancy Leftenant
Robert Smalls	Michael Howard	Henry Johnson
Needham Roberts	William H. Carney	Harriet M. West
Clinton Greaves	Roscoe Robinson	Charles Rogers
William O. Flipper	Margaret E. Bailey	Louise Martin
Clifford Alexander	John Alexander	Hazel W. Johnson
Benjamin O. Davis, Sr.		

◆ Buffalo Soldiers

George W. Williams	Emanuel Stance	Fitz Lee
George Jordan	Thomas Jones	Jones Morgan
Nurse Luticia P. Butler	William Cathy, a woman disguised as a man	

◆ Cavalry

Charles Young	Horace Bivens	George Berry
Henry O. Flipper		

◆ Coast Guard

Daphie Reese	Linda Rodriquez	Bobby C. Wilks
Alex Haley	Pamela Autry	Thomasina Sconiers
Michael Healy	Joseph Jenkins	

◆ Marines

John Martin	Frank E. Petersen	John Earl Rudder
Isaac Walker	Alfred Masters	George O. Thompson
Kenneth J. Tibbs	Frederick C. Branch	Herbert L. Brewer
Annie E. Graham	Ann E. Lamb	Gloria Smith
Kenneth H. Berthoud	Agrippa W. Smith	Edgar R. Huff
Rodney M. Davis	Ralph H. Johnson	

◆ Merchant Marine

Hugh Mulzac	John Godfrey	Adrian Richardson
Clifton Fostic		

◆ National Guard

Thomas J. Hargis

◆ **Navy**

Samuel L. Gravely	Janie Mines	Wesley Brown
Joachim Pease	Bernard Robinson	Leonard Ray Harmon
John Lee	Jesse Brown	Gerald Thomas
Brenda Robinson	Hazel P. McCree	John S. Lawson

Budget: $

Sources:
Davis, Burke, *Black Heroes of the American Revolution,* Harcourt Brace Jovanovich, 1991.

Dennis, Denise, *Black History for Beginners,* Highsmith, 1992.

"General Colin Powell Dedicates a Monument to the Buffalo Soldier—Unsung Black Heroes," *Jet,* September 7, 1992, pp. 34-38.

Low, Augustus, and Virgil A. Clift, eds., *Encyclopedia of Black America,* McGraw Hill, 1981.

Terry, Ted, *American Black History: A Reference Manual,* Myles Publishing, 1991.

Alternative Applications: Have students create a special medal honoring African-American military members. Consider African-American participants in all American conflicts: Revolutionary, Indian, Mexican-American, Civil, Korean, Vietnam, and Persian Gulf wars, World War I, World War II, and invasions of Beirut, Granada, and Panama. If participants have members of the community they wish to add to the list, note branch of service and distinguished conduct.

The Civil War

Age/Grade Level or Audience: All ages.

Description: Present a community study of the Civil War.

Procedure: Open a two-week session with the eleven-hour videotaped series *The Civil War* by Ken Burns. Intersperse small group discussion periods to determine whether African-Americans receive proper credit for their role in shaping America's history.

Budget: $$

Sources:
The nine-part Public Broadcasting Service series *The Civil War* (1990).

Commager, Henry, *Fifty Basic Civil War Documents,* Van Nostrand Reinhold, 1965, reprinted, R.E. Krieger, 1982.

Meltzer, Milton, *Voices from the Civil War: A Documentary History of the Great*

American Conflict, Crowell, 1989.

Murphy, Jim, *The Boy's War: Confederate and Union Soldiers Talk about the Civil War,* Clarion Books, 1990.

Ward, Geoffrey C., Ric Burns, and Ken Burns, *The Civil War: An Illustrated History,* Knopf, 1990.

Alternative Applications: Invite a panel of local social studies teachers, journalists, historians, and civil rights activists to comment on Ken Burns's famous documentary. As a theme song for your session, have a pianist play "The Ashokan Farewell," which was written for the series. Include other musical works from the 1860s, particularly Negro spirituals and period pieces such as "Eating Goober Peas," "Tenting on the Old Campground," "Aura Lee," and "The Bonnie Blue Flag."

Colonialism

Age/Grade Level or Audience: High school and college history, economics, and African-American studies classes.

Description: Conduct an in-depth assessment of the rise of colonialism in Africa and its effect on culture, religion, and world trade.

Procedure: Have students collaborate on a study of colonialism and its impact on Africa. For example, have them study these topics:

- ◆ changes in South African government under foreign governments
- ◆ loss of human rights as a direct outgrowth of the diamond trade
- ◆ decimation of the elephant population by ivory hunters
- ◆ slaughter of animals for hides, teeth, and skulls
- ◆ native deaths from hunger, mistreatment, and exposure to European diseases
- ◆ the spread of colonialism in the Caribbean

Conclude with a comparison to European decimation of Native American populations in the New World.

Budget: $

Sources:

Echewa, T. Obinkaram, *I Saw the Sky Catch Fire,* Plume, 1993.

Kunjufu, Jawanza, *Lessons from History: A Celebration of Blackness,* African American Images, 1987.

Low, W. Augustus, and Virgil A. Clift, eds., *Encyclopedia of Black America,* McGraw Hill, 1981.

Mostert, Noël, *Frontiers: The Epic of South Africa's Creation and the Tragedy of the*

Xhosa People, Knopf, 1992.

Oliver, Roland, *The African Experience*, IconEditions, 1992.

Alternative Applications: Organize a debate between classes or schools. Possible topics of the debate include:

◆ Greed as a motivating force in racism

◆ The trading company's role in introducing African nations to industrial development

◆ The influence of the missionary in keeping African nations subservient to European colonial overlords

◆ The gold-salt trade across the Sahara

◆ The role of Quakers and Mennonites in changing opinions about slavery

The Constitution and Black America

Originator: Michael Sweeney, teacher, Auburn, Washington.

Age/Grade Level or Audience: Middle school and high school history and civics classes.

Description: Organize a study unit on the amendments to the U.S. Constitution that have been most beneficial to black Americans.

Procedure: Name the amendments that have promoted individual freedoms, such as the right to be free, to own property, and to vote. Explain the circumstances that caused these amendments to be added to the Constitution:

◆ **Thirteenth Amendment** (1865) freed the slaves

◆ **Fourteenth Amendment** (1868) passed three years after the Civil War to protect newly freed slaves; extended citizenship and due process to former slaves; denied the rights of former Confederate sympathizers to run for congressional office; forbade states from differentiating among classes of people

◆ **Fifteenth Amendment** (1870) allowed male citizens the vote

◆ **Nineteenth Amendment** (1920) gave women the right to vote

◆ **Twenty-fourth Amendment** (1964) ended poll taxes

Budget: $

Sources:

Hornsby, Alton, Jr., *Chronology of African-American History: Significant Events and People from 1619 to the Present*, Gale, 1991.

Linton, Calvin Darling, *The Bicentennial Almanac: 200 Years of America, 1776-1976*, T. Nelson, 1975.

Alternative Applications: Have individual groups capture the spirit of a particular amendment in a collage or poster. Collect a series to honor these amendments and hang them in a prominent place, such as a foyer, hallway, mall, or billboard.

Courts and Racial Justice

Contributor: Michael McSweeney, teacher, Auburn, Washington.

Age/Grade Level or Audience: All ages.

Description: Create a bulletin board display or handout featuring significant court and legislative decisions.

Procedure: Post background data about the most important court cases and legislative decisions that affect black people. Include the following:

- ◆ *Plessy v. Ferguson* (1896), requiring equal schools for blacks
- ◆ *Smith v. Alwright* (1944), rejecting the exclusion of blacks from the Democratic party primary elections
- ◆ *Brown v. Board of Education* (1954), halting racial segregation in public schools
- ◆ *Hawkins v. Board of Control* (1956), forcing Florida to admit a qualified Negro to a state university graduate program
- ◆ *Edwards v. South Carolina* (1963), rejecting the state's interference with rights of assembly and freedom of speech by arresting demonstrators for disturbing the peace
- ◆ *Gideon v. Wainwright* (1963), providing free legal counsel to indigent defendants in criminal cases
- ◆ *Westberry v. Sanders* (1964), halting gerrymandering, the denial of representation by capricious variances in congressional districting
- ◆ **Civil Rights Act** (1964), declaring an end to discrimination in employment, school integration, voting, and federally funded projects
- ◆ **Voting Rights Act** (1965), ending literacy tests as a means of keeping blacks from registering to vote, allowing the president to send supervisors to register voters, and halting the requirement of poll taxes
- ◆ **Title VII** (1965), ending discrimination in private business
- ◆ *Miranda v. State of Arizona* (1966), requiring police to advise suspects of constitutional rights
- ◆ *Harper v. Virginia Board of Elections* (1966), halting poll taxes in state elections
- ◆ *Loving v. Virginia* (1967), overruling antimiscegenation laws
- ◆ *Swann v. Charlotte-Mecklenburg Board of Education* (1971), upholding busing as a method of ending segregation

Budget: $

Sources:

Films *Awakenings, 1954-1956; Fighting Back, 1957-1962; Ain't Scared of Your Jail, 1960-1961; No Easy Walk, 1961-1963; Mississippi—Is This America?, 1962-1964; Bridge to Freedom, 1965.*

Estell, Kenneth, ed., *The African-American Almanac,* 6th ed., Gale, 1993.

Linton, Calvin Darling, *The Bicentennial Almanac: 200 Years of America, 1776-1976,* T. Nelson, 1975.

Marable, Manning, *Black American Politics: From the Washington Marches to Jesse Jackson,* Schocken Books, 1985.

Wilson, Charles Reagan, and William Ferris, eds., *Encyclopedia of Southern Culture,* University of North Carolina Press, 1989.

Alternative Applications: Utilize a bulletin board during a voter drive. Post voter rights, residency and poll maps, dates, and mock ballots at a public library or other registration site. Hand out printed copies of a time line detailing the rise in black rights. Encourage participation through local media announcements, yard signs, church bulletins, door-to-door campaigns, and billboards.

Each One Teach One

Age/Grade Level or Audience: Adult teachers, librarians, museum curators; community and religious leaders.

Description: Organize a tutorial to educate leaders in black history.

Procedure: Create a consortium of black history experts to present a workshop for teachers, civic leaders, ministers, social workers, writers, editors, and other people who need to know more about the subject in order to perform their jobs adequately.

Budget: $$$

Sources:

"Black Studies: A Select Catalog of National Archives Microfilm Publications," National Archives, P.O. Box 100793, Atlanta, GA 30384.

Brailsford, Karen, "Sacred Ground: Dry Bones Speak," *Emerge,* October 1992, p. 73.

Estell, Kenneth, ed., *The African-American Almanac,* 6th ed., Gale, 1993.

Hornsby, Alton, Jr., *Chronology of African-American History: Significant Events and People from 1619 to the Present,* Gale, 1991.

Kunjufu, Jawanza, *Lessons from History: A Celebration of Blackness,* African American Images, 1987.

Alternative Applications: Have a consortium produce a pamphlet or syllabus to assist immigrants and other newcomers to the area in appreciating local, state, and national black history. Videotape consortium members' speeches or lessons and place them in local libraries and databases for students, teachers, and others to use as an impetus to future black history celebrations.

The Emancipation Proclamation

Age/Grade Level or Audience: Elementary, middle school, and high school history and language students.

Description: Study the background of the Emancipation Proclamation.

Procedure: Provide an array of works on early nineteenth-century America, the presidency of Abraham Lincoln, Fugitive Slave laws, the abolitionist movement, the Missouri Compromise, and the beginnings of the Civil War. Encourage students to form their own opinions as to why Lincoln chose to free the slaves. Compose a handout sheet of the following facts:

- At first, Lincoln did not sympathize with slaves, but pressure from abolitionists and Republicans eventually changed his position on white supremacy.
- Congress began weakening slavery by freeing slaves from the Confederate military, those in the District of Columbia and federal territories, and those belonging to traitors.
- By July 1862, Lincoln revealed to his cabinet his plans to emancipate slaves.
- He announced his plans to end slavery on September 22, 1862.
- Following the Union army's success at Antietam, the proclamation was issued January 1, 1863.
- Its central message was simple:
    And by virtue of the power and for the purpose aforesaid, I do order and declare that all persons held as slaves within said designated States and parts of states are, and hence-forward shall be, free; and that the executive government of the United States, including the military and naval authorities thereof, will recognize and maintain the freedom of said persons.
- Only slaves living in Confederate states (Alabama, Arkansas, Florida, Georgia, Mississippi, North Carolina, South Carolina, Texas, and parts of Louisiana and Virginia) were freed.
- The 800,000 slaves in border states or areas captured by Union troops were not covered.
- To offset further violence, the proclamation urged newly freed slaves to "abstain from all violence, unless in necessary self-defense."
- The proclamation opened the U.S. army and navy to 180,000 black volunteers, who helped turn the tide of the war.

◆ Southern rebels ignored Lincoln's proclamation.

◆ As Union forces liberated territories, more slaves gained their freedom, adding to the growing problem of refugees fleeing the war zone.

◆ The complete abolition of slavery did not occur until December 18, 1865, when Congress passed the Thirteenth Amendment to the Constitution.

Budget: $

Sources:

"The Emancipation Proclamation," National Archives and Records Administration, Washington, DC 20408.

Commager, Henry, *Fifty Basic Civil War Documents,* Van Nostrand Reinhold, 1965, reprinted, R.E. Krieger, 1982.

Evitts, William J., *Captive Bodies, Free Spirits: The Story of Southern Slavery,* Messner, 1985.

Rhodes, Elisha Hunt, *All for the Union: The Civil War Diary and Letters of Elisha Hunt Rhodes,* Vintage Books, 1992.

Alternative Applications: Read aloud from the Emancipation Proclamation or listen to a recorded version. Select a few phrases to explain, especially these:

the executive	aforesaid	thereof
thereto	wherein	countervailing testimony
deemed	by virtue of	suppressing
in accordance with	henceforward	hereby
enjoin	abstain	garrison forts
warranted	thenceforward	

Have students restate the basic idea in their own words. Select a few students to draw up a similar document and post it on the bulletin board. Organize a discussion group to explain why the creation of a Freedman's Bureau was necessary.

Explorers of Africa

Age/Grade Level or Audience: Middle school, high school, and college social studies classes; civic presentations; multicultural festivals; museum displays.

Description: Create an illustrated time line of noted Europeans who explored the "dark continent."

Procedure: Collect names and nationalities of Europeans who explored Africa, noting where they went, how long they stayed, and what they accomplished. Some major figures include the following:

- *Portugal:* Henry the Navigator (1441-60), Pedro de Cintra (1462), Diego Cam (1482-84), Bartholomew Dias (1487-88), Vasco da Gama (1497-98), Finao Gomes (1469-71), Fernao do Po
- *England and Scotland:* Mungo Park (1795-97, 1805-06), Hugh Clapperton (1822-27), Richard L. Lander (1825-27, 1830), Alexander Gordon Laing (1825-26), Richard Pococke (1737-40), James Bruce (1769-72), Richard Francis Burton (1857-59), John Henning Speke (1857-63), David Livingstone (1852-73), John Kirk (1841-55), James A. Grant (1860-63), Samuel Baker (1863-65), Henry Morton Stanley (1871, 1874-77), Joseph Thomson (1883-84)
- *Belgium:* Maurice Adolphe Linant de Bellefonds (1827), Boer settlers
- *France:* Napoleon Bonaparte (1798-1801), René Callié (1827-28), Gaspard T. Mollien, Louis Léon César Faidherbe (1850s), Louis Binger (1887-89), Parfait Louis Monteil (1890-92), Paul Du Chaillu (1840s-60s)
- *Germany:* Ludwig Krapf (late 1840s), John Rebmann (late 1840s), Heinrich Barth (1850-55), Adolf Overweg (1852), Friedrich Gerhard Rohlfs, Gustav Nachtigal, Carl Peters, Count Samuel Teleki von Szek
- *Italy:* Pierre Savorgnan de Brazza (1875-78)

Budget: $

Sources:

"Africa: Its Political Development," *National Geographic,* February, 1980.

Moss, Joyce, and George Wilson, *Peoples of the World: Africans South of the Sahara,* Gale, 1991.

Murphy, E. Jefferson, *Understanding Africa,* Crowell, 1978.

Murray, Jocelyn, ed., *Cultural Atlas of Africa,* Facts on File, 1989.

Alternative Applications: Pinpoint on a large map of Africa the areas explored by these Europeans, particularly James Bruce's search for the source of the Nile, Mungo Park's search for the River Niger, and Richard Francis Burton's journey down the White Nile.

Filming Ancient Africa

Age/Grade Level or Audience: Elementary and middle school history, art, and humanities classes.

Description: Begin preliminary work on a film about ancient Africa.

Procedure: Divide participants into three major groups: one to design sets, one to create costumes, and one to select props for a movie about one of the following topics:

- ◆ The discovery of King Tut's tomb
- ◆ The horse traders of Kanem-Bornu
- ◆ Worship and ritual at the temple at Great Zimbabwe
- ◆ Discovery of the Hope Diamond
- ◆ The first Europeans to visit Kilwa
- ◆ Life in the court of the Oba of Benin
- ◆ The building of the Aswan Dam
- ◆ The first Africans to trade with European slavers
- ◆ Queen Nzingha's life as a warrior-ruler
- ◆ The first Africans to settle in Guyana

Bring together the three groups and map out story boards to guide the director of the movie your group plans to make. Suggest appropriate titles, then explore how the movie will be advertised to draw a large audience.

Budget: $$

Sources:

Brooks, Lester, *Great Civilizations of Ancient Africa,* Four Winds Press, 1971.

Chu, Daniel, and Elliott Skinner, *A Glorious Age in Africa: The Story of Three Great African Empires,* Doubleday, 1965.

Dobler, Lavinia, and William A. Brown, *Great Rulers of the African Past,* Doubleday, 1965.

Green, Richard L., *A Salute to Historic African Kings and Queens,* Empak Enterprises, 1988.

Alternative Applications: Have students select a period of African history to visualize, then have them outline on paper a film, documentary, television drama, miniseries, or video detailing why that period was crucial to black history. Invite students to suggest names of actors to play important roles.

George Washington's Will

Age/Grade Level or Audience: Elementary, middle school, and high school history and language classes.

Description: Study George Washington's will.

Procedure: Read aloud or present by overhead projector George Washington's will (1799), which manumitted his slaves. Invite volunteers to restate in simpler terms the following crucial lines:

- ◆ Upon the decease of my wife, it is my will and desire that all the slaves which I hold in my own right, shall receive their freedom.

◆ And whereas among those who will receive freedom according to this devise, there may be some, who from old age or bodily infirmities, and others who on account of their infancy, that will be unable to support themselves; it is my will and desire that all who come under the first and second description shall be comfortably clothed and fed by my heirs while they live.

◆ The Negroes thus bound are (by their masters or mistresses) to be taught to read and write; and to be brought up to some useful occupation, agreeably to the laws of the commonwealth of Virginia, providing for the support of orphans and other poor children.

◆ And I do hereby expressly forbid the sale, or transportation out of said commonwealth of any slave I may die possessed of, under any pretense whatsoever.

◆ And to my mulatto man William (calling himself William Lee) I give immediate freedom; or if he should prefer it (on account of the accidents which have befallen him, and which have rendered him incapable of walking or of any active employment to remain in the situation he now is), it shall be optional in him to do so. In either case, however, I allow him an annuity of thirty dollars during his natural life, which shall be independent of the victuals and clothes he has been accustomed to receive, if he chooses the last alternative; but in full, with his freedom, if he prefers the first;—and this I give him as testimony of my senses of his attachments to me, and for his faithful services during the Revolutionary War.

Budget: $

Sources:

Estell, Kenneth, ed., *The African-American Almanac,* 6th ed., Gale, 1993.
Walvin, James, *Slavery and the Slave Trade: A Short Illustrated History,* University Press of Mississippi, 1983.

Alternative Applications: Have students discuss the meaning and purpose of manumission and consider the consequences for a black slave who has never known freedom. Make a separate study of each of the following cases:

◆ slaves who do not speak English
◆ illiterate slaves
◆ women with small children
◆ handicapped or aged slaves
◆ slaves born of white parentage
◆ slaves who prefer to remain in their masters' care
◆ slaves guilty of crimes against their owners, such as stealing, assault, poisoning, or arson
◆ slaves who wish to return to Africa

Harlem: Black America's Home Town

Originator: Janet M. Donaldson, Upper Midwest Women's History Center for Teachers, St. Louis Park, Minnesota.

Age/Grade Level or Audience: Middle school, high school, and college history classes; arts societies.

Description: Compose an historical overview of Harlem.

Procedure: Using photographs, filmstrips, books, art prints, sculpture, brochures, or movies, account for the importance of Harlem, New York, to the cultural survival of black America. Include famous people and places and a time line of events. Stress important contributors, such as these:

- ◆ writers Countee Cullen, Zora Neale Hurston, Claude McKay, James Weldon Johnson, Jean Toomer, Jessie Faucet, Rudolph Fisher, Nella Larsen, Langston Hughes
- ◆ musicians Duke Ellington, Eubie Blake, Noble Sissle, Roland Hayes, F. E. Miller, Aubrey Lyle, Billie Holiday, Jelly Roll Morton
- ◆ editors Carter Woodson and W. E. B. Du Bois
- ◆ composers W. C. Handy, J. Rosamond Johnson, Harry J. Burleigh
- ◆ actors Charles Gilpin, Florence Mills, and Paul Robeson
- ◆ dancers Josephine Baker and Katherine Dunham
- ◆ Ethel Ray Nance, National Association for the Advancement of Colored People (NAACP) activist and policewoman
- ◆ entrepreneur Madame C. J. Walker

Create a scrapbook of quotations, aphorisms, poems, memoirs, vignettes, and dialogues created by residents of Harlem, such as Langston Hughes's poems, Zora Neale Hurston's plays and stories, Josephine Baker's memoirs, or W. E. B. Du Bois essays.

Budget: $

Sources:
Films and filmstrips on the Harlem Renaissance; contact Empak Publishing Co., Department C, 520 North Michigan Ave., Suite 1004, Chicago, IL 60611.
Black Writers, Gale, 1989.
Cantor, George, *Historic Landmarks of Black America,* Gale, 1991.
Gilyard, Keith, *Voices of the Self: A Study of Language Competence,* Wayne State University Press, 1991.
Low, W. Augustus, and Virgil A. Clift, eds., *Encyclopedia of Black America,* McGraw Hill, 1981.
Malcolm X and Alex Haley, *The Autobiography of Malcolm X,* Grove Press, 1965, reprinted, Ballantine Books, 1992.

Morrison, Toni, *Jazz,* Knopf, 1992.

Robertson, Sheila C., Kathleen A. O'Brien, and K. G. Woods, *A Social History Describes Six United States Women,* Upper Midwest Women's History Center for Teachers, 6300 Walker St., St. Louis Park, MN 55416.

Smead, Howard, *The Afro-Americans,* Chelsea House Publishers, 1989.

Alternative Applications: Organize a group to create a walking tour or tourist guide to Harlem. Include the following sites:

◆ Abyssinian Baptist Church at 132 West 138th Street, once the pulpit of Adam Clayton Powell, Jr.

◆ Apollo Theater on West 125th Street, home to black dancers, singers, and instrumentalists from the 1920s to current times

◆ Black Fashion Museum at 155 West 126th Street, which features garments covering the entire history of black residence in the New World

◆ Schomburg Center for Research in Black Culture at Lenox Avenue and 135th Street displays published materials that influenced the Harlem Renaissance

◆ St. Nicholas Historical District, an area extending from 137th to 139th streets and from Frederick Douglass Boulevard to Adam Clayton Powell Boulevard, which was once home to Noble Sissle, Claude McKay, James Weldon Johnson, Florence Mills, Eubie Blake, Will Marion Cook, and W. C. Handy, father of the blues

◆ Studio Museum of Harlem at 144 West 125th Street, a folk art center that was once an artists' center containing lecture hall, concert stage, and studio

The Ku Klux Klan

Age/Grade Level or Audience: High school and college social studies, psychology, and sociology classes; history societies; professional and religious groups.

Description: Organize a multimedia study of hate groups, featuring the formation and development of the Ku Klux Klan.

Procedure: Collect information on Ku Klux Klan-sponsored propaganda and violence from a variety of sources, including books, newspaper and magazine articles, histories, films, brochures, leaflets, and interviews. Present findings in a series of illustrated lectures. Illustrate the following facts:

◆ Six Confederate veterans founded the Klan in late spring of 1866 in Pulaski, Tennessee.

◆ The name "Ku Klux" is a corruption of the Greek word "cyclos" for circle.

◆ A major facet of Klan membership was secrecy, which was assured by the donning of white robes with pointed caps pierced by two eyeholes.

◆ The purpose was to harass, humiliate, and otherwise degrade newly freed blacks.

◆ The idea caught on with low-class whites, who felt threatened by hordes of emancipated blacks and who sought empowerment through membership in a secret society.

◆ Other "Old South" supporters, including landowners, judges, doctors, lawyers, and politicians, joined the Klan cause by night while wearing the mask of respectability by day.

◆ To legitimize their hate of blacks, Catholics, Jews, Italians, and other outsiders in the South, Klansmen made a show of religiosity, family devotion, and patriotism.

◆ Methods of annoying blacks worsened to nightriding, cross burning, arson, horsewhipping, rape, emasculation, shooting, tarring and feathering, and lynching.

◆ Targets were usually people who owned land or possessed status, such as someone who owned a successful forge or woodcarving shop or who ran for office.

◆ The conservative press condoned Klan violence on the pretext of protecting Southern women.

◆ Some victims of Klan violence were condemned for a minor slight, such as bumping against a white woman on the street or demanding a receipt in payment of a debt to a white lender.

◆ The Ku Klux Klan Acts of 1870 and 1871 quelled the movement's growth.

◆ From 1882 to 1968, lynchings were common occurrences in Southern states and not unknown as far north as New England; indeed, 4709 lynchings ocurred in a total of forty-three states.

◆ D. W. Griffith's *Birth of a Nation* spawned a resurgence of Klan activity in 1915.

◆ Outraged whites, spurred by the anti-lynching movement led by Ida Wells-Barnett and Jessie Daniel Ames, fought Klan violence.

◆ The Civil Rights movement of the late 1950s and 1960s inspired Klan bombings, often of black churches.

◆ On January 23, 1957, Klansmen forced Montgomery truck driver Willie Edwards, Jr., to jump from a bridge spanning the Alabama River. No one was found guilty of the crime.

◆ On April 25, 1959, eight masked white males dragged Mack Charles Parker from his jail cell in Poplarville, Mississippi, and murdered him, three days before he was to be tried for raping a white woman. Members of the mob included a Baptist minister, health department worker, and the jailer. Juries refused to find the men guilty.

◆ On June 12, 1963, Byron De La Beckwith was charged with murdering civil rights activist Medgar Evers at his Jackson, Mississippi, home. Prosecution of the case continues into the 1990s.

◆ Four young black girls were killed in the bombing of Birmingham's 16th Street Baptist Church on September 15, 1963. Klansman Robert Chambliss was found guilty and imprisoned until 1977.

◆ On May 2, 1964, in Meadville, Mississippi, Klansmen kidnapped Charles Moore and Henry Dee, beat and mutilated them, and threw their bodies into the Mississippi River. Charges against the two suspects were dismissed.

◆ On June 10, 1966, Klansmen shot and killed 67-year-old caretaker Ben Chester White in Natchez, Mississippi. Even with a confession from one Klan member, the jury failed to reach a verdict.

◆ In the 1990s, former Klan official David Duke tried and failed to downplay his earlier role in hate groups in his bid for the governorship of Louisiana.

Publish findings in a series of newspaper articles or professional journals, such as those of a state legal or journalism society or a civil liberties group.

Budget: $$

Sources:

The films *Birth of a Nation* (1915), *Places in the Heart* (1984), and *Mississippi Burning* (1988).

Lester, Julius, *To Be a Slave,* Dial, 1969, reprinted, Scholastic, Inc., 1986.

Mayfield, Mark, "Justice: A Right Denied," *USA Today,* pp. 1A-2A, 4A-5A.

Smead, Howard, *The Afro-Americans,* Chelsea House, 1989.

Walker, Margaret, *Jubilee,* Houghton, 1965, reprinted, Bantam, 1981.

Wilson, Charles Reagan, and William Ferris, eds., *Encyclopedia of Southern Culture,* University of North Carolina Press, 1989.

Alternative Applications: Contrast the rise and fall of Klan activity in the United States with similar hate groups in Russia, Germany, Ireland, Pakistan, India, and South Africa. Note extremist behavior and religious overtones in an attempt to conceal the seriousness of racist crimes. Discuss the importance of such peacekeeping groups as the United Nations, Amnesty International, and the American Civil Liberties Union.

 Library Scavenger Hunt

Originator: Kay Paisley-Callender, teacher and writer, Columbus, Ohio.

Age/Grade Level or Audience: Elementary and middle school history and literature classes.

Description: Research answers to a series of questions about black leaders, entertainers, and sports figures and civil rights history in order to strengthen library resource skills.

Procedure: Have the librarian assemble a group of books, magazines, journals, filmstrips, recordings, software, databases, and other materials on black history. Devise a series of questions and have students locate answers and list sources from which each came. Some significant questions include these:

- ◆ the name of the first abolitionist newspaper
- ◆ the setting of Martin Luther King, Jr.'s "I Have a Dream" speech
- ◆ the singer who popularized "Old Man River" in the musical *Showboat*
- ◆ the product that made Madame Sarah Walker America's first black millionaire
- ◆ the first state to abolish slavery
- ◆ the first free African nation
- ◆ the date that Rosa Parks refused to move to the back of the bus
- ◆ the first black female to seek the U.S. presidency
- ◆ the Constitutional amendment allowing blacks to vote
- ◆ the state that refused to make Martin Luther King, Jr.'s birthday a legal holiday
- ◆ the Supreme Court justice who spearheaded civil rights
- ◆ the first black author to win a Pulitzer Prize
- ◆ the black attorney who accused a Supreme Court nominee of sexual harassment
- ◆ the first black woman astronaut

The first student to list answers and sources will win a prize and/or recognition as a black history expert.

Budget: $$

Sources:

TGABA: Trivia Game about Black Americans, Ali Group, P.O. Box 13093, Columbus, OH 43213; telephone (613)866-7215.

Asante, Molefi K., *Historical and Cultural Atlas of African Americans,* Macmillan, 1991.

Estell, Kenneth, ed., *The African-American Almanac,* 6th ed., Gale, 1993.

Grun, Bernard, *The Timetables of History: A Horizontal Linkage of People and Events,* Simon & Schuster, 1991.

Low, W. Augustus, and Virgil A. Clift, eds., *Encyclopedia of Black America,* McGraw Hill, 1981.

Alternative Applications: Present black history data through a "Question of the Day" contest, which may be accompanied by a list of hints, a photo, drawing, or videotaped or audiotaped clue, such as a segment of a speech or scene from a docudrama, such as *Eyes on the Prize.* Awards should be something small but meaningful, such as a bookmark or listing on a bulletin board.

Matthew Henson

Age/Grade Level or Audience: Elementary or middle school history and science classes.

Description: Present the history of North Pole exploration, highlighting the contribution of Matthew Henson.

Procedure: Explain to students how Matthew Henson became the first explorer to reach the North Pole. Emphasize these points:

- Henson, born in Charles County, Maryland, in 1866, lived in New York.
- At age twelve he went to sea.
- Hired as an explorer of Nicaragua in 1887, Henson assisted Robert E. Peary.
- Henson became the first explorer to reach the North Pole on April 6, 1909.
- He took readings and placed the U.S. flag at the correct spot before Peary arrived.
- In 1912, Henson wrote *A Negro Explorer at the North Pole.*
- He was admitted to the Explorer's Club in 1937.
- President Harry S Truman honored his achievements in 1950 at a Pentagon ceremony.
- Four years later, President Dwight D. Eisenhower honored Henson at the White House.
- Pushed aside as unimportant, he died poor in 1955.
- A plaque erected in 1961 in Annapolis, Maryland, honors Henson's contribution.

Have students draw a map illustrating the entire Peary-Henson voyage.

Budget: $

Sources:

Asante, Molefi K., and Mark T. Masson, *Historical and Cultural Atlas of African Americans,* Macmillan, 1991.

Bigelow, Barbara Carlisle, ed., *Contemporary Black Biography,* Volume 2, Gale, 1992.

Dolan, Sean, *Matthew Henson,* Chelsea House, 1992.

"A Final Resting Place for Matthew Henson," *Ebony,* July 1988, pp. 108-112.

Straub, Deborah G., *Contemporary Heroes and Heroines, Book II,* Gale, 1992.

Alternative Applications: Have students draw illustrations of how they imagine Henson's journey to the North Pole. To stir their thinking, read aloud from a biography of Henson or view films, filmstrips, or *National Geographic* pictures of the North Pole.

Report Writing

Originator: Leatrice Pearson, teacher, Lenoir, North Carolina.

Age/Grade Level or Audience: High school and college history, literature, and African-American studies classes.

Description: Research important aspects of African-American history, such as crucial periods of political influence.

Procedure: Have students utilize media resources and complete a library or research paper or an outline for an oral report on one of the following topics:

- ◆ Carter G. Woodson and Negro History Week
- ◆ Black Soldiers during the Civil War
- ◆ The Jim Crow Laws
- ◆ The Dred Scott Case
- ◆ The "Black Is Beautiful" Movement
- ◆ The Harlem Renaissance
- ◆ The creation of the National Association for the Advancement of Colored People (NAACP)
- ◆ Black Muslims in the United States
- ◆ The speeches of Frederick Douglass
- ◆ Marcus Garvey and the Back to Africa Movement
- ◆ The Buffalo Soldiers and the settlement of the West
- ◆ The Freedman's Bureau
- ◆ The African diaspora
- ◆ The nature and purpose of the Black Codes
- ◆ The creation of the Civil Rights Act of 1867
- ◆ The first Reconstruction Act of 1867
- ◆ The Ku Klux Klan: From Bedford Forest to David Duke
- ◆ The Civil Rights Act of 1875
- ◆ The Civil Rights acts of 1957 and 1960

Assemble individual reports on significant black history topics into an in-house journal, newsletter, assembly program, or database. Retain student writing as resource material. Share reports on IRIS, Prodigy, or other computer networks.

Budget: $

Sources:

The film *The Negro Soldier*, Illinois Film Center; encyclopedias, history books, biographical dictionaries, interviews, recordings, and films and videos on African-American history.

Evitts, William J., *Captive Bodies, Free Spirits: The Story of Southern Slavery*, Messner, 1985.

Hampton, Henry, and Steve Fayer, *Voices of Freedom: An Oral History of the Civil Rights Movement from the 1950s through the 1980s,* Bantam Books, 1990.

Murphy, Jim, *The Boy's War: Confederate and Union Soldiers Talk about the Civil War,* Clarion Books, 1990.

Ray, Delia, *A Nation Torn: The Story of How the Civil War Began*, Lodestar Books, 1990.

Wilson, Amy, "Spirit of the Buffalo," *Detroit Free Press,* July 29, 1992, pp. 1C, 5C.

Wilson, Charles Reagan, and William Ferris, eds., *Encyclopedia of Southern Culture,* University of North Carolina Press, 1989.

Alternative Applications: Organize an annual contest for the best-researched scholarly paper on black history. Invite schools throughout the state to participate. Nominate a multiracial panel to read and evaluate submissions. Offer a stipend, prize, ribbon, medallion, or trophy at a black history assembly or civic function. Name the contest after a prestigious black community member, for example, an educator, inventor, civil rights leader, or entrepreneur.

Slavery and the Caribbean

Age/Grade Level or Audience: Middle school and high school geography and history classes; civic and travel groups.

Description: Create a time line of the history of slavery in the Caribbean.

Procedure: Have students search a variety of sources for information about the Caribbean slaves' experiences. Include these data:

- By 1635, French planters on Guadeloupe were staffing their sugar plantations with African workers.
- By 1640, Nevis's plantation owners were growing rich off the work of black slaves.
- By 1650, France had already established on Martinique a thriving sugar trade, replacing Carib laborers with African slaves.
- By 1667, African slaves staffed sugar plantations in Antigua.
- By 1680, English planters began importing slaves to provide labor for Virgin Gorda's sugarcane and cotton fields.
- As early as 1700, Guadeloupe, utilizing slave work gangs, established itself as a major sugar producer, particularly the Zévalos plantation near St. François.
- In 1726, British sovereignty on Grenada brought the need for more slaves to work the spice mills.
- In 1733, slaves chose to drown in the seas around Minna Neger Ghut, St. John, rather than live in bondage.
- In 1750, Antiguan slave laborers completed a building that now houses the Museum of Antigua and Barbuda. Also, sugar barons of Montserrat, St. Lucia, and St. Kitts were importing West African slaves to work the fields.
- In 1787, Will Blake used slave labor to build Wallblake, his plantation mansion, on Anguilla.
- During the 1790s, Charlotte Amalie, Virgin Islands, was a thriving slave market.
- In 1794, Victor Hugues routed the British from Guadeloupe, liberated the slaves, and sent their masters to the guillotine.

◆ By 1800, slaves marooned on Bonaire's Rode Pan occupied wretched thatched huts and harvested salt for their European masters. Jamaican maroons evolved their famous jerked meat as they hid in remote areas and smoked wild pigs for food.

◆ In 1804, a slave revolt in the Dominican Republic resulted in the creation of Haiti, the first black republic, on the western portion of the island.

◆ In 1807, the slave trade was abolished in Jamaica.

◆ By 1815, Napoleon had reestablished slavery in Guadeloupe.

◆ By 1816, British colonial overseers forced Anguilla into a confederation with St. Kitts and Nevis.

◆ In 1824, runaway slaves from the Freeman Sisters' Underground Railroad sailed aboard the *Turtle Dove* and foundered in Samaná, Dominican Republic, where they made a permanent black settlement.

◆ In 1833, after the demise of slavery in Virgin Gorda, whites abandoned the island to black slaves, who farmed and fished.

◆ In 1834, slavery was abolished on Montserrat.

◆ In 1838, Jamaican slaves were freed.

◆ In 1848, Alsatian Victor Schoelcher helped abolish slavery in Guadeloupe, as did the governor of St. Thomas.

◆ After the American Civil War ended in 1865, planters tried to resurrect the genteel antebellum lifestyle by importing slaves on the Turks and Caicos islands.

Budget: $

Sources:

Fodor's Caribbean: A Complete Guide to 27 Island Destinations, Fodor's Travel Guides, 1993.

Walvin, James, *Slavery and the Slave Trade: A Short Illustrated History,* University Press of Mississippi, 1983.

Alternative Applications: Organize a discussion group to consider why freedom came to some Caribbean slaves decades before the Emancipation Proclamation released American slaves. Consider the following possibilities:

◆ Black populations overwhelmed some islands.

◆ Government by European overseers was ineffective.

◆ The danger of rebellion and sabotage scared off white landowners.

◆ The urge for freedom on one island quickly spread to others as sailors carried the news from port to port.

Slavery Diorama

Age/Grade Level or Audience: High school and college history, sociology, and psychology classes.

Description: Create a diorama or multimedia display describing the African slave trade.

Procedure: Have students depict realistic views of the slave trade, for instance:

- ◆ slave capture in nets and placement in baracoons
- ◆ shackling in coffles for overland transportation to ports
- ◆ the horizontal arrangement of slaves in the holds of slave ships
- ◆ shackling of neck, wrists, and ankles and confinement in stacked layers
- ◆ deck dancing to prevent death from inactivity
- ◆ drowning of troublemakers or diseased slaves
- ◆ display at large auction centers, such as the Charleston, South Carolina, slave market, where blacks were oiled, coated with tar, and branded before being offered for sale
- ◆ bidding, loading on transport wagons, and removal to plantations
- ◆ training in trades, such as blacksmithing, carpentry, cooking and house service, child care, laundry, sugar milling, grain binding, tobacco planting, cotton picking, logging, construction, road building, tanning, and livestock management and slaughter
- ◆ punishment by whipping, amputation, branding, castration, and ham-stringing
- ◆ breeding slaves like prize livestock by selecting strong males to mate with young, vigorous females
- ◆ separation of families as children and elderly slaves were sold to enhance profitability

Budget: $$

Sources:

Evitts, William J., *Captive Bodies, Free Spirits: The Story of Southern Slavery,* Messner, 1985.

Haley, Alex, *Roots: The Saga of an American Family,* Doubleday, 1976.

Kunjufu, Jawanza, *Lessons from History: A Celebration of Blackness,* African American Images, 1987.

Morrison, Toni, *Beloved,* Knopf, 1987.

Alternative Applications: Have students study the psychological effects of dehumanization. Carry this study into the Reconstruction Era when newly emancipated blacks tried to cope with these challenges:

- ◆ responsibilities of caring for themselves and their families
- ◆ migrating from plantations and hostile communities
- ◆ locating housing
- ◆ managing health needs
- ◆ reestablishing scattered families
- ◆ getting jobs

◆ obtaining an education
◆ learning to manage money
◆ countering racist attacks

Draw conclusions about how Darwin's concept of survival of the fittest applies to the former slaves who were most successful at reshaping their lives to conform to white expectations.

What If?

Age/Grade Level or Audience: Elementary, middle school, and high school history and social studies classes.

Description: Organize a thinking game to expand student awareness of racism.

Procedure: Have students name specific changes in U.S. and world history that would have differed if major events had been altered. For example, what if:

◆ African explorers had discovered America
◆ Mennonite and Quaker activists had succeeded in ending slavery during the eighteenth century
◆ the first slaves seized control of New England
◆ Creeks, Choctaws, Seminoles, and Cherokees joined with slaves to over-power European settlers in the Carolinas, Georgia, and Florida
◆ Frederick Douglass had become president of the United States or a cabinet member under Abraham Lincoln
◆ Nelson Mandela had been martyred
◆ trade embargoes had ended apartheid
◆ black athletes had been barred from Olympic participation in 1992
◆ Clarence Thomas's nomination to the Supreme Court had been defeated
◆ Barbara Jordan had been named Bill Clinton's vice president
◆ Jesse Jackson had led a United Nations team in halting famine in Somalia

Budget: $

Sources:

Periodicals such as *Jet, Ebony, Emerge, Life, Time, Newsweek, U.S. News and World Report, Forbes,* and *Black Business* and indexes such as Infotrac and Newsbank.

Asante, Molefi K., *Historical and Cultural Atlas of African Americans,* Macmillan, 1991.

Hornsby, Alton, Jr., *Chronology of African-American History: Significant Events and People from 1619 to the Present,* Gale, 1991.

Low, W. Augustus, and Virgil A. Clift, eds., *Encyclopedia of Black America,* McGraw Hill, 1981.

Alternative Applications: Assign students to compose a news item, tableau, interview, short story, play, poem, hymn, song, movie, or dance expressing a rewritten historical event from the black point of view. For instance:

◆ the Lincoln-Douglass debates
◆ the Gettysburg Address
◆ the unveiling of the Vietnam Memorial
◆ the Virginia reel
◆ Ronald Reagan's peace talks with Mikhail Gorbachev
◆ Kevin Costner's role in *Dances with Wolves*
◆ Edgar Allan Poe's "The Raven"
◆ Mark Twain's "The Celebrated Jumping Frog of Calavaras County"

Journalism

| Africa in the News |

Age/Grade Level or Audience: Elementary, middle school, and high school journalism, language, social studies, and writing classes.

Description: Create an "Africa in the News" bulletin board.

Procedure: Have students comb the popular press for items about Africa. Group together stories on similar topics, such as these:

- ◆ the spread of AIDS
- ◆ hunger and relief efforts in Somalia and Ethiopia
- ◆ Nelson Mandela's speeches and public appearances
- ◆ literature and music by African artists
- ◆ African celebrations and holidays
- ◆ African cooking, fashion, and hair styles
- ◆ new markets for African products, for instance woven goods and foods
- ◆ visits by world leaders and entertainers to Africa
- ◆ attempts to rescue endangered African species, such as the elephant and mountain gorilla

Have students compare articles from different sources.

Budget: $

Sources:
Time, Newsweek, Ebony, Jet, Emerge, Wall Street Journal, U.S. News and World Report, USA Today, and other newspapers and magazines.

Alternative Applications: Have students submit letters to the editor, political cartoons and comic strips, columns, mock interviews, feature articles, fashion sketches, recipes, children's page quizzes and games, and editorials in response to news from Africa or the Caribbean.

African-Americans in the Media

Age/Grade Level or Audience: Middle school, high school, and community college journalism, language, sociology, economics, and history classes.

Description: Study and discuss the emerging role of African-Americans in the popular press.

Procedure: Give each student pairs of scholarly journals, magazines, and newspapers—one from the 1950s and a current issue. Useful choices of publications include the *Wall Street Journal, American Scholar, English Journal, New York Times, Atlanta Constitution, Boston Globe, Washington Post, Christian Science Monitor, Reader's Digest, Time, Newsweek, Sports Illustrated, U.S. News and World Report, Life, Saturday Evening Post,* and *National Geographic.* Have students prepare a set of questions to guide their thinking on the changing role of blacks in the media. For example:

- ◆ What percent of the total advertising space features black models?
- ◆ How many leading articles or news stories depict black Americans in a positive light?
- ◆ What subtle commentary does each publication make about race relations in the United States?
- ◆ What articles refer specifically to black leaders and heroes?
- ◆ How are black women portrayed?
- ◆ What contributions by black artists, scientists, scholars, and entrepreneurs receive cover or lead stories?

Budget: $

Sources:

Guy, Pat, "Magazines Seek Minorities," *USA Today,* October 22, 1992, p. 4B.
Katz, Bill, and Linda Sternberg Katz, *Magazines for Libraries,* Bowker, 1993.

Alternative Applications: Have students conduct an exhaustive investigation of a single day, week, or month from any period in recent time and examine a broad spectrum of news and features about blacks in newspapers, magazines, journals, government publications, movies, and radio and television programs from that period.

 ## African Heroes

Age/Grade Level or Audience: Elementary, middle school, and high school journalism, creative writing, communications, and language classes.

Description: Study great African leaders of the past and present.

Procedure: Provide a selection of resource materials about African history, then have each student select a particular hero or heroine to describe for a school newspaper feature. Some good choices are Patrice Lamumba, Mansa Musa, Desmond Tutu, Nelson Mandela, Shaka, Oliver Tambo, Stephen Biko, Sunni Ali Ber, Askia Muhammad, Affonso I, Idris Alaoma, and Makeda, the Queen of Sheba.

Budget: $$

Sources:
Bigelow, Barbara Carlisle, ed., *Contemporary Black Biography,* Gale, various volumes.
Dobler, Lavinia, and William A. Brown, *Great Rulers of the African Past,* Doubleday, 1965.
Joseph, Joan, *Black African Empires,* Watts, 1974.

Alternative Applications: Have students prepare mock interviews with their heroes and heroines. Suggest the following questions:

  ◆ How did you prepare to lead your people?
  ◆ What was your hardest task?
  ◆ What has fame cost you?
  ◆ Has your family suffered as a result of your political role?
  ◆ What would bring your the greatest happiness?

Videotape the students in costume as they ask questions and learn more about African history.

Backing Police Efforts

Age/Grade Level or Audience: Civic groups; human relations committees.

Description: Lead a campaign backing law enforcement efforts.

Procedure: Have local media leaders meet with city and county officials to consider crime deterrent programs such as these:

  ◆ increased hiring of minority officers
  ◆ pairing black and white officers for community foot patrol
  ◆ opening police annexes in troubled communities where drug dealers or gangs threaten citizens
  ◆ stepping up surveillance to protect the elderly, handicapped, single women, and children

◆ increasing Neighborhood Watch programs
◆ establishing an ombudsman to mediate controversial issues, particularly complaints of police brutality

Budget: $$

Sources:

Consult library sources and state and federal law enforcement agencies for suggestions and models.

Alternative Applications: Offer a reward for Police Officer of the Year or for individual heroic deeds performed by city officials, including fire fighters, social service workers, and rescue departments.

Black Cartoonists

Age/Grade Level or Audience: High school and college journalism and art classes; local newspaper editors and columnists.

Description: Lead a discussion comparing the work of white and black cartoonists.

Procedure: Have participants compare cartoons by Charles Schulz, Kevin Siers, or Doug Marlette; or compare Hanna-Barbera animations with Elmer Simms Campbell's cartoons for Esquire, Ray Billingsley's "Curtis," Robin Harris and Bruce Smith's animated "Bebe's Kids," and Barbara Brandon's "Where I'm Coming From." Also examine the humor of Walt Carr and Gerald Dyes in *Ebony* and the political cartoons of Ron Bryant in *Emerge*. Comment on social values, satire, caricature, dialect, slang, and styles of humor from the black and white perspective.

Budget: $

Sources:
"Bruce Smith: Drawing on a Vision," *Essence,* September 1992, p. 54.
Naylor, Colin, ed., *Contemporary Artists,* 3rd ed., St. James Press, 1989.

Alternative Applications: Have a panel study the frequency with that black characters appear in cartoons, particularly "Peanuts," "Kathy," "Beetle Bailey," "The Wizard of Id," "Sally Forth," "Doonesbury," "For Better or Worse," "Garfield," "Far Side," "Big Jake," and "Kudzu." Comment on the need for positive images in black humor, especially in large metropolitan newspapers and magazines.

Black History Month Newspaper

Age/Grade Level or Audience: Middle school, high school, and community college journalism, communications, and language classes.

Description: Have the regular school newsletter, newspaper, or magazine devote its February issue(s) to black history.

Procedure: Have student reporters write features, news, and editorials on issues relating to black history, for instance:

- ◆ interviews with local civil rights leaders
- ◆ features about little-known American blacks, such as Sally Hemings, Crispus Attucks, Daniel Hale Williams, Edward W. Brooke, Jean Baptiste Pointe du Sable, Toussaint L'Ouverture, Denmark Vesey, Richard Allen, Ida Wells-Barnett, Jan Matzeliger, or Shirley Chisholm
- ◆ editorials concerning affirmative action programs or the need for greater diversity in world and American history studies
- ◆ cartoons and comic strips on black themes
- ◆ critiques of black films and literature
- ◆ quizzes, puzzles, or a question for the day about black inventors, entertainers, filmmakers, Olympic champions, politicians, or sports figures. Offer a prize to the first entrant who submits correct answers.

Budget: $$

Sources:

Asante, Molefi K., *Historical and Cultural Atlas of African Americans,* Macmillan, 1991.
Estell, Kenneth, ed., *The African-American Almanac,* 6th ed., Gale, 1993.

Alternative Applications: For schools that have no newspaper, the February Black History Month Newsletter might be a useful beginning to encourage journalism with a multicultural tone and outreach. A single broadside filled with information about African-American history should include positive information, for instance a description of Kwanzaa activities, fads and fashions, and community projects (e.g., Habitat for Humanity, Meals on Wheels, mother's day out programs, literacy campaigns, and voter registration).

Black Media

Age/Grade Level or Audience: High school and college journalism classes.

Description: Research major African-American publications.

Procedure: Have students select a key African-American publication, such as these newspapers:

Amsterdam News	*Atlanta Daily World*
Baltimore Afro-American	*Berkeley Post Group*
Black Panther	*Black Progress Shopper News*
Buckeye Review	*Capitol Spotlight*
Chicago Citizen	*Chicago Defender*
Chicago South Suburban News	*Forward Times*
Iowa Bystander	*Jamaica's Voice*
Los Angeles Sentinel	*Louisville Defender*
Manhattan Tribune	*Memphis Citizen*
Metro-Sentinel	*Michigan Chronicle*
Muhammad Speaks	*New Pittsburgh Courier*
New York Courier	*Norfolk Journal and Guide*
Seattle Afro-American Journal	*Philadelphia Tribune*
Southern Mediator Journal	*St. Louis Mirror*
Tampa Sentinel-Bulletin	*Tri-State Defender*

and these journals and magazines:

American Visions	*Black Academy Review*
Black Careers	*Black Enterprise*
Black Scholar	*Black Theatre*
Black World	*CLA Journal*
Crisis	*Ebony*
Ebony Jr.	*Emerge*
Essence	*Freedomways*
Harambee	*Jet*
Journal of Negro Education	*Journal of Negro History*
Journal of African Civilizations	*National Medical Association Journal*
Negro History Bulletin	*Negro Traveler and Conventioneer*
New Lady	*Sepia*
Phylon	*Star of Zion*

Trace the publication's founding, philosophy, format, intended audience, and readership. If publication has ceased, note dates and reasons for its demise. Report findings in the form of a library paper, speech, or term paper, complete with outline, thesis statement, annotated text, and exhaustive bibliography.

Budget: $

Sources:

Asante, Molefi K., *Historical and Cultural Atlas of African Americans*, Macmillan, 1991.
Guy, Pat, "Magazines Seek Minorities," *USA Today*, October 22, 1992, p. 4B.
Katz, Bill, and Linda Sternberg Katz, *Magazines for Libraries*, Bowker, 1993.

Smith, Jessie Carney, ed., *Notable Black American Women*, Gale, 1992.

Alternative Applications: Compile a database of the addresses and producers of black broadcast media, such as Black Entertainment TV, Essence TV, Tony Brown's Journal, and Ebony/Jet Showcase, and publishing houses, notably Third World Press, Afro-American Distributors, Africa World/Red Sea Press, Black Class Press, Just Us Books, African American Images, Kitchen table: Women of Color Press, and New Day Press/KARAMU. Use the information to generate an oral report that could be delivered along with tapes and critiques of the medium and capsule biographies of key figures.

Editorials from the Black Perspective

Originator: Leatrice Pearson, teacher, Lenoir, North Carolina.

Age/Grade Level or Audience: High school and college journalism and communications classes; local newspaper editors and columnists.

Description: Provide prompts that will encourage strong editorial writing.

Procedure: Obtain responses to the following quotations:

- ◆ If one managed to change the curriculum in all the schools so that negroes learned more about themselves and their real contributions to this culture, you would be liberating not only negroes, you'd be liberating white people who know nothing about their history. (James Baldwin)
- ◆ Slavery was the black gold that produced America's first wealth and power. Slavery was the breeding ground for the most contagious and contaminating monster of all time—racism. (from *Malcolm X: The Man and His Times*)
- ◆ Hunger has no principles; it simply makes men, at worst, wretched, and at best, dangerous. (James Baldwin)
- ◆ A riot is the language of the unheard. (Martin Luther King, Jr.)
- ◆ A school system without parents at its foundation is just like a bucket with a hole in it. (Jesse Jackson)
- ◆ What the people want is very simple—they want an America as good as its promise. (Barbara Jordan)

Budget: $

Sources:
Bell, Janet Cheatham, *Famous Black Quotations and Some Not So Famous*, Sabayt Publications, 1986.
King, Anita, ed., *Quotations in Black*, Greenwood Press, 1981.

Alternative Applications: Have students create political cartoons or comic strips that illustrate the following bits of wisdom:

◆ He who starts behind in the great race of life must forever remain behind or run faster than the man in front. (Benjamin E. Mays, former president of Morehouse College)

◆ Education is our passport to the future, for tomorrow belongs to the people who prepare for it today. (Malcolm X)

◆ There is no menial work, only menial spirits. (Mary McLeod Bethune)

◆ Our children are what they are taught just as we are what we eat. (Marva Collins)

◆ Anger is like the blade of a sword. Very difficult to hold without harming oneself. (Charles Johnson, *Middle Passage*)

◆ The unprecedented recognition of black male talent in America … is perhaps the greatest story never told by the white media. (Leroy Keith, President of Morehouse College)

◆ We cannot get too comfortable in our houses. The hawk of intolerance still hovers in the air, and restless bigots still talk bigotry in their secret rooms. (Gordon Parks, *Songs of My People*

 The Editorials of J.C. Harris and H.W. Grady

Age/Grade Level or Audience: High school and college journalism and history classes; literary societies; book clubs.

Description: Organize a round table reading and discussion of Joel Chandler Harris's editorials.

Procedure: Have participants read individual editorials from Harris's writings for the *Atlanta Constitution* that seek to ameliorate black/white relations during Reconstruction. Discuss how each might have been healing to Georgians during the bitter era following Sherman's march to the sea and Lee's surrender to Grant at Appomattox Courthouse. Also, invite analysis of Harris's short story "Free Joe and the Rest of the World," which contains this observation:

The problems of one generation are the paradoxes of a succeeding one, particularly if war, or some such incident, intervenes to clarify the atmosphere and strengthen the understanding.

Comment on complementary writings by Henry W. Grady, fellow writer for the *Atlanta Constitution*. Invite discussion of segments of "The New South," Grady's speech to the New England Society on December 21, 1886, which contained this passage:

But what of the Negro? Have we solved the problem he presents or progressed in honor and equity toward solution? Let the record speak to the point. No section shows a more prosperous laboring population than the Negroes of the South, none in fuller sympathy with the employing and land-owning class. He shares our school fund, has the fullest protection of our laws and the friendship of our people.

Budget: $

Sources:
Bickley, R. Bruce, Jr., *Joel Chandler Harris,* University of Georgia Press, 1987.

Bickley, Karen L. Bickley, and Thomas H. English, *Joel Chandler Harris: A Reference Guide,* G. K. Hall, 1978.

Quinn, Arthur Hobson, *American Fiction: An Historical and Critical Survey,* Appleton-Century, 1936.

Alternative Applications: Contrast Joel Chandler Harris and Henry W. Grady's humanistic editorial commentaries with those of William Raspberry, columnist for the *Washington Post,* and Barbara Reynolds, columnist for *USA Today.* Note similarities in their styles and attitudes toward racial harmony.

Extra! Extra!

Age/Grade Level or Audience: Elementary, junior high, high school, and college journalism, history, and writing classes.

Description: Relate major American headlines to black Americans.

Procedure: Organize a round table or symposium to discuss how important events affected the lives of African Americans. Consider these examples:

- ◆ Battleship *Maine* Destroyed (February 16, 1898)—black soldiers join whites in fighting a common enemy during the Spanish-American War
- ◆ German U-Boat Sunk During Attack on U.S. Transports (July 4, 1917)—emphasis on war in Europe draws attention away from the demand for civil rights
- ◆ Negro Lynched in Mississippi (May 21, 1927)—increases pressure on law enforcement to provide equal protection to all citizens
- ◆ Nazis Surrender (May 8, 1945)—returning black soldiers demand more freedom and opportunity
- ◆ Russia Puts Man in Space (April 12, 1961)—United States puts more emphasis on public education, particularly math and foreign languages
- ◆ Martin Luther King Shot to Death (April 5, 1968)—black citizens lose a spokesman, but gain a hero and rallying points
- ◆ "That's One Small Step for Man"—Neil Armstrong (July 21, 1969)—civil rights leaders complain that the growing space program robs poor Americans of funds for education, health, and welfare

Budget: $

Sources:

Asante, Molefi K., *Historical and Cultural Atlas of African Americans,* Macmillan, 1991.

Estell, Kenneth, ed., *The African-American Almanac,* 6th ed., Gale, 1993.

Hornsby, Alton, Jr., *Chronology of African-American History: Significant Events and People from 1619 to the Present,* Gale, 1991.

Alternative Applications: Have students project future events that will affect civil rights for black Americans, such as the following:

- ◆ U.S. Supreme Court decisions affecting abortion rights and funds for poor women
- ◆ drug discoveries relating to the treatment of AIDS and other sexually transmitted diseases, cancer, sickle cell anemia, cystic fibrosis, tuberculosis, high blood pressure, and heart disease
- ◆ legislation affecting the availability of handguns
- ◆ Justice Department investigations of police brutality and interference in suspects' civil rights
- ◆ international strategies to end apartheid
- ◆ laws to end domestic violence
- ◆ Olympic records

 A Future in the Media

Age/Grade Level or Audience: High school and college journalism, film, art, and management classes; camera clubs.

Description: Circulate helpful career information to aspiring young journalists, cinematographers, and directors.

Procedure: Spread information about opportunities in the media. Include the following scholarships and fellowships:

- ◆ Screen and television writing fellowship from Walt Disney Studios. Contact Brenda Vangness, 500 South Buena Vista, Team Disney Building 420K, Burbank, CA 91521-0880.
- ◆ Eddie Murphy Productions/Paramount Pictures fellowship to Howard University or Hampton Institute. Write Jim Arnold, Paramount Pictures, 5555 Melrose Ave., Los Angeles, CA 90038.
- ◆ Black writers program offered by 20th Television. Telephone: (310)203-2273.
- ◆ Assistant director's training program from the Alliance of Motion Picture and Television Producers and the Directors Guild of America. For an application, write Assistant Director's Training Program, 14144 Ventura Blvd., Suite 255, Sherman Oaks, CA 91423.

Post these opportunities on library and school bulletin boards, job counseling services, Employment Security offices, post offices, and community networking centers. Include the data in fraternity and sorority newsletters, church mailings, television and radio career spots, and career fair catalogs.

Budget: $

Sources:
Snodgrass, Mary Ellen, *Contests for Students,* Gale, 1991.

Alternative Applications: Invite media specialists to address journalism and media classes. Promote small group discussion with experts on how minority students should prepare for a career in film, television news, sportscasting, weather, fashion commentary, cartooning, advertising, and editing.

Guest Columnist

Age/Grade Level or Audience: All ages.

Description: Establish a guest column written by a local black leader.

Procedure: Invite a leader of the black community to write a guest column for the local newspaper or deliver it on radio or television. Suggest a number of topics:

- ◆ the purpose of celebrating black history
- ◆ methods of promoting racial harmony
- ◆ the role of cultural divergence in community life
- ◆ the future of the community
- ◆ support for black political candidates
- ◆ ways to help minority youth achieve
- ◆ awareness of black history as a year-round project
- ◆ support for the black family

Distribute the material on brochures at street fairs, through the chamber of commerce, or as inserts to the daily newspaper. Include a calendar of events for Black History Month.

Budget: $

Sources:
Any local newspaper, newsletter, media news program, or in-house business publication.
Ravitch, Diane, *The American Reader: Words That Moved a Nation,* HarperCollins, 1990.
Sandoz, Ellis, *Political Sermons of the American Founding Era,* Liberty Press, 1991.

Alternative Applications: Have local media reprint famous speeches by great black leaders, particularly Martin Luther King, Jr., Sojourner Truth, Frederick Douglass, Jesse Jackson, Thurgood Marshall, Maya Angelou, Carol Moseley Braun, Fannie Lou Hamer, Faye Wattleton, or Barbara Jordan. Print these speeches or excerpts from them in a Black History Month feature. Expand this program to appear in church bulletins, civic newsletters, or PTA publications.

Honoring the Past

Age/Grade Level or Audience: All ages.

Description: Establish a "Five, Ten, and Twenty-Five Years Ago in the Black Community" section in the newspaper.

Procedure: During Black History Month, feature events and photographs of individuals, businesses, church, school, and social activities, and other evidence of community contributions in a special column that looks to the past. Update information with stories about famous people and how their lives have been affected by the events, for example, war heroes or scholarship winners who have returned to serve in public office or to establish local professional practices or businesses.

Budget: $$

Sources:
Newspaper obituaries; library, museum, and private collections; diaries, clipping files, and photo albums; census reports.
Hornsby, Alton, Jr., *Chronology of African-American History: Significant Events and People from 1619 to the Present,* Gale, 1991.
Trager, James, *The People's Chronology,* Henry Holt, 1992.

Alternative Applications: Compose a demographic study of local citizens. Include a study of population by race, personal income, home ownership, literacy, leadership roles, black-owned businesses and newspapers, churches, private schools, segregated country clubs and social organizations, street gangs, and crime. Have newspapers, radio, and television editors prepare feature articles stressing the growth and achievement of the black community, including the following data:

- ◆ number of churches and church attendance
- ◆ increase in educational attainment through literacy programs
- ◆ number and diversity of the local work force
- ◆ professional awards and attainments, such as architectural refinements
- ◆ recreational facilities and opportunities for youth
- ◆ anti-crime, domestic violence, and drug awareness programs

◆ support for families, including outreach to single mothers
◆ philanthropic and volunteer organizations, particularly soup kitchens, halfway houses, and shelters for the homeless, runaway children, AIDS victims, or battered women.

Publicize your findings during Black History Month in newspaper, television, or radio reports. Invite the public to respond.

Lead Story Roundup

Age/Grade Level or Audience: Elementary, middle school, and high school journalism, communications, English, and history classes.

Description: Create headlines about civil rights.

Procedure: Provide students with information about famous black Americans, then have individuals or groups compose twenty-five headlines about famous events in African-American history along with the date that each occurred. Follow these models:

◆ Diego el Negro Sails with Columbus Aboard *Capitana* (July, 1502)
◆ Maryland Passes First Antimiscegenation Law (September 20, 1664)
◆ Declaration of Independence Approved after Deletion of Antislavery Clause (July 4, 1776)
◆ William Lloyd Garrison Founds *The Liberator* (January 1, 1831)
◆ Harriet Tubman Escapes Slavery in Maryland (July 1849)
◆ James Stone First Black to Fight for Union Army (August 23, 1861)
◆ Richard T. Greener First Black to Graduate from Harvard (November 1873)
◆ Harry T. Burleigh Wins Spingarn Medal for Creative Music (November 1917)
◆ Dr. Percy Julian Joins Glidden Staff (1936)
◆ Dr. Ruth Love Named Superintendent of Chicago Schools (March 1981)
◆ Dusable Museum of African-American History Opens in Chicago (1972)
◆ Andy Razaf Enters Songwriters Hall of Fame (May 1972)
◆ Fannie Lou Hamer Registers to Vote (December 1962)
◆ Thousands March in Selma (1955)
◆ Muhammad Ali Takes Heavyweight Boxing Championship from George Foreman in Kinshasa, Zaire (October 26, 1974)
◆ Loretta Glickman Elected Mayor of Pasadena (May 6, 1982)
◆ Max Robinson, American Network TV's First Black Anchor, Dies of AIDS (December 20, 1988)
◆ Nelson Mandela Tours the U.S. (June 20-30, 1990)
◆ Whoopi Goldberg Stars in *Sister Act* and *Sarafina!*

Budget: $

Sources:

Asante, Molefi K., *Historical and Cultural Atlas of African Americans,* Macmillan, 1991.

Hampton, Henry, and Steve Fayer, *Voices of Freedom: An Oral History of the Civil Rights Movement from the 1950s through the 1980s,* Bantam Books, 1990.

Hornsby, Alton, Jr., *Chronology of African-American History: Significant Events and People from 1619 to the Present,* Gale, 1991.

Low, W. Augustus, and Virgil A. Clift, eds., *Encyclopedia of Black America,* McGraw-Hill, 1981.

Alternative Applications: Have students organize an overview of African-American history through a series of banner headlines for front page leads. For instance:

- ◆ First Slaves Auctioned in Western Hemisphere
- ◆ Underground Railroad Leads Captives to Freedom in Canada
- ◆ Lincoln Signs Emancipation Proclamation
- ◆ Shirley Chisholm Runs for U.S. Presidency
- ◆ Jesse Jackson Organizes Rainbow Coalition

Race and Controversy

Age/Grade Level or Audience: College civics and journalism classes; letters to the editor; public debate.

Description: Make a study of public reaction to controversial and/or pornographic references in works by black artists and entertainers.

Procedure: Determine the limits on freedom of speech, which is guaranteed in the Bill of Rights. Examine the outcry over the work of black artists, photographers, rock performers, comedians, or film stars, particularly routines by Eddie Murphy and Richard Pryor, Malcolm X's speeches, Sister Souljah's public interviews, Eldridge Cleaver's prison memoir *Soul on Ice,* and Ice-T's song "Cop Killer." Compare your definitions of freedom with those of the religious right, Citizens for the American Way, Citizens for Decency, and crusades led by Tipper Gore and Anita Bryant. Debate the use of movie ratings and warning labels on records, tapes, and compact discs that are sold to minors.

Budget: $$

Sources:

The Bill of Rights to the U.S. Constitution; *Time, Newsweek, Essence, Ebony,* and other news and popular magazines.

Mooney, Louise, *Contemporary Newsmakers,* Gale, various volumes.

Alternative Applications: Organize a local panel to suggest ways in which parents can protect children from controversy without violating the rights of others to express dissent (e.g., late-night scheduling of violent television programs and X-rated movies; rating and labeling systems for musical recording).

Volunteers without Borders

Age/Grade Level or Audience: All ages.

Description: Compose a newspaper feature or guest column on *Medecins sans Frontiers* or *Aviation sans Frontiers.*

Procedure: Research in on-line, newspaper, or magazine articles the history and purpose of *Medecins sans Frontiers* (Doctors without Borders) or *Aviation sans Frontiers* (Pilots without Borders), a Belgian-based medical relief and evacuation agency. Compose a journalistic feature or guest column on this European volunteer medical group's work in Africa.

Budget: $

Sources:
Write the main office in care of Leon Didden, Administrator, Brussels National Airport, Building 2, Local C142, Zaventem, Belgium; or Maison des Ailes, Rue Montoyer 1, 1040, Brussels, Belgium.

Alternative Applications: Compose editorials to encourage local support for relief efforts by publishing names, addresses, and photos of agencies that assist the poor, sick, illiterate, neglected, or oppressed. Include these:

- ◆ Amnesty International
- ◆ UNICEF
- ◆ Big Brothers and Big Sisters of America
- ◆ Christian Children's Fund
- ◆ Habitat for Humanity
- ◆ the Quilt Project
- ◆ United Negro College Fund
- ◆ American Civil Liberties Union
- ◆ Reading Is Fundamental
- ◆ Meals on Wheels
- ◆ Junior Police

Who's Writing News

Age/Grade Level or Audience: Elementary and middle school journalism classes.

Description: Create an in-house newsletter.

Procedure: During Black History Month, have students create a school newsletter featuring news of the day. Include in each issue a thumbnail sketch of a noted black journalist, editor, cartoonist, cinema director, or sportscaster, especially Ida Wells-Barnett, Ed Bradley, Spike Lee, Alice Dunnigan, Bernard Shaw, Cheryl Miller, Mal Goode, Bryant Gumbel, Barbara Brandon, Stephanie Stokes Oliver, Ahmad Rashad, William Raspberry, Barbara Reynolds, or Venice Tipton Spraggs.

Budget: $$$

Sources:
Brelin, Christa, ed., *Who's Who among Black Americans, 1992-1993*, 7th ed., Gale, 1992.
Bigelow, Barbara Carlisle, ed., *Contemporary Black Biography*, Gale, various volumes.
Smith, Jessie Carney, ed., *Notable Black American Women*, Gale, 1992.

Alternative Applications: Collect thumbnail sketches of black journalists, editors, cartoonists, movie directors, or sportscasters in a scrapbook or database. Next to each, cite an original essay, editorial, article, or familiar quotation.

 You Are There

Age/Grade Level or Audience: High school and college journalism, drama, and history classes.

Description: Conduct an on-the-spot interview with participants in major events in African-American history.

Procedure: Assign students to work in pairs or small groups to interview famous black Americans at the scene of some major occurrence. Tape record the interviews. For example:

- ◆ Rosa Parks refusing to give up her seat on the bus
- ◆ the promotion of Colin Powell to general
- ◆ the publication of Lewis Latimer's textbook on electric lighting systems

◆ Daisy Bates encouraging nine students to integrate Central High in Little Rock, Arkansas
◆ Quincy Jones winning honors at the 24th Annual Grammy Awards in Los Angeles
◆ Hank Aaron hitting has 715th home run to earn the nickname "Home Run King"
◆ the airing of Diahann Carroll's television series "Julia"
◆ Guion Bluford just completing his medical experiments in outer space
◆ Fanny Jackson Coppin's leadership of the Black Women's Rights movement
◆ the premiere of Spike Lee's film *Malcolm X*
◆ Carol Moseley Braun's election to the U.S. Senate.

Play the tape over local radio stations in celebration of Black History Month.

Budget: $$

Sources:
Infotrac, Newsbank, articles from *Ebony, Jet, Emerge, Newsweek, Time, U.S. News and World Report, USA Today,* and other current sources.
Asante, Molefi K., *Historical and Cultural Atlas of African Americans,* Macmillan, 1991.
Estell, Kenneth, ed., *The African-American Almanac,* 6th ed., Gale, 1993.
Trager, James, *The People's Chronology,* Henry Holt, 1992.

Alternative Applications: Form a panel of students impersonating famous black Americans. Have these illustrious guests discuss a crucial topic, such as:

◆ improvement of life in the inner city
◆ low-income housing
◆ day-care for single parents
◆ formation of black-owned businesses
◆ films by and about blacks
◆ community literacy
◆ voter registration programs
◆ equal rights in the military
◆ drugs, alcohol, gang violence, AIDS, and other killers of the young
◆ particular issues facing your own community

Language

Afrocentrism

Age/Grade Level or Audience: All ages.

Description: Invite a guest speaker or panel to present a program on Afrocentrism.

Procedure: Have participants explain the meaning and purpose of Afrocentrism and its effect on black people. Include information about these topics:

- Black Muslims
- Afrocentric schools
- reclaiming the black culture
- reducing family and street violence
- identifying and conquering self-destructive behavior, particularly drug dependence, alcoholism, and smoking
- strengthening the black family
- creating strong self-image in young people
- Afrocentrism as a cohesion mechanism
- Afrocentrism as a means of combatting ghetto mentality
- cultivating safer, more enjoyable cities

Conclude with handouts, press releases, and brochures to be distributed through black history classes, museums, libraries, scout troops, police youth clubs, churches, and the chamber of commerce.

Budget: $$$

Sources:

Contact African American Images, 9204 Commercial, Suite 308, Chicago, IL 60617-4585; telephone (800)552-1991.

Adler, Jerry, "African Dreams," *Newsweek*, September 23, 1991, pp. 43-45.

Bray, Rosemary, "Reclaiming Our Culture," *Essence,* December 1990, pp. 84-87.

Estell, Kenneth, ed., *The African-American Almanac,* 6th ed., Gale, 1993.

Low, W. Augustus, and Virgil A. Clift, eds., *Encyclopedia of Black America,* McGraw-Hill, 1981.

Alternative Applications: List other ethnic groups that have been slighted by Eurocentric American history. For example, include native Americans, Hispanics, and Asian Americans, particularly the victims of Japanese internment camps such as Manzanar, which imprisoned innocent people during much of World War II.

Apartheid

Age/Grade Level or Audience: High school and college sociology and world civilization classes; religious groups; civic organizations.

Description: Define and explain *apartheid.*

Procedure: Provide participants with background information on apartheid, South Africa's formal segregation of races, including its origins, purpose, and social and political ramifications. Provide handouts of the following time line:

- ◆ As early as 1652, white settlers of South Africa supported a system of apartness from black natives.
- ◆ "Apartheid" became the Afrikaner National Party slogan in the 1940s.
- ◆ In 1948, separation of races intensified as Nationalists gained power.
- ◆ In 1956, Miriam Makeba sang in the antiapartheid documentary *Come Back Africa.*
- ◆ In 1961, because of United Nations condemnation, South Africa withdrew from the English Commonwealth.
- ◆ During the 1970s, public condemnation of apartheid-style racism brought boycotts and trade embargoes from many nations.
- ◆ In 1990 Miriam Makeba and Nelson Mandela were allowed to return to South Africa.
- ◆ In 1992, Nelson Mandela toured the United States to raise funds to fight apartheid.

Read aloud from books and magazine articles describing rigid laws affecting land ownership, inheritance, schools, public transportation, government representation, medical care, and marriage. Lead a discussion of the moral implications of a political and social system that allows a white minority to tyrannize a black majority.

Then organize a support group to assist Jeffry Hadebe and the Mpumalanga Teacher Training College in Hammersdale, South Africa, who are attempting to eradicate the educational and linguistic apartheid of black children. Their major needs are for pens, pencils, and books. Send reading material that is not political, such as sets of children's *Highlights* or *National Geographic World,* elementary, secondary, and college textbooks, novels—any reading matter that will develop competency in English. To save on the high cost of international shipping, mail your parcels to: Dr. Thulani Langa, 172 Putnam Ave., Apartment 2, Cambridge, MA 02139.

Budget: $

Sources:
Films *Cry Freedom* (1987), *Sarafina!* (1992), and *The Power of One.*

Debroey, Steven, *South Africa to the Sources of Apartheid,* University Press of America, 1989.

Mathabane, Mark, *Kaffir Boy: The True Story of a Black Youth's Coming of Age in Apartheid South Africa,* New American Library, 1987.

Mostert, Noel, *Frontiers: The Epic of South Africa's Creation and the Tragedy of the Xhosa People,* Knopf, 1992.

Ndibe, Okey, "South Africa's Circle of Violence," *Emerge,* December 1992, pp. 15-16.

Woods, Donald, *Apartheid: A Graphic Guide,* Henry Holt, 1988.

Woods, *Biko,* Henry Holt, 1991.

Alternative Applications: Turn this study into a public forum by inviting public officials and business leaders to debate the issues that question trade with South Africa. Include the following topics:

- ◆ Are liberal nations morally obligated to boycott trade with South Africa?
- ◆ Does the cessation of trade do more harm than good to the black cause?
- ◆ Are white South African leaders moving toward an end to racism?
- ◆ How can bloodshed be stopped during the transition years?
- ◆ What should be the U.S. role in alleviating racism in South Africa?
- ◆ What can outside agencies do to promote better living conditions for black citizens of South Africa?

Black English

Age/Grade Level or Audience: Middle school, high school, and college language classes.

Description: Study the emergence of a separate branch of English among black people.

Procedure: Lead students in a group study of black linguistic patterns, such as the use of the verb "to be," idioms such as "sweet mouth" and "juke and jive," and characteristic pronunciations, particularly "ax" for "ask." Select early writings by black authors for examples of black English. For instance, Frederick Douglass's poem "Jubilee-Beaters":

We raise de wheat
Dey gib us de corn;
We bake de bread
Dey gib us de cruss;
We sif de meal
Dey gib us de huss;
We peel de meat
Dey gib us de skin,
And dat's de way
Dey takes us in.
We skim de pot
Dey gib us de liquor
And say dat's good enough for nigger.
Walk over! Walk over!
Tom butter and de fat;
Poor nigger you can't get over dat;
Walk over!

Budget: $

Sources:

Draper, James P., *Black Literature Criticism*, Gale, 1992.
Low, W. Augustus, and Virgil A. Clift, eds., *Encyclopedia of Black America*, McGraw-Hill, 1981.

Alternative Applications: Study spirituals and the works of dialect writers, particularly these:

- ◆ Zora Neale Hurston's *Mule Bone*
- ◆ the poetry of Mari Evans, Langston Hughes, and Nikki Giovanni
- ◆ Edgar Alan Poe's "The Gold Bug"
- ◆ Joel Chandler Harris's "Uncle Remus" tales
- ◆ Susan Straight's *I Been in Sorrow's Kitchen and Licked Out All the Pots*
- ◆ Virginia Hamilton's *Drylongso*
- ◆ Theodore Taylor's *The Cay*

List variances in dialect by comparing phrases and words to standard English. Note the dropping of letters and endings and the alteration of inflections and auxiliary verbs.

 ## Black History Glossary

Age/Grade Level or Audience: Middle school and high school language and history classes.

Description: Create an alphabetized glossary of terms crucial to African-American history.

Procedure: Assign individual students to define and explain the origin of important terms, such as these:

dark continent	white man's burden
white flight	chickenbone special
apartheid	Motown
Negro National Anthem	civil disobedience
multiculturalism	WASP
Jim Crow laws	Fifteenth Amendment
Ku Klux Klan	grandfather clause
NAACP	rainbow coalition
affirmative action	equal opportunity employer
Poor People's March	nonviolence
PUSH	slave trade triangle
Dred Scott decision	separate but equal
Uncle Tom	garbage workers' strike
Islam	Black Power
Pan-Africanism	diaspora
Black Is Beautiful	high-tech lynching
SNCC	A.N.C.
Harlem Renaissance	de facto segregation
Buppy	Rodney King
tokenism	quotas
Willie Horton ads	Freedmen's Bureau
civil rights	Reconstruction
patroller	pass
Brown v. Board of Education	Watts riot
mulatto	octoroon
Oreo	Symbionese Liberation Army
block busting	Back to Africa movement
maroons	copperhead
indentured servant	negrito
Great Society	miscegenation
nightriders	afrocentrism

Where possible, have students supply a date or an era to which these terms apply and place each term and a definition on a poster. Arrange posters chronologically in a display to indicate their importance in history and politics, particularly election campaigns, civil rights victories, wars, and periods of racial unrest. For example, place *Great Society* during Lyndon Johnson's presidency and *Rodney King* during George Bush's presidency.

Budget: $

Sources:

Asante, Molefi K., *Historical and Cultural Atlas of African Americans,* Macmillan, 1991.

Hornsby, Alton, Jr., *Chronology of African-American History: Significant Events and People from 1619 to the Present,* Gale, 1991.

Kunjufu, Jawanza, *Lessons from History: A Celebration of Blackness,* African American Images, 1987.

Low, W. Augustus, and Virgil A. Clift, eds., *Encyclopedia of Black America,* McGraw-Hill, 1981.

"Woman Who Changed Laws That Prevented Mixed Marriage Tells What It Was Like Then," *Jet,* November 9, 1992, pp. 12-15.

Alternative Applications: Place the "Term of the Day" on the chalkboard. Explain and discuss each, such as *separate but equal* and *de facto segregation.* Review terms from previous days and show their relationship to each other and to the current state of race relations. At the end of the study, collect terms in a database.

 Black Language Roundup

Age/Grade Level or Audience: Middle school, high school, and college language, history, and black studies classes.

Description: Name and locate geographically the languages spoken by members of the black race.

Procedure: Utilize media resources to identify the languages spoken by most of the world's black races, including these:

Acholi	Afrikaan	Akan	Arabic
Bambara	Bantu	Bari	Cajun
Dinka	Dyula	Ewe	French
Fulani	Gambai	Gbaya	Gullah
Hausa	Hindi	Ijo	Kanuri
Khoisan	Kiswahili	Kongo	Krio
Kwa	Lendu	Lingala	Lugbara
Luo	Madi	Malinka	Mande
Mangbetu	Maasai	Mende	Mossi
Lango	Nandi	Nubian	Portuguese
Rwanda	Sango	Swahili	Tswana
Twi	Voltaic	Wolof	Xhosa
Yoruba	Zulu		

Budget: $

Sources:

Baugh, Albert Croll, *A History of the English Language,* Prentice-Hall, 1993.
Crystal, David, *Cambridge Encyclopedia of Language,* Cambridge University Press, 1987.
McCrum, Robert, *The Story of English,* Penguin Books, 1993.
Murray, Jocelyn, ed., *Cultural Atlas of Africa,* Facts on File, 1989.
Ulufudu, *The Zulu Bone Oracle,* Wingbow Press, 1989.

Alternative Applications: Assign students to prepare a word list of English terms that came from African languages. Provide numerous dictionaries, language histories, and etymologies for participants to compare histories. Have them choose a word to illustrate on a poster. For example:

- ◆ **aardvark,** the Afrikaan term for "earth pig" dating to 1833 names a large digging animal.
- ◆ **aardwolf,** the Afrikaan term for "earth wolf" dating to 1833 names a striped mammal of the hyena family.
- ◆ **banana,** an African term dating to 1597 names a soft tropical fruit.
- ◆ **banjo,** from the Kimbandu word *mbanza* and dating to 1739 names a four- or five-stringed musical instrument.
- ◆ **baobab,** an African name dating to 1640 names a broad tropical tree.
- ◆ **basenji,** from the Bantu word dating to 1933 names a small brown barkless dog.
- ◆ **benne,** from the Mandingo *bene* and dating to 1769 names a synonym for sesame.
- ◆ **bongo,** from the Bobangi *mbangani* and dating to 1861 names a small central African antelope.
- ◆ **boogie,** a black American slang term dating to 1902 and denoting a good time or spirited dance.
- ◆ **chimpanzee,** from the Kongo word *chimpenzi* dating to 1738 names a small tree ape.
- ◆ **cocktail,** from the Krio term *kaktel* dating to 1806, which derives from a scorpion with a stinger on its tail and refers to an alcoholic drink.
- ◆ **dashiki,** from the Yoruba *danshiki* dating to 1968 names a loose tunic.
- ◆ **dik-dik,** an East African name dating to 1883 refers to a small antelope.
- ◆ **duiker,** from the Afrikaan *duik* meaning "dive" and dating to 1777 names a family of antelopes.
- ◆ **ebony,** from the Egyptian *hbnj* dating to the fourteenth century denotes a tropical hard wood.
- ◆ **eland,** the Afrikaan word dating to 1600 names a spiral-horned elk.
- ◆ **gerenuk,** from the Somali *garanung* dating to 1895 denotes an East African antelope.
- ◆ **gnu,** from the Bushman *nqu* and dating to 1777 names a large African antelope with curved horns.
- ◆ **goober,** from the Kongo *nguba* and dating to 1833 is a synonym for peanut.
- ◆ **guinea,** African place name dating to 1664 which was transferred to the coins made from native gold; also refers to the region's plants and animals, such as guinea hens and guinea corn.

- **gumbo**, a Bantu word derived from *ochinggombo* and dating to 1845 is a synonym for okra; also refers to soup thickened with okra or to a mixed Creole dialect.
- **hoodoo**, from the Hausa *hu'du'ba* and dating to 1875 is a jinx or evil spell.
- **Hottentot**, an Afrikaan word dating to 1677 refers to Bush people and Bantu natives in South Africa.
- **juju**, from the Hausa *djudju* and dating to 1894 is a synonym for amulet, fetish, or charm.
- **juke**, derived from the Bambara term *dzugu* and dating to 1939 originally meant "wicked" and was applied to roadhouses and jukeboxes; currently it is used as a verb meaning to dance or frolic.
- **kopje**, from the Afrikaan *koppie* and dating to 1848 is a hillock.
- **kudu**, the Afrikaan *koedoe* and dating to 1777 names a large spiral-horned antelope.
- **mamba**, the Zulu *im-amba* dating to 1862 names a venomous snake of the cobra family.
- **mojo**, a black teenage expression of the 1960s refers to a seasoning, potion, or concoction that has power over the emotions.
- **mumbo-jumbo**, an African deity mentioned in 1738 currently refers to complex rituals or language.
- **nyala**, the Zulu *inxala* dating to 1894 names a southeastern African antelope.
- **obeah**, derived from the Twi *abia,* a vine used to make a charm, and dating to 1760 is a general term for voodoo or sorcery.
- **okapi**, the Mbuti term from *o'api* dating to 1900 names a short-necked member of the giraffe family that is marked by a striped rump and reddish skin.
- **okra**, an African word dating to 1679 that names a tall vegetable plant and its edible pods.
- **Rastafarian**, derived from the Ethiopian name of Haile Selassie and dating to 1955 refers to a Jamaican religious cult.
- **springbok**, the Afrikaan term dating to 1775 names a graceful gazelle.
- **steenbok**, the Afrikaan term dating to 1775 names a small antelope.
- **tote**, dating to 1677 is a synonym for carry; also refers to a burden, load, or satchel.
- **tsetse**, from the Tswana word dating to 1849 names a south African fly.
- **veldt**, the Afrikaan term for field dating to 1852 is a synonym for grassland or savanna.
- **voodoo**, from the Ewe *vodu* and dating to 1850 names an African form of ancestor worship.
- **wildebeest**, from the Afrikaan dating to 1838 is a synonym for gnu.
- **yum yum**, an African lip sound dating to 1883, it expresses delight or anticipation.
- **zombie**, from the Kongo *nzambi* and dating to 1871 refers to a corpse reanimated by a supernatural power.

Extend the list to include Caribbean terms, such as reggae, buckra, gris-gris, and dreadlocks. Assist students in making an oversized crossword puzzle to decorate a wall for a banquet, assembly, or celebration.

Expatriates

Age/Grade Level or Audience: High school and college English and history classes.

Description: Search for a broader definition of *expatriate* by examining the lives of several black expatriates.

Procedure: Have students discuss the motivations behind an individual's choosing to leave one's native land by using examples from the lives of Paul Robeson, Josephine Baker, and James Baldwin. Explain the social, political, and economic reasons for each defection, such as Robeson's investigation by the House Un-American Activities Commission, Baldwin's ease with French artists, and Baker's open reception by the people of Paris. Discuss what social and professional advantages these people gained by leaving their homeland and living elsewhere.

Budget: $

Sources:
Asante, Molefi K., *Historical and Cultural Atlas of African Americans,* Macmillan, 1991.
Carlisle, Barbara Bigelow, ed., *Contemporary Black Biography,* Gale, various volumes.
Low, W. Augustus, and Virgil A. Clift, eds., *Encyclopedia of Black America,* McGraw-Hill, 1981.

Alternative Applications: Lead a discussion about World War II and its liberating influence on black Americans through contact with Europeans, particularly the French, who welcomed nonwhite people, including their own Algerian citizens. Describe how the return of veterans to the United States altered attitudes toward segregation and discrimination.

Gullah

Age/Grade Level or Audience: High school and college language and literature classes; literary societies; reading theaters.

Description: Study literary works that depict Gullah.

Procedure: Discuss the following data about black language:

- the isolation felt by slaves from differing lingual groups
- the advantage to slave owners in keeping workers ignorant of each other's language
- the advantage to slaves of creating a common language
- the creation of pidgin or creole languages as a means of communication among people of varying lingual backgrounds
- stylistic and linguistic mechanisms of Gullah that set it apart from the other prominent Southern dialects, notably tidewater, southern mountain, Uncle Remus, Geechee, Cajun, and Creole, and from Caribbean languages, notably Krio and Afrish
- minority groups' needs to be bilingual when dealing with business, government, or the media

Conclude with a study group to read aloud from Susan Straight's novel *I Been in Sorrow's Kitchen and Licked Out All the Pots* or Virginia Hamilton's children's book *Drylongso.*

Budget: $$

Sources:

Films *Conrack* (1974) and *Daughters of the Dust* (1992).

Creel, Margaret W., *A Peculiar People: Slave Religion and Community—Culture among the Gullahs,* New York University Press, 1988.

Hamilton, Virginia, *Drylongso,* Harcourt Brace Jovanovich, 1992.

Straight, Susan, *I Been in Sorrow's Kitchen and Licked Out All the Pots,* Hyperion, 1992.

Taylor, Theodore, *The Cay,* Cornerstone Books, 1990.

Alternative Applications: Present black filmmaker Julie Dash's video *Daughters of the Dust,* which describes the migration of a Gullah family northward from Sea Islands, Georgia. Organize a panel to describe feminist themes, for example:

- Gullah women's concepts of morality and social order
- the courage of women in leading their families during hard times
- the role of matriarchs or elder female leaders
- women and rites of passage
- the mother's role in stabilizing a fragmented family

Hieroglyphics

Age/Grade Level or Audience: Elementary and middle school language classes.

Description: Study the origin and meaning of hieroglyphics.

Procedure: Point out the existence of a highly developed black civilization that evolved pictographs by having students write reports on the hieroglyphic form of writing. Incorporate the writing of common words and names in Egyptian pictographs.

Budget: $$

Sources:
Budge, E. A. Wallis, *An Egyptian Hieroglyphic Dictionary,* Dover Publications, 1978.
Budge, *Egyptian Language: Easy Lessons in Egyptian Hieroglyphics,* Routledge & Keegan Paul, 1966, reprinted, Dover Publications, 1983.
Roehrig, Catherine, *Fun with Hieroglyphs,* available from Metropolitan Museum of Art, 255 Gracie Station, New York, NY 10028-9998; telephone: (800)468-7386.
Rossini, Stephane, *Egyptian Hieroglyphics: How to Read and Write Them,* Dover Publications, 1989.
Spence, Lewis, *Ancient Egyptian Myths and Legends,* Dover Publications.

Alternative Applications: Have students duplicate an Egyptian frieze written in pictographic form or create a new frieze delineating a great moment in Egyptian history, such as the interment of a pharaoh, a harvest ritual, arrival of a visiting dignitary from the south, capture and display of jungle animals, or creation of a bust, temple, or obelisk to honor Cleopatra, Hatshepsut, Tutankhamen, or Ramses II.

Jump Rope Rhymes

Age/Grade Level or Audience: Elementary school students.

Description: Create jump rhymes by imitating the rhyming ditties of black children.

Procedure: Present a two-line prompt to establish style and rhythm. Have children work in small groups to supply more couplets. For instance:

- ◆ I was born in a frying pan
  Just to see how old I am…
- ◆ Little Sally Walker
  Sitting in the saucer…
- ◆ Hey girl
  Whatcha got?…
- ◆ My momma and your momma
  Lives across the street…

◆ Miss Sue, Miss Sue
    Miss Sue from Alabama…
◆ I have a boyfriend
    Nabisco…
◆ Oh, sailor went to sea sea sea
    To see what he could see see see…
◆ I wish I had a nickel
    I wish I had a dime…
◆ Apples on a stick
    Make me sick…
◆ Miss Mary Mack Mack Mack
    All dressed in black black black…
◆ Way down yonder,
    On the East Coastline…
◆ Mister Brown, Mister Brown,
    I come to court your daughter…

Then have students use their rhymes to keep time with activities involving hop-scotch, hand clapping, hula hooping, bean bag toss, line and circle dancing, circle games, ball passing, and follow-the-leader.

Budget: $

Sources:

Cole, Joanna, *Anna Banana: 101 Jump-rope Rhymes,* Morrow Junior Books, 1989.
Jones, Bessie, and Bess Lomax Hawes, *Step It Down: Games, Plays, Songs, and Stories from the Afro-American Heritage,* Harper & Row, 1972, reprinted, University of Georgia Press, 1987.
Lankford, Mary D., *Hopscotch around the World,* Morrow Junior Books, 1992.
Michels, Barbara, and Bettye White, *Apples on a Stick: The Folklore of Black Children,* Coward-McCann, 1983.

Alternative Applications: Use African-American folk rhymes as the basis of choral reading during which children act out, clap, pantomime, and sway to the words they recite. For example:

Hambone

Hambone, Hambone, where you been?
Around the world and I'm goin' agin.
Hambone, Hambone, what'd you do?
I caught the train and the ferry too.
Hambone, Hambone, where'd you go?
Sailed right up to Lucy's door.
I asked sweet Lucy would she be mine,
She said she's willin' if Papa don't mind.

Kwanzaa Flash Cards

Originator: Dr. Laurie Rozakis, teacher, editor, and writer, Farmingdale, New York.

Age/Grade Level or Audience: Kindergarten and elementary school language classes; religious schools.

Description: Create a set of flash cards to illustrate the seven lessons or *nguzo saba* of Kwanzaa, a holiday created in 1966 by African-American leader Maulana Karenga.

Procedure: On a large card print the word "Kwanzaa" surrounded by pictures of pumpkins, gourds, cabbages, onions, corn, bananas, coconuts, pineapples, and other harvested vegetables and fruits. Have students compare the December festival with the American concept of Thanksgiving. Explain that Kwanzaa means "first fruits of the harvest" and that it takes place annually from December 26 until January 1. Then introduce the seven lessons of Kwanzaa, one per card.

- ◆ **brotherhood:** Have students pantomime a scene featuring brothers and sisters playing a ring game in harmony.
- ◆ **self-determination:** Ask a volunteer what it means to be determined. Explain why determination must begin with the individual and radiate out to the community.
- ◆ **cooperation:** Have two students lock hands on the other's wrists to form a chair. Ask a third student to sit on the improvised seat.
- ◆ **sharing:** Make an oral list of places in the United States where people share with those who are poor, homeless, sick, or in danger, such as the Red Cross, Goodwill, UNICEF, Salvation Army, and church charities.
- ◆ **creativity:** Ask students how they would spend a rainy Saturday if they could have any supplies they needed, such as paper, cardboard, crayons, markers, string, and glue.
- ◆ **purpose:** Have a volunteer explain why it is important to set personal goals and achieve them. Ask every student to name at least three goals for the school year.
- ◆ **faith:** Have students explain why they trust their country, neighbors, families, and churches to make the best possible world.

Budget: $

Sources:

Ebony Jr., December 1981, pp. 9-10.

Karenga, Maulana, *The African American Holiday of Kwanzaa: A Celebration of Family, Community, and Culture*, University of Sankore Press, 1988.

McClester, Cedric, *Kwanzaa: Everything You Always Wanted to Know But Didn't Know Where to Ask*, Gumbs and Thomas, 1985.

Porter, A. P., *Kwanzaa*, Carolrhoda Books, 1991.

Walter, Mildred Pitts, *Have a Happy...*, Lothrop, Lee, & Shepard, 1989.

Alternative Applications: For older groups, place the African terms for the seven lessons on the backs of each card. They should read as follows:

- ◆ **unity: umoja** [u-mow'-jah]
- ◆ **self-determination: kujichagulia** [koo'-jee-sha-goo'-lyah]
- ◆ **cooperation: ujima** [u-gee'-mah]
- ◆ **sharing: ujamma** [u-jahm'-mah]
- ◆ **creativity: kuumba** [koo-oom'-bah]
- ◆ **purpose: nia** [nee'-ah]
- ◆ **faith: imani** [ee-mah'-nee]

Have the students read the words with you as you identify the meaning of each and explain its importance to the holiday and to the idea of community. Note that celebrants exchange gifts, give thanks, share a feast, and look forward to another year. Discuss how this idea relates to the first Thanksgiving, when native Americans shared their food with pilgrims. Then have students explain why the world as a whole needs to develop a sense of brotherhood, self-determination, cooperation, sharing, creativity, purpose, and faith.

 Language Pairs

Age/Grade Level or Audience: Elementary, middle school, and high school foreign language classes and clubs.

Description: Make a chart of Swahili words and their equivalent in a target language.

Procedure: Have French, Spanish, German, Italian, or Latin classes create a chart pairing Swahili with the language they are studying. For example:

French
- ◆ buba/chemise: blouse
- ◆ chakula/viande: food
- ◆ loppa/joupe: skirt
- ◆ kofi/chapeau: hat

German
- ◆ tafadali/bitte: please
- ◆ toto/kind: child
- ◆ tutaonana/Auf Wiedersehen: good-bye
- ◆ peya/birne: pear

Italian
- ◆ jambo/saluto: hello

- ◆ kanzu/vestito: robe
- ◆ wototo/ragazzi: children
- ◆ tufa/mela: apple

Latin

- ◆ boga/melopepo: pumpkin
- ◆ dashiki/tunica: tunic
- ◆ matunda/frumentum: fruit
- ◆ zazibu/uvae: grapes

Spanish

- ◆ fundi/maestro or maestra: teacher
- ◆ gele/adorno: turban
- ◆ karamu/fiesta: feast
- ◆ nanasi/ananá: pineapple

Translate the seven Swahili concepts of Kwanzaa into a target language. For example, in Latin:

- ◆ unity: umoja/concordia
- ◆ self-determination: kujichagulia/constantia
- ◆ cooperation: ujima/consociatio
- ◆ sharing: ujamma/partiens
- ◆ creativity: kuumba/cogitatio
- ◆ purpose: nia/consilium
- ◆ faith: imani/fides

Budget: $

Sources:

Kunjufu, Jawanza, *Lessons from History: A Celebration of Blackness,* African American Images, 1987.

Shumaker, David, *Seven Language Dictionary,* Arenel Books, 1978.

Alternative Applications: Listen to the French-African poems read by Paul Mankin, which are available on cassette from Smithsonian/Folkways. Compare to the rhythms, images, and diction of poems by Charles Baudelaire, Victor Hugo, Paul Verlaine, Arthur Rimbaud, and other French poets.

New Names for Old

Age/Grade Level or Audience: Middle school and high school history and language classes.

Description: Collect early names for African countries.

Procedure: Make a list of current countries of Africa. Beside each, give former names. Include these out-of-date names:

Abyssinia	Ashanti	Basutoland
Bechuanaland	Cape Colony	Congo Free State
Dahomey	Darfur	Eritrea
French Somalia	German East Africa	Gold Coast
Kamerun	Madagascar	Merina
Northern Rhodesia	Nyasaland	Orange Free State
Portuguese Guinea	Southern Rhodesia	Southwest Africa
Spanish Sahara	Tanganyika	Togoland
Transvaal	Ubangui-Shari	United Arab Republic

Budget: $

Sources:

Asante, Molefi K., *Historical and Cultural Atlas of African Americans,* Macmillan, 1991.

Bissell, Richard E., and Michael Radu, *Africa in the Post-Decolonization Era,* Transaction Books, 1984.

Crowder, Michael, ed., *The Cambridge History of Africa,* Cambridge University Press, 1986.

Murray, Jocelyn, ed., *Cultural Atlas of Africa,* Facts on File, 1989.

Alternative Applications: Create a series of color-coded maps of colonies that were once ruled by Belgium, France, Germany, Great Britain, Italy, Portugal, Spain, and Turkey. Show them in chronological order to demonstrate the gradual withdrawal of colonial governments as African nations obtained freedom.

Sharing Words from Different Worlds

Originator: Dr. Laurie Rozakis, teacher, editor, and writer, Farmingdale, New York.

Age/Grade Level or Audience: Elementary and middle school language classes; church schools.

Description: Learn Swahili terms.

Procedure: Make illustrated handouts demonstrating the meaning of the following Swahili words:

◆ **asante** [ah-sahn'-tay]: thank you
◆ **bendera** [ben-de'-rah]: the red, black, and green-striped flag of Africa

◆ **bibi** [bee'-bee]: Mrs.
◆ **boga** [bo'-gah]: pumpkin
◆ **buba** [boo'-buh]: an African blouse
◆ **bwana** [bwah'-nuh]: Mr.
◆ **chakula** [sha-koo'-lah]: food
◆ **chungwa** [chuhng'-wah]: orange
◆ **daktari** [dahk-tah'-ree]: doctor
◆ **dashiki** [dah-shee'-kee]: an African man's open-necked tunic
◆ **duka** [doo'-kuh]: shop
◆ **fundi** [fuhn'-dee]: teacher or mentor
◆ **gele** [gay'-lay]: an African woman's head cloth or turban
◆ **habari** [hah-bah'-ree]: How are you?
◆ **jambo** [jahm'-bo]: hello
◆ **kanzu** [kan'-zoo]: an African man's robe
◆ **karamu** [kah-rah'-moo]: a thanksgiving or harvest feast, held on the last day of Kwanzaa week
◆ **kofi** [ko'-fee]: an African hat
◆ **kwaheri** [kwa-heh'-ree]: goodbye
◆ **loppa** [lahp'-pah]: an African skirt
◆ **matunda** [mah-toon'-dah]: fruit
◆ **nanasi** [nah-nah'-see]: pineapple
◆ **nazi** [nah'-zee]: coconut
◆ **ndizi** [nuh-dee'-zee]: banana
◆ **peya** [pay'-yah]: pear
◆ **tafadali** [tah-fah-dah'-lee]: please
◆ **toto** [toh'-toh]: child
◆ **tufa** [too'-fah]: apple
◆ **tutaonana** [too-tow-nah'-nah]: good-bye
◆ **wototo** [wo-to'-to]: children
◆ **zazibu** [zah-zee'-boo]: grapes

Budget: $

Sources:

Karenga, Maulana, *The African American Holiday of Kwanzaa: A Celebration of Family, Community, and Culture,* University of Sankore Press, 1988.

Kunjufu, Jawanza, *Lessons from History: A Celebration of Blackness, African* American Images, 1987.

McClester, Cedric, *Kwanzaa: Everything You Always Wanted to Know But Didn't Know Where to Ask,* Gumbs and Thomas, 1985.

Porter, A. P., *Kwanzaa,* Carolrhoda Books, 1991.

Alternative Applications: Assign a group of students to draw a mural illustrating an African harvest feast where participants wear traditional dress. Have them label examples from the word list above plus these terms:

- **kikomba cha umoja** [kee-kuhm'-bah sha u-mow'-jah]: the shared juice cup
- **kinara** [kee-nah'-rah]: a candleholder
- **mazao** [mah-zah'-oh]: fresh vegetables and fruit
- **mishumaa saba** [mee-shoo'-mah-ah sah'-bah]: seven holiday candles, with three red on the left, a black in the middle, and three green on the right
- **mkeka** [muh-keh'-kuh]: table mat
- **muhindi** [moo-heen'-dee]: corn
- **zawadi** [zah-wah'-dee]: presents to exchange with friends

Translating Lyrics

Age/Grade Level or Audience: Middle school, high school, and college foreign language classes.

Description: Have students listen to Cajun songs and isolate phrases they can translate into French.

Procedure: Present works by a black zydeco group, such as Queen Ida and the Bon Temps Zydeco Band, Chubby Carrier and the Bayou Swamp Band, Clifton Chenier and his Red-Hot Louisiana Band, Rockin' Dopsie and the Zydeco Twisters, and Buckwheat Zydeco. Have French students contrast Cajun lyrics with standard French. On the chalkboard, make a list of differences, such as the elision of *mes amis* into *zamis* or the Cajun pronunciation of *cher* [chahr] and *Louisiane* [loo-zahn'].

Budget: $$

Sources:
Records, cassettes, and compact discs from local libraries; French dictionaries.

Alternative Applications: Once the lyrics are completely translated into French, have the students perform a capella versions of the songs or play them on authentic or home-made Cajun or African instruments.

Literature

LITE

African Authors

Age/Grade Level or Audience: Middle school, high school, and college literature classes; literary societies; library programs.

Description: Provide a wide selection of noted African literature for perusal, small group discussion, and writing and art projects.

Procedure: Guide readers in the selection of materials from the following possibilities:

- Peter Abraham, *Wild Conquest, Mine Boyu, The Path of Thunder, Tell Freedom,* and *Return to Goli*
- Chinua Achebe, *Things Fall Apart, No Longer at Ease, Arrow of God,* and *Man of the People*
- Mongo Beti, *Le Pauvre Christ de Bomba, Mission Terminée,* and *Le Roi Miraculé*
- J. P. Clark, *Song of a Goat, The Masquerade,* and *The Raft*
- H. I. E. Dhlomo, *Valley of the Thousand Hills*
- Muga Gicaru, *Land of Sunshine*
- A. C. Jordan, *The Wrath of the Ancestors*
- Joseph Kariuki, *Mau Mau Detainee*
- Alex la Guma, *A Walk in the Night* and *And a Threefold Cord*
- Thomas Mofolo, *Pitseng, Chaka,* and *Traveler to the East*
- Ezekiel Mphahlele, *Down Second Avenue, The African Image, Man Must Live, The Living and Dead,* and *Shaka Zulu*
- James Ngugi, *Weep Not Child* and *The River Between*
- Ben Okri, *The Famished Road*
- Sembene Ousmane, *Le Docker Noir, O Pays, Mon Beau Peuple!, Les Bouts de Bois de Dieu,* and *L'Harmattan*
- Ferdinand Oyono, *Le Vieux Nègre et la M'daille, Une Vie de Boy,* and *Chemins d'Europe*

- ◆ Okot p'Bitek, *Are Your Teeth White?*
- ◆ Sol T. Plaatje and Mwalimu Joseph Nyerere, translations of Shakespeare's plays
- ◆ Wole Soyinka, *The Interpreters, The Road, A Dance of the Forests, Kongi's Harvest, The Strong Breed, The Lion and the Jewel, The Trials of Brother Jero,* and *The Swamp Dwellers*
- ◆ Amos Tutuola, *The Palm Wine Drunkard* and *My Life in the Bush of Ghosts*
- ◆ B. W. Vilakazi, *In the Gold Mines, Zulu Horizons,* and *Zulu Songs*
- ◆ the poems of Jacob Stanley Davies, Adelaide Casley-Hayford, Mabel Dove Danquah, Léopold Sédar Senghor, Léon Damas, David Diop, Édouard Maunick, Elolongué Epanya-Yondo, Tchicaya U'Tamsi, Malick Fall, and A. B. C. Merriman Labor
- ◆ anthologies, particularly *Contos d'Africa, Novos Contos d'Africa,* and *Poesia Negra de Expressão Portuguesa*

Budget: $$

Sources:

Black Writers, Gale, 1989.
Draper, James P., *Black Literature Criticism,* Gale, 1992.
Moses, Knolly, "A Dialogue with Chinua Achebe," *Emerge,* December 1992, pp. 11-13.
Rosenberg, Donna, ed., *World Literature,* National Textbook Co., 1992.

Alternative Applications: Hold a reading circle in which volunteers cite passages by black African authors that compare or contrast similar segments by white writers. For example, consider the following paired readings:

- ◆ the Dahomey "Song for the Dead" and Christina Rossetti's "Song" or "Remember"
- ◆ Adelaide Casely-Hayford's "Mista Courifer" and George Orwell's "Shooting an Elephant"
- ◆ Bernard Dadié's "Dry Your Tears, Africa" and Carl Sandburg's "Chicago"
- ◆ David Diop's "Africa" and Walt Whitman's "I Hear America Singing"
- ◆ Chinua Achebe's "Marriage Is a Private Affair" and Rudyard Kipling's "Without Benefit of Clergy"

Have participants locate lines illustrating rhetorical devices, such as personification, metaphor, extended metaphor, image, simile, sense impression, parallel construction, onomatopoeia, euphony, cacophony, paradox, alliteration, rhyme, caesura, apostrophe, rhetorical question, and symbolism.

"Between the World and Me"

Originator: Leatrice Pearson, teacher, Lenoir, North Carolina.

Age/Grade Level or Audience: Middle school, high school, and college literature classes; literary societies.

Description: Discuss the imagery in Richard Wright's poem "Between the World and Me."

Procedure: Explain what rhetorical devices Wright uses to communicate his horror at discovering the scene of a lynching. Have readers answer the following questions:

- ◆ How does he give life to inanimate objects?
- ◆ Where did the lynching take place?
- ◆ How was the victim tormented?
- ◆ How and why does the speaker identify with the victim?
- ◆ What irony attaches to his "baptism"?
- ◆ How does the event affect his attitude?
- ◆ What does the sun symbolize?

Explain how Wright's use of sense impressions—sound, taste, smell, sight, and touch—enables the reader to identify with the victim. Why does the ground grip his feet? Contrast the mood and tone of "Between the World and Me" with Wright's "I Have Seen Black Hands," "The FB Eye Blues," and "Red Clay Blues" or Dudley Randall's "Ballad of Birmingham," which eulogizes four black children murdered in Birmingham, Alabama, in 1963.

Budget: $

Sources:
Bontemps, Arna, ed., *American Negro Poetry*, Hill & Wang, 1974.
Chapman, Abraham, ed., *Black Voices: An Anthology of Afro-American Literature*, St. Martin's Press, 1970.
Gayle, Addison, Jr., *Richard Wright: Ordeal of a Native Son,* Anchor Press, 1980.

Alternative Applications: Make a study chart or series of posters illustrating rhetorical devices. Draw illustrations from poems, essays, short stories, plays, novels, or speeches by black writers. For example:

- ◆ **metaphor**
  Hope is a crushed stalk
  Between clenched fingers.
    (Pauli Murray, "Dark Testament")

- ◆ **simile**
  I'm certain that if she could
  Tutor these potential protégés, as
  Quick as Aladdin rubbin his lamp, she would.
    (Margaret Danner, "Dance of the Abakweta")

◆ **aphorism**

Much growth is stunted by too careful prodding,
Too eager tenderness.
The things we love we have to learn to leave alone.
  (Naomi Long Madgett, "Woman with Flower")

◆ **slang**

she slid past
so fly and outtasight
that whistles
didn't phase her
  (Marvin Wyche, "And She Was Bad")

◆ **hyperbole**

Lately, I've become accustomed to the way
The ground opens up and envelops me
Each time I go out to walk the dog.
  (LeRoi Jones, "Preface to a Twenty Volume Suicide Note")

◆ **parallel structure**

I am an invisible man. No, I am not a spook like those who haunted Edgar
Allan Poe; nor am I one of your Hollywood-movie ectoplasms. I am a man
of substance, of flesh and bone, fiber and liquids—and I might even be said
to possess a mind.
  (Ralph Ellison, Invisible Man)

◆ **dialect**

You sang:
Walk togedder, chillen,
Dontcha git weary ...
  (Sterling A. Brown, "Strong Men")

◆ **periodic sentence**

Consciousness of my environment began with the sound of talk.
  (J. Saunders Redding, No Day of Triumph)

◆ **allusion**

i
am the result of
President Lincoln
World War I
and Paris
the
Red Ball Express
white drinking fountains
sitdowns and
sit-ins...
  (Mari Evans, "Status Symbol")

◆ **dialogue**

'Jim, I cannot let my baby go.' Her mother's words, although quiet, were carefully pronounced.

'Maybe,' her father answered, 'it's not in our hands. Reverend Davis and I were talking day before yesterday how God test the Israelites, maybe he's just trying us.'

'God expects you to take care of your own,' his wife interrupted.
    (Diane Oliver, "Neighbors")

◆ **rhyme**

However,
even the F. F. V. pate
is aware that laws defining a Negro
blackjack each other with*in* and with*out* a state.
    (Melvin B. Tolson's "PSI")

◆ **alliteration**

The lariat lynch-wish I deplored.
The loveliest lynchee was our Lord.
    (Gwendolyn Brooks, "The Chicago Defender Sends a Man to Little Rock")

Have students work in small groups to collect more illustrations, such as cacophony, masculine and feminine rhyme, onomatopoeia, blank verse, metonomy, apostrophe, caesura, enjambment, paradox, internal rhyme, and other rhetorical devices.

Black Book Fair

Age/Grade Level or Audience: All ages.

Description: Help Friends of the Library organize a black book fair.

Procedure: Obtain sponsorship for a black book fair. Offer shoppers calendars, bookmarks, videos, games, comics, posters, art prints, magazines, photographs, greeting cards, and other memorabilia as well as fiction and nonfiction by and about blacks. Help black families select works to introduce children to their heritage, such as atlases of Africa, explanations of Kwanzaa, biographies of great black entertainers, scholars, and sports figures, and collections of stories, myths, and poems by Caribbean, African, and African-American authors. Make the black book fair an annual event during Library Week, American Education Week, or Martin Luther King Day.

Budget: $$$

Sources:
Request assistance from professional booksellers, particularly B. Dalton, Scholastic, and Waldenbooks; look for titles in *Books in Print, Publisher's Weekly,* or *Library Journal.*

Alternative Applications: Request that local department stores, discount markets, and booksellers provide a shelf or corner devoted to black literature. Encourage others to patronize vendors who feature black authors, children's books, and bestsellers.

 Black History Book Collection

Age/Grade Level or Audience: All ages.

Description: Organize a special room dedicated to books about black history.

Procedure: Invite local book clubs, civic groups, Friends of the Library, and donors to add books to a special collection of works on black history. Include reference books, atlases, poster collections, recordings, photographs, sculpture, videos, and other material. Raise money for costly volumes by selling donated books, magazines, prints, or other items.

Budget: $$$

Sources:
Consult *Books in Print* or *Publisher's Weekly* and keep a "wish list" of the titles that would be most helpful.

Alternative Applications: Post notices on the library bulletin board or in local newspapers encouraging people to donate a book as a memorial to a community member. Offer a prioritized list of materials that the library needs. Supply an appropriate bookplate to mark books given in memory of a deceased person.

 Black on White

Age/Grade Level or Audience: Middle school, high school, and college literature and black studies classes; literary societies; book clubs; library workshops.

Description: Study literature that depicts how blacks get along with people of other races.

Procedure: Select short stories or books that detail a black/white relationship, such as these:

- ◆ Mark Twain, *Pudd'nhead Wilson* or *Huckleberry Finn*
- ◆ Margaret Mitchell, *Gone with the Wind*

◆ William Styron, *The Confessions of Nat Turner*
◆ Jean Rhys, *Wide Sargasso Sea*
◆ William Blinn, *Brian's Song*
◆ E. R. Braithwaite, *To Sir with Love*
◆ Elizabeth Kata, *A Patch of Blue*
◆ J. H. Griffith, *Black Like Me*
◆ Eddy L. Harris, *Native Stranger*
◆ Thomas Tryon, *Lady*
◆ Alan Paton, *Cry the Beloved Country*
◆ William Faulkner, "That Evening Sun Go Down," *Intruder in the Dust, The Unvanquished*, or *The Sound and the Fury*
◆ William E. Barrett, *Lilies of the Field*
◆ Chinua Achebe, *Things Fall Apart*
◆ Jess Mowry, *Way Past Cool*
◆ Theodore Taylor, *The Cay*
◆ Carson McCullers, *The Member of the Wedding*
◆ Harper Lee, *To Kill a Mockingbird*

Complete the study with a roundtable discussion of the coping mechanisms that facilitate peaceful coexistence.

Sources:

The primary texts and criticism on the works.
Black Writers, Gale, 1989.
Draper, James P., *Black Literature Criticism*, Gale, 1992.

Budget: $$

Alternative Applications: Have readers select significant passages of dialogue to read aloud or dramatize, such as these:

◆ Dilsey's interaction with the Compson children in *The Sound and the Fury*
◆ Homer Smith's arguments with the nuns in *Lilies of the Field*
◆ Jem Finch's attempts to understand the plight of a black man accused of raping a white woman in *To Kill a Mockingbird*
◆ Philip's experience before and after the hurricane in *The Cay*
◆ Berenice's rejection of the orange dress in *A Member of the Wedding*
◆ Brian Piccolo's first meeting with his roommate, Gale Sayers, in *Brian's Song*

Black Study Group

Age/Grade Level or Audience: Adult literary societies.

Description: Organize serious readers into a black study group.

Procedure: Consult the *Encyclopedia of Associations* for organizations that might be interested in supporting a black study group. Consider studying new black voices, such as novelist Darryl Pinckney, author of High Cotton, filmmaker Spike Lee, composer Quincy Jones, or Nobel Prize-winner Derek Walcott. Advertise the creation of a black study group on college or university bulletin boards, in the media, and through newsletters of Mensa, League of Women Voters, and American Association of University Women. Hold an organizational meeting to decide what types of studies will be included, such as current fiction, feminism, civil rights, political issues, community improvement, film, or other programs. Create a spin-off black studies group for high school or grade school students. Have volunteers from the parent group involve young members in readings, skits, discussions, and debates.

Budget: $$$

Sources:

Black Writers, Gale, 1989.

Brown, Stewart, ed., *Caribbean Poetry Now*, Edward Arnold, 1992.

Hughes, Langston, ed., *An African Treasury: Articles, Essays, Stories, Poems by Black Africans*, Crown, 1960.

Popkin, Michael, *Modern Black Writers*, Ungar, 1978.

Schuman, Michael, "We've Come a Long Way…," *Forbes*, February 14, 1992, pp. 196-214.

Alternative Applications: Design a library, college, or university bulletin board featuring a map of the following countries and their black authors. Place a star by those writing in French or any other language other than English. For example:

AFRICA

    Benin

        Olympe Bhely-Quénum

    Cameroon

        Mongo Beti, Elolongué Epanya-Yondo, Ferdinand Oyono

    Cape Verde Islands

        Nuno Miranda

    Congo

        Tchicaya U Tam'si*

    French Guyana

        Léon-Gontran Damas

    Gambia

        Lenrie Peters

    Ghana

        Ama Ata Aidoo, Ayi Kwei Armah, George Awooner-Williams, Adelaide Casley-Hayford, Mabel Dove Danquah

    Guinea

        Camara Laye, Léon Damas

Guyana

Wilson Harris, Edgar Mittelholzer

Ivory Coast

Bernard Binlin Dadié

Kenya

Muga Gicaru, Josiah Kariuki, James Ngugi

Lesotho

Thomas Mofolo

Mauritius

Édouard Maunick

Nigeria

Chinua Achebe, Timothy Aluko, Elechi Amadi, John Pepper Clark, Cyprian Ekwensi, Onuora Nzekwu, Gabriel Okara, Christopher Okigbo, Wole Soyinka, Amos Tutuola

Rhodesia

Dennis Brutus

São Tomé

Francisco Jose Tenreiro

Senegal

Birago Diop, David Diop, Malick Fall, Cheikh Hamidou Kane, Sembène Ousmane, Léopold Sédar Senghor

Sierra Leone

Jacob Stanley Davies, A. B. C. Merriman Labor

South Africa

Peter Abrahams, H. I. E. Dhlomo, Bessie Head, A. C. Jordan, Mazisi Kunene, Alex La Guma, Ezekiel Mphahlele, S. E. K. Mqhayi, Sol T. Plaatje, B. W. Vilakazi

Uganda

Okot p'Bitek

CARIBBEAN

Barbados

Edward Brathwaite, George Lamming

Haiti

Jacques-Stéphen Alexis, Pierre Marcelin, Jacques Roumain, Philippe Thoby-Marcelin

Jamaica

Peter Abrahams, Claude McKay

Martinique

Aimé Césaire, René Maran

St. Lucia

Derek Wolcott

NORTH AMERICA

United States

Maya Angelou, William Armstrong, William Attaway, James Baldwin, Toni

Cade Bambara, Amiri Baraka, Arna Bontemps, Gwendolyn Brooks, Sterling A. Brown, Ed Bullins, Charles W. Chesnutt, Countee Cullen, Paul Laurence Dunbar, Ralph Ellison, Mari Evans, Ernest J. Gaines, Lorraine Hansberry, Robert Hayden, Chester Himes, Langston Hughes, Zora Neale Hurston, James Weldon Johnson, William Melvin Kelley, John Oliver Killens, Toni Morrison, Ishmael Reed, Wallace Thurman, Melvin B. Tolson, Jean Toomer, Alice Walker, Margaret Walker, John A. Williams, Richard Wright

Create a display of articles, poems, short stories, plays, speeches, children's literature, novels, autobiographies, and nonfiction works in print and on tape for visitors to browse and sample.

 Books for Summer

Age/Grade Level or Audience: All ages.

Description: Organize a summer reading program.

Procedure: Help the local library compile a special collection of books about black history or by black authors. Offer prizes as an incentive to encourage people to read. For example, give coloring books or posters to children or selected paperbacks to adults who reach a target of thirty books in a three-month period. Include books on tape for handicapped or illiterate library members. Provide titles in foreign languages to serve local populations who don't read English.

Budget: $$$

Sources:
Recruit volunteers, particularly the Friends of the Library, to donate books or help raise funds to add to the library's collection of works suited to the summer reading program. Consult book catalogs and multicultural catalogs, particularly those of Perma-Bound, Vandalia Rd., Jacksonville, IL 62650; telephone: (800)637-6581. *Scan Books in Print, Publisher's Weekly,* or *Library Journal* for appropriate titles.

Alternative Applications: Organize volunteers to start a black history clipping file for the local library, museum, school library, or historical society. Have a regular staff of volunteers comb newspapers, magazines, travel guides, journals, and other print sources for materials. Laminate articles, maps, and charts to ease handling and reduce wear on fragile pieces. Ask local readers to donate or photocopy articles, particularly those in color, such as maps and articles from *National Geographic.*

Comparing Wisdom

Age/Grade Level or Audience: Middle school and high school literature and language classes; civic groups; book clubs; literary societies.

Description: Compare common American aphorisms with the wise sayings of Africans.

Procedure: Present the group with a list of African aphorisms. For example:

- ◆ The head of a man is a secret storage place. (Chagga)
- ◆ The heart of a man is like an intricately woven net. (Tswana)
- ◆ The fool says, "This world is a virgin girl"; the wise man knows the world is old. (Hausa)
- ◆ The heart of the wise man lies quiet like limpid water. (Cameroon)
- ◆ There is no medicine to cure hatred. (Ashanti)
- ◆ The humble pay for the mistakes of their betters. (Baguirmi)
- ◆ It is best to bind up the finger before it is cut. (Lesotho)
- ◆ He who hunts two rats, catches none. (Buganda)
- ◆ What is said over the dead lion's body, could not be said to him alive. (Zaire)
- ◆ The frog wanted to be as big as the elephant, and burst. (Ethiopia)
- ◆ Move your neck according to the music. (Galla)
- ◆ If there were no elephant in the jungle, the buffalo would be a great animal. (Ghana)
- ◆ One camel does not make fun of the other camel's hump. (Guinea)
- ◆ Save your fowl before it stops flapping. (Ivory Coast)
- ◆ Thunder is not yet rain. (Kenya)
- ◆ A little rain each day will fill the rivers to overflowing. (Liberia)
- ◆ The end of an ox is beef, and the end of a lie is grief. (Madagascar)
- ◆ A cutting word is worse than a bowstring; a cut may heal, but the cut of the tongue does not. (Mauritania)
- ◆ There is no medicine against old age. (Niger)
- ◆ Some birds avoid the water, ducks seek it. (Nigeria)
- ◆ One little arrow does not kill a serpent. (Malawi)
- ◆ The monkey does not see his own hind parts; he sees his neighbors'. (Zimbabwe)
- ◆ In a court of fowls, the cockroach never wins his case. (Rwanda)
- ◆ If a centipede loses a leg, it does not prevent him from walking. (Senegal)
- ◆ Only a monkey understands a monkey. (Sierra Leone)
- ◆ In the ocean, one does not need to sow water. (Somalia)
- ◆ Let rats shoot arrows at each other. (Sudan)
- ◆ A sheep cannot bleat in two different places at the same time. (Tanzania)
- ◆ A roaring lion kills no game. (Uganda)
- ◆ A horse has four legs, yet it often falls. (Zululand)

Have volunteers restate the idea in English.

Budget: $

Sources:

Bell, Janet Cheatham, *Famous Black Quotations and Some Not so Famous,* Sabayt Publications, 1986.

King, Anita, ed., *Quotations in Black,* Greenwood Press, 1981.

Leslau, Charlotte, and Wolf Leslau, *African Proverbs,* P. Pauper Press, 1982.

Alternative Applications: Have participants work in pairs to create a comparative list of African and American sayings, such as one of Poor Richard's sayings, a verse from the book of Proverbs, or one of Aesop's homilies. Select the most striking pairs to write in calligraphy on poster paper or on wall hangings or book markers, or transfer some to cloth and create needlework to be framed or made into pillows. Proverbs to use, for example, include:

- ◆ Seeing is different from being told. (Kenya)
  Seeing is believing.
- ◆ Before healing others, heal thyself. (Nigeria)
  Physician, heal thyself.
- ◆ Evil knows where evil sleeps. (Nigeria)
  Evil begets evil.
- ◆ A little shrub may grow into a tree. (Sudan)
  The mighty oak was once an acorn.
- ◆ Hunger is felt by a slave and hunger is felt by a king. (Ashanti)
  All men put on their pants one leg at a time.
- ◆ Little by little grow the bananas. (Zaire)
  The best way to eat an elephant is one bite at a time.

"D.P."

Age/Grade Level or Audience: Middle school and high school literature and humanities classes.

Description: Discuss Kurt Vonnegut's short story "D.P."

Procedure: Read Kurt Vonnegut's story aloud. Lead a discussion of the author's purpose in choosing the orphaned "blue-eyed colored boy" as his focus.

Budget: $

Sources:

Simmons, John S., and Malcolm E. Stern, *The Short Story and You: An Introduction to Understanding and Appreciation,* National Textbook Co., 1986.

Vonnegut, Kurt, *Welcome to the Monkey House,* Franklin Library, 1981.

Alternative Applications: Organize discussion groups to ponder the fate of offspring of black G.I.s in Korea, Vietnam, Panama, Granada, and the Persian Gulf.

- ◆ Enumerate suggestions for how the United States can prevent racial discrimination against these multiracial children.
- ◆ Report on the Pearl Buck Foundation, which was established to ease the burden of the children born to Asian mothers and American G.I. fathers.
- ◆ Locate source material explaining the hard life of unwanted biracial children in Asia, especially Vietnamese orphans known as "the dust."

Derek Walcott

Age/Grade Level or Audience: Middle school, high school, and college literature classes; literary societies; book clubs.

Description: Hold a public reading of the works of poet and playwright Derek Walcott, 1992 Nobel Prize winner for literature.

Procedure: Hold a Derek Walcott reading at a school, library, museum, or public assembly. Select some of his verse, such as segments of Omeros, his 325-page Caribbean epic, or short works, such as *The Light of the World, The Lighthouse,* "Sea Grapes," "A Far Cry from Africa," or "Sunday Lemons." Concentrate on thought-provoking, evocative lines, for instance:

Where shall I turn, divided to the vein?
I who have cursed
   the drunken officer of British rule, how choose
Between this Africa and the English tongue I love?
Betray them both, or give back what they give?

Have participants note syncopated cadences, slang, Creole patois, sense impressions, and rich island images. Conclude the reading with a comparison of Walcott's view of Caribbean life with that of other literary views, such as Lynn Joseph's *Coconut Kind of Day,* Theodore Taylor's *The Cay,* Jean Rhys's *Wide Sargasso Sea,* or Ernest Hemingway's *The Old Man and the Sea* or *Islands in the Stream.*

Budget: $

Sources:
Brown, Stewart, ed., *Caribbean Poetry Now,* Edward Arnold, 1992.
"Derek Walcott, Famed Poet, Playwright, awarded 1992 Nobel Prize in Literature," *Jet,* October 26, 1992, p. 14.

Gray, Paul, "Bard of the Island Life," *Time,* October 19, 1992, p. 65.

Walcott, Derek, *The Arkansas Testament* (poetry), Farrar, Straus, 1987.

Walcott, *Collected Poems,* 1945-1984, Farrar, Straus, 1986.

Walcott, *Dream on Monkey Mountain and Other Plays,* Farrar, Straus, 1970.

Walcott, *The Fortunate Traveller* (poetry), Farrar, Straus, 1981.

Walcott, *The Joker of Seville and O Babylon!: Two Plays,* Farrar, Straus, 1978.

Walcott, *Midsummer* (poetry), Farrar, Straus, 1984.

Walcott, *Remembrance and Pantomime: Two Plays,* Farrar, Straus, 1980.

Walcott, *The Star-Apple Kingdom* (poetry), Farrar, Straus, 1979.

Walcott, *Three Plays,* Farrar, Straus, 1986.

Alternative Applications: As an introduction to Walcott's life and work, post a bulletin board display of facts about his life and career. Include these data:

- ◆ Walcott was born of Dutch, English, and African ancestry in 1930 in Castries, St. Lucia.
- ◆ Educated at St. Mary's College and the University of the West Indies, Kingston, Jamaica, he published his first book of verse at the age of eighteen.
- ◆ He followed with nine more volumes in his lengthy career as poet, playwright, and teacher and stresses the blend of African and European influences on Caribbean thought and culture.
- ◆ In 1959, he founded the Trinidad Theatre Workshop.
- ◆ Spending equal amounts of time in Boston, Massachusetts, and Port of Spain, Trinidad, he now teaches literature and creative writing at Boston University.
- ◆ His first significant prize was a MacArthur Foundation grant in 1981.
- ◆ In October 1992, Walcott won the Nobel Prize for literature, totaling $1.2 million.

Feminist Writers

Originator: Leatrice Pearson, teacher, Lenoir, North Carolina.

Age/Grade Level or Audience: High school and college literature classes; literary societies.

Description: Present a program of female African-American poets.

Procedure: Read aloud from works by Nikki Giovanni, Mari Evans, Gwendolyn Brooks, Naomi Long Madgett, Clarissa Scott Delany, Helene Johnson, Margaret Walker, Julia Fields, Toni Morrison, Rita Dove, Brandi Barnes, Helen Armstead Johnson, Lucille Clifton, Maya Angelou, and Mona Lake Jones, particularly her "Room Full of Sisters," which proclaims, "A sisterhood of modern sojourners today / Still out in front, blazing the way," and from "Black Culture," which drolly comments "'Black folks don't have any culture' I heard somebody say / and I just put my hand on my hip, rolled my eyes and looked the other way."

Budget: $$

Sources:

A Salute to Historic Black Women, Empak Enterprises, 1984.
Black Writers, Gale, 1989.
Bontemps, Arna, ed., *American Negro Poetry,* Hill & Wang, 1974.
Chapman, Abraham, ed., *Black Voices: An Anthology of Afro-American Literature,* St. Martin's Press, 1970.
Smith, Jessie Carney, *Notable Black American Women,* Gale, 1992.

Alternative Applications:
Lead a discussion of the black woman's unique point of view as demonstrated by her poetry. Determine how hardship has made her strong and humor has preserved her balance, as described in Mari Evans's poem "I Am a Black Woman":

tall as a cypress
strong
beyond all definition still
defying place
and time
and circumstance
assailed
impervious
indestructible.

Compare these assertions to Sojourner Truth's "Ain't I a Woman" speech, Helen Reddy's popular song "I Am Woman," Gloria Steinem's introduction to *Revolution from Within,* or Maya Angelou's epic poem *Now Sheba Sings the Song.*

Freedom's Journal

Age/Grade Level or Audience: Middle school, high school, and college literature and writing classes.

Description: Discuss *Freedom's Journal,* the first black newspaper in the United States.

Procedure: Read aloud from the first edition of Samuel Cornish and John B. Russworm's *Freedom's Journal.* Have students discuss the significance of the following paragraphs:

◆ We wish to plead our own cause. Too long have others spoken for us. Too long has the public been deceived by misrepresentations, in things which concern us deeply, though in the estimation of some mere trifles; for though there are many in society who exercise towards us benevolent feelings; still (with sorrow we confess it) there are others who make it their business to enlarge upon the least trifle, which tends to the discredit of any person of colour and pronounce anathemas and denounce our whole body for the misconduct of this guilty one. We are aware that there are many instances of vice among us, but we avow that it is because no one has taught its subjects to be virtuous; many instances of poverty, because no sufficient efforts accommodated to minds contracted by slavery, and deprived of early education have been made, to teach them how to husband their hard earnings, and to secure to themselves comfort.

◆ Education being an object of the highest importance to the welfare of society, we shall endeavour to present just and adequate views of it, and to urge upon our brethren the necessity and expediency of training their children, while young, to habits of industry, and thus forming them for becoming useful members of society. It is surely time that we should awake from this lethargy of years, and make a concentrated effort for the education of our youth. We form a spoke in the human wheel, and it is necessary that we should understand our dependence on the different parts, and theirs on us, in order to perform our part with propriety.

◆ If ignorance, poverty and degradation have hitherto been our unhappy lot; has the eternal decree gone forth, that our race alone are to remain in this state, while knowledge and civilization are shedding their enlivening rays over the rest of the human family? The recent travels of Denham and Clapperton in the interior of Africa, and the interesting narrative which they have published; the establishment of the republic of Haiti after years of sanguinary warfare; its subsequent progress in all the arts of civilization; and the advancement of the liberal ideas in South America, where despotism has given place to free governments, and where many of our brethren now fill important civil and military stations, prove the contrary.

Budget: $

Sources:

Estell, Kenneth, ed., *The African-American Almanac,* 6th ed., Gale, 1993.

Low, W. Augustus, and Virgil A. Clift, eds., *Encyclopedia of Black America,* McGraw Hill, 1981.

Alternative Applications: Have students contribute paragraphs to the first issue of the newspaper in which they support abolitionism and suggest other reasons why slavery should be abolished.

Gertrude Johnson Williams Award

Age/Grade Level or Audience: All ages.

Description: Submit a short story to the Gertrude Johnson Williams Literary Award contest.

Procedure: Obtain contest rules, which describe the requirements for an original short story of 2,500 words or less. The contest criteria stress a positive outlook "to raise the level of consciousness and hope of African-American writers and readers." Contestants must be nonpublished authors of African descent. The annual awards total $10,000.

Budget: $

Sources:
Ebony, September 1992, p. 60.

Alternative Applications: Read past winners of the award, which are published each April in *Ebony* magazine. Determine what qualities influenced judges, such as sincerity, organization, concrete examples, and theme. Create a writing class assignment based on these qualities.

The Latest in Books by Black Authors

Age/Grade Level or Audience: All ages.

Description: Advertise current works by black authors.

Procedure: Create a bulletin board of book jackets of works by Caribbean, African, or African-American authors. Organize the display according to age and interest level. Feature a variety of books from reference and nonfiction to poetry, drama, novels, and short stories, for example:

- ◆ poems by Nobel laureate Derek Wolcott
- ◆ Patricia McKissack's biography *Jesse Jackson*
- ◆ Anna Kosof's *The Civil Rights Movement and Its Legacy*
- ◆ Mildred D. Taylor's *Roll of Thunder, Hear My Cry*
- ◆ John Agard's *The Calypso Alphabet*
- ◆ Joyce Powzyk's *Tracking Wild Chimpanzees*
- ◆ Donna Bailey and Anna Sproule's *We Live in Nigeria*
- ◆ Judith Hoffman Corwin's *African Crafts*

◆ Martin Gibrill's *African Food and Drink*
◆ Molefi K. Asante and Mark T. Mattson's *Historical and Cultural Atlas of African Americans*
◆ Toni Morrison's *Jazz*

Budget: $

Sources:

Collect book jackets from the technical services division of a city, county, or school library. For more information about books, consult the Perma-Bound Multicultural Catalog, Vandalia Road, Jacksonville, IL 62650; telephone: (800)637-6581.

Miller-Lachmann, Lyn, *Our Family, Our Friends, Our World: An Annotated Guide to Significant Multicultural Books for Children and Teenagers,* Bowker, 1992;

Alternative Applications: Encourage more readers to sample black authors. Use these methods:

◆ Distribute book lists by mail or at the checkout desk of the library.
◆ Share the information with the book editor of a local newspaper.
◆ Have the Friends of the Library include new book information in their newsletters.
◆ Include suggested titles that the library would like to purchase and which donors or support groups may supply as gifts or memorials.
◆ Hold a pre-holiday Afrocentric book fair.
◆ Make Afrocentric bookmarks to distribute free. List a book title on each one.

Lyndon Johnson and the Black Panthers

Age/Grade Level or Audience: High school and college literature and history classes; civic clubs.

Description: Compare the philosophy of President Lyndon B. Johnson's voting rights address of 1965 with the Black Panther Manifesto of 1966.

Procedure: Note the differences in phrasing and intent in these two works. Consider Johnson's comments and goals:

◆ There is no Negro problem. There is no Southern problem. There is no Northern problem. There is only an American problem.
◆ There is no issue of states rights or national rights. There is only the struggle for human rights.
◆ We must preserve the right of free speech and the right of free assembly.
◆ We will guard against violence, knowing it strikes from our hands the very weapons which we seek—progress, obedience to law, and belief in American values.

◆ So we want to open the gates to opportunity. But we're also going to give all our people, black and white, the help that they need to walk through those gates.

◆ I want to be the president who helped to feed the hungry and to prepare them to be taxpayers instead of tax eaters.

Contrast these thoughts with the Black Panther Party's demands:

◆ We want freedom. We want power to determine the destiny of our Black Community.

◆ We want full employment for our people.

◆ We want an end to the robbery by the capitalist of our Black Community.

◆ We want decent housing, fit for shelter of human beings.

◆ We want education for our people that exposes the true nature of this decadent American society. We want history that teaches us our true history and our role in the present-day society.

◆ We want an end to police brutality and murder of black people.

◆ We want land, bread, housing, education, clothing, justice and peace.

Budget: $

Sources:

Estell, Kenneth, ed., *The African-American Almanac,* 6th ed., Gale, 1993.
Heath, G. Louis, ed., *The Black Panther Party Leaders Speak,* Scarecrow, 1976.
Seale, Bobby, *Seize the Time: The Story of the Black Panther Party and Huey P. Newton,* Random House, 1970.

Alternative Applications: Debate the more controversial of the Black Panther demands:

◆ We want all black men to be exempt from military service.

◆ We want freedom for all black men held in federal, state, county and city prisons and jails.

◆ We want all black people when brought to trial to be tried in court by a jury of their peer group or people from their black communities, as defined by the Constitution of the United States.

◆ When a long train of abuses and usurpations, pursuing invariably the same object, evinces a design to reduce [black people] under absolute despotism, it is their right, it is their duty, to throw off such government, and to provide new guards for their future security.

Melville and Slavery

Age/Grade Level or Audience: High school and college literature classes; literary societies; book clubs.

Description: Analyze the theme of Herman Melville's novella *Benito Cereno*.

Procedure: Launch a thorough study of the theme of *Benito Cereno*, Herman Melville's novella concerning the debilitating effect of the slave trade on European adventurers. Consider several controlling motifs:

- ◆ the imprisoning microcosm of the ship
- ◆ miscommunication between Captain Delano and Don Benito
- ◆ desperation of transported slaves
- ◆ evil begetting evil
- ◆ the duplicity and greed that undergird the foundations of America

Budget: $$

Sources:

Howard, Leon, *Herman Melville,* University of Minnesota Press, 1961.

Karcher, Carolyn L., *Shadow over the Promised Land: Slavery, Race, and Violence in Melville's America,* Louisiana State University Press, 1980.

Melville, Herman, *Benito Cereno,* Imprint Society, 1972.

Sealts, Merton M., *Pursuing Melville, 1940-1980: Chapters and Essays,* University of Wisconsin Press, 1982.

Alternative Applications: Contrast Melville's horrific tale with other authors' views, particularly these:

- ◆ Harriet Beecher Stowe, *Uncle Tom's Cabin*
- ◆ William Faulkner, *Absalom, Absalom*
- ◆ Arthur Miller, *The Crucible*
- ◆ Toni Morrison, *Beloved*
- ◆ Margaret Walker, *Jubilee*
- ◆ William Styron, *The Confessions of Nat Turner*
- ◆ Ann Petry, *Tituba of Salem Village*
- ◆ Paula Fox, *Slave Dancer*

Incorporate into your study the words of W. E. B. Du Bois on race:

The problem of the twentieth century is the problem of color. This double-consciousness, this sense of always looking at one's self through the eyes of others, of measuring one's soul by the tape of a world that looks on in amused contempt and pity. One ever feels his twoness—an American, a Negro; two souls, two thoughts, two unreconciled strivings, two warring ideals in one dark body, whose dogged strength alone keeps it from being torn asunder.

Decide whether Du Bois's description of "twoness" is still relevant to American life.

Militant Verse

Originator: Leatrice Pearson, teacher, Lenoir, North Carolina.

Age/Grade Level or Audience: Middle school, high school, and college literature classes; literary societies.

Description: Assess the tone and timeliness of Raymond R. Patterson's poetry.

Procedure: Invite volunteers to read aloud stanzas of Raymond R. Patterson's "A Traditional Ballad," "Birmingham 1963," "For the Bombed Negro Children," and "Riot Times U.S.A.," which concludes:

Yes, I trust the things one hears—
Times will get better
Than they presently are—
About as far as I can throw
Three hundred years,
And up to now
That hasn't been far.

Encourage each reader to make a personal response or evaluation of each verse, particularly as it applies to recurrent urban unrest, as seen in the Los Angeles riots in spring 1992.

Budget: $

Sources:
Black Writers, Gale, 1989.
Patterson, Raymond R., *Twenty-six Ways of Looking at a Black Man and Other Poems*, Award Books, 1969.

Alternative Applications: Invite readers to append their own stanzas concerning restlessness, racism, hatred, and vengeance. Collect responses on a single handout and share with the group. Have students compare their style with Patterson's command of rhythm, tone, point of view, image, and diction.

Read, Read, Read

Originator: Dr. Sandra E. Gibbs, Director of Special Programs, National Council of Teachers of English, 1111 Kenyon Rd., Urbana, IL 61801; telephone: (217)328-3870.

Age/Grade Level or Audience: All ages.

Description: Launch a community African-American read-in.

Procedure: Encourage community members to familiarize themselves with African-American authors. Use a variety of methods, including these:

- Help the public library prepare for the read-in by raising money to buy additional books and magazines by black authors and publishers by holding bake sales, silent auctions, progressive dinners, and book swaps.
- Organize reading circles for families and clubs. For large gatherings, provide an interpreter to sign for the deaf; in bilingual settings, provide a translator.
- Read excerpts from works by black authors over the public address system in a mall, factory, school, or business.
- Have local radio announcers read selections on the air.
- Print selections in newspapers.
- Get a sorority or fraternal organization to sponsor free paperbacks for underprivileged people.
- Select a team of young readers to visit retirement homes, hospitals, and veterans' homes to read aloud.
- Provide large print volumes or books on tape for visually impaired and illiterate people.
- At the library create a separate shelf of books in translation for non-English speaking readers.
- Offer small rewards to children who read twenty-five books during Black History Month.
- Pair readings with movies, for instance, read aloud from Alex Haley's *Roots,* William Armstrong's *Sounder,* Ernest Gaines's *The Autobiography of Miss Jane Pittman,* Alice Walker's *The Color Purple,* or *The Autobiography of Malcolm X,* then view the film.
- Introduce a book club to the novels and shorter works of Chester Himes, including *If He Hollers Let Him Go, The Heat's On, A Rage in Harlem, Cotton Comes to Harlem, Black on Black, Run Man Run,* and *Pinktoes* or the detective novels of Walter Mosley, such as *Butterfly.*
- Tape readings and create a reference collection for use by schools, book clubs, and church groups.

Budget: $$$$

Sources:

For information about the National African American Read-In Chain, contact Dr. Jerrie C. Scott, African-American Read-In Chain, Central State University, Urban Literacy, Lower Library, Wilberforce, OH 45384; telephone: (513)376-6535, or Dr. Sandra E. Gibbs, Director of Special Programs, NCTE, 1111 Kenyon Rd., Urbana, IL 61801; telephone: (217)328-3870. Order multicultural catalogs from Perma-Bound, Vandalia Rd., Jacksonville, IL; telephone: (800)637-6581.

Bates, Karen Grigsby, "Possessing the Secrets of Success," *Emerge,* October 1992, pp. 47-49.

Alternative Applications: Launch the "Year of the Black Author." Divide the calendar into segments, allotting different time spans for novels, short stories, plays, essays, poems, lyrics, speeches, sermons, editorials, biographies, autobiographies, and aphorisms. For example, begin with these:

- ◆ stories by Toni Cade Bambara, such as "Blues Ain't No Mockingbird"
- ◆ Langston Hughes's children's book *Tales of Simple*
- ◆ Margaret Walker's novel *Jubilee*
- ◆ the spiritual "Oh, Freedom"
- ◆ Malcolm X's autobiography (written with Alex Haley)
- ◆ Gwendolyn Brooks's poem "We Real Cool"
- ◆ Derek Walcott's epic poem *Omeros*
- ◆ Alain Locke's essay "The New Negro"
- ◆ the prologue to Ralph Ellison's novel *Invisible Man*
- ◆ Darwin Turner's critical essay "The Negro Dramatist's Image of the Universe, 1920-1960"
- ◆ Toni Morrison's literary treatise *Playing in the Dark: Whiteness and the Literary Imagination*
- ◆ Martin Luther King, Jr.'s speech "I Have a Dream"
- ◆ Lerone Bennett, Jr.'s history *Made in the Water: Great Moments in Black American History*
- ◆ Lorraine Hansberry's play *A Raisin in the Sun*

Reading the Black Female Writer

Age/Grade Level or Audience: College women's studies groups; adult civic clubs, such as Business and Professional Women's League, American Association of University Women, National Organization of Women, and League of Women Voters.

Description: Organize a reading circle to discuss black feminism as revealed through current fiction.

Procedure: Have different members volunteer to read short works by contemporary black female authors, particularly Margaret Walker's "Lineage," Nikki Giovanni's "Mothers," June Jordan's "For My Mother," and Alice Walker's "Women," "Uncles," and "For My Sister Molly Who in the Fifties." Provide each reader a list of themes and issues to examine, for example:

- ◆ empowerment
- ◆ emotional strengths
- ◆ male/female parental roles
- ◆ commitment
- ◆ health issues
- ◆ reproductive issues

- ◆ education issues
- ◆ employment issues
- ◆ social equality
- ◆ alienation
- ◆ family violence
- ◆ spirituality

Budget: $$

Sources:

Provide a wide selection from these choices:

Angelou, Maya, *And Still I Rise* (poetry), Random House, 1978.

Angelou, *I Know Why the Caged Bird Sings,* Random House, 1970.

Angelou, *Now Sheba Sings the Song,* Dial Books, 1987.

Campbell, Bebe Moore, *Your Blues Ain't Like Mine,* Putnam, 1992.

Cary, Lorene, *Black Ice,* Vintage Books, 1992.

Giovanni, Nikki, *My House,* Morrow, 1972.

Golden, Marita, *And Do Remember Me,* Doubleday, 1992.

Jordan, June, *Things That I Do in the Dark: Selected Poetry,* Random House, 1977.

Lewis, Mary, *Herstory: Black Female Rites of Passage,* African American Images, 1988.

McMillan, Terry, *Waiting to Exhale,* G. K. Hall, 1993.

Morrison, Toni, *Beloved,* Knopf, 1987

Morrison, *Jazz,* Knopf, 1992.

Morrison, *Song of Solomon,* Knopf, 1977

Morrison, *Sula,* Knopf, 1973.

Naylor, Gloria, *Bailey's Cafe,* Harcourt Brace Jovanovich, 1992.

Naylor, *The Women of Brewster Place,* Viking, 1982.

Pemberton, Gayle, *The Hottest Water in Chicago: On Family, Race, Time, and American Culture,* Faber & Faber. 1992.

Petry, Ann, *Tituba of Salem Village,* Crowell, 1964.

Stetson, Erlene, *Black Sister: Poetry by Black American Women, 1746-1980,* Indiana University Press, 1981.

Walker, Alice, *The Color Purple,* Harcourt Brace Jovanovich, 1982.

Walker, *Possessing the Secret of Joy,* Harcourt Brace Jovanovich, 1992.

Walker, *Revolutionary Petunias and Other Poems,* Harcourt Brace Jovanovich, 1973.

Walker, Margaret, *Jubilee,* Houghton, 1965, reprinted, Bantam, 1981.

Alternative Applications: Study pairs of feminist poets, essayists, novelists, dramatists, journalists, orators, and short story writers, one black and one non-black. Some likely white writers include Margaret Atwood, Anne Tyler, Margaret Sanger, Kate Chopin, Gloria Steinem, Amy Tan, Susan Faludi, Edith Wharton, Ellen Gilchrist, Molly Ivins, Ellen Goodman, Florence King, Katharine Anne Porter, Susan B. Anthony, Olive Ann Burns, Sara Teasdale, Molly Yard, Françoise Sagan, Carolyn Kiser, Emma Goldman, Harriette Arnow, Robin Morgan, Helen Brownmiller, and Susan Straight. Determine the relative significance of racism and sex.

Steinbeck on American Racism

Age/Grade Level or Audience: Middle school and high school literature and history classes; civic groups; literary societies and book clubs.

Description: Read selections from John Steinbeck's *Travels with Charley* and *America and Americans*.

Procedure: Read aloud from John Steinbeck's observations on forced integration in New Orleans, Louisiana, found in Book Four of *Travels with Charley*. Follow up with his essay on slavery in America and Americans. Make the following interpretive comments:

◆ While traveling America during the volatile 1960s, Steinbeck chose to watch the forced integration of public schools.

◆ He described the blatant racism of white women directed at small black children "a kind of frightening witches' Sabbath.... These were a crazy actors playing to a crazy audience."

◆ He compared his own childhood experiences in Salinas, California, but had too little contact with black people to place himself in the position of southerners.

◆ He commented, "I knew I was not wanted in the South. When people are engaged in something they are not proud of, they do not welcome witnesses. In fact, they come to believe the witness causes the trouble."

◆ In *America and Americans,* he accounted for the strength of black people by explaining how humble diet, hard work, and struggle accomplished what Charles Darwin described as strengthening of the race by "survival of the fittest."

Budget: $

Sources:
Steinbeck, John, *America and Americans,* Viking Press, 1966.
Steinbeck, *Travels with Charley: In Search of America,* Viking Press, 1962, reprinted, Penguin Books, 1986.

Alternative Applications: Ask students to role-play parts in the first forced integrations of public schools. Display photographs of the era showing state police, governors George Wallace and Lester Maddox, and Orville Faubus, James Meredith, and Autherine Lucy, all of whom played prominent parts in the mixing of races in schools.

Math

An African-American Profile

Age/Grade Level or Audience: High school and community college math, computer science, and economics classes.

Description: Present an audio-visual overview of the black American's standard of living in contrast with whites, Asian-Americans, Hispanics, and native Americans.

Procedure: Have students create overhead transparencies, computer disks and databases, or original filmstrips of charts, graphs, and maps featuring data about the lifestyle of the black population in the United States. Individual graphics should cover these topics:

- population numbers and distribution among states
- property and business ownership
- entrepreneurial success
- birth, death, marital, and health statistics
- participation in the military
- literacy and educational attainment
- crime and prison population
- welfare statistics
- representation in the Senate and House of Representatives
- numbers of black police chiefs, mayors, governors, judges, and other municipal and state authorities and other pertinent governmental facts

Budget: $$

Sources:

Software programs such as Get S.M.A.R.T., PCensus-USA, and Statmaster Desktop Demographics from American Demographics, P.O. Box 68, Ithaca, NY 14851; telephone: (800)828-1133, fax: 607-273-3196.

Asante, Molefi K., *Historical and Cultural Atlas of African Americans,* Macmillan, 1991.

"Black Income Up … Slightly," *Emerge,* October 1992, p. 14.

Chadwick, Bruce A., and Tim B. Heaton, eds., *Statistical Handbook on the American Family,* Oryx Press, 1992.

Horton, Carrell Peterson, and Jessie Carney Smith, *Statistical Record of Black America,* 2nd ed., Gale, 1993.

Johnson, Dwight L., "We, the Black Americans," U.S. Department of Commerce, Bureau of the Census, 1986.

Kane, Joseph Nathan, *Facts about the States,* H. W. Wilson, 1989.

Kazin, Alfred, "Cry, the Beloved Country," *Forbes,* September 14, 1992, pp. 140-56.

Shantz, Nancy B., and Patricia Q. Brown, "Trends in Racial/Ethnic Enrollment in Higher Education," U.S. Department of Education, Office of Educational Research and Improvement, 1990.

Alternative Applications: Present an oral report contrasting the lifestyles of all races. Draw correlations between these topics: education and attainment; urban residence and crime; major illnesses and availability of health care; infant morality and prenatal care; and dietary deficiency and household income. Use the facts and figures as a basis for developing computer graphics in line, vertical bar, and horizontal bar graphs and pie charts. Present your findings in lectures, local newspapers, or other forums.

 ## An African-American Theme Park

Age/Grade Level or Audience: High school geometry, computer science, business, and drafting classes.

Description: Lay out an African-American theme park.

Procedure: Have students utilize computer equipment or drafting boards to plot a schematic drawing of a large theme park based on the culture, history, lifestyle, and interests of African-Americans. Include food courts, rides, nature trails, halls of history, displays, and trading centers where African commodities and African-American books, tapes, jewelry, pottery, carvings, decorations, tableware, and clothing are sold.

Budget: $

Sources:

Emulate other theme parks, such as Disneyland, Disney World, Six Flags over Georgia, or Busch Gardens. Refer to visual stimuli, such as the filmstrip "Black Odyssey: Migration to the Cities" from the Center for the Humanities, or *The History of Africa,* a computer program from KnowMaster.

Alternative Applications: Have students divide into groups and make mock-up attractions of an African-American theme park out of cardboard, clay, balsa wood, styrofoam, or other light, malleable materials. Conclude by assembling the attractions on a sand table or library display case. Invite students interested in business to think up posters, television and radio spots, billboards, T-shirts, coffee mugs, magazine layouts, and other forms of advertisement for the park.

An African Museum

Age/Grade Level or Audience: Middle school, high school, and college drafting, computer science, physics, art, architecture, and history classes.

Description: Design a museum to house a black art collection.

Procedure: Have students select a focus for a museum collection, such as early African art, African culture, African-American lifestyles and art, African influences on Caribbean watercolor, architecture, and nature photography, or other topics. Then have the group design a building to display the collection so that people of all ages and backgrounds can gain from the experience of visiting and viewing the displays. Include the following data:

- ◆ accessible entries for the handicapped
- ◆ height and angle of ceilings
- ◆ lighting sources and types
- ◆ lengths of hallways
- ◆ acoustical enhancements
- ◆ special groupings, such as African works of the precolonial period
- ◆ revolving display cases for delicate works, such as woven goods and delicate masks
- ◆ interactive showings for children
- ◆ art workshops
- ◆ security systems

Create a brochure that will guide visitors to the displays. Arrange materials in logical order: for example, list displays chronologically or by content, such as African clothing, cooking vessels, jewelry, weapons, musical instruments, and games.

Budget: $$

Sources:

Bomani, Asake, and Belvie Rooks, *African and Caribbean Artists in Paris,* Q.E.D. Press, 1992.

Bomani and Rooks, *Paris Connections: African American Artists in Paris,* Q.E.D. Press, 1992.

Felix, Marc L., *Mwana Hiti: Life and Art of the Matrilineal Bantu of Tanzania,* F. Jahn, 1990.

McElroy, Guy, Facing History: *The Black Image in American Art, 1710-1940*, edited by Christopher C. French, Bedford Arts/Corcoran Gallery, 1990.

Turle, Gillies, *The Hidden Art of the Maasai: Always Something New and Strange out of Africa,* Knopf, 1992.

Alternative Applications: Create a memorable, functional monument to African-American contributions. Design a geometric shape that will appeal to the eye and establish a cohesive impression. Select building materials, landscaping, sculpture, bas-relief, and/or inscription. Choose a significant location, such as a city on the banks of the Mississippi River or near the Charleston Slave Market Museum.

Census Comparisons

Age/Grade Level or Audience: Middle school and high school math and computer science classes.

Description: List and compare the black urban population centers of the United States.

Procedure: Have students collect census figures on the growth of urban centers, particularly New York, Chicago, Los Angeles, Seattle, Detroit, Philadelphia, Washington, D.C., Baltimore, Houston, Atlanta, Dallas, Newark, St. Louis, San Francisco, New Orleans, Memphis, Cleveland, Miami, Birmingham, Norfolk, and Pittsburgh. Assign charts illustrating shifts in racial concentrations in these areas, including the growth of Hispanic, native American, and Asian populations. Have students include figures on areas that have the least diversity of racial population, especially the upper Midwest.

Budget: $

Sources:

Asante, Molefi K., *Historical and Cultural Atlas of African Americans,* Macmillan, 1991.

"Black Income Up ... Slightly," *Emerge,* October 1992, p. 14.

Boyer, Richard, and David Savageau, *Places Rated Almanac: Your Guide to Finding the Best Places to Live in America,* Prentice-Hall Travel, 1989.

Carpenter, Allan, *Facts about the Cities,* H. W. Wilson, 1992.

Horton, Carrell Peterson, and Jessie Carney Smith, *Statistical Record of Black America,* 2nd ed., Gale, 1993.

Johnson, Dwight L., "We, the Black Americans," U.S. Department of Commerce, Bureau of the Census, 1986.

Kazin, Alfred, "Cry, the Beloved Country," *Forbes,* September 14, 1992, pp. 140-156.

"Rise in Diverse Populations," *American Demographics,* October 91, p. 26.

Shantz, Nancy B., and Patricia Q. Brown, "Trends in Racial/Ethnic Enrollment in Higher Education," U.S. Department of Education, Office of Educational Research and Improvement, 1990.

Alternative Applications: Organize a roundtable to discuss the "what-ifs" of demographics. Consider these possibilities:

- ◆ equal distribution of races among all states
- ◆ integrated housing patterns
- ◆ job opportunities and small business starts for nonwhites
- ◆ a greater number of mixed race people
- ◆ enforcement of equal opportunity laws

Counting in Swahili

Age/Grade Level or Audience: Kindergarten through primary grades.

Description: Teach students to count from one to ten in Swahili.

Procedure: Present a brief description of Swahili, how old a language it is, where it is spoken, and who speaks it. Then repeat the first ten numbers in Swahili until students have them memorized.

- 1: **moja** [mow'-jah]
- 2: **mbili** [uhm'-bee'-lee]
- 3: **tatu** [tah'-too]
- 4: **nne** [uhn'-nay]
- 5: **tano** [tah'-no]
- 6: **sita** [see'-tah]
- 7: **saba** [sah'-buh]
- 8: **nane** [nah'-nay]
- 9: **tisa** [tee'-suh]
- 10: **kumi** [koo'-mee]

Refer to these numbers in future counting exercises.

Budget: $

Sources:
Haskins, Jim, *Count Your Way through Africa,* Carolrhoda Books, 1989.

Alternative Applications: Use each number alongside its pronunciation and a uniquely African representation of the meaning:

- ◆ one Mount Kilimanjaro or Niger River
- ◆ two wildebeest or gnus
- ◆ three ostriches or emus
- ◆ four yams or bowls of fufu
- ◆ five grass huts or village compounds

    ◆ six Ashanti drums or finger pianos
    ◆ seven diamonds or pyramids
    ◆ eight Maasai women or Mali children
    ◆ nine hyenas or hippos
    ◆ ten baobab trees or pyrethrum daisies

Graphing Racial Data

Age/Grade Level or Audience: Middle school, high school, and college mathematics, economics, and computer science classes.

Description: Create a series of graphs that depict African or Caribbean lifestyles.

Procedure: Have students locate and discuss demographic studies of African, Caribbean, and African-American peoples, particularly these topics:

    ◆ urbanization and industrialization
    ◆ marriage and divorce
    ◆ disease, death, and birth rates
    ◆ religions
    ◆ education and literacy
    ◆ commerce and standard of living
    ◆ location and patterns of migration.

Refer to *USA Today* for ideas on graphing. Have students utilize these facts as they practice drawing, illustrating, and coloring horizontal and vertical bar, pie, or line graphs, either by hand or on the computer. Suggest captions for each graph. Arrange the finished graphs in a school, museum, civic, or library display or a newspaper feature.

Budget: $$

Sources:

"Black Population in the United States: A Chartbook," U.S. Department of Commerce, Bureau of the Census, 1990.

Foley, June, Mark Hoffmann, and Tom McGuire, eds., *World Almanac,* Pharos Books, 1992.

Horton, Carrell Peterson, and Jessie Carney Smith, *Statistical Record of Black America,* 2nd ed., Gale, 1993.

Kane, Joseph Nathan, *Facts about the States,* H. W. Wilson, 1989.

Kone-Diabi, Aissatu, "Family Planning," *World Health,* August-September 1986, pp. 10-12.

Nordland, Rod, "Africa in the Plague Years," *Newsweek,* November 24, 1986, pp. 44-47.

Steinhart, Peter, "Beyond Pills and Condoms: As Africa's Population Mounts, What More Can Be Done?" *Audubon,* January 1991, pp. 22-25.

Alternative Applications: Have students present a select body of data using all four methods of computer graphing. For example, present the following facts and assign groups of students to think of ways to demonstrate the following body of facts about white and black population figures for the United States:

Date	% Black	Black	White
1620	1.0	20	2,180
1630	2.0	60	4,586
1640	2.2	597	26,037
1650	3.2	1,600	47,768
1660	3.9	2,920	72,138
1670	4.0	4,535	107,400
1680	4.6	6.971	144,536
1690	8.0	16,729	193,643
1700	11.1	27,000	223,000
1710	13.5	44,000	286,000
1720	14.8	68,000	397,000
1730	14.5	91,000	538,000
1740	17.7	160,000	745,000
1750	20.2	236,000	934,000
1760	20.4	325,000	1,267,000
1770	21.4	459,000	1,688,000
1780	20.7	575,000	2,204,000
1790	19.3	757,000	3,172,000
1800	18.9	1,002,000	4,306,000
1810	19.0	1,378,000	5,862,000
1820	18.4	1,772,000	7,867,000
1830	18.1	2,329,000	10,537,000
1840	16.8	2,874,000	14,196,000
1850	15.7	3,639,000	19,553,000
1860	14.1	4,442,000	26,923,000
1870	13.5	5,392,000	33,589,000
1880	13.1	6,581,000	43,403,000
1890	12.3	7,389,000	55,101,000
1900	11.6	7,760,000	66,809,000
1910	10.7	9,827,000	81,364,000
1920	9.9	10,463,000	94,120,000
1930	9.7	11,891,000	108,864,000
1940	9.7	12,865,000	118,214,000
1950	9.9	15,042,000	134,982,000
1960	10.5	18,871,000	158,831,000
1970	11.1	22,530,000	177,748,000
1980	11.7	26,495,000	227,061,000
1990	12.1	29,986,000	249,924,000

Have groups work together to answer the following questions utilizing conclusions drawn from a study of the data:

◆ Why do population shifts occur, such as migrations or resettlements?

◆ What missing information skews this study of racial population, such as ways of categorizing mixed blood people?

◆ How could war, disease, natural catastrophes, and laws affect a rise or fall in percentage?

◆ What change in figures might a demographer predict for the coming century?

◆ How might methods of studying census affect future data?

The Migrant Scene

Age/Grade Level or Audience: Middle school, high school, and college computer science, sociology, and history classes.

Description: Write a history of the evolution of migrant labor as a significant aspect of Southern agriculture.

Procedure: Organize a paper to cover the following aspects of the history of migrant labor. Through computer graphics, generate facts and figures to depict the migrant situation state by state, which clearly indicates that black people do *not* comprise a major portion of seasonal workers. Include figures on race, age, health, education, on-the-job injuries, and longevity:

◆ Because of the demands of the job, 70 percent of migrant workers are young, averaging 31 years.

◆ Only 4 percent are under the age of 18.

◆ The average age of African-American migrants is 40.

◆ Only 29 percent of seasonal farm workers are women.

◆ 64 percent of migrants are married.

◆ 29 percent have never been married.

◆ Only 38 percent are U.S.-born, the rest coming from Asia, the Caribbean, and Latin America. Only 2 percent of American migrants are black.

◆ Of U.S. citizens who follow the harvests for a living, 60 percent are white, 34 percent Hispanic, and 5 percent black. The remaining 1 percent are mostly Asian and native American.

Budget: $

Sources:

Rose Lucas, Association of Farmworker Opportunity Programs, 408 Seventh St. S.E., Washington, DC 20003; telephone: (202)543-3443, fax: 202-546-2331.

Ashabranner, Brent, *Dark Harvest: Migrant Farmworkers in America,* Dodd, Mead, 1985.

Kane, Joseph Nathan, *Facts about the States,* H. W. Wilson, 1989.

Alternative Applications: In the text of an analytic paper, indicate the following conclusions:

- ◆ how migrant labor replaced slave labor during the Reconstruction Era
- ◆ where migrant labor has become most profitable in the South
- ◆ a racial breakdown of the migrant labor force, including illegal workers from Haiti and other parts of the Caribbean
- ◆ lifestyles of migrant families
- ◆ debilitating problems faced by migrants, notably interruption of education, alcoholism and illegal drug use, infant mortality, malnutrition, health problems, substandard housing and sanitation, domestic violence, and work-related accidents
- ◆ congressional efforts to improve life for migrants
- ◆ private philanthropic groups that help migrants break the poverty cycle, such as Habitat for Humanity, National Farm Worker Ministry, National Migrant Workers Council, National Association of State Directors of Migrant Education, Migrant Dropout Reconnection Program, Interstate Migrant Education Council, Farmworker Justice Fund, East Coast Migrant Health Project, Association of Farmworker Opportunity Programs, and Amnesty International

Schematic Drawings

Age/Grade Level or Audience: Middle school and high school geometry and computer drafting classes.

Description: Create a gallery of schematic drawings of inventions by African-Americans.

Procedure: Have students study important inventions by black scientists and engineers, such as these:

- ◆ Garret Augustus Morgan's four-way traffic signal and gas mask
- ◆ Andrew J. Beard's automatic railcar coupler
- ◆ Henry Blair's corn and cotton planters
- ◆ Benjamin Banneker's wooden clock
- ◆ Norbert Rillieux's sugar refiner
- ◆ Granville T. Woods's railroad telegraph
- ◆ David N. Crosthwait's vacuum heating system
- ◆ Otis Boykin's stimulator for an artificial heart
- ◆ Lewis Temple's improved whaling harpoon
- ◆ Ozzie S. Williams's radar search beacon
- ◆ Elijah J. McCoy's automatic lubricating cup

Assign the class to draw multiple views of the mechanisms.

Budget: $$

Sources:

Haber, Louis, *Black Pioneers of Science and Invention,* Harcourt Brace Jovanovich, 1970, reprinted, 1991.

International Library of Negro Life and History, Publishers Co., 1969.

James, Portia P., *The Real McCoy: African-American Invention and Innovation, 1619-1930*, Smithsonian Institution Press, 1989.

Klein, Aaron E., and Cynthia L. Klein, *The Better Mousetrap: A Miscellany of Gadgets, Labor-saving Devices, and Inventions that Intrigue,* Beaufort Books, 1982.

Logan, Rayford W., and Michael R. Winston, eds., *Dictionary of American Negro Biography,* Norton, 1982.

Alternative Applications: Pair drawings illustrating earlier models that these inventions improved on. For example, illustrate the more primitive sugar-making systems used on Caribbean and Southern plantations as opposed to Norbert Rillieux's modernized version, which reduced the tedium of labor-intensive work and spared the workers from accidents such as burns, drowning, and scalding; or contrast Benjamin Banneker's wooden clock with time systems of earlier civilizations, such as water clocks, slotted candles, and sundials.

Music

African Musical Instruments

Age/Grade Level or Audience: Elementary and middle school music and crafts classes; religious schools; scout troops; 4-H clubs.

Description: Present pictures and information about African musical instruments.

Procedure: Using reference books, recordings, films, filmstrips, and videos, acquaint students with the sounds and uses of African musical instruments, such as the notched flute, musical bow, gondje, kalungu, double gong, drumstick, xylophone, tambourine, apentemma drum, atumpan or talking drum, fontomfrom drum, donno drum, harp, lyre, zither, trumpet, bells, fiddle, mibra or thumb piano, and hand rattle. Point out that audiences played their own bodies by slapping their hands and legs, stamping their feet, vibrating their tongues against the roofs of their mouths, and clicking their fingers and tongues.

Divide African musical instruments into four basic categories:

- **aerophones:** instruments that make music from air vibration, such as the notched flute, animal horn or calabash trumpet, reed flute, oboe, clarinet, double-reed pipe, mouth bow, and whistle
- **chordophones:** instruments that coax musical tones from string vibrations, such as the lyre, zither, lute, one-string fiddle, earth-bow, hand piano, and harp
- **idiophones:** instruments that vibrate in every part, as with the thumb piano, calabash rattles, scrapers, xylophones, marimbas, beaded nets, lithophones, clappers, sistrum, and bells
- **membranophones:** instruments that require a tightly stretched membrane or skin to carry the vibration caused by a blow of the hand or a stick, as with the talking drum, tension drum, hourglass drum, slit drum, friction drum, water drum, and iron gong

Note that a few instruments combine techniques, for example the tambourine, which mates a vibrating membrane with the sound of clashing metal disks.

Budget: $$

Sources:

Bebey, Francis, *African Music: A People's Art,* Harrap, 1975.

Nketia, J. H. Kwabena, *The Music of Africa,* Gollancz, 1975.

Sing Children Sing: Songs of the Congo, Caedmon Records.

Warren, Dr. Fred, and Lee Warren, *The Music of Africa: An Introduction,* Prentice-Hall, 1970.

Alternative Applications: Present recorded African songs for special occasions, such as homecomings, weddings, harvest festivals, coming-of-age ceremonies, coronations, and funerals.

- ◆ Discuss the mood that each song evokes, such as patriotism, pride, grief, gratitude, hope, or joy.
- ◆ Have students write their reactions to each song. Discuss the roles of the cantor or leader and the griot, the tribal narrator who educated citizens by reciting the tribe's history.
- ◆ Differentiate between monotonal Arab style, polyphonic Negro style, and yodeling, polyphonic Bushman-Pygmy style.
- ◆ Include technical information, such as the importance of syncopation, rhythmic patterns, and descant.
- ◆ Have a volunteer group make a finger piano from strips of bamboo cut in varied lengths and laid across a half gourd, which serves as an echo chamber.

African Music American Style

Age/Grade Level or Audience: High school, college, and adult music groups and societies.

Description: Discuss similarities between traditional African music and the styles of famous black American singers.

Procedure: Play recordings of traditional African music, then play the works of these performers:

Stevie Wonder	B. B. King	Ray Charles
Natalie Cole	Brook Benton	Louis Armstrong
Cab Calloway	Bob Marley	Lou Rawls
Lionel Ritchie	Ella Fitzgerald	Pearl Bailey
Bessie Smith	Count Basie	Billie Holiday

Lena Horne	Mahalia Jackson	Lionel Hampton
Ethel Waters	Fats Domino	Smokey Robinson
Louis Jordan	Jelly Roll Morton	Charlie Pride
Jimi Hendrix	Sarah Vaughan	Roland Hayes
Marian Anderson	Mary Wells	Harry Belafonte
Herbie Hancock	BeBe and CeCe Winans	Bo Diddley
Diana Ross	John Coltrane	Roberta Flack
Otis Redding	Ronny Jordon	

Lead a discussion of hints of African tradition in American soul, calypso, ragtime, reggae, black country, jazz, hip-hop, be-bop, swing, hymns, scat, gospel, spirituals, protest songs, and rhythm and blues.

Budget: $$

Sources:
Recordings such as the soundtrack from the PBS series *The Civil War,* "Great Gospel Performances, Vols. 1 & 2," "Count Basie and His Orchestra: Ain't Misbehavin'," "Nat King Cole: The Trio Recordings," "Happy Birthday Duke, Vols. 1-5," "The Essential Jimi Hendrix," "The Rhythm of Resistance: Music of Black South Africa," "Ladysmith Black Mambazo: Journey of Dreams," "Sing! The Songs of Joe Raposo," and "Louis Armstrong: The California Concerts."

Bordowitz, Hank, "Jazz Videos Take Us Back to Yesterday," *Emerge,* October 1992, p. 72.

Duncan, Amy, "Ambassadors of Afropop," *Christian Science Monitor,* October 1989, pp. 74-77.

Friedwald, Will, *Jazz Singing: America's Great Voices from Bessie Smith to Bebop and Beyond,* Scribner's, 1990.

Jennings, Nicholas, "Africa's Cult Musician," *Maclean's,* October 13, 1986, pp. 8-9.

Labate, John, "Africa's Hot New Export: Music," *Fortune,* May 4, 1992, p. 18.

Alternative Applications: Organize a panel to discuss recurrent themes in African, Caribbean, and African-American music, such as love, relationships between men and women, hardship, yearning for freedom, trust in God, and work. Compare these themes to those of Appalachian folk tunes, country and western, songs from films, and show tunes. For example:

Nobody Knows de Trouble I See
Nobody knows de trouble I see,
Nobody knows but Jesus;
Nobody knows de trouble I see,
Glory hallelujah.
Sometimes I'm up
Sometimes I'm down,
Oh, yes, Lord;
Sometimes I'm almost to de groun',

Oh, yes, Lord.
Altho' you see me goin' 'long so,
Oh, yes, Lord;
I have my troubles here below,
Oh, yes, Lord.

African Rhythm Band

Age/Grade Level or Audience: Kindergarten and elementary music and crafts classes; religious schools; classes for the handicapped.

Description: Create and play African instruments.

Procedure: Help participants to make their own African musical instruments. For example, try these:

◆ Make a banjo from a shoe box lid with a hole cut in it. Stretch thick and thin rubber bands lengthwise across the box. Pluck strings separately or strum them in a series.

◆ Make a xylophone from wooden tomato stakes cut into two one-foot lengths. Lay them parallel to each other and about three inches apart. Place varying lengths of aluminum or plastic pipe or bamboo strips horizontally across the two stakes. Tap with a mallet made from wooden dowels with a rubber ball pushed onto the end.

◆ Make a thumb piano by gluing bamboo strips or popsicle sticks of varying lengths between two wooden blocks. Play by plucking with the fingers.

◆ Make pairs of finger cymbals by pushing thick rubber bands through holes cut into two bottle caps or metal lids.

◆ Make bongos from oatmeal boxes with the ends removed. Attach two rubber circles cut from heavy balloons by fitting them over each end and lacing with heavy twine. Play with the tips of your fingers.

Budget: $$$

Sources:
Bebey, Francis, *African Music: A People's Art,* Harrap, 1975.
Nketia, J. H. Kwabena, *The Music of Africa,* Gollancz, 1975.
Simons, Robin, *Recyclepedia: Games, Science Equipment, and Crafts from Recycled Materials,* Houghton Mifflin, 1976.
Sing Children Sing: Songs of the Congo, Caedmon Records.
Warren, Dr. Fred, and Lee Warren, *The Music of Africa: An Introduction,* Prentice-Hall, 1970.

Alternative Applications: Play African or Caribbean songs and have band members keep time with homemade or purchased rhythm band instruments. Include simple rhythm instruments, such as sticks, scrapers, gourds, tambourines, shakers, and rattles.

Antiphonal Chant

Age/Grade Level or Audience: Elementary and middle school music classes; music societies.

Description: Explore the African system of arranging songs into antiphonal chants.

Procedure: Hand out song sheets that depict the separation of lines into those sung by the cantor or leader and the reply of the assembly or chorus. For example:

Go Down Moses
Cantor: When Israel was in Egypt's land,
Chorus: Let my people go.
Cantor: Oppress'd so hard they could not stand,
Chorus: Let my people go.
Cantor: Go down, Moses,
Way down in Egypt lan'
Tell ole Pharaoh,
Chorus: Let my people go!

I Ain't Gwine Study War No More
Cantor: Gwine to lay down my burden,
Chorus: Down by the riverside,
down by the riverside,
down by the riverside.
Cantor: Gwine to lay down my burden,
Chorus: Down by the riverside, to study war no more.

Swing Low, Sweet Chariot
Cantor: I looked over Jordan and what did I see,
Chorus: Comin' fo' to carry me home.
Cantor: A band of angels comin' after me,
Chorus: Comin' fo' to carry me home.
Cantor: If you get there before I do,
Chorus: Comin' fo' to carry me home.
Cantor: Tell all my friends I'm comin' too,
Chorus: Comin' fo' to carry me home.

Brother Rabbit

Cantor: Brother rabbit, brother rabbit your ears mighty long,
Chorus: Yes, brother possum, I b'lieve they're put on wrong, however,
Unison: Ev'ry little soul must shine, shine,
Ev'ry little soul must shine,
Rise and shine, rise and shine, rise and shine.

Wade in the Water

Cantor: See that ban' all dress'd in white?
Chorus: It look lak the childr'n of the Israelite.
Cantor: See that ban' all dress'd in red?
Chorus: It look lak the ban' that Moses led.
Unison: Wade in de water
Wade in de water,
Wade in de water.
God's a-gonna trouble de water.

I'm Gonna Sing

Cantor: Oh, I'm a-gonna sing,
Chorus: Gonna sing, gonna sing,
Gonna sing all along the way.
Cantor: One day you'll hear the trumpet sound
Chorus: Gonna sing all along the way.
Cantor: The trumpet sound the world around
Chorus: Gonna sing all along the way.
Cantor: Oh, Jordan's stream is wide and cold,
Chorus: Gonna sing all along the way.
Cantor: It chills the body but not the soul,
Chorus: Gonna sing all along the way.

Budget: $

Sources:

Video- or audiocassettes of the films *Glory* (1990) and the nine-part PBS series, *The Civil War* (1990).

Silverman, Jerry, *Songs of Protest and Civil Rights,* Chelsea House, 1992.

Alternative Applications: Lead a discussion of the interplay between a cantor or spokesperson and an assembly. Play a recording or videotape of Martin Luther King, Jr.'s "I Have a Dream" speech or some of the speeches of Jesse Jackson to illustrate how antiphony affects American assemblies, where black people follow African patterns by replying to the cantor's statements.

Band Music

Originator: Bob Taylor, trumpeter, band director, retired teacher, Hickory, North Carolina.

Age/Grade Level or Audience: High school, college, and community bands and jazz ensembles.

Description: Offer a program of serious or classical band music featuring black themes and composers.

Procedure: Present a program of works by black composers. Some possibilities include these:

- ◆ Quincy Jones's *The Pawnbroker, For Love of Ivy, The Wiz, Cactus Flower, In Cold Blood,* "Even When You Cry," "Grace," and "Ironsides"
- ◆ selections from Stevie Wonder's *Songs in the Key of Life,* particularly "Love's in Need of Love Today" and "Isn't She Lovely"
- ◆ W. C. Handy's "St. Louis Blues"
- ◆ James P. Johnson's "Carolina Shout" or "Mule Walk"
- ◆ Harry T. Burleigh's "Six Plantation Melodies"
- ◆ Thomas "Fats" Waller's "Ain't Misbehavin'"
- ◆ Pinetop Smith's "Pinetop's Boogie-Woogie"
- ◆ Meade Lux Lewis's "Honky Tonk Train Blues"
- ◆ "When the Saints Go Marchin' In"
- ◆ Kid Ory's "Society Blues"
- ◆ Jelly Roll Morton's "Black Bottom Stomp"
- ◆ Duke Ellington's "Cotton Tail," "Black and Tan Fantasy," "Mood Indigo," "Satin Doll," "Black, Brown and Beige," "Liberian Suite," "A Drum Is a Woman," "My People," and "New Orleans Suite"
- ◆ Billy Strayhorn's "Take the A Train," "Chelsea Bridge," "Warm Valley," and "Jack the Bear"
- ◆ Count Basie's "One O'Clock Jump," "Swingin' the Blues," "Send for You Yesterday, and Here You Come Today," and "Boogie-Woogie"
- ◆ Erskine Hawkins's "Tuxedo Junction"
- ◆ Trummy Young's "It Ain't What You Do, It's the Way That You Do It"
- ◆ Thelonius Monk's "Criss Cross," "Misterioso," and "Round Midnight"
- ◆ Tad Dameron's "If You Could See Me Now," "Dial B for Beauty," "Our Delight," and "The Scene Is Clean"

Budget: $$$

Sources:

Anderson, E. Ruth, *The Contemporary American Composers: A Biographical Dictionary,* G. K. Hall, 1982.

International Who's Who in Music and Musicians' Directory, 11th ed., Melrose, 1988.

Jones, James T., "Choirs Use Funky Means to Give God Name Recognition," *USA Today,* August 26, 1992, p. 9D.

Tischler, Alice, *Fifteen Black American Composers: A Bibliography of Their Works,* Harmonie Park Press, 1981.

Black Music Videos

Age/Grade Level or Audience: All ages.

Description: Spark up a Black History Month celebration with a music video.

Procedure: Hold a neighborhood, church, civic, or school celebration featuring a great black musician or musical movement. Show a music video, for example:

- *Aretha Franklin: Queen of Soul*
- *Aretha Franklin: Ridin' on the Freeway*
- *B. B. King and Friends: A Night of Red Hot Blues*
- *B. B. King: Live at Nicks*
- *B. B. King: Live in Africa*
- *Chaka Khan: Live*
- *Diana Ross: In Concert*
- *Diana Ross: Visions of Diana*
- *Fats Domino and Friends*
- *Harlem Harmonies*
- *Herbie Hancock: Jazz Africa*
- *Ike and Tina Turner Show*
- *The Incomparable Nat King Cole, Volumes I and II*
- *Johnny Mathis: Chances Are*
- *Konkombe: The Nigerian Pop Music Scene*
- *La Toya Jackson*
- *Louis Armstrong: Satchmo*
- *Mahalia Jackson*
- *Marvin Gaye: Greatest Hits Live*
- *Marvin Gaye: Motown Presents*
- *Natalie Cole: The Unforgettable Concert*
- *Otis Redding: Live in Monterey*
- *Pointer Sisters: Live in Africa*
- *Quincy Jones: A Celebration*
- *Reggae Superstars in Concert*
- *Spike Lee: A Cappella*
- *Thelonious Monk: Music in Monk's Time*
- *Whitney Houston: Welcome Home Troops*

◆ *Wynton Marsalis: Blues and Swing*
◆ *Ziggy Marley and the Melody Makers*

Budget: $$$

Sources:
Tapes from video rental services.
Furtaw, Julia C., *The Video Source Book,* 14th ed., Gale, 1993.

Alternative Applications: Have a volunteer outline major musical movements, such as hip-hop, swing, rock, rap, be-bop, rhythm and blues, jazz, and reggae. List top performers in each category.

Choral Music

Age/Grade Level or Audience: High school, college, and community chorus; church choir.

Description: Offer a program of serious or classical choral music by black composers or arrangers.

Procedure: Present a variety of choral works and solos that underscore the hardships and joys of the black experience. A worthy modern composer to feature is Leslie Adams (1932-), creator of Psalm 21, *The Ode to Life, Hosanna to the Son of David, Madrigal, Creole Girl, The Heart of a Woman, I Want to Die Easy, Man's Presence, Prayer, The Righteous Man, Since You Went Away, Under the Greenwood Tree, Vocalise, We Shall Overcome, For You There Is No Song, Dunbar Songs, There Was an Old Man, Tall Tales,* and the opera *Blake.* Other possibilities include these:

◆ Quincy Jones's *The Wiz, Give Me the Night, E.T.,* "We Are the World"
◆ Anthony Davis's opera *The Life and Times of Malcolm X*
◆ Edward Boatner's *The Story of the Spirituals*
◆ Harry Lawrence Freeman's *Voodoo* or *Martyr*
◆ Robert Nathaniel Dett's *The Chariot Jubilee*
◆ Harry T. Burleigh's *Spirituals,* "Southland Sketches," "The Lovely Dark and Lonely One," "Little Mother of Mine," "Deep River," "The Prayer"
◆ James A. Bland's "Carry Me Back to Old Virginny"
◆ Wallace Saunders's "Casey Jones"
◆ Jester Hairston and Harry Robert Wilson's *Negro Spirituals and Folk Songs*
◆ Lee Adams and Charles Strouse's "No More," from the Broadway musical *Golden Boy*
◆ Robert de Cormier's "Wayfaring Stranger" and "Ain't-a That Good News"
◆ Thomas A. Dorsey's "Precious Lord, Take My Hand," "There'll Be Peace in the Valley," "If I Don't Get There," and "Say a Little Prayer for Me"

- Edwin Hawkins Singers's "Oh Happy Day"
- Tramaine Hawkins's "Spirit Fall Down on Me"
- Charles Harrison Mason's "I'm a Soldier in the Army of the Lord" and "My Soul Loves Jesus"
- William Grant Still's "Troubled Island" and "Plain Chant for America"
- Will Marion Cook's operetta *Clorinda*

Comment on the background of black composers and arrangers, particularly Harry T. Burleigh, famous collector of secular, religious, and spiritual songs, Jester Hairston, and Edward Boatner.

Budget: $$$

Sources:

For more information about Leslie Adams, consult Management Consultants, 15830 Van Aken Blvd., No. 302, Cleveland, OH 44120; telephone: (216)752-4973.

Anderson, E. Ruth, *The Contemporary American Composers: A Biographical Dictionary,* G. K. Hall, 1982.

International Who's Who in Music and Musicians' Directory, 11th ed., Melrose, 1988.

Jones, James T., "Choirs Use Funky Means to Give God Name Recognition," *USA Today,* August 26, 1992, p. 9D.

Tischler, Alice, *Fifteen Black American Composers: A Bibliography of Their Works,* Harmonie Park Press, 1981.

Alternative Applications: Coordinate a program on the subject of justice and liberty. Feature choral works such as Randall Thompson's *Testament of Freedom* or *The Last Words of David* or Pablo Casals's "Nigra Sum."

Dueling Pianos

Age/Grade Level or Audience: All ages.

Description: Hold a piano solo competition.

Procedure: Divide entrants into beginner, intermediate, and advanced categories. Have each performer play one personal choice and one selection from a required list, such as these:

- segments of Harry Lawrence Freeman's operas *Martyr* or *Voodoo*
- Scott Joplin's "Bethena," "The Entertainer," or "Maple Leaf Rag"
- Thomas A. Dorsey's "Precious Lord, Take My Hand"
- Nat King Cole's "Straighten Up and Fly Right"
- Edwin Hawkins Singer's "Oh Happy Day"

Provide judges with a professional evaluation sheet rating students from one to ten on musicality, stage presence, rhythm, fingering, and phrasing.

Budget: $$

Sources:
Brodt Music Company, P.O. Box 9345, Charlotte, NC 28299; telephone: (700)438-4129.

Alternative Applications: Include other types of keyboard performance categories, particularly duet, duo piano, vocal accompaniment, choral accompaniment, pipe or electric organ, electronic keyboard, and piano and another instrument, such as violin, viola, or flute.

A History of African-American Music

Age/Grade Level or Audience: Middle school, high school, and college music classes; music societies; civic groups.

Description: Create an audio-visual music festival to celebrate the history of African-American music.

Procedure: Assign participants a particular segment of music history to study and portray through an audio-visual presentation. Assemble the segments into a chronological whole, beginning with slave songs, hymns, work songs, and minstrel performances and working up through jazz, be-bop, doo-wop, soul, rock, rhythm and blues, opera, reggae, zydeco, black country, West Indian soca, and rap. Include these facts:

- ◆ In the 1870s, the Fisk Jubilee Singers of Nashville, Tennessee, popularize spirituals among white audiences.
- ◆ In 1871, John Esputa organizes the Colored Opera Company.
- ◆ In 1875, Massachusetts blacks form the Boston Musical Union.
- ◆ In 1876, black musicians organize the Philharmonic Society of New York.
- ◆ In 1893, Harry Lawrence Freeman's opera *Martyr* is performed in Denver. That same year, Frederick Douglass's grandson, violinist Joseph Douglass, tours the United States for the Victor Talking Machine Company.
- ◆ In 1897, Scott Joplin produces the first ragtime hit, "Maple Leaf Rag."
- ◆ By 1903, the Samuel Coleridge-Taylor Musical Society of Washington, D.C., reaches a membership of 200.
- ◆ In 1908, Shepard N. Edmons founds a black-owned music publishing house.
- ◆ In 1912, Robert Nathaniel Dett composes *Magnolia*, a five-piano suite.
- ◆ In 1921, Thomas A. Dorsey begins writing gospels with "If I Don't Get There."

- In 1925, Florence B. Price becomes the first black woman to win the Wanamaker Award for musical composition.
- In 1928, Harry Lawrence Freeman's *Voodoo* is produced on Broadway.
- In 1932, Thomas A. Dorsey is proclaimed father of gospel after publishing "Precious Lord, Take My Hand."
- In 1943, Nat King Cole sells half a million copies of his first composition, "Straighten Up and Fly Right," and in 1948 he becomes the first black to star in his own radio series.
- In 1946, Pearl Bailey debuts on stage in *St. Louis Woman.*
- In 1947, Nat King Cole records "Christmas Song."
- In 1955, Leontyne Price sings in a televised production of *Tosca.*
- In 1960, Odetta performs at Carnegie Hall.
- In 1969, Edwin Hawkins Singers bring gospel to the pop charts with "Oh Happy Day."
- In 1968, Thomas J. Anderson composes his *Chamber Symphony.*
- In the fall of 1992, Kathleen Battle sings at the New York Philharmonic's 150th anniversary.

Budget: $$$

Sources:

Films and videos such as *Lady Sings the Blues* (1972), *Mahogany* (1976), *Roots* (1977), *Glory* (1990), and *The Songs Are Free* (1991).

Davis, Anthony, *The Life and Times of Malcolm X* (opera score), G. Schirmer Rental Library, 1987.

Estell, Kenneth, ed., *The African-American Almanac*, 6th ed., Gale, 1993.

Hornsby, Alton, Jr., *Chronology of African-American History: Significant Events and People from 1619 to the Present*, Gale, 1991.

McLane, Daisann, "Caribbean Soul: From Calypso to Reggae, Salsa to Soca," *Black Enterprise*, May 1991, pp. 92-93.

"Music from around the Hemisphere," *Americas*, September-October 1985, pp. 62-63.

Palmer, Don, "Sounds of the Caribbean: The Music of Trinidad, Tobago, Martinique, Guadeloupe and Jamaica," *Black Enterprise*, May 1987, pp. 42-44.

Alternative Applications: Invite local talent to illustrate each segment of the chronological study with songs or lip-syncing.

Joplin Expo

Age/Grade Level or Audience: All ages.

Description: Present a discussion and performance of the music of Scott Joplin.

Procedure: Present an overview of Scott Joplin's life, including these facts:

◆ The son of a former slave, Joplin was born November 24, 1868, in Tex-arkana, Texas.

◆ He moved to St. Louis, Missouri, in 1885, to play ragtime piano and tour on the vaudeville circuit.

◆ At George Smith College, he studied harmony and music theory.

◆ In 1897, while working at the Maple Leaf Club in Sedalia, Missouri, he composed his greatest hit, "Maple Leaf Rag," which sold over a million copies.

◆ From 1899 to 1909 he played marches, two-steps, ragtime, serenades, cake walks, and waltzes in saloons and bordellos.

◆ In 1903, he composed his first opera, *Guest of Honor.*

◆ In 1904, he wrote "The Cascades" for the 1904 World's Fair.

◆ Resettled in St. Louis, in 1911 he wrote two operas, *The Entertainer and Treemonisha,* which he dedicated to his mother.

◆ Seriously mentally ill, he died penniless in a New York hospital in 1917 and was buried in an unmarked grave in St. Michael's Cemetery, Brooklyn.

◆ The Atlanta Symphony performed *Treemonisha* in 1972.

◆ In 1974, Joplin tunes were revived by Gunther Schuller.

◆ "The Entertainer" made the Top Forty and won Oscars for best title song and best sound track for the movie *The Sting.*

Play recordings of Joplin's ragtime originals, particularly "Bethena," "Maple Leaf Rag," "The Chrysanthemum," "The Cascades," "The Entertainer," "Swipesy," and "Solace." Compare them with other typically African-American styles, such as reggae, rhythm and blues, calypso, spirituals, or soul tunes.

Budget: $$

Sources:

Sound track from the film *The Sting* (1973).

Low, W. Augustus, and Virgil A. Clift, eds., *Encyclopedia of Black America,* McGraw-Hill, 1981.

Alternative Applications: Study the works of Joplin alongside those of Thomas Milton Turpin or James Scott's "Ragtime Oriole." Show the video or movie *Ragtime.* Compare with similar themes and background music in *The Sting.*

Motown

Age/Grade Level or Audience: Middle school, high school, and college music and music history classes.

Description: Prepare a history of Motown.

Procedure: Organize students into groups to take notes on the history of Motown, Berry Gordy, Jr.'s African-American corporation that turned many singing groups and soloists into recording and performing stars. Assign individual groups to study Smokey Robinson and the Miracles, Diana Ross and the Supremes, Martha and the Vandellas, the Temptations, the Jackson Five, and the Four Tops. Have the groups create wall charts of each group's most popular hits and the number of records sold. Use symbols to indicate gold and platinum records. Include important dates such as these:

◆ In 1957, former boxer Berry Gordy cowrote "Reet Petite," his first modest hit.
◆ The next year Gordy wrote "Lonely Teardrops."
◆ In 1959, at age thirty, he borrowed $800 to start his Detroit recording business.
◆ In 1960, his first major success, "You Got What It Takes," was recorded by Marv Johnson.
◆ In 1961, he made his first gold record with the Miracles, "Shop Around."
◆ In 1962, Motown reached a major portion of the recording audience with "Two Lovers," "You Beat Me to the Punch," "Do You Love Me," and "You Really Got a Hold on Me."
◆ A record year, 1964 saw the production of "My Guy, "Baby Love," "Where Did Our Love Go," and "Chapel of Love."
◆ By 1966, three-quarters of Motown's output was successful, ranging from doo-wop to soul, rhythm and blues, gospel, rock and roll, and pop.
◆ In 1972, Motown moved to Los Angeles.
◆ Gordy sponsored the filming of *Lady Sings the Blues,* starring Diana Ross as Billie Holiday.

Budget: $

Sources:

Cantor, George, *Historic Landmarks of Black America,* Gale, 1991.

Low, W. Augustus, and Virgil A. Clift, eds., *Encyclopedia of Black America,* McGraw-Hill, 1981.

Lamarr, Renee, "The Rise and Fall of Motown," *Interview,* April 1986, pp. 185-186.

"Motown Memories," *Rolling Stone,* August 23, 1990, pp. 79-83.

"Singer Eddie Kendricks Mourned by Music World," *Jet,* October 26, 1992, pp.53-54, 60.

Waller, Don, *The Motown Story,* Scribner, 1985.

Alternative Applications: Hold a Motown Day. Organize a variety of activities, such as these:

◆ Have students demonstrate dances associated with the rise of Motown, such as the shag and the funky chicken.
◆ Suggest that groups dress up like famous groups, particularly Diana Ross and the Supremes, the Temptations, Four Tops, Spinners, Gladys Knight and the Pips, Martha and the Vandellas, Isley Brothers, Jr. Walker and the All Stars, Marvelettes, Pointer Sisters, Smokey Robinson and the Miracles, Commodores, or Jackson Five.

◆ Invite groups to sing or lip-sync Motown favorites, such as "Under the Boardwalk" and "My Guy."
◆ Post charts of the numbers of records sold by Stevie Wonder, Diana Ross, Marvin Gaye, Smokey Robinson, Tammi Terrell, Billy Eckstine, Mary Wells, Lionel Ritchie, Chaka Khan, and other Motown successes.

Music Workshop

Age/Grade Level or Audience: All ages.

Description: Locate black musicians to staff a music workshop.

Procedure: Invite black professionals to teach the fundamentals of guitar, piano, trumpet, banjo, drums, string bass, or vocal music. Provide the workshop free to assist indigent community members in improving their skills. For the youngest participants, teach note reading, scales, and beginning harmonics. Conclude the music workshop with a group performance.

Budget: $$$

Sources:
Consult local school, college, and university music departments, night clubs, private music teachers, or bands for suggested personnel to staff music workshops.

Patois

Originator: Susan L. Henry, librarian and book dealer, Charlotte, North Carolina.

Age/Grade Level or Audience: Elementary, middle school, high school, and college music classes; music societies; civic choruses.

Description: Sample African music that mixes languages other than English.

Procedure: Distribute song sheets containing the original words to songs in Louisiana Creole or Gullah patois. Discuss how the lyrics blend English with other tongues and dialects. For example, "Aurore Pradère," "Fais Do Do, Colas," "Kum Ba Yah," and "Sanguree."

> **Kum Ba Yah**
> Someone's singin', Lord, Kum ba yah.
> Someone's singin', Lord, Kum ba yah.

Someone's shoutin', Lord, Kum ba yah.
Oh, Lord, Kum ba yah.

Fais Do Do, Colas

Fais do do, Colas, mon 'tit frere.
Fais do do, chere cochon, mon 'tit frere.
T'auras du gateau Papa e aura,
Et moi j'un aurai,
Fais do do, mon chere.

Budget: $$

Sources:

Recordings such as Sweet Honey in the Rock's *All for Freedom* and Warren-Mattox Productions' *Shake It to the One That You Love the Best.*
Bebey, Francis, *African Music: A People's Art,* Harrap, 1975.
Nketia, J. H. Kwabena, *The Music of Africa,* Gollancz, 1975.
Warren, Dr. Fred, and Lee Warren, *The Music of Africa: An Introduction,* Prentice-Hall, 1970.

Alternative Applications: Organize a rhythm band to accompany a capella singing to taped or recorded African songs, such as "Calypso Freedom," "Amen," "Loop de Loop," "Ya, Ya, Ya," "Gone to the Mailboat," "Kum Ba Yah," "Ise Oluwa," "Juba," "Alunde and the Story of Ono," "The Little Shekere," and "Bob-a-Needle." Include cymbals, bongo drums, sticks, bells, tambourines, and triangles.

Porgy and Bess

Age/Grade Level or Audience: Middle and high school music classes; music clubs.

Description: Present a short version of the folk opera *Porgy and Bess.*

Procedure: Discuss the historical foundations of the plot and the setting on Catfish Row and islands off the South Carolina coast. Then summarize the action of the opera, interspersing recorded lyrics, particularly "Summertime," "I Got Plenty of Nothing," "I'm on My Way," and "Bess, You Is My Woman." Note the following social, religious, and economic themes:

- ◆ religious societies
- ◆ male and female roles
- ◆ family
- ◆ the drug culture and gambling
- ◆ fate and superstition
- ◆ faith and determination

Budget: $$

Sources:
Heyward, DuBose, *Porgy and Bess* (recording), Philips, 1985.

Alternative Applications: Perform the play in tableau shadow screen style. As the narrator summarizes each segment of the action, have actors take their places on a stage or behind a screen. Because there is less need for props, makeup, costumes, and scenery, the shadow screen technique will require less preparation and minimize costs.

Rap Wrap-Up

Age/Grade Level or Audience: School, civic, and church groups.

Description: Explore the purpose and style of rap music.

Procedure: Play some rap recordings, such as songs by Sons of the Ghetto, Takagi Kan's "Hip Hip Fork," or Yolanda "Yo Yo" Whitaker's "Black Pearl." Invite local rap groups to perform. Encourage a discussion of pervasive themes, particularly outrage, poverty, and pride. Stress the importance of energy, feeling, and wit in the creation of rap lyrics. List rap slang, which has permeated the languages of other countries, such as France, Japan, Russia, and Brazil.

Budget: $$

Sources:
Taped segments of local radio shows; record shops; films such as *Boyz 'n the Hood* (1991) and *Grand Canyon* (1991).
Collins, Gail, "Rap as a Second Language," *Ms.,* January-February 1989, pp. 56-58.
Collum, Danny Duncan, "Roots to Rap: A Mother Lode in the Ethnic Gap," *National Catholic Reporter,* February 28, 1992, p. 14.
Dobb, Edwin, "Thrice Blessed," *Reader's Digest,* December 1992, pp. 65-71.
Hampton, Dream, "Rap Happiness," *Parenting,* February 1992, p. 24.
Holden, Stephen, "From Rock to Rap," *New York Times Magazine,* April 26, 1987, p. 46.
McCluskey, Ian, "Rap Around the Globe," *Time,* October 19, 1992, pp. 70-71.
Samuels, David, "The Rap on Rap: The 'Black Music' That Isn't Either," *New Republic,* November 11, 1991, pp. 24-28.
Simpson, Janice C., "Yo! Rap Gets on the Map: Led by Groups Like Public Enemy, It Socks a Black Message to the Mainstream," *Time,* February 5, 1990, pp. 60-62.
Teachout, Terry, "Rap and Racism," *Commentary,* March 1990, pp. 60-62.

Alternative Applications: Organize a round-robin rap session. Have one participant compose opening lines, then pass the poem to the next writer. Have a recorder type up a list of stanzas and distribute to readers, print in booklet form, or post on a bulletin board.

 ## Rhythm of Resistance

Age/Grade Level or Audience: Middle school, high school, and college music and social studies classes; literary and music societies; library study groups.

Description: Hold an African music festival.

Procedure: Play recordings by African musicians, such as these:

Babsy Mlangeni	Perefere Malomba	Mahotella Queens
Ebenezer Obey	Sipho Mchunu	Dumisani Maraire
Hassan Hakmoun	Foday Musa Suso	Oumou Sangare
Sanougue Kouyate	Sona Diabate	Umthombowase Golgota
Balafon	Aster Aweke	Lilly Tchlumba
M'Bella Bel	Miriam Makeba	Ladysmith Black Mambazo
Mthembu Queens	Nahawa Doumbia	Sophie Mgcinas
Stella Chiwese	Tshala Muana	Angelique Kidjo
Tabu Ley Rochereau	Youssou N'Dour	

Have students draw conclusions about how rhythm, repetition, and musical style communicate social and political opinions.

Budget: $$

Sources:

The videos "Rhythm of Resistance: Music of Black South Africa" and "Johnny Clegg and Savuka: Cruel, Crazy, Beautiful World"; consult Laurie J. Fuchs, Director of Ladyslipper, Box 3124-R, Durham, NC 27715; telephone: (800)634-6404.

Bordowitz, Hank, "Jazz Videos Take Us Back to Yesterday," *Emerge,* October 1992, p. 72.

Cocks, Jay, "Legacy with a Future," *Time,* October 19, 1992, p. 77.

Duncan, Amy, "Ambassadors of Afropop," *Christian Science Monitor,* October 1989, pp. 74-77.

Jennings, Nicholas, "Africa's Cult Musician," *Maclean's,* October 13, 1986, pp. 8-9.

Labate, John, "Africa's Hot New Export: Music," *Fortune,* May 4, 1992, p. 18.

Alternative Applications: Contrast African protest songs with works by these Reggae singers:

Bob Marley	Linton Kwesi Johnson	Burning Spear
Bunny Wailer	Ranking Ann	Sister Carol

Ziggy Marley	Amazulu	Cedelia Marely Booker
Deltones	Foxy Brown	I-Three
Judy Mowatt	Lillian Allen	Marcia Griffiths
Rita Marley	Peter Tosh	

Screen the documentary *Time Will Tell*, which describes Bob Marley's fervent fans, who extend from Jamaica outward to distant parts of the world. The film also includes footage of his 1978 "One Love" Peace Concert, held in Kingston, Jamaica, and attended by Ethiopian emperor Haile Selassie. Have volunteers research Marley's role in the Rastafarian movement and assign small groups to discuss protest themes in his most famous songs, "I Shot the Sheriff," "Lively Up Yourself," "War," "The Harder They Come," and "Them Belly Full."

1776

Age/Grade Level or Audience: High school and college black studies and American history classes; adult music and civic groups.

Description: Discuss the premise of the musical comedy *1776*.

Procedure: Screen the musical *1776* and lead a group discussion of the movie's implications for later episodes in American history, particularly the Civil War and the Emancipation Proclamation. Have volunteers answer these questions:

- ◆ How might the nation have been different if Rutledge's proposal had failed?
- ◆ What does Rutledge's song "Molasses, Rum, and Slaves" imply about the purity of New England abolitionism?
- ◆ How does colonial economics impinge on the Declaration of Independence?
- ◆ What stand does slave-holder Thomas Jefferson take in the controversy?
- ◆ Why does John Adams capitulate to the Southern bloc?
- ◆ In what respect does the argument against King George's tyranny condemn the colonists's attitude toward slavery?

Budget: $$

Sources:
The musical comedy *1776* (1972), and other tapes from video rental services.
Evitts, William J., *Captive Bodies, Free Spirits: The Story of Southern Slavery*, Messner, 1985.

Alternative Applications: Evaluate the film *1776* from a modern perspective. Decide how modern legislators would vote on ethical matters such as the right of Southern states to import slaves, the value of the slave trade to the economy, or the moral implications of slave ownership.

Sing-along

Age/Grade Level or Audience: All ages.

Description: Organize musicians and singers for a sing-along to honor Black History Month. Citizens will assemble in a hall, auditorium, gymnasium, or church and join in the singing of a variety of familiar songs, spirituals, hymns, and patriotic anthems.

Procedure: Distribute song sheets featuring known and less familiar lyrics to songs by and about Negroes, such as "Deep River," "Swing Low, Sweet Chariot," "Joshua Fit the Battle of Jericho," "Great Day," "Follow the Drinking Gourd," "Soon I Will Be Done with the Troubles of the World," "Amazing Grace," "The Battle Hymn of the Republic," "We Shall Overcome," "Oh, Freedom," "I'm So Glad," and "The Negro National Anthem." Tell the backgrounds of these works and note their significance to the civil rights movement. For instance:

- ◆ "The Negro National Anthem" is also known as "Lift Ev'ry Voice and Sing."
- ◆ It was written by James Weldon Johnson (1871-1938).
- ◆ Johnson's brother Rosamond set the lyrics to music.
- ◆ The first performance was at a Lincoln Day celebration on January 12, 1900, where five hundred school children sang it in unison.
- ◆ By 1920, the anthem spread throughout the South and into other parts of the United States.
- ◆ The theme of the song is faith, perseverance, and hope.

Budget: $$

Sources:
Ebony, February 1992, p. 117.
Ride On, King Jesus: Florence Quivar Sings Black Music of America, available from Rose Records, 214 South Wabash Ave., Chicago, IL 60604; telephone: (800)955-ROSE.
Silverman, Jerry, *Songs of Protest and Civil Rights*, Chelsea House, 1992.
Southern, Eileen, *The Music of Black Americans: A History*, Norton, 1983.

Alternative Applications: Show a video or movie such as *Driving Miss Daisy, I Know Why the Caged Bird Sings, Conrack, Boyz 'n the Hood, The Learning Tree, Places in the Heart, Daughters of the Dust, The Autobiography of Miss Jane Pittman*, or *Sounder*. Follow with a songfest. To strengthen community participation, feature local soloists, instrumentalists, singing or dancing groups, or folklorists. Conclude with a panel discussion of the importance of music in African-American life, both past and present.

Slavery and Negro Spirituals

Age/Grade Level or Audience: Elementary, middle school, and high school music classes; adult music societies; church and civic groups.

Description: Study the lyrics of Negro spirituals for clues to the hardships and longings inherent in slavery.

Procedure: Invite singing groups to present a medley of Negro spirituals. Include a mix of elegiac, philosophical, and exuberant songs, such as "Sweet Little Jesus Boy," "Soon I Will Be Done with the Troubles of the World," "Get on Board, Little Children," "Steal Away," "Listen to the Lambs," and "De Gospel Train." Pass out song sheets including lyrics and commentary on how each song relates to some aspect of slavery, such as these:

- ◆ separation of families
- ◆ hard, boring, dirty, and dangerous labor
- ◆ poor health
- ◆ hunger
- ◆ despair
- ◆ expectation of liberation
- ◆ fear of the future
- ◆ reliance on religious faith

Budget: $$

Sources:

Low, W. Augustus, and Virgil A. Clift, eds., *Encyclopedia of Black America,* McGraw-Hill, 1981.

Ride On, King Jesus: Florence Quivar Sings Black Music of America, available from Rose Records, 214 South Wabash Ave., Chicago, IL 60604; telephone: (800)955-ROSE.

Southern, Eileen, *The Music of Black Americans: A History,* Norton, 1983.

Alternative Applications: Introduce the words to "Oh, Freedom" or "This Train":

Oh, Freedom!

Oh, freedom! Oh, freedom!
Oh freedom over me.
An' before I'd be a slave
I'd be buried in my grave,
An' go home to my Lord
An' be free, an' be free.

This Train

This train is boun' for glory, this train,

This train is boun' for glory, this train
This train is boun' for glory.
If you want to get to heb'n
Then you got to be holy.
This train is boun' for glory, this train.

Invite professional musicians to discuss the musical, religious, and thematic aspects of the songs, particularly dialect, repetition, escapism, and affirmation of faith.

 Songs of Protest

Age/Grade Level or Audience: All ages.

Description: Create a bulletin board display featuring lyrics from songs sung by protesters and civil rights marchers.

Procedure: Select a song verse to place at the center of a display of facts, maps, photographs, drawings, and memorabilia from the civil rights struggle. Some possible choices include:

Carry It On
If you can't go on no longer,
Take the hand held by your brother;
Every victory gonna bring another,
Carry it on, carry it on.

If You Miss Me from the Front of the Bus
If you miss me from the front of the bus,
And you can't find me nowhere,
Come on up to the driver's seat,
I'll be drivin' up there.

My People Will Rise
Let's all unite
And make a stand
And share in the profit
Of our grand, rich land.

We Are Soldiers in the Army
I'm glad I am a soldier,
I've got my hand on the gospel plow;
But one day I'll get old, I can't fight anymore,
I'll just stand here and fight on anyhow.

Budget: $

Sources:
Silverman, Jerry, *Songs of Protest and Civil Rights,* Chelsea House, 1992.

Alternative Applications: Have students write new verses to describe other aspects of the struggle for freedom, such as these:

- ◆ support of the victims of Apartheid
- ◆ court cases, such as *Brown v. Board of Education*
- ◆ the abolition of slavery in Haiti
- ◆ the end of segregation in the U.S. military
- ◆ the fight to end famine in Somalia and Ethiopia
- ◆ famous firsts, particularly Thurgood Marshall's appointment to the U.S. Supreme Court or Mae Jemison's space flight
- ◆ Ron Brown's presidency of the National Democratic Party
- ◆ the clean-up efforts and creation of enterprise zones following urban riots in Los Angeles, California

We Shall Overcome

Age/Grade Level or Audience: All ages.

Description: Arrange a viewing of the Emmy Award-winning musical documentary *We Shall Overcome,* narrated by Harry Belafonte.

Procedure: Have the audience respond individually to the film and its presentation of powerful emotions and segments of history. Encourage participants to answer the following questions:

- ◆ Where did the song "We Shall Overcome" originate?
- ◆ Why did it become a rallying cry of tobacco workers of the 1930s and 1940s?
- ◆ Why was the song suitable for campus sit-ins and civil rights marches of the 1960s and 1970s?
- ◆ Why is the song often sung while people stand together and hold hands?
- ◆ What role did the following people play in its use: Pete Seeger, Martin Luther King, Jr., Guy Carwan, Joan Baez, the Freedom Singers?
- ◆ How does the song compare to other statements of purpose and beliefs, for example "Eyes on the Prize"?
- ◆ What do varying rhythms indicate about the song?
- ◆ Why has the song spread to oppressed peoples in India, South Africa, Lebanon, Russia, and Korea?
- ◆ How does the song relate to antiwar and nuclear protest rallies?

Budget: $$

Sources:

The documentary musical *We Shall Overcome* (1988).

Hampton, Henry, and Steve Fayer, *Voices of Freedom: An Oral History of the Civil Rights Movement from the 1950s through the 1980s,* Bantam Books, 1990.

Alternative Applications: Discuss why the song "We Shall Overcome" has been called "unifying," "stabilizing," "reassuring," "connecting," "uplifting," and "sustaining." Explain why the following variations are meaningful:

- ◆ We are not afraid.
- ◆ I will see the Lord.
- ◆ I will overcome.
- ◆ Blacks and whites together.
- ◆ We will win our rights.

Teach a group the most common set of lyrics to "We Shall Overcome":

We shall overcome,
We shall overcome,
We shall overcome someday.
Oh, deep in my heart
I do believe
That we shall overcome some day.

Work Songs

Contributor: Rick Glover, First Sergeant, U.S. Army, Retired, Hickory, North Carolina; Roberta Brown, teacher, Fort Bragg, North Carolina; Susan L. Henry, librarian and book dealer, Charlotte, North Carolina; Dennis Buff, video consultant, Hickory, North Carolina.

Age/Grade Level or Audience: Middle school and high school music classes; adult music societies.

Description: Discuss the emotional release found in work, marching, hunting, rowing, or convict songs.

Procedure: Present recordings and songsheets of the work songs "Hammer Man," "Tol' My Cap'n," "Trouble Don't Last Always," "Water Boy," and "You Can Dig My Grave." Have a small group present their reactions to the emotionalism, injustice, despair, and protest inherent in the lyrics and describe the dramatic scenario that the song portrays.

Hammer Man
Take this hammer, carry it to the cap'n,

Tell him I'm gone, tell him I'm gone.
Cap'n called me lazy good fer nothin'
Ain't my name, ain't my name.
If he asks you, was I runnin'
Tell him I'm flyin', tell him I'm flyin'.

Tol' My Cap'n

Tol' my cap'n my han's wuz swole,
"Devil take yo' han's, boy,
Let the wheelers roll!"
Tol' my cap'n my feet wuz sore,
"Devil take yo' feet, boy,
Bother me no more."

Trouble Don't Last Always

Keep your eye on the sun
See how she run
Don't let me catch you with your work undone.
I'm a-troubled, I'm a-troubled,
Trouble don't last always.

Water Boy

Water boy, where you been hidin'?
If you don't come, gwine tell yo' Mammy.
There ain't no hammer
That's on this mount'in
That ring like mine, son,
That ring like mine.

You Can Dig My Grave

You can dig my grave with a silver spade
'Cause I ain't gonna be here no longer!
There's a little white robe in the heb'n for me
'Cause I ain't gonna be here no longer!
There's a golden harp in the heb'n for me.
You just touch one string and the whole heb'n rings
'Cause I ain't gonna be here no longer!

Budget: $

Sources:

The songs "John Henry," "Dinah," "Shrimp Boat's a-Comin'," and "Banana Boat Song";
  Gardner Read's "You Can Dig My Grave"; Jester Hairston's "Hold My Mule While I
  Dance, Josey," "Dis Ol' Hammer," and "Pay Me My Money Down"; Avery Robinson's
  "Water Boy"; and Eugene Thamon Simpson's "Hold On"; the film *The Power of One.*
Dorson, Richard M., *American Folklore,* University of Chicago Press, 1980.
Heyward, DuBose, *Porgy and Bess* (recording), Philips, 1985.

Lester, Julius, *To Be a Slave*, Dial, 1969, reprinted, Scholastic, Inc., 1986.

Metcalf, Doris Hunter, *African Americans: Their Impact on U.S History*, Good Apple, 1992.

Alternative Applications: Assign a committee to compose a work song based on a particular local job, such as truck driving, grave digging, heavy construction, fishing or shrimping, farm labor, livestock management, lumbering, mining, or marching. Stress the importance of cadence and repetition to fit natural work rhythms and repetitious hand and body motions, as with the stacking of lumber, hauling of fishnets, or the placement of items in crates. For example:

Tain't No Mo' Sellin' Today

Tain't no mo' sellin' today.
Tain't no mo' hirin' today.
Tain't no mo' pullin' off shirts today.
It's stomp down freedom today.
Stomp it down!
Stomp down freedom today.

Many Thousand Gone

[Marching song of the First Arkansas Unit]
No more iron chain for me
No more, no more,
No more iron chain for me,
Many thousand gone.

Airborne Running Cadence

[Sung to "Bo Diddley"]
Bo Diddley, Bo Diddley, have you heard?
We're going to jump from a big iron bird.
Refrain: Hey Bo Diddley, Hey hey Bo Diddley Bo.
C-130 sitting on the strip;
Airborne trooper going to take a little trip.
Stand up, hook up shuffle to the door;
Jump right out and count to four.
If my main don't open wide,
I've got another one by my side.
If that one don't open too,
Look out below I'm coming through.
If I die on the old drop zone,
Box me up and send me home.
Pin my wings upon my chest;
Tell my friends I done my best.

Marching Cadence

I used to wear some old blue jeans
Now I'm wearing army green
Hey, Mom, I want to go—

But they won't let me go—
Home.
I used to drive a Chevrolet;
Now I'm marching every day.
Hey, Mom, I want to go—
But they won't let me go—
Home.
I used to date a teenage queen;
Now I pack an M-16.
Hey, Mom, I want to go—
But they won't let me go—
Home.

Marching Song

[Marching song of the 1st Arkansas Unit; set to tune of "John Brown's Body"]
We have done with hoeing cotton;
We have done with hoeing corn.
We are color Yankee soldiers now
As sure as you are born.
When the Master hears us yelling,
They'll think it's Gabriel's horn,
As we go marching on.

Blood on the Risers

[As sung by Airborne-school graduates]
He was just a rookie trooper
And he surely shook with fright.
As he checked all his equipment
And made sure his pack was tight.
He had to sit and listen to those awful engines roar.
You ain't gonna jump no more.
"Is everyone happy?" cried the sergeant, looking up.
Our Hero, feebly answered "yes" and then they stood him up.
He leaped right out into the blast, his static line unhooked.
He ain't gonna jump no more.

Sweet Potatoes

Sweet potato, yellar yam,
Lord have mercy
Heah I am!
String beans, green corn, I got okra too.
Ev'rything is fresh for you.

Sandy Anna

Hey heave hi ho!
Work on the levee all day.
Seaman what's the matter? Heave ray hooray heave!
Seaman what's the matter? Heave Sandy Anna heave!

Street Medley

Chairs to mend, old chairs to mend,
Rush or cane-bottomed.
New mackerel, new mackerel.
Old rags, any old bones,
Take money for your rags,
Any hard skins or rabbit skins.

Seller's Chant

Here's yo col' ice lemonade,
It's made in de shade,
It's stirred wid a spade.
Come buy my col' ice lemonade.
It's made in de shade
An' sol' in de sun.
Ef you hain't got no money,
You cain't git none.
One glass fer a nickel,
An' two fer a dime,
Ef you hain't got de chink,
You cain't git mine.
Come right dis way,
Fer it sho' will pay
To git candy fer de ladies
An' cakes fer de babies.

Religion and Ethics

Advice from Marian Wright Edelman

Age/Grade Level or Audience: All ages.

Description: Create a bulletin board or series of posters featuring advice from Marian Wright Edelman.

Procedure: Highlight these twenty-five precepts with illustrations, pictures cut from magazines, or paper flowers:

- ◆ Don't expect anything for free. Work for what you get.
- ◆ Choose your aims wisely and make a workable plan for achieving them.
- ◆ Take charge of what you do.
- ◆ Work for reasons other than pay or prestige.
- ◆ Allow room for failure and disappointments.
- ◆ Think of parenting as a serious responsibility.
- ◆ Accept your spouse as an equal and a friend.
- ◆ Create families to last.
- ◆ Be truthful, even when it is inconvenient or painful.
- ◆ View yourself as part of the entire human race.
- ◆ Give up pretense for the real you.
- ◆ Keep trying.
- ◆ Accept a crucial role in change.
- ◆ Keep learning.
- ◆ Show your children that hard work is necessary.
- ◆ Let yourself enjoy life.
- ◆ Select friends you can be proud of.
- ◆ Keep a positive attitude.
- ◆ Let go of painful memories.
- ◆ Assist those in need.
- ◆ Let your voice speak for the real you.
- ◆ Take charge of your outlook.

◆ Honor the family, state, nation, and race to which you belong.

◆ Don't be a quitter.

◆ Remember that you are not alone.

Budget: $

Sources:

Edelman, Marian Wright, *The Measure of Our Success: A Letter to My Children and Yours,* Beacon Press, 1992.

Smith, Jessie Carney, ed., *Notable Black American Women,* Gale, 1992.

Alternative Applications: Present Edelman's twenty-five precepts as topics for a writing and/or poster contest. Distribute the statements on handouts or fliers around the community. Advertise them in the newspaper. Publish the results in a booklet of advice to live by. Hold a public reading at a PTA meeting, club gathering, or radio or television broadcast. Invite participants to suggest additions to the original list.

African Meditation Methods

Age/Grade Level or Audience: All ages.

Description: Study the importance of meditation in African religions.

Procedure: Collect data on the method and use of meditation in African religion, particularly the "ankh" life-force in Egypt, "ntu" in South Africa, and "nkra" in Ghana. Contrast with the meditative methods arising from other religions, particularly transcendental meditation, the Catholic rosary, Buddhist mandala, Hasidic recitation, yoga, contemplation of the Russian Orthodox icon, Zen koan, Taoist tai-chi, charismatic Christian laying on of hands and prayer circles, and Christian Science spontaneous healing.

Budget: $

Sources:

Drewel, Margaret Thompson, "Ritual Performance in Africa Today," *Drama Review,* Summer 1988, pp. 25-30.

Jamal, Isma'el, "African Meditation," *Upscale,* June/July 1992, pp. 60-61.

Lawson, E. Thomas, *Religions of Africa,* Harper & Row, 1984.

Alternative Applications: Lead a group in meditation. Stress breath control, posture, relaxation, visualization of a positive image, focus, and awareness of revitalization. Discuss the effects on heartbeat, body temperature, blood pressure, attitudes, fears, and thought processes.

"Amazing Grace" and the Slave Trade

Age/Grade Level or Audience: Middle school and high school history and black studies classes; church gatherings.

Description: Present a chalk talk about the composition of "Amazing Grace."

Procedure: Outline on a chalkboard, overhead projector, or handout the life of John Newton, religious convert who abandoned the slave trade. Include data such as these:

◆ John Newton was born July 24, 1775, in England.
◆ At age eleven, he followed the trade of his father, a sea captain.
◆ By fifteen, Newton had become so wicked and profane that he lost a job in Alicant, Spain.
◆ The next year, Newton was impressed into the British navy aboard the *Harwich*.
◆ He deserted. After his capture, he was put in irons and whipped.
◆ In shame, he fled England and lived in Guinea.
◆ Later, in Sierra Leone, he joined a white slaver and stood guard over six hundred victims on ship; only three hundred survived the voyage.
◆ Aboard a vessel bound for Brazil, Newton read about Christianity.
◆ After surviving a storm at sea, he believed that he had been saved so that he could perform important Christian work.
◆ In 1742, Newton married Mary Catlett, a sweet-natured woman who influenced his behavior. They adopted a daughter.
◆ To rid himself of the taint of the slave trade, he became a minister.
◆ In 1764, he wrote *An Authentic Narrative,* confessing his role in slavery and referring to himself as "the old African blasphemer."
◆ In 1779, he and William Cowper composed 281 hymns, including "Amazing Grace."
◆ He served English pulpits until his death in 1807.

Conclude the presentation with a discussion of the hymn and its emotional response to the slave trade, which Newton considered his greatest sin.

Budget: $

Sources:
Newton, John, *John Newton: Letters of a Slave Trader,* Moody Press, 1983.
Pollock, John, *Amazing Grace: John Newton's Story,* Harper & Row, 1981.
Snodgrass, Mary Ellen, *Late Achievers: Famous People Who Succeeded Late in Life,* Libraries Unlimited, 1992.
Walvin, James, *Slavery and the Slave Trade: A Short Illustrated History,* University Press of Mississippi, 1983.

Alternative Applications: Lead a discussion of Abraham Lincoln's famous comment, "As I would not be a slave, so I would not be a master." Explain how these words describe the evil that corrupted John Newton's life. Comment on the return of his self-esteem and sense of purpose after he left the slave trade and confessed his crimes.

Black Evangelism

Age/Grade Level or Audience: Middle school, high school, and college religion and history classes; religious study groups; museums; historical societies.

Description: Generate a database or time line detailing major periods of black evangelism.

Procedure: Assign volunteers particular decades to research. Assemble information, including names, places, styles, and impact of evangelism in a database or on a wall frieze to hang in a church, library, museum, school, or public building during Black History Month. Note the following events:

- ◆ David George's description of black worship in 1773.
- ◆ Founding of the first black Baptist church in Augusta, Georgia, in 1773.
- ◆ Absalom Jones's rejection of segregation in the St. George's Methodist Episcopal Church of Philadelphia, Pennsylvania, in 1787.
- ◆ Ordination of Absalom Jones as the first black Episcopal priest in 1804.
- ◆ Josiah Bishop's purchase of freedom and in 1810 his pastorate of the Abyssinian Baptist Church of New York.
- ◆ John Gloucester's founding of the first African Presbyterian Church in Philadelphia in 1807.
- ◆ Richard Allen's establishment of the African Methodist Episcopal Church in 1816.
- ◆ Daniel Alexander Payne's election as bishop of the African Methodist Episcopal Church in 1852.
- ◆ The establishment of the Church of God in Christ in Lexington, Mississippi, in 1897.
- ◆ Ordination of Pauli Murray as the first female Episcopal priest in 1977.

Budget: $

Sources:

Hornsby, Alton, Jr., *Chronology of African-American History: Significant Events and People from 1619 to the Present,* Gale, 1991.

Lawson, E. Thomas, *Religions of Africa,* Harper & Row, 1984.

Wilson, Charles Reagan, and William Ferris, eds., *Encyclopedia of Southern Culture,* University of North Carolina Press, 1989.

Alternative Applications: Invite a historian or specialist in liturgy to comment on periods of revival and evangelism in American history, such as the evangelism of Charles Emanuel "Sweet Daddy" Grace, founder of the United House of Prayer, Charles Harrison Mason, one of the founders of the Church of God in Christ, Adam Clayton Powell, Jr., Martin Luther King, Jr., Jesse Jackson, and other charismatic leaders.

Black Moses

Age/Grade Level or Audience: Elementary and middle school history and writing classes.

Description: Compose an explanation of Harriet Tubman's nickname, "Black Moses."

Procedure: Have students compare the accomplishments of Harriet Tubman and Moses, the epic leader of the Hebrew people. Suggest that they include the following items of interest:

- ◆ Harriet Tubman's escape from bondage
- ◆ Moses' role in leading the Israelites out of Egypt
- ◆ Routes followed by Tubman on the Underground Railroad
- ◆ Moses' route out of Egypt
- ◆ Laws that hampered Tubman's crusade for freedom
- ◆ Moses' racial problems after his adoption into the royal Egyptian court

Budget: $

Sources:

Bradford, Sarah, *Harriet Tubman: The Moses of Her People,* 1886, reprinted, Corinth, 1961.

Hornsby, Alton, Jr., *Chronology of African-American History: Significant Events and People from 1619 to the Present,* Gale, 1991.

Low, W. Augustus, and Virgil A. Clift, eds., *Encyclopedia of Black America,* McGraw-Hill, 1981.

Smith, Jessie Carney, ed., *Notable Black American Women,* Gale, 1992.

Alternative Applications: Have students describe other leaders who parallel Harriet Tubman's bravery, such as these:

- ◆ Mary Baker Eddy, founder of the Christian Science Church
- ◆ Corrie ten Boom's assistance to Jews fleeing the Nazis
- ◆ Miep van Santen's concealment of Anne Frank's family
- ◆ Joseph Smith, who led Mormon pioneers to Utah
- ◆ Brigham Young, who founded Salt Lake City

Black Muslims

Age/Grade Level or Audience: High school and college sociology and religion classes; religious schools; civic groups.

Description: Describe the emergence of the Black Muslims.

Procedure: Provide a chronological overview of the development of the Black Muslims, noting the key leaders and significant events that helped shape the Nation of Islam. Include these facts:

◆ In 1897, Robert Poole, later called Elijah Muhammad, began a study of the causes of black poverty.

◆ In the 1920s, the Nation of Islam, founded by Wallace Delaney Fard and headquartered in Detroit, Michigan, insisted on the superiority of the black race.

◆ Fard, also known as F. Muhammad Ali, asserted that the earliest humans were black, and that one day whites would face divine retribution for mistreatment and suppression of blacks.

◆ Elijah Muhammad replaced Fard in 1934 and at a second temple in Chicago, Illinois, served as messenger of Allah or God.

◆ Fard disappeared.

◆ The Nation of Islam carried its message to prisoners, street people, and the hopeless.

◆ In 1942, Muhammad went to jail in Michigan when he failed to register for the draft.

◆ In 1946, he left prison and began recruiting followers, many from large urban centers and prisons.

◆ One of the most significant converts was Malcolm Little, a 21-year-old native of Omaha, Nebraska, who was imprisoned in Massachusetts in February 1946 for robbery and selling drugs.

◆ Little began studying Islam and corresponding with Muhammad.

◆ In 1952, Little, renamed Malcolm X to symbolize his loss of identity through slavery, obtained parole and ministered to blacks in New York and Philadelphia, Pennsylvania.

◆ In 1961, C. Eric Lincoln published *The Black Muslims in America,* an overview of the Islamic sect.

◆ Mohammed Abdul-Rauf allied Black Muslims with all Islam.

◆ Following the death of President John F. Kennedy in 1963, Malcolm X rejoiced. His remarks caused a permanent rift with Muhammad, who banned him from public speaking.

◆ By 1964, Malcolm X chose separatism and formed the Organization of Afro-American Unity, a more radical group.

◆ He journeyed to Mecca and renamed himself El-Hajj Malik El-Shabazz.

◆ Abandoning the fiery rhetoric of his earlier days, Malcolm X supported the civil rights movement and change through violence. In his words, "Nobody can give you freedom. Nobody can give you equality… if you're a man, you take it."

◆ On February 21, 1965, while delivering a speech at Harlem's Audubon Ballroom, Malcolm X was assassinated by three black gunmen—Norman Butler, Thomas Johnson, and Thomas Hagan—associated with the Nation of Islam. The trio were found guilty and jailed.

◆ Malcolm X left six daughters and a wife, Betty Shabazz.

◆ By the 1970s, the Black Muslims, headquartered in Chicago, had built segregated schools, churches, businesses, and community networks among America's blacks.

◆ In 1975, Muhammad died. His son Warith Deen began his own version of Islam based on the tenets of Malcolm X.

◆ Louis Farrakhan perpetuated Muhammad's views.

◆ Gradually, the middle class began to accept the Islamic faith for its push for decency and lawful behavior.

◆ In 1988, Black Muslim teams helped suppress drug dealing in Washington, D.C.

◆ In 1992, Deen became the first Muslim to pray in the U.S. Senate.

◆ By 1992, Thomas Hagan remained in jail. His accomplices were paroled.

Budget: $

Sources:

The films *The Story of Islam* (1989) and *Malcolm X* (1992).

Cantor, George, *Historic Landmarks of Black America*, Gale, 1991.

"Daughter's View of Malcolm X," *USA Today,* November 16, 1992, p. 15A.

Davis, Angela, "Malcolm X," *Emerge*, December 1992, pp. 35-37.

Estell, Kenneth, ed., *The African-American Almanac*, 6th ed., Gale, 1993.

Glasse, Cyril, *The Concise Encyclopedia of Islam*, Harper & Row, 1989.

Hornsby, Alton, Jr., *Chronology of African-American History: Significant Events and People from 1619 to the Present*, Gale, 1991.

Low, W. Augustus, and Virgil A. Clift, eds., *Encyclopedia of Black America*, McGraw-Hill, 1981, reprinted, Da Capo Press, 1984.

Malcolm X and Alex Haley, *Autobiography of Malcolm X,* Grove Press, 1965, reprinted, Ballantine Books, 1992.

"Nation of Islam," *USA Today,* November 18, 1992, pp. 1A-2A.

Alternative Applications: Lead a workshop on the differences between religious philosophy and political activism. Incorporate the following activities:

◆ Discuss the rise in violence and infighting that characterized the growth of the Black Muslims.

◆ Contrast the Islamic beliefs in self-help and family values with traditional Judeo-Christian ideals.

◆ Account for Islam's call for segregation of whites and blacks and a condemnation of whites as devils.
◆ Contrast white and black reactions to Spike Lee's film *Malcolm X.*

Quakers and the Underground Railroad

Age/Grade Level or Audience: Adult discussion groups.

Description: Study the reasons for the Quakers' assistance to runaway slaves.

Procedure: Have individuals research different denominations during slave times and their response to the slave trade, the Fugitive Slave Law, abolitionism, and other issues crucial to the ending of the institution of slavery. Feature the work of Levi Coffin and other Quakers, who were the first to press for an end to slavery. Emphasize the role of Quakers in organizing and staffing the Underground Railroad. Mention specifically other groups, particularly Unitarians, Baptists, Mennonites, Methodists, Presbyterians, Lutherans, Episcopalians, Catholics, and Jews.

Budget: $

Sources:
The novels or film versions of Jessamyn West's *Friendly Persuasion* (Harcourt Brace Jovanovich, 1945, reprinted, Buccaneer Books, 1982) and *Except for Me and Thee* (Harcourt, 1969).

Cantor, George, *Historic Landmarks of Black America,* Gale, 1991.

Estell, Kenneth, ed., *The African-American Almanac,* 6th ed., Gale, 1993.

Hornsby, Alton, Jr., *Chronology of African-American History: Significant Events and People from 1619 to the Present,* Gale, 1991.

Low, W. Augustus, and Virgil A. Clift, eds., *Encyclopedia of Black America,* McGraw-Hill, 1981.

Windley, Lathan A., *Runaway Slave Advertisements: A Documentary History from the 1730s to 1790,* Greenwood Press, 1983.

Alternative Applications: Compose a newsletter or newspaper article about the work of George Keith, George Fox, William Penn, John Woolman, Levi Coffin, Anthony Benezet, Quakers Garrett Henderich, Derick Op de Graeff, Francis Daniel Pastorius, Abram Op de Graeff, and Richard Worrell. Contrast the abolitionist movement with organized efforts to help Jews escape Nazi death camps.

Religions of Africa

Age/Grade Level or Audience: Middle school, high school, and college history, religion, and sociology classes; church groups; literary societies.

Description: Study the variety of religious customs and practices throughout Africa's history.

Procedure: Provide participants with guest lecturers, art prints, photographs, travelogues, videos, filmstrips, films, and reference books on religions in Africa, particularly Islam, Amenism, Atenism, fetishism, totemism, Copt, Baha'i, Ethiopian, animism, Santeria, voodoo, Catholicism, and Protestantism. Organize discussion groups to consider these topics:

- ◆ Pharaoh Akhenaten's establishment of monotheism through the worship of Amon-Ra
- ◆ contrasts between Eastern Orthodoxy, Roman Catholicism, Protestantism, and Coptic Christianity
- ◆ the Black Muslim emphasis on the family
- ◆ Baha'i activism against prejudice and racism
- ◆ differences in style of worship, such as singing and clapping, ceremonies and feasts, processions, musical accompaniment, rites of passage, scarification, and circumcision
- ◆ effects of religion and ethics on cultural, social, and governmental structures
- ◆ meaning and use of religious symbols, such as the ankh and idols
- ◆ places of worship, such as shrines, particularly Spain's Shrine of the Black Madonna, which was adapted from the Moors
- ◆ Zulu methods of divination by "throwing the bones"
- ◆ Yoruba voodoo and witchcraft as outgrowths of nature lore
- ◆ Santeria and animal sacrifice

Note how native African religions were influenced by other religious groups, such as Mormons, Seventh Day Adventists, Presbyterians, Lutherans, Catholics, Baptists, members of the Church of Scotland, Moravian Brethren, and Methodists.

Budget: $$

Sources:
Ali, Ahmed, *The Holy Qur'an,* Sterling Printing and Publishing, 1964.
Aunapu, Greg, "Shedding Blood in Sacred Bowls," *Time,* October 19, 1992, p. 60.
Ben-Jochannon, Yosef, *African Origins of the Major "Western Religions,"* Alkebu-lan Books, 1970.
Brown, Karen McCarthy, *Mama Lola: A Vodou Priestess in Brooklyn,* University of California Press, 1991.

Budge, E. A. Wallis, *Tutankhamen: Amenism, Atenism and Egyptian Monotheism with Hieroglyphic Texts of Hymns to Amen and Aten,* B. Blom, 1971.

Drewel, Margaret Thompson, "Ritual Performance in Africa Today," *Drama Review,* Summer 1988, pp. 25-30.

Glasse, Cyril, *The Concise Encyclopedia of Islam,* Harper & Row, 1989.

Lawson, E. Thomas, *Religions of Africa,* Harper & Row, 1984.

Murray, Jocelyn, ed., *Cultural Atlas of Africa,* Facts on File, 1989.

Nketia, J. H. Kwabena, *The Music of Africa,* Gollancz, 1975.

Spence, Lewis, *Ancient Egyptian Myths and Legends,* Dover Publications, 1990.

Alternative Applications: Have participants study headdresses, masks, priests' robes, ritual vessels, face paints, kente cloths, asipim chairs, umbrellas, and other artifacts connected with African worship. Present materials detailing music, dance, processions, divination, marriage and funeral rites, coming-of-age and healing ceremonies, naming rituals, and tableaux as African methods of worship.

Religious Themes in Negro Spirituals

Age/Grade Level or Audience: High school and college religion and literature classes; book clubs; church groups; literary societies.

Description: Listen to recordings of common Negro spirituals, then discuss prevalent biblical scenes and themes.

Procedure: Present songsheets of classic Negro Spirituals, especially these:

- ◆ "Sometimes I Feel Like a Motherless Child"
- ◆ "Stan' Still Jordan"
- ◆ "Good News"
- ◆ "Were You There"
- ◆ "Weepin' Mary"
- ◆ "Ev'ry Time I Feel De Spirit"
- ◆ "Couldn't Hear Nobody Pray"
- ◆ "Wade in de Water"
- ◆ "Joshua Fit de Battle of Jericho"
- ◆ "All God's Chillun"
- ◆ "Oh Dem Golden Slippers"
- ◆ "Rock-a-My Soul"
- ◆ "Roll, Jordan, Roll"
- ◆ "Little David, Play on Your Harp"
- ◆ "Steal Away"
- ◆ "By an' By"
- ◆ "De Blin' Man Stood on de Road an' Cried"

◆ "De Gospel Train"
◆ "Deep River"
◆ "I'm Jus' a Wanderer"

Invite volunteers to explain connections between names, places, and events in the songs with similar incidents in the Bible, for example, frequent mention of the Children of Israel, Pharaoh, Moses, Daniel, Gabriel, King David, Joshua, Mary, Joseph, Christ's birth and crucifixion, Paul, Silas, and the Jordan River.

Budget: $$

Sources:

Southern, Eileen, *The Music of Black Americans: A History,* Norton, 1983.
Wilson, Charles Reagan, and William Ferris, eds., *Encyclopedia of Southern Culture,* University of North Carolina Press, 1989.

Alternative Applications: Organize a Black History Month hymn sing. Invite multi-ethnic church groups to join in singing the most familiar songs. Feature a different hymn each week. Provide handouts to explain the background and significance of spirituals to slave morale. Indicate black code terms, such as River Jordan for Underground Railroad, Pharaoh for slave owners, and Hebrew children for slaves.

Things Fall Apart

Age/Grade Level or Audience: High school and college sociology and literature classes; book clubs; literary societies.

Description: Read and discuss the religious implications of Chinua Achebe's novel *Things Fall Apart.*

Procedure: After participants have read the book, organize round table discussions of the stabilizing influence of traditional religions. Concentrate on the theme of change and how it destroys the main characters' lives. Propose the following questions:

◆ What is the religious and ethical system before the arrival of missionaries?
◆ Why is childbirth significant to the tribe?
◆ Why are the souls of dead children suspect?
◆ How does life change during the main character's exile?
◆ Why is the main character estranged from his son?
◆ Why does the main character help murder his foster son?
◆ What forces lead to the main character's suicide?
◆ How does the new missionary destroy black pride and tradition?

Budget: $

Sources:
Achebe, Chinua, *Things Fall Apart*, Heinemann, 1958, reprinted, Fawcett, 1988.
Carroll, David, *Chinua Achebe*, Twayne, 1970.
Killam, G.D., *The Novels of Chinua Achebe*, Africana Publishing, 1969.

Alternative Applications: Have participants discuss why Achebe gave his book the name *Things Fall Apart*. Consider whether similar institutional changes are damaging African family life and worship, particularly industrialization, modernization, independence, communications, depletion of animal and plant species, and pollution.

Science

African and Caribbean Fruits and Spices

Age/Grade Level or Audience: Middle school, high school, and college biology or life science classes.

Description: Do an oral presentation about the cultivation, harvesting, and use of African and Caribbean spices, fruits, and vegetables.

Procedure: Supply information from a variety of sources. Have students select a particular plant to describe, such as these:

banana	cabbage	cardamom	cassava
cinnamon	coconut	coriander	corn
cumin	date	eggplant	egusi
ginger root	gourd	mango	millet
onion	peanut	pepper	pineapple
plantain	pumpkin	rice	squash
spinach	tomato	turmeric	

Arrange samples of fragrant or tasty plants for students to smell and taste. Include coconut, onion, cumin, turmeric, various types of pepper, banana oil, dates, ginger, and coriander. Then blindfold participants and have them identify substances by taste and smell.

Budget: $

Sources:

Harris, Jessica B., "A Taste of the Islands: Spicy, Sweet, and Savory," *Black Enterprise,* May 1987, pp. 47-48.

Nabwire, Constance, and Bertha Vining Montgomery, *Cooking the African Way,* Lerner Publications, 1988.

Trillin, Calvin, "Flying Fish on Baxter's Road: Eating One's Way through Barbados," *House and Garden,* September 1986, pp. 82-86.

Trillin, "Grazing in Guadeloupe: Ragout of Goat, Conch Curry, and Fricassee of Octopus from the Island's Celebrated Chefs," *House and Garden,* January 1988, pp. 46-49.

Alternative Applications: Make a chart of ways in which native plants are used in industry. For example:

- peanuts produce oil, makeup, mulch, and fertilizer
- rice powder is added to cosmetics, puddings, paper, and baby foods
- flax is made into linen for bags, rope, cloth, and wallpaper
- papyrus was formed into paper
- gourds are carved into utensils, bowls, and musical instruments
- coconut palms are stripped of leaves and bark for rope and weaving material and parts are cooked as a vegetable

African Butterflies and Moths

Age/Grade Level or Audience: Middle school, high school, and college biology, entomology, life science, and art classes.

Description: Describe the habitats and life cycles of African butterflies.

Procedure: Isolate the most common butterflies of Africa by name and describe where and how they live. Emphasize adaptive coloration, which enables the delicate insects to elude predators. Include these species:

- black-bordered charaxes
- false acraea
- *Deilephila nerii* or oleander hawk
- *Euchloron megaera*
- *Bunaea alcinio*
- *Papilio dardanus*
- *Lycaenidae kallimoides* or hairstreak
- *Danaidae linnaeus* or tiger butterfly
- *Papilio demoleus* or orange-dog swallowtail
- *Morpho portis*
- *Gonepteryx rhamni* or brimstone butterfly
- *Pieris brassicae* or white and yellow cabbage butterfly
- *Vanessa atalanta* or red admiral butterfly
- *Cupido minimus* or small blue butterfly
- *Lycaena phlaeas* or small copper butterfly
- *Iphiclides podalirius* or scarce swallowtail
- *Papilio antimachus* or giant swallowtail
- *Satyridae elymnias* or brown butterfly

- *Nudaurelia zambesina* or giant silkworm moth
- *Argema mittrei* or moon moth
- *Hemaris fuciformis* or bee hawk moth

Sketch posters of the most colorful species. Use the sketches for a bulletin board display; to decorate tables, napkins, invitations, or thank-you notes; or to illustrate a display on African wildlife.

Budget: $$

Sources:

Brown, Leslie, *Africa: A Natural History,* Random House, 1965.

D'Abrera, Bernard, *Butterflies of the Afrotropical Region,* Lansdown Editions, 1980.

Jourdan, Eveline, *Butterflies and Moths around the World,* Lerner Publications, 1981.

Kingdon, Johnathan, *Island Africa: The Evolution of Africa's Rare Animals and Plants,* Princeton University Press, 1989.

Alternative Applications: Conduct detailed research on other insects that are indigenous to the African ecosystem, particularly the termite, dune beetle, driver ant, mantid, cicada, bot fly, caddis fly, trapdoor spider, desert locust, tsetse fly, simulium fly, anopheles mosquito, honeybee, grub, tenebrionid beetle, silverfish, cerbalus spider, tick, locust, Guinea threadworm, and grasshopper. Note connections between insect infestations and disease, as with the *Aedes aegypti* mosquito and yellow fever; the botfly and respiratory diseases of sheep, cattle, horses, and humans; ticks and encephalitis; or the *anopheles* mosquito and malaria.

African Habitats

Age/Grade Level or Audience: Kindergarten, elementary, middle school, high school, and college biology and life science classes.

Description: Study variations in African habitats.

Procedure: Divide students into two teams. Have each team collect data on the requirements for survival in one of two widely contrasting areas of the African continent. Choose from among areas such as these: desert, savanna, bush, nyika or wilderness, semi-arid scrub, tropical rain forest, mountain, coastal, shore, swamp, woodland, or jungle. Subjects of research should include geology, weather, sources of water, plants, animals, predators, disease, and human adaptation.

Budget: $

Sources:

Aardema, Verna, *Bringing the Rain to Kapiti Plain,* Dial Press, 1981.

Brown, Leslie, *Africa: A Natural History,* Random House, 1965.

"Etosha Park," *National Geographic,* March 1983.

Isadora, Rachel, *Over the Green Hills,* Greenwillow Books, 1992.

"Journey up the Nile," *National Geographic,* May 1985.

Kasza, Keiko, *A Mother for Choco,* Putnam, 1992.

Kingdon, Johnathan, *Island Africa: The Evolution of Africa's Rare Animals and Plants,* Princeton University Press, 1989.

Lemonick, Michael D., "The World in 3300 B.C.," *Time,* October 26, 1992, pp. 66-69.

Lester, Julian, *How Many Spots Does a Leopard Have? And Other Tales,* Scholastic, Inc., 1989.

MacClintock, Dorcas, *African Images,* Scribner, 1984.

"Serengeti," *National Geographic,* May 1986.

Alternative Applications: Have students augment their research by simulating a desert or jungle habitat in a terrarium or greenhouse. Collect local plants common to Africa, such as philodendron, papyrus, eucalyptus, lantana, or bamboo. For large habitats, add indigenous lizards, snakes, and birds.

African Healers

Age/Grade Level or Audience: Middle school, high school, and college biology and life science classes.

Description: Compose a report on ethnobiology and African plants that are beneficial to medicine.

Procedure: In an oral presentation, give details about these medicinal plants:

- *water lily bulbs* used to combat fever and the *maytenus vine* to treat cancer, gathered from the Shimba Hills of Kenya
- *fara,* a Senegalese cure for malaria, eye disease, and stomachache, *palinkumfo* for intestinal parasites, *katirao* for snakebite, and *datura* for breast cancer
- *rosy periwinkle* from Ghana and Madagascar to treat liver disorders and to save children suffering from leukemia
- *mousingi* from the Central African Republic as a possible cure for AIDS
- *enantia* from Cameroon as an antimalarial compound, *African cherry* to relieve prostate inflammation, and *voacanga* and *strobanthus gratus* to stimulate the heart
- Egyptian squill to treat ulcers and swelling, *castor oil* to combat warts, lesions, and bronchitis, *roasted ox liver* to improve eyesight, *poppy juice* to ease colic, *willow bark* to treat infection and asthma, *moldy bread* to encourage healing, *pomegranate* and *wormseed* for intestinal parasites, *copper salt solution* to ease eye infection, *sea onion juice* to strengthen a weak heart

◆ *ginger, chinaberry, ouabain vine, snakeroot, calamus*, and *wormseed*, which Africans transplanted to the American south and the Caribbean

Budget: $

Sources:

Aikman, Lonnelle, *Nature's Healing Arts: From Folk Medicine to Modern Drugs*, National Geographic Society, 1977.

Kingdon, Johnathan, *Island Africa: The Evolution of Africa's Rare Animals and Plants*, Princeton University Press, 1989.

Alternative Applications: Have students extend their study of folk cures with additional treatments derived from other parts of Africa, as well as Central, North, and South America, New Zealand, Japan, China, and Australia. Create drawings and brief explanations of each treatment for a database or library, school, museum, or civic display.

An African Window Garden

Age/Grade Level or Audience: Kindergarten and elementary school science classes; religious schools; 4-H clubs; Brownie and Cub Scouts; retirement homes; classes for the handicapped.

Description: Start a window garden of African plants.

Procedure: In a variety of pottery dishes, peat pots, or glass containers plant cuttings, slips, bulbs, or seeds of the following plants common to Africa:

acacia	acanthus	arum lily	bamboo
clivia	coffee	cowpea	deiffenbachia
eucalyptus	fern	flax	gourd
guava	heather	hemlock	hibiscus
hydrangea	lantana	laurel	liana
mallow	milkweed	millet	mint
moss	myrtle	nettle	okra
oleander	palm	papyrus	pepper
philodendron	pumpkin	rose	rubber tree
sedge	squash	yam	

Budget: $$$

Sources:

Brown, Leslie, *Africa: A Natural History,* Random House, 1965.

Kingdon, Johnathan, *Island Africa: The Evolution of Africa'a Rare Animals and Plants,* Princeton University Press, 1989.

Alternative Applications: Create an African display with plants borrowed from local gardeners. Include massed sweet potato plants growing in water or deiffenbachia, fern, hibiscus, philodendron, aloe, or coffee plants. Add paper cutouts of butterflies, snakes, lizards, monkeys, and other animals native to Africa.

All That Glitters

Age/Grade Level or Audience: Middle school, high school, and college natural science and geology classes.

Description: Present a unit of study on the African diamond trade.

Procedure: Use a variety of media to emphasize the importance of the diamond to the history and economics of Africa. For example:

◆ Present handouts explaining how diamonds, the world's hardest substances, are formed, mined, and shaped.

◆ Make a chalkboard list of industrial uses, such as crushing, grinding, sanding, polishing, drilling, and cutting.

◆ Name the trades that depend on diamonds, particularly auto and aircraft manufacturing, electronics, petroleum, mining, tool and dye making, dentistry, and glass and optical manufacturing.

◆ Explain how diamonds are graded and why they come in shades of yellow, pink, black, blue, gray, and champagne.

◆ Organize a small group to draw examples of famous African diamonds, notably the largest, the Cullinan (1905), from which the Star of Africa was cut and set in the British royal scepter, as well as the Eureka (1867), Excelsior (1893), Jonker, Jubilee, Star of Sierra Leone (1972), Star of South Africa (1869), Tiffany, and Victoria.

◆ Have several volunteers make geometric sketches of common crystalline configurations of diamond shapes, notably the marquise, baguette, brilliant, round, pear, teardrop, and emerald cuts.

◆ Present and discuss technical terms connected with diamonds, especially facet, lapidary, schist, isometric, mineralogy, pipe, carat, Mohs scale, alluvial, diatreme spinel, adamantine, refraction, and octahedron.

◆ Assign reports on the following minerals: kimberlite, peridotite, olivine, garnet, pyroxene, ilmenite, serpentine, chlorite, calcite, and mica.

◆ Discuss how in 1880 James Ballantyne Hannay, a Scottish chemist, synthesized diamonds from lithium.

◆ Locate on a map the African cities and mines most closely connected with the diamond trade:

Bafi-Sewa	Bakwanga	Beyla	Birim River
Brazzaville	Bultfontein	Bushimale	Cafunfo
Carnot	Chicapa	Chiumbe	De Beers
Dutoitspan	Elandsfontein	Hopetown	Jagersfontein
Kanshi	Kimberley	Kissidougou	Luachimo
Luembe	Marahoue River	Mwadui	Namaqualand
Nzako	Oranjemund	Ouadda	Premier
Shinyanga	Tortiya	Wesselton	

Budget: $

Sources:

Clarendon Press Cartographic Department Staff, *The Oxford Economic Atlas of the World,* Oxford University Press, 1972.

Frazier, Si, and Ann Frazier, "South of the Equator," *Lapidary Journal,* August 1990, pp. 36-47.

Gall, Timothy L., and Susan B. Gall, *Consumers' Guide to Product Grades and Terms,* Gale, 1993.

Herbert, Ivor, *The Diamond Diggers: South Africa 1866 to the 1970s,* Tom Stacy, 1972.

Koskoff, David, *The Diamond World,* Harper & Row, 1981.

McCloud, Scott, "Diamonds Aren't Forever," *Time,* October 12, 1992, p. 73.

Alternative Applications: Discuss social and economic issues that relate to the diamond trade, particularly apartheid, colonialism, and smuggling. Name people who have made their fortunes in diamonds, especially Barney and Harry Barnato, Cecil Rhodes, Ernest Oppenheimer, and Anton Dukelsbuhler. Explain how the diamond has been both boon and curse to Africans of Ghana, Guinea, Sierra Leone, Angola, Zaire, Liberia, Ivory Coast, Central African Republic, Tanzania, and South Africa.

Animal Express

Age/Grade Level or Audience: Elementary, middle school, and high school biology classes; college zoology classes; ecology clubs; animal preservation societies.

Description: Conduct a detailed study of African animals.

Procedure: Open the session with the film *Gorillas in the Mist* (1988), or a National Geographic Society videotape, such as *Gorilla* (1956) or *Lions of the African Night.* Lead a discussion of the importance of preserving African animals in their natural habitats. Consider the following topics:

- ◆ raising endangered species in game reserves or laboratories
- ◆ providing food for endangered species

- frozen sperm banks and artificial insemination to propagate endangered species
- embargoes and importation bans on hides, teeth, bones, and horns of endangered species
- media campaigns aimed at preserving wildlife and raising money for protective measures, such as antipoaching patrols
- tagging migratory animals to determine habits
- treatment centers for injured or diseased animals
- vaccination programs

Budget: $$

Sources:

Attenborough, David, *Atlas of the Living World,* Houghton Mifflin, 1989.

Brown, Leslie, *Africa: A Natural History,* Random House, 1965.

Carty, Winthrop P., and Elizabeth Lee, *The Rhino Man and Other Uncommon Environmentalists,* Seven Locks Press, 1992.

Douglas-Hamilton, Ian, and Oria Douglas-Hamilton, *Among the Elephants,* Penguin Books, 1978.

Kingdon, Johnathan, *Island Africa: The Evolution of Africa's Rare Animals and Plants,* Princeton University Press, 1989.

Martin, Chryssee, and Esmond Bradley Martin, *Run, Rhino, Run,* Chatto & Windus, 1982.

Moss, Cynthia, *Elephant Memories,* Morrow, 1988.

Williams, John G., *A Field Guide to the Birds of East Africa,* Collins, 1980.

Alternative Applications: Conduct a study of the endangered species of Africa and the United States. Compare the ecological problems of both nations, such as these:

- poachers and hunters
- fire
- the illegal ivory trade
- clear-cutting of ancient forests
- industrialization
- acid rain
- strip mining
- erosion
- polluted air, streams, and rivers
- noisy highways, rail lines, and airports

Baobab: The Tree of Life

Age/Grade Level or Audience: Elementary school life science classes; scout troops; 4-H clubs; religious schools.

Description: Explain why the baobab tree is important to Africans.

Procedure: Read aloud a book about the baobab or monkey-bread tree. Point out the difference between biological facts and legends about the tree. Emphasize these facts:

◆ The baobab is one of the world's oldest plants.
◆ It can live as long as one thousand years.
◆ It can grow sixty feet high, forty feet wide, and ten feet thick.
◆ It is sometimes called the upside-down tree because, when the leaves fall, its stunted limbs, protruding from a grotesquely thickened trunk, look like roots pointing at the sky.
◆ The baobab is a succulent plant so soft that a bullet can pass through it.
◆ Its spongy inner tissue stores water to help it survive drought.
◆ The tree produces a gourd-like fruit hanging from long twigs.
◆ The baobab's ability to adapt to changes in the environment accounts for its long life.

Budget: $$

Sources:
Attenborough, David, *Atlas of the Living World,* Houghton Mifflin, 1989.
Bash, Barbara, *Tree of Life: The World of the African Baobab,* Little, Brown, 1989.
Brown, Leslie, *Africa: A Natural History,* Random House, 1965.

Alternative Applications: Explain why Africans revere the gnarled baobab and its role in the African ecosystem. Mention these facts:

◆ The baobab is a nesting place for birds, such as the yellow-collared lovebird, mosque swallow, orange-billed parrot, lilac-breasted roller, red-headed buffalo weaver, honey guide bird, pygmy falcon, superb starling, and yellow-billed hornbill.
◆ Insects make their homes in the bark, limbs, and leaves of the baobab.
◆ Bats pollinate the baobab's flowers.
◆ Natives pick the leaves and cook them like spinach.
◆ Elephants eat the smooth, glossy purplish-gray bark.
◆ Waxy flowers turn into firm-shelled fruit, which can be cracked and eaten.
◆ Parts of the tree are used for weaving, drinks, fertilizer, packaging, drinking cups, musical instruments, and candy.
◆ The spongy wood is light enough to make fishing floats, canoes, and housing material.
◆ As a medicine, the baobab is used to cure malaria, dysentery, fever, earache, and kidney infection.
◆ The acid in the baobab nut is used to curdle milk or harden rubber.
◆ A burning solution of baobab pulp rids animals of insect pests.

Brainstorming

Age/Grade Level or Audience: Elementary, middle school, high school, and college science classes.

Description: Brainstorm the design and use of significant inventions.

Procedure: Assemble models or drawings of items invented or improved upon by black engineers and scientists. Have students work in groups to examine the items and analyze how they save labor. Discuss scientific principles that undergird the design of each. Include the following:

- James S. Adams's airplane propeller
- George E. Alcorn's semiconductors
- Benjamin Banneker's wooden clock
- James A. Bauer's coin changer
- Andrew J. Beard's automatic railcar coupler
- Henry Blair's corn and cotton planters
- Otis Boykin's stimulator for an artificial heart
- Henrietta Bradbury's torpedo discharger
- Leander M. Coles's mortician's table
- Cap B. Collins's portable electric light
- David N. Crosthwait's vacuum heating system
- Joseph Hunter Dickinson's player piano
- Charles Richard Drew's blood bank
- James Forten's sail raising device
- Albert Y. Garner's flame retardant
- Meredith C. Gourdine's electradyne paint spray gun
- Edward Hawthorne's heart monitor
- Harry C. Hopkins's hearing aid
- Thomas L. Jennings's dry cleaning process
- John Arthur Johnson's monkey wrench
- Frederick M. Jones's portable X-ray machine
- Percy Lavon Julian's glaucoma treatment
- J. L. Love's pencil sharpener
- Elijah J. McCoy's automatic locomotive lubricator
- Garret Augustus Morgan's gas mask or four-way traffic signal
- W. B. Purvis's machine to make paper bags
- Norbert Rillieux's sugar refiner
- Dewey S. C. Sanderson's urinalysis meter
- J. H. Smith's lawn sprinkler
- P. D. Smith's mechanical potato digger
- Richard Spikes's automatic transmission
- Lewis Temple's improved whaling harpoon

◆ Sarah Walker's hair straightener
◆ Ozzie S. Williams's radar search beacon
◆ Granville T. Woods's railroad telegraph
◆ Louis Tompkins Wright's treatment for head and neck injuries

Budget: $$$

Sources:

Asante, Molefi K., *Historical and Cultural Atlas of African Americans,* Macmillan, 1991.

Haber, Louis, *Black Pioneers of Science and Invention,* Harcourt Brace Jovanovich, 1970, reprinted, 1991.

International Library of Negro Life and History, Publisher's Co., 1969.

James, Portia P., *The Real McCoy: African-American Invention and Innovation, 1619-1930,* Smithsonian Institution Press, 1989.

Klein, Aaron E., and Cynthia L. Klein, *The Better Mousetrap: A Miscellany of Gadgets, Labor-saving Devices, and Inventions that Intrigue,* Beaufort Books, 1982.

Logan, Rayford W., and Michael R. Winston, eds., *Dictionary of American Negro Biography,* Norton, 1982.

Terry, Ted, *American Black History: Reference Manual,* Myles Publishing, 1991.

Alternative Applications: Have students compose a group report on how one of these inventions could be improved by applying more current technology, such as microchips, laser, memory, digital readout, remote control, fiber optics, solar panels, solid state construction, or space age metals.

Deadly Organisms

Age/Grade Level or Audience: Middle school, high school, and college biology and life science classes.

Description: Study diseases caused by fungi, protozoa, spirochetes, bacteria, and viruses carried by organisms such as the snail, rat, tsetse fly, blood fluke, tick, louse, flea, and Aedes aegypti, *Aedes africanus,* and *anopheles mosquito.*

Procedure: Lead students in a study of the tropical organisms responsible for malaria, black water fever, polio, cholera, syphilis, tetanus, typhus, trachoma, leprosy, dengue fever, encephalitis, yellow fever, hookworm, diphtheria, plague, schistosomiasis, Q-fever, and sleeping sickness in humans as well as nagana and onchocerciasis in livestock. Show on maps the yellow fever belt of Africa and the malaria belt of Haiti, the Dominican Republic, Africa, and other parts of the world. Create a time line of the resurgence and eradication of major diseases through organism control. Feature these data:

◆ A crippled Egyptian mummy dating to 3700 B.C. may be the world's oldest evidence of polio.

- During the fifth century B.C., Hippocrates classified varieties of malaria.
- Smallpox ravaged North Africa in A.D. 647.
- European explorers brought malaria to the Western Hemisphere in the fifteenth century.
- In the 1630s, Spanish missionaries discovered that quinine, extracted from the cinchona tree, prevented malaria.
- The Dutch first infected South Africans with smallpox in 1713.
- In 1734, John Atkins described the neurological symptoms of sleeping sickness.
- From 1764 to 1778, yellow fever surfaced in Sierra Leone and Senegal.
- The importation of African slaves to Cuba in 1803 brought sleeping sickness to the Caribbean.
- In 1822, Fever J. Campbell reported that Rhodesians inoculated healthy people with smallpox to weaken the disease.
- In the 1820s, African slaves carried yellow fever to American port cities.
- Dengue from Africa first attacked the Caribbean and coastal United States in 1827.
- In 1852, Bilharz discovered the microbe that causes schistosomiasis.
- In 1872, Armauer G. Hansen discovered the bacteria that cause leprosy or Hansen's disease.
- In 1880, Charles Laveran discovered that protozoa infested the blood of Algerian malaria victims.
- In the 1880s, David Bruce studied the organisms that cause tetanus, sleeping sickness, and nagana.
- From 1881 to 1882, cholera swept through Egypt.
- In 1884, Loffler isolated the diphtheria microbe.
- In 1885, Pfeiffer isolated the bacteria that cause typhus and typhoid fever.
- Nigerians first suffered sleeping sickness in 1890.
- In the 1890s, Juan Finlay hypothesized that the *Aedes aegypti* mosquito spread yellow fever.
- In 1898, Ronald Ross of Great Britain connected the bite of female *Anopheles* mosquito with transmission of malaria. That same year, Italians Amico Bignami, Giuseppe Bastianelli, and Giovanni Battista Grassi made detailed studies of how the disease develops in the human body.
- Plague invaded South Africa in 1899.
- By 1900, Walter Reed proved Juan Finlay's ideas by isolating the virus that causes yellow fever.
- In 1905, William Gorgas initiated a program of insecticide spray and draining of standing pools of water to control mosquitoes.
- From 1912 to 1946, plague killed 70 percent of the residents of French West Africa.
- A London commission studied the eradication of sleeping sickness in 1925.
- From 1925 to 1936, hygienists attempted to eradicate hookworm among South African miners.
- The mortality rate for diphtheria in Egypt in 1932 was more than 45 percent.

◆ In 1939, Paul Miller, a Swiss chemist, created DDT to control the mosquitoes that carry malaria.

◆ In 1940, a yellow fever epidemic afflicted the Nuba Mountains of the Sudan.

◆ During World War II, more effective malaria treatments replaced quinine.

◆ In 1947, cholera again swept Egypt.

◆ By 1948, sleeping sickness was virtually eradicated in the Congo.

◆ In 1954, yellow fever beset Trinidad.

◆ In 1955, the World Health Organization (WHO) attempted to conquer malaria by spraying DDT over areas infested with mosquitoes.

◆ In 1959, yellow fever returned to Trinidad. Also, rifampicin was discovered as a treatment for leprosy.

◆ In 1961, a severe yellow fever epidemic hit Ethiopia.

◆ In 1965, the Rockefeller Foundation signed an agreement with the government of St. Lucia to study the control of schistosomiasis by treating the sick and eradicating the disease-bearing snail.

◆ An outbreak of cholera in 1971 ravaged seventeen African countries.

◆ In 1980, researchers studied an antimalaria vaccine.

◆ By 1984, WHO declared the St. Lucia method of schistosomiasis control a success.

Budget: $

Sources:

Beausoleil, E. G., "Malaria and Drug Resistance," *World Health,* August-September 1986, pp. 7-9.

Brown, Leslie, *Africa: A Natural History,* Random House, 1965.

Friedman, Milton J., and William Trager, "The Biochemistry of Resistance to Malaria," *Scientific American,* March 1981.

Gibson, Diana, "Together, We Have Defeated Oncho," *World Health,* October 1985, pp. 6-8.

Goodfield, June, *Quest for the Killers,* Hill & Wang, 1987.

Gordon, Harrison A., *Mosquitoes, Malaria, and Man: A History of the Hostilities since 1880,* Dutton, 1978.

Kingdon, Johnathan, *Island Africa: The Evolution of Africa's Rare Animals and Plants,* Princeton University Press, 1989.

Marks, Geoffrey, and William K. Beatty, *Epidemics,* Scribner, 1976.

Mumper, Sharon E., "AIDS in Africa: Death is the Only Certainty," *Christianity Today,* April 8, 1988, pp. 36-39.

Walsh, John, "Return of the Locust: A Cloud over Africa," *Science,* October 3, 1986, pp. 17-19.

"Winged Marauders," *The Economist,* October 22, 1988, p. 48.

Alternative Applications: Make a similar study of Africa's most dangerous insects and reptiles, particularly the locust, scorpion, crocodile, cobra, viper, and black mamba. Determine how victims are treated and their chances of surviving attack.

Note modern chemicals that ward off insects and protect swimmers from crocodiles.

Early Humans in Africa

Age/Grade Level or Audience: Middle school, high school, and college biology and life science classes.

Description: Study the early humans of Africa. Highlight anthropological discoveries of hominid fossils more than five million years old.

Procedure: Discuss why knowledge of primitive social institutions, nutrition, disease, warfare, and survival methods are significant to the survival of *Homo sapiens* on this planet. Include the following breakthroughs in cultural anthropology in your presentation:

- England's A. R. Radcliffe-Brown's study of social cohesion and ritual in African tribal society
- The 1925 discovery of the Taung Baby in South Africa
- Explorations of Louis and Mary Leakey on Rusinga Island, where remains of Proconsul led to a fuller understanding of human evolution from primates
- Leakey's study of the Kikuyu of Kenya from 1937 to 1939
- Leakey's extensive work in 1942 in the Olduvai Gorge of Tanzania, where hominid fossils and obsidian tools attested to the existence of the *Zinjanthropus boisei,* peoples living nearly two million years ago.
- The significance of *Australopithecus boisei,* a prehuman life form
- Mary Leakey's discovery of the Zinj skull of the "Nutcracker Man" in Tanzania
- Evidence of toolmaking in homo habilis in 1960
- The establishment of the Coryndon Memorial Museum in Nairobi
- The discovery in the Olduvai Gorge between 1959 and 1965 of *Homo erectus,* who dates back one million years
- Studies of *Ramapithecus* and *Kenyapithecus wickeri* near Fort Ternan and Rusinga near Lake Victoria
- Leakey's encouragement of Jane Goodall and Dian Fossey in studies of primates, particularly chimpanzees and gorillas
- The continuation of the Leakey family's interest in anthropology with the work of their son Richard, who concentrated on *Australopithecines* of East Africa and the Omo River region of Ethiopia and Lake Turkana, Kenya

Budget: $$

Sources:

Bishop, Walter W., and J. Desmond Clark, *Background to Evolution in Africa,* University of Chicago Press, 1967.

Cole, Sonia M., *Leakey's Luck: The Life of Louis Seymour Bazett Leakey, 1903-1972,* Harcourt Brace Jovanovich, 1975.

Leakey, Louis, *By the Evidence: Memoirs, 1932-1951,* Harcourt Brace Jovanovich, 1974.

Leakey, L., *Stone Age Cultures of Kenya Colony,* Anthropological Publications, 1970.

Leakey, L., *Stone Age Races of Kenya,* F. Cass, 1971.

Leakey, L., *Unveiling Man's Origins: Ten Decades of Thought about Human Evolution,* Methuen, 1970.

Leakey, L., *White African: An Early Autobiography,* Schenkman Publishing Co., 1966.

Leakey, Mary, *Africa's Vanishing Art: The Rock Paintings of Tanzania,* Doubleday, 1983.

Leakey, M., *Disclosing the Past: An Autobiography,* Doubleday, 1984.

Leakey, M., *Olduvai Gorge: My Search for Early Man,* Collins, 1979.

Leakey, Richard, *The Making of Mankind,* Dutton, 1981.

Leakey, R., *One Life: An Autobiography,* Salem House, 1984.

Leakey, R., and Robert Lewin, *People of the Lake: Mankind and its Beginnings,* Anchor Press, 1978.

"Man's Family Tree Rooted in Africa," *USA Today,* August 1989, pp. 10-11.

Murray, Jocelyn, ed., *Cultural Atlas of Africa,* Facts on File, 1989.

Alternative Applications: Write a history of the search for the !Kung and San peoples, who may have been Africa's original inhabitants. Also, differentiate among the varying racial types in Africa, including the Forest Negroids, Nilotics, Pygmies, Bushman-Hottentots, Fulani, Somali, and Caucasoids. List the human "missing links," such as *Homo erectus, Homo habilis,* and *Homo sapiens,* and discuss the significance of each.

Elephant Lore

Age/Grade Level or Audience: Kindergarten, elementary, and middle school life science classes.

Description: Research and present elephant lore.

Procedure: Compile scientific data as well as history, stories, films, cartoons, and poems about elephants, such as *Dumbo,* Rudyard Kipling's "The Elephant Child," and George Orwell's essay "Shooting an Elephant." Make a bulletin board display, database, booklet, research paper, or multimedia show from your findings. Include different types of elephants as well as their uses in agriculture, logging, zoos, and circus acts. Include the following facts:

- ◆ The elephant uses its trunk to gather food and as a sensory organ.
- ◆ The trunk is also called a proboscis.
- ◆ A trunk can siphon water.

◆ Because of their rounded legs and sturdy feet, elephants can move rapidly over rough terrain.

◆ Savanna elephants are larger than their cousins, the forest elephants.

◆ Diet consists of fresh greenery.

◆ All elephants fight off enemies with their tusks.

◆ Calves take nearly twenty-two months to gestate.

◆ Elephants, which are social animals, live in clans.

◆ Because they gradually wear out their molars, aged elephants starve to death.

◆ The clan gathers to help and comfort wounded or dying members.

Budget: $$

Sources:

Brown, Leslie, *Africa: A Natural History,* Random House, 1965.

Douglas-Hamilton, Ian, and Oria Douglas-Hamilton, *Among the Elephants,* Penguin Books, 1978.

"Elephant Talk," *National Geographic,* August 1989.

Heim, Burt, "Elephants in Trouble," *Boys' Life,* September 1990, p. 18.

Kingdon, Johnathan, *Island Africa: The Evolution of Africa's Rare Animals and Plants,* Princeton University Press, 1989.

MacClintock, Dorcas, *African Images,* Scribner, 1984.

Morais, Richard C., "Save the Elephants!" *Forbes,* September 14, 1992.

Moss, Cynthia, *Elephant Memories,* Morrow, 1988.

Owens, Mark, and Delia Owens, *The Eye of the Elephant: An Epic Adventure in the African Wilderness,* Houghton Mifflin, 1992.

Tarshis, Lauren, "A Race Against Extinction," *Scholastic Update,* March 23, 1990, pp. 22-23.

Alternative Applications: Have students compare the size, strength, and habits of elephants with other work animals, such as burros, horses, oxen, llamas, camels, and dogs.

George Washington Carver, Inventor

Age/Grade Level or Audience: Middle school, high school, and college biology classes; garden clubs; museums; agricultural societies; 4-H clubs.

Description: Present a study of George Washington Carver's contributions, discoveries, and inventions.

Procedure: Present an illustrated lecture on how George Washington Carver aided poor farmers by teaching them about nutrition and about turning a profit from the peanut. Mention that peanuts have no cholesterol, are rich sources of protein, vitamin B, and polyunsaturated fat, and contain significant amounts of magnesium, iron, calcium, phosphorus, and potassium. Illustrate your lecture with a large poster showing how peanuts form underground from low-growing bushes.

Name varieties of peanuts, particularly Virginia, runner, Spanish, and valencias. Note that peanut production is still associated with black farmers, particularly those of North and South Carolina, Georgia, Florida, Alabama, Texas, and Oklahoma as well as Malawi, Nigeria, Senegal, Sudan, and South Africa.

Budget: $$

Sources:

National Peanut Council, 1000 Sixteenth St. N.W., Suite 506, Washington, DC 20036; telephone: (202)659-5656; National Peanut Festival Association, 1691 Ross Clark Circle S.E., Dothan, AL 36301; telephone: (205)793-4323.

Asimov, Isaac, *Asimov's Biographical Encyclopedia of Science and Technology: The Lives and Achievements of 1510 Great Scientists from Ancient Times to the Present,* Doubleday, 1982.

Elliott, Lawrence, *George Washington Carver: The Man Who Overcame,* Prentice-Hall, 1966.

Holt, Rackham, *George Washington Carver: An American Biography,* Doubleday, 1963.

Jenkins, Edward S., *American Black Scientists and Inventors,* National Science Teachers Association, 1975.

McMurry, Linda O., *George Washington Carver: Scientist and Symbol,* Oxford University Press, 1981.

Rienow, Robert, and Leona Rienow, "From Orchids to Peanuts," *The Rotarian,* December 1964-January 1965.

Wilson, Charles Reagan, and William Ferris, eds., *Encyclopedia of Southern Culture,* University of North Carolina Press, 1989.

Alternative Applications: Create a display tracing the arrival of the peanut in Africa, Europe, and Asia from its origination point in Brazil, South America. Note the following facts about peanuts:

◆ The word *goober* derives from the Kongo word *nguba.*
◆ The peanut formed a significant part of the soldier's diet during the Civil War, when meat and other protein sources were in short supply.
◆ Peanut growing was originally associated with poverty, particularly in the South.
◆ Peanuts rose in popularity as a snack food around 1875.
◆ Around 1900, inventors devised machines to plant, cultivate, harvest, and shell peanuts.
◆ As peanut production became cheaper and less labor intensive, the kernels were used for oil, peanut butter, candy, and salted snack food.
◆ Demand for peanut products grew during World War II.

- ◆ Peanuts can be made into other foods, for example, milk, cheese, and ice cream.
- ◆ Nonfood uses for peanuts include face cream, shaving cream, ink, bleach, metal polish, washing powder, wallboard, shoe polish, medicine, cosmetics, linoleum, rubber, soap, and salve.

Include facts about Carver's career, such as these:

- ◆ Booker T. Washington hired Carver to teach at Tuskegee Institute in 1869.
- ◆ Carver began raising living standards for poor black farmers by teaching them to rotate crops by planting sweet potatoes, corn, cowpeas, soybeans, and peanuts along with cotton.
- ◆ While a professor at Tuskegee Institute, Carter developed more than three hundred uses for peanuts.
- ◆ In 1921, Carver urged the Congressional Ways and Means Committee to protect American peanut farmers from foreign competition.
- ◆ As unofficial champion of poor blacks, he influenced newspaper publishers, liberal congressmen, agricultural commissions, and other notables.
- ◆ Carver received honorary doctorates and numerous prestigious awards, including the Theodore Roosevelt Medal, honors from the Edison Foundation and London's Royal Society of Arts, and the National Association for the Advancement of Colored People's (NAACP) Spingarn Medal.
- ◆ In 1936, Tuskegee recognized Carver's fortieth year on the faculty by honoring him as the school's most productive teacher and researcher. Both the Prince of Wales and President Theodore Roosevelt visited Carver's lab.
- ◆ In 1940, in honor of his service to humanity, the Carver Foundation established the Carver Memorial Museum and preserved the Tuskegee laboratory.
- ◆ In 1973, Carver was elected to the Hall of Fame for Great Americans.
- ◆ Congress designated January 5 as George Washington Carver Day.

Health Tips

Age/Grade Level or Audience: All ages.

Description: Post health tips for handy reference.

Procedure: Keep a continuing series of news about black health problems on a central bulletin board at a school, post office, medical center, restaurant, retirement home, recreation department, library, or civic center. Include data such as these:

- ◆ Smoking during pregnancy causes low infant birth weight.
- ◆ Drinking alcohol during pregnancy can harm a newborn for life.
- ◆ AIDS spreads from shared needles and unprotected sex.
- ◆ A balanced diet of protein, vitamins, and calcium is essential for unborn babies.

◆ Drugs and violence are the most common killers of young blacks.

◆ Lead poisoning is a silent destroyer of poor children who chew on plaster and paint flakes.

◆ New treatments can ease the pain of sickle cell anemia.

◆ Children need a second vaccination against measles.

◆ To prevent death from stroke, adults should get regular blood pressure evaluations.

◆ To control weight, people should eat more steamed and broiled foods and less fatty, fried meats.

◆ Colon, rectal, and prostate cancer kills more black men than white men because black men seek help too late.

◆ Women over forty need annual mammograms to detect breast cancer.

◆ Adults and children can lower stress and ease depression by exercising with a group.

◆ Certain groups—the elderly, people who have had pneumonia, heavy smokers, asthma and emphysema sufferers, teachers, and health care workers— should get a flu shot every fall.

Budget: $$

Sources:

Chambers, Veronica, "Our Hungry Children," *Essence,* September 1992, p. 142.

"Diet, Weight and Exercise Help to Nix Hypertension," *Jet,* November 9, 1992, p. 16.

"Drug Holds Promise for Easing Sickle Cell Anemia," *Jet,* September 7, 1992, p. 16.

Kanamine, Linda, and James Harney, "Cities Amid Metallic Epidemic," *USA Today,* October 21, 1992, p. 13A.

Kunjufu, Jawanza, *Countering the Conspiracy to Destroy Black Boys,* African American Images, 1990.

"Lead Poisoning Not Confined to Poor Areas, CDC Says," *Jet,* September 7, 1992, p. 16.

"Why Hypertension Strikes Twice as Many Blacks as Whites," *Ebony,* September, 1992, pp. 36-41.

Alternative Applications: Hold a health fair. Distribute free brochures from the American Cancer Society, AIDS Coalition, Weight Watchers, Planned Parenthood, American Heart Association, March of Dimes, National Institute of Mental Health, Meals on Wheels, and other groups. Staff a booth with volunteers to provide free blood pressure checks, breast exams, stool sample kits, urinalysis, Mantoux tests, flu shots, prenatal care, and vaccinations. To create a positive image of health care, provide refreshments for adults and balloons and activities for children.

Herbs, Tonics, Teas, and Cures

Age/Grade Level or Audience: All ages.

Description: Demonstrate Southern black folk remedies.

Procedure: Collect samples of the following herbal preparations, which slaves and rural blacks relied upon when medical care was not available:

- Add **bergamot** to shampoo and hair pomade to promote healthy growth. Also, dice bergamot leaves in salads or boil into tea.
- Make a tea of **catnip** to ease pain and cure cough, flu, or bronchitis.
- Rely on **chamomile** tea to ease menstrual cramps and to sooth the nerves.
- Mix chamomile with **ground ivy** for a tea to cure heartburn. Also, blend chamomile with grease or lotion for a poultice to draw out inflammation.
- To cure gout, rheumatism, and joint pain, slice **dandelion** root and leaves in salads, boil as a bracing drink, or shred into stews and soups.
- Simmer **dill** weed or seed and drink to settle a queasy stomach.
- Tie **fatback** over a splinter to make it rise to the surface.
- Drink **fennel** tea to rid the intestines of gas and to promote a healthy sexual appetite and cure hiccups.
- Drink **feverfew** tea to rid the intestines of worms, settle nerves, or regulate menstrual periods.
- Add **garlic** to stews, beans, and other foods to stop asthma attacks.
- Drink hot **ginger** tea to cure menstrual cramps. Ground ginger root is also a tasty additive to roast pork, turkey, or chicken.
- Stir honey into **horehound** tea to loosen a rattling chest cough or ease a sore throat.
- Make a tea of **lemon mint** to add to bubble bath or shampoo.
- Give **mint** tea to invalids to relieve depression and weakness.
- Place **nightshade** leaves over a sore to promote healing.
- Promote health by adding **paprika** to foods.
- Serve **parsley** tea to rid the body of excess fluid.
- Ease a head cold or sinus infection by eating foods with lots of **pepper.**
- Soak or boil **persimmon** bark in water and sip as a cure for diarrhea.
- Bind **plantain** leaves on boils or abscesses.
- Blend **pine bark** with boiling water for a strong spring tonic.
- Keep **rosemary** in corn meal and flour as a deterrent to bugs. Also, rinse hair in rosemary and borax to promote shine. Place a compress of rosemary tea on the forehead to ease sinus headache.
- Keep dry **sage** on hand as an additive to tea. Sweeten with honey to relieve arthritis and chest colds.
- Drink **sassafras** tea to cure constipation.
- Sip **tansy** tea to kill intestinal parasites.
- Make a paste of wet **tobacco** to draw the sting out of chiggers, mosquito bites, or bee stings.
- Soak brown paper in **vinegar** and place over a bruise or stiff joint to ease soreness. Also, sip vinegar water sweetened with honey every morning to prevent arthritis.

Budget: $$

Sources:

Aikman, Lonelle, *Nature's Healing Arts: From Folk Medicine to Modern Drugs,* National Geographic Society, 1977.

Buchman, Dian Dincin, *Dian Dincin Buchman's Herbal Medicine: The Natural Way to Get Well and Stay Well,* Gramercy, 1980.

Reader's Digest, *Magic and Medicine of Plants,* Reader's Digest Association, 1986.

Alternative Applications: Compare black herbal lore with the folk remedies of native Americans, who often relied on similar local plants for medication.

In the Rice Fields

Age/Grade Level or Audience: Middle school, high school, and college biology and life science classes.

Description: Make a display describing the labor-intensive nineteenth-century method of rice cultivation.

Procedure: Create a bulletin board showing slaves performing each stage of rice cultivation. Show how seed was rolled underfoot to mix with clay; how workers sowed, hoed, flooded, and harvested the crop; and how rice was hulled, winnowed, and stored. Explain in side notes why rice was a profitable crop and is a nutritious dish. Give similar facts about tobacco, indigo, corn, and cotton.

Budget: $

Sources:

Agricultural Research Service, "Rice in the United States: Varieties and Production," U.S. Government Printing Office, 1973.

Hess, Karen, *The Carolina Rice Kitchen: The African Connection,* University of South Carolina Press, 1992.

Straight, Susan, *I Been in Sorrow's Kitchen and Licked Out All the Pots,* Hyperion, 1992.

Alternative Applications: On a handout, list facts about rice plantations, along with drawings of the rice plant during different stages of its growth. Give useful information about rice, such as:

- ◆ varieties, including *Orgyza sativa, Orgyza globerrima,* and *Zizania aquatica*
- ◆ nutritional value of rice (i.e., high starch content and low protein and vitamins)
- ◆ use of rice to make oil, beer, flour, baby food, cereal, nonallergenic food, makeup, fuel, mulch, fertilizer, solvent, fodder, chicken feed, thatch, brooms, rope, mats, bedding, sandals, hats, paper, mats, bags, and plastics

♦ cultivation of rice in Tennessee, Florida, Missouri, Oklahoma, South Carolina, Louisiana, Mississippi, Arkansas, and California
♦ introduction of rice to South Carolina after Captain J. Turber's ship was blown off course in 1685
♦ how South Carolina led the nation in rice production

Invent-O-Rama

Originator: Roberta Brown, teacher, Fort Bragg, North Carolina.

Age/Grade Level or Audience: Kindergarten, elementary, and middle school science classes; scout troops; 4-H clubs.

Description: Display the names of African-American inventors alongside objects or drawings to illustrate their work.

Procedure: Arrange on a shelf or in a display case objects, drawings, or pictures cut from magazines representing the discoveries and designs of the following inventors, designers, and technologists:

♦ James S. Adams—airplane propeller
♦ George E. Alcorn—semiconductors
♦ Archie Alexander—Whitehurst Freeway, Washington, D.C.
♦ Virgie M. Ammons—fireplace damper tool
♦ Charles S. Bankhead—composition printing
♦ Benjamin Banneker—America's first clock
♦ James A. Bauer—coin changer
♦ Andrew J. Beard—automatic railcar coupler
♦ Charles R. Beckley—folding chair
♦ Alfred Benjamin—scouring pads
♦ Miriam E. Benjamin—signal chair
♦ J. W. Benton—oil derrick
♦ Henry Blair—corn and cotton planters
♦ Sarah Boone—folding ironing board
♦ Otis Boykin—stimulator for an artificial heart
♦ Henrietta Bradbury—torpedo discharger
♦ Phil Brooks—disposable syringe
♦ Marie Van Brittan Brown—home security system
♦ Robert F. Bundy—signal generator
♦ J. A. Burr—lawn mower
♦ George Washington Carver—crop rotation, recycling, paint, cosmetics and lotions, wood stain
♦ Albert J. Cassell—method of manufacturing silk

◆ W. Montague Cobb—color chart of the human heart
◆ Leander M. Coles—mortician's table
◆ Cap B. Collins—portable electric light
◆ David N. Crosthwait—vacuum heating system
◆ Joseph Hunter Dickinson—player piano
◆ Charles Richard Drew—blood bank
◆ James Forten—sail raising device
◆ Albert Y. Garner—flame retardant
◆ Sarah E. Goode—folding bed
◆ Meredith C. Gourdine—smoke control, electradyne paint spray gun
◆ W. S. Grant—curtain rod support
◆ Solomon Harper—thermostatic hair curlers
◆ M. C. Harvey—lantern
◆ Lincoln Hawkins—coatings for communication cable
◆ Edward Hawthorne—heart monitor, blood pressure control
◆ H. C. Haynes—improved razor strap
◆ William Hinton—test for syphilis
◆ Dorothy E. Hoover—aeronautical research
◆ Harry C. Hopkins—hearing aid
◆ Thomas L. Jennings—dry-cleaning process
◆ John Arthur Johnson—monkey wrench
◆ Frederick M. Jones—truck refrigeration, starter generator, portable X-ray machine
◆ Leonard Julian—sugar cane planter
◆ Percy Lavon Julian—glaucoma treatment, synthetic cortisone
◆ Ernest Everett Just—studies of cell division
◆ Samuel L. Kountz—improved kidney transplants
◆ Robert Benjamin Lewis—oakum picker
◆ J. L. Love—pencil sharpener
◆ Elijah J. McCoy—automatic locomotive lubricator
◆ James Winfield Mitchell—method of purifying chemicals
◆ Garret Augustus Morgan—gas mask, four-way traffic signal
◆ Benjamin T. Montgomery—boat propellor
◆ George Olden—postage stamp
◆ W. B. Purvis—fountain pen, machine to make paper bags
◆ J. W. Reed—dough roller and kneader
◆ Norbert Rillieux—sugar refiner
◆ G. T. Sampson—folding clothes dryer
◆ Dewey S. C. Sanderson—urinalysis meter
◆ C. B. Scott—street sweeper
◆ J. H. Smith—lawn sprinkler
◆ P. D. Smith—mechanical potato digger
◆ Richard Spikes—automatic carwash, car directional signals, automatic transmission, beer keg
◆ J. A. Sweeting—cigarette roller

◆ Stewart and Johnson—metal bending machine
◆ Lewis Temple—improved whaling harpoon
◆ Charles H. Turner—method of studying the habits of insects
◆ Sarah Walker—hair straightener, face cream, hot comb
◆ Anthony Weston—improved threshing machine
◆ Daniel Hale Williams—first emergency open-heart surgery
◆ Ozzie S. Williams—radar search beacon
◆ J. R. Winter—fire escape ladder
◆ Granville T. Woods—railroad telegraph
◆ Louis Tompkins Wright—treatment for head and neck injuries

Budget: $

Sources:

Asante, Molefi K., *Historical and Cultural Atlas of African Americans,* Macmillan, 1991.

Haber, Louis, *Black Pioneers of Science and Invention,* Harcourt Brace Jovanovich, 1970, reprinted, 1992.

James, Portia P., *The Real McCoy: African-American Invention and Innovation, 1619-1930,* Smithsonian Institution Press, 1989.

Klein, Aaron E., and Cynthia L. Klein, *The Better Mousetrap: A Miscellany of Gadgets, Labor-saving Devices, and Inventions that Intrigue,* Beaufort Books, 1982.

Logan, Rayford W., and Michael R. Winston, eds., *Dictionary of American Negro Biography,* Norton, 1982.

Alternative Applications: Use inventors' names as subjects for individual written or oral reports or scientific studies of how mechanical devices work. Have students replicate the theory behind a particular device or treatment such as Charles Drew's blood bank, Otis Boykin's stimulator for an artificial heart, Louis Wright's neck brace, Garret Morgan's gas mask, or Percy Julian's glaucoma treatment as subjects for science fairs or computer drafting projects. Feature drawings and scientific explanations in a series of school, radio, television, or newspaper public address spots highlighting an inventor a day throughout Black History Month.

The Palm Tree

Age/Grade Level or Audience: Middle school, high school, and college biology and life science classes.

Description: Create a bulletin board display of facts about the palm tree and its role in tropical societies.

Procedure: Post drawings of various types of palm trees, fronds, flowers, and fruit, especially the date and coconut palms. Include a map detailing where palm trees are most common, such as the African coast and Madagascar as well as the Caribbean. Emphasize these facts about the trees:

- ◆ Palms vary from other trees because they have no branches, only a leafy crown of fan-shaped or elongated fronds.
- ◆ Dating back 220 million years, the palm is one of the earth's oldest trees.
- ◆ About 117 species are native to Africa.
- ◆ Palm trees are said to have a thousand uses. For centuries, people have woven palm huts, sunhats, mats, brooms, flooring, fans, umbrellas, clothing, visors, bags and baskets, plaited rope and twine, and planted palms for shade, wind protection, and ornamentation.
- ◆ Palm wood is useful for making walls and buildings, garden tools, and utensils.
- ◆ Palm also provides coconuts for food, milk and sap for drinking, and plant matter for fertilizer.
- ◆ The African palm also provides copra, which is made into an oil that is used in drugs and ointments, soap, candles, cosmetics, margarine and vegetable oil, vinegar, candies, tin-plating, rattan furniture, and lubricants.
- ◆ The leaf of the African toddy palm can be cooked as a vegetable.

Budget: $

Sources:

Brown, Leslie, *Africa: A Natural History,* Random House, 1965.

McCoy, Randolph E., "What's Killing the Palm Trees?" *National Geographic,* July 1988, pp. 120-130.

Tangley, Laura, and Julie Ann Miller, "The Caribbean—An Ecosystem in Crisis," *Bio-Science,* May 1988, p. 319.

Alternative Applications: Make a report comparing the variety of uses for the palm with those of the oak, sugar maple, rubber tree, pine, teak, and other trees. Comment on which plants are most disease resistant, widest spread, fastest growing, and easiest to harvest and replant.

Sickle Cell Anemia

Age/Grade Level or Audience: High school and college science and pre-med classes; museums; science centers.

Description: Present facts about the occurrence and treatment of sickle cell anemia.

Procedure: Make available a series of posters and graphs delineating the virulence and effects of sickle cell anemia and the percentage of black people who suffer from it. Include the following information:

- ◆ a map showing parts of North, Central, and South America, Africa, Asia, and Europe where the disease occurs
- ◆ a drawing of a normal cell and the crystallization of the twisted rod-like shapes of sickle cells, which impede absorption of oxygen and obstruct small blood vessels
- ◆ a list of causes of abnormal hemoglobin in red blood cells
- ◆ an explanation of how the disease, through chemical malfunction, can cause abdominal, skeletal, and muscle pain, kidney stress, tissue damage, anemia, shortness of breath, jaundice, fever, and bleeding
- ◆ a discussion of the genetic transference of the disease
- ◆ the relationship between sickle cells and malarial infection
- ◆ definitions of *HbA*, *HbS*, *heterozygous*, and *homozygous*
- ◆ a description of treatment, involving antibiotics, analgesics, rest, hot packs, and blood transfusion
- ◆ a chart contrasting the number of carriers (1 in 10) with the 65,000 U.S. victims (1 in 400)

Budget: $

Sources:

Dr. Lillian E. C. McMahon, Boston Sickle Center, Boston City Hospital, 818 Harrison Ave., FGH 2, Boston, MA 02118; telephone: (617)424-5727; Dr. Oswaldo Castro, Howard University Center for Sickle Cell Disease, 2121 Georgia Ave. N.W., Washington, DC 20059; telephone: (202)806-7930.

Gerster, George, "Fly of the Deadly Sleep: Tsetse," *National Geographic,* December 1986, pp. 814-833.

Karlen, Arno, *Napoleon's Glands and Other Ventures in Biohistory,* Little, Brown, 1984.

Serjeant, Graham R., *The Clinical Features of Sickle Cell Disease,* American Elsevier Publishing, 1974.

Song, Joseph, *Pathology of Sickle Cell Disease,* Thomas, 1971.

Alternative Applications: Describe the search for a cure for sickle cell anemia, such as Linus Pauling's study of blood cells. Note any breakthroughs in protecting families from transferring the tendency, particularly genetic screening and amniocentesis. Also, study other diseases that ravage black people in Africa and the Caribbean, including these:

AIDS	amebiasis	amoebic dysentery
bejel	bilharziasis	black water fever
brucellosis	cholera	dengue fever
Guinea threadworm	hemorrhagic fever	hookworm
kwashiorkor	Lassa fever	leprosy
malaria	marasmus	onchocerciasis
plague	polio	schistosomiasis

| sleeping sickness | smallpox | tuberculosis |
| typhus | yaws | yellow fever |

Note that all of these diseases are spread and exacerbated by malnutrition, unsanitary conditions, bacteria, virus, insects, and protozoa.

Two-Feet, Four-Feet, Wings, Fins, and Tail

Age/Grade Level or Audience: Kindergarten and elementary science classes.

Description: Draw a frieze that categorizes two-footed, four-footed, winged, crawling, and finned animals from Africa.

Procedure: Make available a collection of illustrated children's dictionaries, reference books, posters, storybooks, filmstrips, and computer programs that classify animals. Have students select animals from Africa from each category to draw on a frieze.

Budget: $$

Sources:
Kingdon, Johnathan, *Island Africa: The Evolution of Africa's Rare Animals and Plants,* Princeton University Press, 1989.
MacClintock, Dorcas, *African Images,* Scribner, 1984.
Norden, Carroll R., *The Jungle,* Raintree Children's Books, 1988.
Owens, Mark, and Delia Owens, *Cry of the Kalahari,* Collins, 1985.
Podendorf, Illa, *Jungles,* Children's Press, 1982.
Purcell, John Wallace, *African Animals,* Children's Press, 1982.
Scott, Peter, and Philippa Scott, *Animals in Africa,* C. N. Potter, 1962.

Alternative Applications: Have students create five separate oversized booklets from poster paper, one each for two-footed, four-footed, winged, crawling, and finned animals. Assign separate groups to letter names of animals and add details of their habitats, such as rivers, sandy soil, mountain tops, burrows, cliffs, and vines.

Zoo's Who

Age/Grade Level or Audience: Elementary and middle school science classes.

Description: Prepare posters of African animals and their habits.

Procedure: Have students draw one animal per poster and position it in a natural setting, such as on a plain, hill country, or mountain slope or in a lake, wetland, seashore, or river. Include these:

aardvark	aardwolf	alcelaphine	antelope
baboon	bongo	bat-eared fox	blackfly
black mamba	boomslang	buffalo	bushbaby
bushpig	bush warbler	caracal	cheetah
chevrotain	chimpanzee	civet	cobra
colobus	cony	cormorant	crane
crocodile	dik-dik	duiker	dung beetle
egret	eland	elephant	flamingo
fruit bat	gazelle	gekko	gemsbok
genet	gerenuk	giant frog	gnu
gorilla	guinea fowl	hartebeest	heron
hippo	hirola	hornbill	hyena
hyrax	jacana	jackal	kestrel
kingfisher	klipspringer	kob	kongoni
korhaan	kudu	leopard	lion
mandrill	marabou stork	mongoose	mousebird
nyala	okapi	oryx	ostrich
peacock	pelican	plover	porcupine
puff adder	python	reedbuck	rhino
scarab beetle	secretary bird	serval	shrew
sitatunga	springbok	springhare	squirrel
steenbok	vervet	tickbird	topi
tsetse fly	turaco	vulture	warthog
waterbuck	wildebeest	zebra	zebu

Divide animal posters into identifiable groups and subgroups (i.e., scavenger, migratory, nocturnal, hoofed, insectivore, herbivore or browser, carnivore, omnivore, ruminant, feline, and primate). Have each student add a paragraph to the back of the poster telling about the animal's habits, diet, size, color, and natural enemies. For example, feature one of these unusual species:

- ◆ arboreal boomslang, a venomous tree snake that feeds on birds and chameleons
- ◆ southern carmine bee eater, a long-billed bird with deep rose body and blue head and underside that breeds on banks overlooking rivers
- ◆ whistling rat, a burrowing rodent of the Kalahari
- ◆ rangei, a web-footed nocturnal desert lizard

Budget: $$

Sources:

National Geographic Society videotape *Among the Wild Chimpanzee.*
Brown, Leslie, *Africa: A Natural History,* Random House, 1965.

Kingdon, Johnathan, Island Africa: *The Evolution of Africa's Rare Animals and Plants,* Princeton University Press, 1989.

MacClintock, Dorcas, *African Images,* Scribner, 1984.

Norden, Carroll R., *The Jungle,* Raintree Children's Books, 1988.

Owens, Mark, and Delia Owens, *Cry of the Kalahari,* Collins, 1985.

Owens and Owens, "Light in the Darkness," *Sports Illustrated,* December 17, 1990, pp. 102-114.

Podendorf, Illa, *Jungles,* Children's Press, 1982.

Purcell, John Wallace, *African Animals,* Children's Press, 1982.

Richardson, Philip R. K., "The Lick of the Aardwolf," *Natural History,* April 1990, pp. 79-85.

Scott, Peter, and Philippa Scott, *Animals in Africa* C. N. Potter, 1962.

Alternative Applications: Organize a large frieze depicting the unique animals of Africa set in their natural habitats. Include plants such as these:

acacia	acanthus	arum lily	bamboo
banana tree	baobab	bindweed	breadfruit
camellia	chickweed	cinnamon	clivia
clover	coffee	cowpea	deiffenbachia
ebony	epiphyte	eucalyptus	fern
flax	guava	guinea grass	heather
hemlock	hibiscus	hydrangea	lantana
laurel	liana	lichen	mahogany
mallow	milkweed	millet	mint
moss	myrtle	nettle	Nile cabbage
okra	oleander	palm	papyrus
pepper	philodendron	pococa	quinine
rattan	rice	rose	rubber tree
sedge	teak	vanilla	water hyacinth
yam	ziziphus		

Have students present their part of the frieze orally to a parents' group or another class, or videotape for later presentation.

Sewing and Fashion

Banner Bolster

Age/Grade Level or Audience: Middle school and high school sewing and crafts classes; museum workshops; church schools; scout troops; civic clubs; 4-H clubs.

Description: Design and display a series of uplifting banners to counter racism, community tensions, or elitism.

Procedure: Have groups of volunteers sew or paint an inspirational quotation on a banner. Choose quotations from a variety of sources, for example, the Bible, Mahatma Gandhi, Martin Luther King, Jr., Maya Angelou, Abraham Lincoln, Toni Morrison, Louis Armstrong, Malcolm X, Jesse Jackson, Frederick Douglass, or Langston Hughes.

Budget: $$

Sources:
Bell, Janet Cheatham, *Famous Black Quotations and Some Not So Famous,* Sabayt Publications, 1986.
King, Anita, ed., *Quotations in Black,* Greenwood Press, 1981.
Leslau, Charlotte, and Wolf Leslau, *African Proverbs,* P. Pauper Press, 1982.

Alternative Applications: Organize a march, candlelight vigil, or informational picket in which groups carry inspirational banners to encourage community involvement, neighborliness, voting, parent involvement in education, literacy, concern for world hunger, or campaigns against drugs, alcohol, guns, AIDS, racism, or gang violence.

 **Corn Rows**

Age/Grade Level or Audience: All ages.

Description: Organize a demonstration of how to cornrow hair.

Procedure: Create a booth at a street fair or neighborhood festival where volunteers cornrow hair for a small fee. Post a sign explaining these facts:

- ◆ Cornrowing dates to the reign of early Egyptian queens, including Sheba and Nefertiti.
- ◆ The rows symbolize order and symmetry.
- ◆ Hair plaiting is common among the Yoruba, Jamaicans, and Haitians.
- ◆ It often tops the heads of queens, priestesses, and dignitaries.
- ◆ The first cornrowing indicates a young girl's place among women.
- ◆ Marriage is symbolized by elaborate cornrowing, which winds to a small crown on the back of the head.
- ◆ Elaborate or ceremonial cornrowing often follows a conical shape rising to a crown.

Add other services, such as face painting for small children. Establish a goal and use the money from the cornrowing and face painting to pay for a school, museum, library, or recreation center project. Advertise the purpose of the booth in local media, newsletters, bulletin boards, and PTA meetings.

Budget: $$

Sources:

Kunjufu, Jawanza, *Lessons from History: A Celebration of Blackness,* African American Images, 1987.

Murray, Jocelyn, ed., *Cultural Atlas of Africa,* Facts on File, 1989.

Thomas, Valerie, *Accent African: Traditional and Contemporary Hairstyles for the Black Woman,* Col-Bob Associates, 1973.

Yarbrough, Camille, *Cornrows,* Coward, McCann & Geoghehan, 1979.

Alternative Applications: Using wigs, create a school, museum, or mall display of traditional African hair styles for men, women, and children, including braids, locs, interlocs, African twists, Nubian twists, cones, and corkscrews. Present an illustrated pamphlet with each style giving step-by-step instructions plus grooming tips.

 A Handful of Puppets

Age/Grade Level or Audience: Kindergarten and elementary school classes; religious schools; scout troops; classes for the handicapped.

Description: Present a Black History Month puppet theater.

Procedure: Have students place hands flat on brown paper. Draw around palm, little finger, the three middle fingers, and thumb. Leave a two-inch margin. Trace the pattern on two pieces of felt and cut out. Sew front and back together to make a two-handed puppet, in which the thumb and little finger operate the puppet's hands. Have students draw or stitch faces with crayons, liquid markers, embroidery, buttons, and scraps of fabric or felt. Select favorite Afrocentric stories to tell with hand puppets.

Budget: $$$

Sources:
Alexander, Lloyd, *The Fortune-Tellers,* Dutton Children's Books, 1992.
Cameron, Ann, *Julian's Glorious Summer,* Random House, 1987.
Carter, Polly, *Harriet Tubman and Black History Month,* Silver Press, 1990.
Clark, Charlotte R., *Black Cowboy: The Story of Nat Love,* E. M. Hale, 1970.
Gray, Nigel, *A Country Far Away,* Orchard Books, 1989.
Greenfield, Eloise, *Grandpa's Face,* Philomel Books, 1988.
Grifalconi, Ann, *The Village of Round and Square Houses,* Little, Brown, 1986.
Grifalconi, *Osa's Pride,* Little, Brown, 1989.

Alternate Applications: Use puppets in tableaus or skits to teach young children health and safety tips about clean teeth, good diet, study, friendship, after-school safety, and how to avoid drugs, alcohol, tobacco, guns, and violence.

Kite Flags

Age/Grade Level or Audience: Elementary, middle school, and high school sewing classes; Brownie and Cub Scouts; religious schools; classes for the handicapped.

Description: To display pride in Africa, create kites featuring the colors and designs of African flags.

Procedure: Examine reference books on African flags, and select colors and designs that can be used to decorate simple rectangular kites with colored streamers for tails. For example, the Liberian flag, designed by Marcus Garvey, features red, black, and green stripes that symbolize struggle, the black race, and the green of Africa. This project might also apply to the making of banners and windsocks, wall designs, jackets, T-shirts, tote bags, and other items.

Budget: $$

Sources:

Atlases and encyclopedias.

Moss, Joyce, and George Wilson, *Peoples of the World: Africans South of the Sahara,* Gale, 1991.

Murphy, E. Jefferson, *Understanding Africa,* Crowell, 1978.

Murray, Jocelyn, ed., *Cultural Atlas of Africa,* Facts on File, 1989.

Alternative Applications: Have flag makers sew copies of African flags from scraps of silk, polyester, or cotton, or draw or paint flag designs on plain muslin or paper. Use the finished flags as the focal point of a Black History Month banquet, convocation, or multimedia presentation. Have a reader present the following facts about African flags on a chalkboard, handout, or overhead projector:

◆ Angola's flag, which is red and black, features a machete, cog wheel, and star to symbolize farmers, industrial workers, and socialism.

◆ Benin's flag, which copies the flag of Ethiopia and was adopted in 1960, contains three rectangles in green, yellow, and red.

◆ After Botswana gained independence in 1966, the people of this desert land chose a blue flag halved by a black stripe edged in white to represent their need for water.

◆ In 1984, Burkina Faso designed a flag featuring a red top over a green bottom and a gold star at the center.

◆ Independent since 1962, Burundi adopted a complicated flag: split into four sections by a white cross, its top and bottom portions are red and its side portions green. At the center of the cross is a white circle and three red stars edged in green symbolizing unity, peace, and progress.

◆ Cameroon's flag is divided vertically into thirds. The colors are green, red, and yellow. A yellow star, representing unity, adorns the center.

◆ The flag of the Cape Verde Islands sports a simple design decorated with an ornate insignia. To the right are horizontal rectangles of yellow and green. The left portion is a vertical stripe of red centered with a black star surrounded by corn husks, two ears of corn, and a seashell at the connecting point.

◆ The Central African Republic's flag, adopted in 1960, is split by a vertical strip of red. To the left and right are four rectangles in blue, white, green, and yellow. On the first blue stripe to the left gleams a yellow star, symbol of unity.

◆ Chad, which once was governed by the French, adopted a simple flag in 1960. It is divided into three vertical rectangles colored blue, yellow, and red.

◆ The flag of the Comoro Islands, adopted in 1978, is a green background centered with a white crescent moon and four stars.

◆ The flag of Djibouti, designed in 1972, features a white triangle radiating from the left and bordering two stripes, blue at the top and green at the bottom. Centering the triangle is a red star.

◆ Gambia's flag, composed of five horizontal stripes, features red at the top, blue in the middle, and green at the bottom. Separating these bright colors are two smaller white stripes.

◆ One of Africa's most artistic flags is that of Kenya. Like Gambia's flag, it has five horizontal stripes, the top black, the center red, and the bottom green. Separating these three rectangles are two white stripes. At the center is a red, white, and black shield covering crossed spears.

◆ In 1966, Lesotho, also creative with its flag, chose a diagonal design. The left rectangle, centered with a brown shield, crossed club and spear, and crocodile, is white; the center stripe blue; and the right rectangle green.

◆ Because Liberia was colonized by American slaves, its flag reflects the colors and shape of the U.S. flag. Eleven horizontal stripes alternate red with white. A blue square occupies the left corner and is topped by a white star.

◆ In contrast to these elaborate flags, the Libyan banner is solid green.

◆ Namibia's flag, like Lesotho's, is a diagonal design. A red stripe edged with white separates two triangles, the top blue and the bottom green. In the upper left corner shines a twelve-rayed golden sunburst.

◆ Nearly square in shape, Niger's flag, adopted in 1959, is comprised of three horizontal stripes ranging from orange at the top to white in the center and green at the bottom. In the center is an orange circle, symbolic of the sun.

◆ The flag of Rwanda, divided vertically into thirds, ranges from red to yellow to green. In the center stands a large black "R."

◆ One of the most graceful banners, adopted in 1977, symbolizes the Seychelles and features a wide red top and narrower green bottom separated by a white curve.

◆ Reflecting the influence of the United Nations is Somalia's flag. Adopted in 1960, it consists of a simple blue rectangle centered by a large white star.

◆ A complex design adorns Uganda's flag. Six horizontal stripes, colored black, yellow, red, black, yellow, red, set off a white circle containing a crane, the national bird, which is yellow, red, black, and gray.

◆ Zaire, possessor of one of the most romantic flag motifs, adopted a green background centered with a yellow circle that contains a forearm clenching the flaming torch of freedom.

Finished flags might be used as decorations for a Black History Month processional or street fair. Place the speaker's comments along with colored model flags on handouts or favors for a banquet, reception, or conference.

Native Fashions

Age/Grade Level or Audience: Civic, church, and school groups; 4-H clubs; sorority assemblies; department stores.

Description: Sponsor an African-American fashion show.

Procedure: Select models to display fashions with a distinctive Caribbean, African, or African-American flair. Invite a black fashion consultant to narrate. Use native African music and decor as background, such as Kente cloth, Kwanzaa symbols, palms, hibiscus, native birds and butterflies, or displays of fruits and vegetables.

Budget: $$$$

Sources:

"Ebony Fashion Fair 'Living the Fantasy' Dazzles Nation's Capital," *Jet,* November 9, 1992, pp. 26-29.

"Flaps, Tubes, Peekaboos," *New York Times Fashion,* November 22, 1992, p. 23.

Gregory, Deborah, "Native," *Essence,* August 1992, pp. 50-57.

Alternative Applications: Sponsor a jewelry fair featuring native African accessories, particularly torques, arm bands, bracelets, rings, necklaces, barrettes, earrings, hair clusters, toe rings, and anklets. Display on mannequins. Invite area crafters to sell their work. Suggest that part of the fair's profits be donated to a scholarship to help a black student study fashion history or design.

 Proud Stitches

Age/Grade Level or Audience: Home economics and adult sewing classes.

Description: Develop sewing techniques while cultivating black pride.

Procedure: Introduce basic sewing techniques by teaching beginning sewers to emulate the hallmarks of Afrocentric fashions. Display fashions along with pattern numbers that will produce similar designs. Feature the following African touches:

- ◆ Kente trim
- ◆ batiked fabrics
- ◆ metallic braid, bells, beading, and metal ornaments
- ◆ ethnic prints and colors, particularly black, red, gold, and purple
- ◆ regal headdresses and headbands with matching belts and sashes
- ◆ animal prints
- ◆ kikois and kitenges (sarong skirts) and harem pants
- ◆ kangas and kanzus (caftans)
- ◆ jalabas and dashikis (tunics)
- ◆ appliqued X's to honor Malcolm X

Budget: $$$

Sources:

Essence Catalog, P.O. Box 62, Hanover, PA 17333-0286; telephone: (800)882-8055.

Alexander, Lloyd, *The Fortune-Tellers,* Dutton Children's Books, 1992.

Asante, Molefi K., *Historical and Cultural Atlas of African Americans,* Macmillan, 1991.

"Flaps, Tubes, Peekaboos," *New York Times Fashion,* November 22, 1992, p. 23.

Gregory, Deborah, "Native," *Essence,* August 1992, pp. 50-57.

Saitoti, Tepilit Ole, *Maasai,* Abradale Press, 1980.

Alternative Applications: Offer an award to the design or sewing student who creates the best example of Afrocentric fashion for men, women, or children. Display fashion ensembles as sketches or on a model, mannequin, or doll. Feature notable examples in a shop window, county fair, mall, library, school home economics department, textile show, or museum display.

Sociology

African Culture in the Sea Islands

Age/Grade Level or Audience: Middle school, high school, and college sociology, black studies, and history classes; civic groups.

Description: Present an overview of African influence on black communities along the Atlantic coast.

Procedure: Using crafts, recordings of Gullah songs and stories, videos, and handouts, present information about African culture on the Atlantic islands off the coasts of Georgia and North and South Carolina. Include the following information:

- perpetuation of an extended family rather than the European nuclear family
- living African style in compounds and enclaves rather than separate residences
- group work habits, such as laughter, conversation, and singing among groups weaving baskets, harvesting, cooking, and repairing fishing nets
- husbands taking more than one wife and maintaining more than one household
- matriarchs serving as teachers of culture, religion, and ethics to community children
- the effects of outside influences, particularly service in World War II and changes brought about by the civil rights movement, such as the Headstart program
- use of Gullah among old and young, with people in the middle range adapting to standard English to facilitate relations with mainland business
- perpetuation of African names, for example Kojo, Fiba, Cunjie, Ayo, Yao, Twia, Minna, Jibba, Boogah, Bodick, Kiya, and Yacky
- erratic patterns of school attendance
- syncretism of Christian worship with African Santeria, Umbunda, and Voodoo
- beliefs in "haints" and "ghosses"
- decoration and annual cleaning of family graves

◆ reliance on herbal and folk remedies
◆ family disruption through migrant labor
◆ seasonal rhythms tied to rice and cotton culture, oyster and crab gathering, livestock and poultry raising, and vegetables such as potatoes, beans, tomatoes, cucumbers, cabbage, broccoli, squash, turnips, and melons

Budget: $$

Sources:

The films *Conrack* (1974) and *Daughters of the Dust* (1992).

Fancher, Betsy, *The Lost Legacy of Georgia's Golden Isles,* Larlin, 1978.

Hamilton, Virginia, *Drylongso,* Harcourt Brace Jovanovich, 1992.

Wilson, Charles Reagan, and William Ferris, eds., *Encyclopedia of Southern Culture,* University of North Carolina Press, 1989.

Woods, Peter, *The Black Majority: Negroes in Colonial South Carolina from 1670 through the Stono Rebellion,* Norton, 1975.

Alternative Applications: Present a map of the Atlantic coast islands, highlighting areas with the strongest African influences. Note the location and cultural significance of these places:

Edisto	St. Helena	Jekyll Island
Ladies	Kiawah	Ossabaw
Daufuskie	Skidaway	Tybee
Sapelo	Wadmalaw	Yamacraw
Mt. Pleasant	Johns	Dataw
Younge's Island	Hilton Head	Harris Neck
St. Catherines	St. Simons	Butler
Darien	Ridgeway	Thunderbolt

 ## Black Excellence

Age/Grade Level or Audience: All ages.

Description: Organize a workshop spotlighting black excellence.

Procedure: Screen the *Ebony/Jet Guide to Black Excellence,* an inspirational video featuring Oprah Winfrey, Joshua Smith, and John Johnson, with Avery Brooks narrating. Appoint a panel of local business and civic leaders, educators, and ministers to discuss how and why black people are achieving. Compose a task force to target areas in which adults can lead young people toward excellence. For example:

◆ Form a neighborhood watch to report crime and drug trade.
◆ Organize a support system of parents and neighbors to keep children in school.

◆ Organize a Friends of the Library group to aid in the procurement of worthy reading materials about black success and to encourage participation at library activities.

◆ Petition city, county, state, and federal officials to support black businesses, scholarships, health clinics, and community development.

◆ Appoint a committee of local stringers to report area successes to newspapers, radio and television stations, newsletters, and magazines. Suggest that each story be accompanied by photographs or videos of events such as ground breaking ceremonies, openings of new businesses and wellness clinics, and scholarship ceremonies.

Budget: $$

Sources:

Ebony/Jet, Johnson Publishing, 820 South Michigan Ave., Chicago, IL 60605; phone: (800)342-0443.

Alternative Applications: Invite a local camera club to create an overview of local examples of black excellence. Display pictures or videos in shopping malls, business and college recruitment fairs, church assemblies, civic club meetings, or school festivals. Select someone with a strong speaking voice, such as a disc jockey, sports announcer, drama student, or speech teacher, to narrate a tape to accompany the display.

The Black Experience

Originator: Leatrice Pearson, teacher, Lenoir, North Carolina.

Age/Grade Level or Audience: Middle school and high school sociology, history, and anthropology classes; historical societies; museums.

Description: Organize a colloquium to discuss the unique position of African-Americans in U.S. history.

Procedure: Open a roundtable discussion of Malcolm X's statement, "Education is our passport to the future; for tomorrow belongs to the people who prepare for it today." Present the following ideas for consideration:

◆ Slavery prevented Africans from retaining a knowledge of their past.
◆ To squelch communication and the possibility of a revolt, slaveholders separated members of the same tribe or purchased members of different tribes.
◆ To quell revolts and halt religious practices, slaves were forbidden to own drums or firearms and stopped from assembling in large groups without a white person present.

◆ Slaves were not allowed to engage in enterprise, such as selling carvings and baskets or bartering vegetables for clothing or furniture.

◆ To maintain order, lawmakers forbade slaves to learn to read and write English or to write native languages.

◆ Families were often split up and sold to owners in different parts of the country.

◆ Black testimony was rejected in courts.

◆ Blacks were not allowed to ward off white attackers or to strike white people.

◆ Black Americans grew up with a hunger for their roots, which had been forcefully taken from them.

◆ Even free blacks who made new lives in the North and Canada did not feel welcome in white society.

◆ Runaway slaves who went south found acceptance among Seminoles, Creeks, and Cherokees.

◆ Discrimination, bigotry, and hatred discourages black Americans from participating fully in citizenship, particularly at election time.

Conclude with an explanation of why black and white citizens should ponder these statements and learn more about racism in the United States.

Budget: $

Sources:

Films and videos such as *Roots* (1977), *Eyes on the Prize* (1986), *Mississippi Burning* (1988), *The Civil War* (1990), and *Malcolm X* (1992).

"Candidates Bush and Clinton Talk about Jobs, Racism, Affirmative Action," *Jet*, October 26, 1992, pp. 4-9.

Cheek, William F., *Black Resistance before the Civil War*, Glencoe Press, 1970.

David, Jay, ed., *Growing Up Black: From Slave Days to the Present: Twenty-five African-Americans Reveal the Trials and Triumphs of Their Childhoods*, Avon Books, 1992.

Kunjufu, Jawanza, *Lessons from History: A Celebration of Blackness*, African American Images, 1987.

Low, W. Augustus, and Virgil A. Clift, eds., *Encyclopedia of Black America*, McGraw-Hill, 1981.

Morrison, Toni, *Beloved*, Knopf, 1987.

Sandoz, Ellis, *Political Sermons of the American Founding Era*, Liberty Press, 1991.

Alternative Applications: Discuss the importance of teaching African-American history to black and white students so that both races can appreciate African-American contributions to history, culture, and citizenship. Select concepts that will enable black youths to develop strong self-images so that they can achieve. For instance, introduce Paul Cuffe and Martin Delany's concept of Pan-Africanism, through which black people everywhere share fellowship and unity. Discuss Frederick Douglass's reminder, "If there is no struggle, there is no progress."

Black Pride Day

Originator: Leatrice Pearson, teacher, Lenoir, North Carolina.

Age/Grade Level or Audience: All ages.

Description: Organize a procession to demonstrate black pride.

Procedure: Delegate tasks to organizers. Include these:

- ◆ Invite bands, majorettes, and pep clubs.
- ◆ Make posters and banners with uplifting quotations from memorable African-Americans.
- ◆ Invite civic, church, and school groups to make floats or dress as clowns, ride unicycles and go-carts, juggle, perform magic tricks, or walk on stilts.

Begin the parade at a central location, such as city hall or a railroad depot, and march to a significant location in the black community, for example, a school, library, civic center, retirement home, housing project, or museum. Hold the black pride procession in the morning so that activities can culminate in a food court, where vendors sell soul food, homemade pies and cakes, and lemonade.

Budget: $$$$

Sources:
Call on the chamber of commerce and visitors bureau to support the procession, which will draw outsiders to your area.
Asante, Molefi K., *Historical and Cultural Atlas of African Americans,* Macmillan, 1991.
Estell, Kenneth, ed., *The African-American Almanac,* 6th ed., Gale, 1993.
Low, W. Augustus, and Virgil Clift, eds., *Encyclopedia of Black America,* McGraw Hill, 1981.
Smith, Jessie Carney, ed., *Notable Black American Women,* Gale, 1992.

Alternative Applications: Hold a miniature black pride parade in a shopping mall, school, civic center, auditorium, gymnasium, retirement home, or street. Invite civic clubs, school groups, scout troops, or churches to decorate a wagon, wheelbarrow, bicycles, or cart to depict some aspect of black pride, such as the achievements of early African civilizations, African-American participation in the Olympics, or the role black women have played in gaining women's rights. Invite a local civil rights advocate or elected official to serve as grand marshall. Include marching units, such as junior police or hospital candy stripers, musicians, clowns, acrobats, and balloons. Have the parade pass a reviewing stand. Offer prizes for the most original, the best display of black pride, the youngest participant, and the most spirited performer.

Black Social Doctrine

Age/Grade Level or Audience: High school and college sociology classes; adult study groups.

Description: Discuss the implications of opinions expressed by black leaders.

Procedure: Read aloud the social philosophies of important black leaders on various topics. Lead a discussion of their applicability to all people. For example:

Feminism

◆ Black women are not here to compete or fight with you, brothers. If we have hang-ups about being male or female, we're not going to be able to use our talents to liberate all of our black people. (Shirley Chisholm)

◆ I want the same thing for blacks, Hispanics, and whites that I want for myself and my child. And that is the ability to take charge of our lives and not be victimized by reproduction. (Faye Wattleton)

◆ Look at me! Look at my arm! I have plowed and planted, and gathered into barns, and no man could head me—and ain't I a woman? I could work as much and eat as much as a man (when I could get it), and bear de lash as well—and ain't I a woman? I have borne thirteen chillern and seen 'em mos' all sold off into slavery and when I cried out with a mother's grief, none but Jesus heard—and ain't I a woman? (Sojourner Truth)

Civil Rights

◆ The major threat to blacks in America has not been oppression, but rather the loss of hope and absence of meaning. (Cornel West)

◆ The challenge is to become part of the struggle, to make a positive difference. (David Satcher)

Racism

◆ This constant reminder by society that I am "different" because of the color of my skin, once I step outside my door, is not my problem—it's theirs. I have never made it my problem and never will. I will die for my right to be human—just human. (Cicely Tyson)

◆ To be black is to shine and aim high. (Leontyne Price)

Budget: $

Sources:

David, Jay, ed., *Growing Up Black: From Slave Days to the Present: Twenty-five African-Americans Reveal the Trials and Triumphs of Their Childhoods,* Avon Books, 1992.

King, Anita, ed., *Quotations in Black,* Greenwood Press, 1981.

Lester, Julius, *To Be a Slave,* Dial, 1969, reprinted, Scholastic, Inc., 1986.

Alternative Applications: Contrast comments by black philosophers, lecturers, teachers, and writers with those of Socrates, Marcus Aurelius, Solomon, Confucius, Buddha, Black Elk, Chief Seattle, Chief Joseph, Mahatma Gandhi, John Kennedy, Abraham Lincoln, Gloria Steinem, Henry David Thoreau, or Eleanor Roosevelt. Pair comments daily on the chalkboard or a bulletin board during February.

Black Towns

Age/Grade Level or Audience: Middle school, high school, and college sociology and history classes; civic and historical groups.

Description: Discuss the formation of all-black towns and communities.

Procedure: Present information about the creation of all-black towns and communities, such as:

- General Rufus Saxon's creation of a black peasant community on Georgia's Sea Islands following the Civil War
- John Eaton's establishment of a black community in Davis Bend, Mississippi
- South Carolina's creation of black communities through its Land Commission during the decade following the Civil War
- formation of Nicodemus, Kansas, a black town, in 1877
- Isaiah Montgomery's creation of Mound Bayou, Mississippi, in 1888
- Edward P. McCabe's establishment of Langston, Oklahoma, in 1890
- incorporation of Boley, Oklahoma, in 1904

Budget: $

Sources:

Bethel, Elizabeth Rauh, *Promiseland: A Century of Life in a Negro Community,* Temple University Press, 1981.

Wilson, Charles Reagan, and William Ferris, eds., *Encyclopedia of Southern Culture,* University of North Carolina Press, 1989.

Alternative Applications: Lead a debate on the practicality of an all-black town. Consider the following difficulties:

- commercial relationships with outside suppliers, labor unions, and financial institutions
- representation in county, state, and national government
- legal entanglements with antidiscrimination laws
- loss of contact with national values
- cultural isolation

Contrast the formation of all-black towns with the establishment of Indian reservations.

▮ | Black Women in the Third World |

Originator: Janet M. Donaldson, Upper Midwest Women's History Center for Teachers, St. Louis Park, Minnesota.

Age/Grade Level or Audience: High school and college sociology and women's studies classes; adult study groups.

Description: Hold a workshop centered on the struggles of black women in the Third World.

Procedure: Present handouts, activities, posters, discussion topics, slide programs, and videos detailing serious social problems for black women in the Third World, particularly these:

- ◆ male preference
- ◆ low self-esteem
- ◆ female circumcision
- ◆ lack of empowerment
- ◆ fatherless families
- ◆ subsistence farming
- ◆ manual labor
- ◆ sexism

Budget: $$$

Sources:

"Black Woman," *National Geographic,* August 1989.

Gross, Susan Hill, *Wasted Resources, Diminished Lives: Contemporary Issues for Women in Africa South of the Sahara; Meeting the Third World through Women's Perspectives;* and *Third World Women: Family, Work, and Empowerment,* available through the Upper Midwest Women's History Center, Central Community Center, 6300 Walker St., St. Louis Park, MN 55416.

Saitoti, Tepilit Ole, *Maasai,* Abradale Press, 1980.

Alternative Applications: Compare unhealthy and discriminatory practices in Africa to problems plaguing women in the United States, notably eating disorders, diminished academic performance and career expectations, workplace exploitation and sexual harassment, low self-esteem, high suicide rates, incest, rape, and other forms of violence toward women. Make up a list of positive suggestions to benefit young black women. For example:

- ◆ community, school, and church support of sex education
- ◆ job placement and child care assistance for young mothers
- ◆ tutorials for female students

◆ centralized referral information on athletic and academic scholarships, grants, loans, and other inducements
◆ shelters for homeless or abused women
◆ halfway houses for substance abusers
◆ support for women who are HIV positive
◆ budget workshops that feature details on how to establish credit
◆ GED programs to encourage older women to complete their education

Famine in Ethiopia and Somalia

Age/Grade Level or Audience: High school and college sociology classes; adult study groups; journalists.

Description: Compose a short history of famine in Somalia.

Procedure: Utilizing local sources, draw up a time line of events that have devastated Ethiopia and Somalia and of the relief efforts launched by the United Nations, Red Cross, Disaster Relief, World Health Organization (WHO), UNICEF, *Medecins sans Frontieres,* Church World Service, and other groups. Explain how malnutrition affects not only this generation but the next as well. Include these facts about the slow, painful bodily depletion brought on by marasmus or starvation:

◆ Without nutrition, the body begins to devour its reserves of fat.
◆ Growth is stunted.
◆ Hunger encourages desperation and violent behavior and discourages learning.
◆ The heart loses strength.
◆ The immune system, weakened by loss of protein, fails.
◆ Diseases such as colds and flu become life threatening.
◆ Communicable diseases such as measles and tuberculosis spread among the malnourished.
◆ Skin loses its elasticity.
◆ Boils, lesions, and other eruptions increase discomfort.
◆ Flies and maggots corrupt the eyes, mouth, and open sores.
◆ Appetite is suppressed.
◆ Decreased brain activity causes loss of concentration.
◆ The eyes are unable to focus.
◆ Hair falls out.
◆ Unclean water introduces gastrointestinal infection.
◆ Diarrhea robs the body of strength.
◆ Extreme diarrhea leads to rectal prolapse and further risks of infection.
◆ Dehydration may lead to unconsciousness or death.

Publish your findings in a local newspaper or church bulletin, or deliver your data in an oral report to a civic or philanthropic organization. Encourage contributions to these agencies:

American Red Cross
P.O. Box 37243
Washington, DC 20013

CARE
660 First Ave.
New York, NY 10016

Mennonite Board of Missions
1251 Virginia Ave.
Harrisonburg, VA 22801-2497
(800)999-3534

World Concern
P.O. Box 33000
Seattle, WA 98133

International Medical Corps
5933 West Century Blvd., No. 310
Los Angeles, CA 90045

Budget: $

Sources:

Infotrac, Newsbank, and other electronic information sources.
"Africa's Stricken Sahel," *National Geographic,* August 1987.
Castro, Josue de, *The Geography of Hunger,* Little, Brown, 1952.
Morrow, Lance, "Africa: The Scramble for Existence," *Time,* September.

Alternative Applications: Use information about Somalia's famine to launch a club, church, or community project to help people trapped in an endless cycle of rebellion, reproduction, disease, starvation, migration, and death. Collect nonperishable food, dry milk, medicines, blankets, money, and volunteers to bring relief to the hopeless, or adopt a child through Christian Children's Fund or social services in your area. Because people of black and Hispanic or native American parentage are often deleted from relief programs, consider sponsoring a family of mixed race.

Human Relations Report Card

Age/Grade Level or Audience: All ages.

Description: Post a giant race relations report card.

Procedure: Utilize an electronic bulletin board, wall sign, banner, or other central location to post a community race relations report card. Select people of all races, ages, educational backgrounds, and income levels to participate on the evaluation committee. Have them consider the following points:

◆ number of community-sponsored events throughout the year
◆ museums, historic sites, and concerts featuring multicultural themes and offered free to the public

- ◆ sensitivity of press, television, and radio to racial issues, such as hiring practices, availability of public transportation, polling information, and health and economic resources
- ◆ percentage of nonwhites appointed to standing committees, study commissions, and other honors
- ◆ quality of educational facilities in all parts of town
- ◆ relationships between citizens and law enforcement officers and judges

Budget: $$$

Sources:

Chamber of commerce, League of Women Voters, or community relations committees.

Alternative Applications: Encourage the local newspaper editor to run the race relations report card in a February issue. Post an update within three to six months to show progress in weak areas. Provide a "wish list" of items that would improve life for black citizens, such as stockpiles of emergency food, medicine, furniture, and clothing for disaster victims; telephone homework help; tutorial services; organized activities and sports for young children; computer classes; AIDS and drug prevention; and mobile wellness clinics for infants, the handicapped, and the elderly.

Maasai Seasons

Age/Grade Level or Audience: Middle school, high school, and college sociology, history, and literature classes.

Description: Draw up a calendar of the seasons from the Maasai point of view.

Procedure: Have participants volunteer to submit information about various aspects of Maasai life as it reflects the seasons. Include the following details:

- ◆ pasturing, branding, and tending cattle, goats, and sheep
- ◆ preparing to hunt game
- ◆ going on retreat to garner strength for battle
- ◆ dressing meat for cooking
- ◆ anticipating May's short rains
- ◆ repairing huts with dung after the November rainy season
- ◆ feasting during initiation ceremonies
- ◆ making useful items from horn, hides, and gourds
- ◆ repairing fences and *kraals* or compounds
- ◆ storing water for the May-to-October dry season
- ◆ moving herds to available water

 ◆ drinking blood when milk is scarce
 ◆ watching for predators and rustlers
 ◆ acquiring firewood for July and August, the cold months

Budget: $

Sources:
Bentsen, Cheryl, *Maasai Days,* Anchor Books, 1991.
Saitoti, Tepilit Ole, *Maasai,* Abradale Press, 1980.
Saitoti, *The Worlds of a Maasai Warrior,* Abradale Press, 1980.

Alternative Applications: Join with several partners to create a poem or
song defining the periods of time that form the Maasai seasons. Alter tone and images
to indicate hope and thanks to the gods for plenty of grass and rain. Chant your poem
to the accompaniment of drum, flute, shekere, finger cymbals, scrapers, or thumb piano.

Mr. Johnson

Age/Grade Level or Audience: All ages.

Description: Study the film *Mr. Johnson.*

Procedure: Present the seriocomic film *Mr. Johnson* and invite a panel to dis-
cuss themes in the movie, particularly colonial exploitation of West African people and
the methods by which subjugated people adapt to colonialism.

Budget: $

Sources:
The film *Mister Johnson* (1991).

Moss, Joyce, and George Wilson, *Peoples of the World: Africans South of the Sahara,*
 Gale, 1991.

Murray, Jocelyn, ed., *Cultural Atlas of Africa,* Facts on File, 1989.

Oliver, Roland, *The African Experience,* IconEditions, 1992.

Spillman, Susan, "Film Fest Extols African Heritage," *USA Today,* October 15, 1992, p.
 8D.

Alternative Applications: Have small groups consider various aspects
of African life as revealed in the film *Mr. Johnson,* which is set in Nigeria: rites, ceremonies, and worship; food, clothing, and dance; work styles and methods; bureau-
cracy; women's rights; and the Hausa hierarchy. Conclude the study with an
explanation of Mr. Johnson's actions and the reasons he dies for his efforts. Compare
with the films *The Power of One, La Vie Est Belle, Heritage Africa, Daughters of the Dust,
Sarafina,* and *Come Back Africa.*

Out of Africa

Age/Grade Level or Audience: High school and college sociology, literature, and history classes; book clubs.

Description: Discuss paternalistic attitudes toward Africans in Isak Dinesen's *Out of Africa.*

Procedure: Screen the film *Out of Africa* and invite participants to sample some of the essays by Karen Blixen (who wrote under the pseudonym Isak Dinesen) about life among the Kikuyu in her books *Out of Africa* and *Shadows on the Grass.* Lead a discussion about her attitude toward hiring, educating, healing, and defending the Kikuyu as English colonialism usurped increasing amounts of their land.

Budget: $$

Sources:
The film *Out of Africa* (1985).
Dinesen, Isak, *Out of Africa,* Putnam, 1937, reprinted, Crown, 1987.
Dinesen, *Shadows on the Grass,* Random House, 1961.
Johannesson, Eric O., *The World of Isak Dinesen,* University of Washington Press, 1961.

Alternative Applications: Report on Blixen's relationship with her African neighbors. Contrast her coexistence and altruism with the medical and missionary work of Albert Schweitzer, the explorations and missionary work of Henry Stanley and David Livingston, the scientific investigations of paleontologists Louis, Mary, and Richard Leakey, and the animal activism of Dian Fossey and Jane Goodall.

Peoples of Africa

Age/Grade Level or Audience: Middle school and high school sociology and anthropology classes; adult study groups.

Description: Study the varied lifestyles of African peoples.

Procedure: Assign groups of students to outline important aspects of African life. Include the following:

- ◆ tribal societies
- ◆ matrilineal and patrilineal descent
- ◆ affined groups allied by marriage
- ◆ population distribution

♦ adaptation to climate and topography
♦ extended families
♦ sedentary versus nomadic peoples
♦ stateless societies based on clan and kinship

Keep a database of research information for future reference.

Budget: $$

Sources:

Abraham, Willie E., *The Mind of Africa,* University of Chicago Press, 1962.

"Africa Adorned," *National Geographic,* November 1984.

Bascom, William R., and Melville J. Herskovits, *Continuity and Change in African Culture,* University of Chicago Press, 1959.

Moss, Joyce, and George Wilson, *Peoples of the World: Africans South of the Sahara,* Gale, 1991.

Nketia, J. H. Kwabena, *The Music of Africa,* Gollancz, 1975.

Alternative Applications: Have students draw comparisons between African lifestyles and other social groups, particularly the varied lifestyles of the natives of North, Central, and South America, Gypsies, migrant workers, stateless Palestinians, Kurds, Montagnards, Haitian refugees, Lapps, Australian aborigines, New Zealanders, Polynesians, and other peoples of Oceania.

The Rights of the Child

Age/Grade Level or Audience: High school and college sociology, history, and literature classes; civic and church groups.

Description: Organize a study of the United Nations Declaration of the Rights of the Child, adopted November 20, 1959.

Procedure: Lead a group discussion of the goal and effectiveness of the U.N. declaration, which promises a better world to children. Comment on these tenets:

♦ Mankind owes the child the best it has to give.
♦ Children deserve equal treatment, regardless of race, sex, national origin, religion, and political background.
♦ Each should be protected and treated with dignity.
♦ Each deserves a name and nationality.
♦ Each has a right to care, nutrition, and medicine before and after birth.
♦ Handicapped children should receive special treatment and education.
♦ Each deserves loving, responsible parents.
♦ Each deserves free and compulsory education.

◆ Each deserves a chance to play and grow under the guidance of adults.

◆ Each should be protected from neglect, cruelty, and exploitation.

Compare these precepts with the ideas of Marian Wright Edelman.

Budget: $

Sources:

David, Jay, ed., *Growing Up Black: From Slave Days to the Present: Twenty-five African-Americans Reveal the Trials and Triumphs of Their Childhoods,* Avon Books, 1992.

Estell, Kenneth, ed., *The African-American Almanac,* 6th ed., Gale, 1993.

Newton, David E., *Gun Control: An Issue for the Nineties,* Enslow Publishers, 1992.

Alternative Applications: Discuss how these precepts have failed to protect the poor and abused of Somalia, South Africa, Haiti, Jamaica, the Dominican Republic, Antigua, and parts of the United States. Ask volunteers to join a panel to discuss key problems in child protection:

◆ random shootings and other unpredictable forms of violence

◆ malnutrition

◆ incomplete immunization against serious diseases

◆ irregular or absent health care

◆ improper parenting

◆ poor self-image

◆ a limited future

Stayin' Alive

Age/Grade Level or Audience: High school and college sociology and psychology classes; adult study groups.

Description: Study the coping mechanisms that enabled slaves to endure bondage.

Procedure: Discuss in small groups the efficacy of these methods:

◆ joking and lampooning

◆ singing folk rhymes, ironic work songs, spirituals, and hymns

◆ use of code names, such as Moses and the children of Israel for the Underground Railroad conductor and escapees or Canaan for Canada

◆ pretending to be dim-witted, sick, hard of hearing, or obsequious and subservient

◆ telling symbolic stories, particularly the Uncle Remus fables

◆ leaving the spigots of kegs open, sabotaging farm machinery and chimneys, fouling wells and cisterns, and breaking tools

- deliberately losing, hiding, or dropping into a river important equipment and tools
- crippling horses and leaving gates and fences open so animals could wander
- self-mutilation of toes, fingers, eyes, and teeth
- untying boats from their moorings
- setting fires to barns, silos, warehouses, or ripening cane and cotton fields
- using a light-skinned slave as a cover for an escape
- punishing or killing black turncoats and spies
- organizing sit-down strikes and other forms of mutiny
- poisoning or murdering overseers and masters

Budget: $

Sources:

Cheek, William F., *Black Resistance before the Civil War,* Glencoe Press, 1970.

Cleaver, Eldridge, *Soul on Ice,* McGraw, 1968.

Mannix, Daniel, and Malcolm Cowley, *Black Cargoes: A History of the Atlantic Slave Trade, 1518-1865,* Viking Press, 1962.

Walvin, James, *Slavery and the Slave Trade: A Short Illustrated History,* University Press of Mississippi, 1983.

Alternative Applications: Read aloud from slave narratives and rhymes that illustrate coping mechanisms. For instance, in his memoir, Peter Randolph describes an exchange with his master:

"Pompey, how do I look?"
"Oh, massa, mighty!"
"What do you mean by 'mighty,' Pompey?"
"Why, Massa, you look noble."
"What do you mean by 'noble'?"
"Why, sar, you look just like one lion."
"Why, Pompey, where have you ever seen a lion?"
"I seen one down in yonder field the other day, massa."
"Pompey, you foolish fellow, that was a jackass."
"Was it, massa? Well you look just like him."

An ironic rhyme recited by William Wells Brown in *My Southern Home* depicts the slave blend of dialect, good humor, and satire:

De big bee flies high,
    De little bee makes de honey,
De black man raise de cotton,
    An' de white man gets de money.

A more pointed rhyme, recounted in Brown's *Clotel* describes the glee of slaves celebrating the master's death:

Hang up the shovel and the hoe—
Take down the fiddle and the bow

Old master has gone to the slaveholder's rest;
He has gone where they all ought to go.

Conclude with a tribute to black history from the final chapter of Eldridge Cleaver's *Soul on Ice:*

I watched the Slaver's lash of death slash through the opposing air and bite with teeth of fire into your delicate flesh, the black and tender flesh of African Motherhood, forcing the startled Life untimely from your torn and outraged womb, the sacred womb that cradled primal man, the womb that incubated Ethiopia and populated Nubia and gave forth Pharaohs unto Egypt, the womb that painted the Congo black and mothered Zulu, the womb of Mero, the womb of the Nile, of the Niger, the womb of Songhay, of Mali, of Ghana, the womb that felt the might of Chaka before he saw the sun.

"Stop the Drugs" Campaign

Age/Grade Level or Audience: All ages.

Description: Organize a "Stop the Drugs" campaign.

Procedure: Sponsor a writing contest requiring students to state in two thousand words or less the physical, moral, and psychological damage wrought by alcohol and illegal drugs in a community. Emphasize the damage done to the unborn, particularly fetal alcohol syndrome and crack-addicted babies. Make the connection between AIDS and shared needles. Offer separate prizes for children, teen, and adult divisions.

Budget: $$$

Sources:
Johnson, Lucas L., "Crack in the Family," *Essence*, August 1992, p. 38.
Newton, David E., *Gun Control: An Issue for the Nineties*, Enslow Publishers, 1982.
Safran, Claire, "Mama Hale and Her Little Angels," *Reader's Digest*, September 1984, pp. 49-53.

Alternative Applications: Assist science students in creating anti-drug, gun, alcohol, and tobacco projects for science fairs. Consider the following topics:

- ◆ designer drugs and their effects on the nervous system
- ◆ marijuana and the adverse effects on users' offspring
- ◆ cocaine and respiration
- ◆ methods of ending drug dependency
- ◆ methadone and recidivism
- ◆ alcoholism as substance abuse
- ◆ emotional problems among the children of alcoholics
- ◆ smoking and cancer of the lip and tongue

◆ smoking and its effects on the unborn

◆ guns and violence

◆ poverty and street gangs

Have students use charts and graphs to support their assertions. Categorize data by race, age, sex, and location.

 Studying the Bones

Age/Grade Level or Audience: All ages.

Description: Demonstrate the Zulu method of prognostication.

Procedure: Explain how Zulu diviners studied animal ankle and knuckle bones, fruit pits, seeds, shells, bits of glass, horn, ivory, fangs, wooden carvings, claws, beaks, hooves, stones, and coins to interpret dreams, commune with spirits, and make predictions about marriage, work, and planting. Comment on the importance of these elements:

◆ selection of the correct pieces to make up a set of thirteen

◆ protecting the pieces

◆ designation of five special bones: man, woman, warrior, chief, and cattle

◆ determination of purpose, whether to heal, interpret, advise, or curse

◆ phrasing a question for the bones to answer

◆ chanting or crooning to accompany a trance

◆ shaking the container

◆ blowing four breaths on the pieces

◆ pouring out the pieces onto a table or mat

◆ choosing pieces that are worth reading and pieces that refuse to cooperate

◆ assessment of location and spacing of bones

◆ counting the points, which carry these messages:

1: freedom

2: separation

3: good sign

4: cooperation

5: caution

6: strength and wisdom

7: trust God

8: prepare for a fight

9: creativity

10: wish fulfillment

11: communion with spirits

12: abundance

13: harmony

Budget: $

Sources:
Lawson, E. Thomas, *Religions of Africa,* Harper & Row, 1984.
Ulufudu, *The Zulu Bone Oracle,* Wingbow Press, 1989.

Alternative Applications: Contrast the use of bone oracles with other types of divination, for example, the I Ching, Tarot, Ouija, nature lore, seances, palmistry, reading tea leaves, phrenology, astrology, and dream interpretation.

Voting Patterns

Age/Grade Level or Audience: Middle school, high school, and college sociology, civics, black studies, and American history classes.

Description: Make a study of the racial voting patterns in your area.

Procedure: Study factors affecting the racial voting patterns of your city, county, and state. Note periods when voter registration was heaviest and comment on factors that influenced participation, particularly voter registration campaigns, college drives to attract young voters, mobile registration sites, and neighborhood advertising urging voter participation.

Budget: $

Sources:
League of Women Voters, National Association for the Advancement of Colored People (NAACP), courthouse records, almanacs and legislative records, local registrars, newspaper articles.

Alternative Applications: Generate a report on a voting-related topic, such as bloc voting, liberal versus conservative candidates, one-issue voters, and overt racism. Interview people who vote consistently and find out how their attitudes toward participation have varied over time. Present your findings in a series of school or local newspaper articles.

Who Does the Work?

Age/Grade Level or Audience: Middle school, high school, and college sociology, economics, and labor history classes.

Description: Research statistics on the types of jobs held by black Americans.

Procedure: Make a study of the labor markets that are traditionally open to black workers. Extend this study to include earlier economic periods, such as the Great Depression, the Eisenhower Era, the Great Society, and Reconstruction. Separate data by into categories, such as sex, age, state, handicaps, skilled, semi-skilled, professional, unskilled, rural, suburban, and urban. Use this study to launch a local campaign to improve job opportunities for black workers. Present findings to key personnel managers, job fair coordinators, and school counselors.

Budget: $

Sources:

U.S. Department of Labor; data from the Pennsylvania State Data Center, telephone: (717)948-6178.

Cook, Roy, *Leaders of Labor,* Lippincott, 1966.

Horton, Carrell Peterson, and Jessie Carney Smith, *Statistical Record of Black American,* 2nd ed., Gale, 1992.

Alternative Applications: Invite black entrepreneurs, lawyers, teachers, scholars, engineers, doctors, dentists, accountants, and other role models to offer advice to young people seeking to break out of stereotypical black jobs. Compile and distribute the information through school and job counselors, ministers, libraries, and the chamber of commerce.

Speech and Drama

Action and Words

Originator: Theodore Shorack, teacher, Los Angeles, California.

Age/Grade Level or Audience: Kindergarten and elementary school students; PTA and parent night programs; religious schools; scout, 4-H, and other club programs.

Description: Teach young children to recite and act out the poem "Boats, Boats."

Procedure: Have students perform the following actions as they recite Theodore Shorack's "Boats, Boats." Note the gestures for the group and for its student leader.

Boats, Boats

Boats, Boats off the coast,
robbing Africans of what they love most.
>   (*Rowing; leader shading eyes and gazing toward shore.*)

Chains, Chains, choking their throats
packed in tight on the slavery boats.
>   (*Pulling at chains on throats; leader raising hands to the sky.*)

Dollars, Dollars, the auctioneer hollers.
White men taking Blacks by their collars.
>   (*Counting out money; leader stuffing bills into imaginary wallet.*)

Whip, Whip, they long to break free,
Doing what they can to escape and flee.
>   (*Lashing out with imaginary whips; leader cowering in pain and fear.*)

North, North follow that star.
Safe in the darkness, traveling far.
>   (*Looking skyward; leader pointing to the North Star.*)

Danger, Danger, during the day.
Hound dogs and hunters along the way.
> *(Holding hands up like dog ears and lolling their tongues; leader guiding an imaginary dog by a leash.)*

Train, Train, not on a rail.
Going house to house on the freedom trail.
> *(Circular chugging motions; leader knocking on door.)*

Home, Home, where will that be?
North in Canada they can be free!
> *(Hugging each other; leader waving to audience.)*

Invite students to create new verses that follow the same pattern of repetition, rhythm, and rhyme.

Budget: $

Sources:

Original verse.

Bontemps, Arna, ed., *American Negro Poetry*, Hill & Wang, 1974.

Chapman, Abraham, ed., *Black Voices: An Anthology of Afro-American Literature*, St. Martin's Press, 1970.

Alternative Applications: Organize an elementary or middle school group to decide on gestures and dramatization for a choral reading of "Remember the Preacher-man."

Remember the Preacher-man

On a bus rode a woman named Rosa Parks.
'had to give up her seat because her skin was dark.
A white man saw Rosa in a seat he desired,
but she wouldn't get up—she said, "My feet are tired!"
The driver-man said, "You're going to jail,
unless you give that seat to the man who's pale!"
So she went to jail—as if she'd done something bad.
Black folks in Montgomery were fighting mad.
A young preacher-man, Dr. Martin Luther King,
said, "Rosa, my friend, you did the right thing!"
He told all the Black folks who were ready to fight,
"Let's *get* what we deserve, but let's do it right."
Dr. King knew his history—indeed, he was a scholar.
He said, "Don't fight with guns; trust the Lord and use the dollar."
So dark-skinned people chose to walk instead of ride
and the busses lost the battle to a growing Black pride.
There were many more battles and many remain today.
Sharing his dream of justice, Dr. King led the way.
But the power of hate couldn't resist temptation
while this man of love was changing a nation.

While he was taking his dream to Memphis town,
a white man with a rifle gunned the peaceful man down.
Now as we decide how to do the right thing,
remember the preacher-man, Dr. Martin Luther King.

Africa's Liberation

Age/Grade Level or Audience: High school and college speech, drama, and language classes; banquets, civic meetings, church assemblies; Toastmasters clubs.

Description: Present a speech on the evolving freedom among African countries.

Procedure: Deliver an address covering the liberation of African countries. Include the following details:

Description: Present a speech on the evolving freedom among African countries.

- ◆ On March 6, 1957, Ghana evolved from the former Gold Coast and three years later became a republic.
- ◆ Gambia dropped its colonial ties with England and became a free nation on February 18, 1965.
- ◆ On March 12, 1968, the island of Mauritius abandoned 158 years of British control and declared independence.
- ◆ Uganda evolved slowly, freeing itself of British control in 1962, but requiring five more years to become a republic.
- ◆ Also slow to achieve freedom, Zimbabwe struggled against British control from 1966 to 1972 and claimed independence on April 18, 1980.
- ◆ Breaking with Rhodesia, Zambia became a republic on October 24, 1964.
- ◆ After ending Belgian control in the Congo on June 30, 1960, the nation named Zaire suffered tribal squabbles until 1965.
- ◆ Zanzibar threw off British rule in 1961 and, as Tanganyika, became independent.
- ◆ German Togoland became a free republic on April 27, 1960.
- ◆ Freed of its miserable history as a source of slaves, Nigeria embraced freedom on October 1, 1960.
- ◆ In 1958, Guinea voted to separate itself from French control.
- ◆ Gabon, also a French possession, became free on August 17, 1960.
- ◆ Another French territory, Chad achieved freedom in 1960.
- ◆ Upper Volta, which separated from French control in 1960, adopted the name Burkina Faso on August 4, 1984.

◆ Following four years of turmoil, Burundi stabilized as a republic in 1966.
◆ The former Bechuanaland, once controlled by the British, became the free nation of Botswana in 1966.
◆ The former Dahomey suffered repeated uprisings until 1975, when it achieved independence and was named Benin.
◆ South Africa, the last stronghold of colonial racism, came under the control of the National Party and apartheid in 1948 and still struggles for freedom.

Budget: $

Sources:

Grun, Bernard, *The Timetables of History: A Horizontal Linkage of People and Events,* Simon & Schuster, 1991.

Moss, Joyce, and George Wilson, *Peoples of the World: Africans South of the Sahara,* Gale, 1991.

Murray, Jocelyn, ed., *Cultural Atlas of Africa,* Facts on File, 1989.

Alternative Applications: Select individuals to describe each nation's struggle in a short presentation. Arrange the program in order of each country's liberation. Include details about colonial history, languages, peoples, customs, leaders, flags, natural resources, and current outlook. As each contributor concludes, pin the colored shape of the country to a blank map of Africa.

At Home in Africa

Age/Grade Level or Audience: Nursery school and kindergarten classes.

Description: Describe life as an African animal.

Procedure: Display pictures, read stories, or show videos or filmstrips about African animals. Have students select an animal with which to identify. Have each participant answer the following questions:

◆ What color are you?
◆ What do you eat?
◆ Where do you live?
◆ What do you do all day?

Budget: $$

Sources:

Aaseng, Nathan, *Animal Specialists,* Lerner Publications, 1987.

Aaseng, *Horned Animals,* Lerner Publications, 1987.

Aaseng, *Prey Animals,* Lerner Publications, 1987.

Brennan, John, and Leonie Keaney, *Zoo Day,* Carolrhoda Books, 1989.

Cherfas, Jeremy, *Animal Builders,* Lerner Publications, 1991.

Cherfas, *Animal Communications,* Lerner Publications, 1991.

Cherfas, *Animal Defenses,* Lerner Publications, 1991.

Cherfas, *Animal Parents,* Lerner Publications, 1991.

Cherfas, *Animal Societies,* Lerner Publications, 1991.

Taylor, David, *Animal Olympians: Sporting Champions of the Animal World,* Lerner Publications, 1989.

Alternative Applications: Have each student select an African animal to have as an imaginary pet. Distribute art supplies so that students can create the following drawings: a home for the pet; feeding time; a bath and pedicure; brushing, combing, and fluffing; a collar and leash; training; and competition at an African pet show.

Benjamin Franklin and Slavery

Age/Grade Level or Audience: Middle school, high school, and college speech, history, and writing classes.

Description: Organize a panel to discuss Benjamin Franklin's condemnation of slavery.

Procedure: Have students form small groups to discuss the following comments from an address of November 9, 1798, to the Pennsylvania Society for Promoting the Abolition of Slavery and the Relief of Free Negroes Unlawfully Held in Bondage, in which the group's president, Benjamin Franklin, castigated the Constitutional Convention for failing to include Thomas Jefferson's antislavery proposal. Emphasize these lines:

- ◆ Slavery is such an atrocious abasement of human nature, that its very extirpation, if not performed with solicitous care, may sometimes open a source of serious evils.
- ◆ The unhappy man, who has long been treated as a brute animal, too frequently sinks beneath the common standard of the human species. The galling chains that bind his body do also fetter his intellectual faculties, and impair the social affections of his heart.
- ◆ Accustomed to move like a mere machine, by the will of a master, reflection is suspended; he has not the power of choice; and reason and conscience have but little influence over his conduct because he is chiefly governed by the passion of fear.

◆ He is poor and friendless; perhaps worn out by extreme labor, age, and disease.

Budget: $

Sources:

Concise Dictionary of American Literary Biography, Volume 1: *Colonization to the American Renaissance, 1640-1865,* Gale, 1988.

Estell, Kenneth, ed., *The African-American Almanac,* 6th ed., Gale, 1993.

Alternative Applications: Have students make a brief oral explanation of the method by which abolitionists could alleviate the following difficulties inherent in manumission:

◆ how to teach slaves to utilize their freedom
◆ how to train former slaves for the labor market
◆ how to provide employment suitable to people of different ages, sexes, and talents
◆ how to provide education for young black children
◆ how to protect newly freed blacks from racist violence

 ## Black Philosophies

Age/Grade Level or Audience: High school and college American speech and history classes; debate societies.

Description: Present opinion papers supporting or refuting the views of controversial black leaders.

Procedure: Have students study the speeches, essays, and philosophies of famous black leaders, particularly Clarence Thomas, Spike Lee, Thurgood Marshall, Barbara Jordan, Louis Farrakhan, Jesse Jackson, Stokely Carmichael, H. Rap Brown, Malcolm X, Angela Davis, Claude Brown, Martin Luther King, Jr., Frederick Douglass, Eldridge Cleaver, Marcus Garvey, W. E. B. Du Bois, and Booker T. Washington. Encourage each student to select an idea to support or refute by logic and example.

Budget: $

Sources:

Black Writers, Gale, 1989.

Hampton, Henry, and Steve Fayer, *Voices of Freedom: An Oral History of the Civil Rights Movement from the 1950s through the 1980s,* Bantam Books, 1990.

King, Anita, ed., *Quotations in Black,* Greenwood Press, 1981.

Lester, Julius, *To Be a Slave,* Dial, 1969.

Ravitch, Diane, *The American Reader: Words That Moved a Nation,* HarperCollins, 1990.

Alternative Applications: Pair students who choose opposite sides of a particular issue, such as the Back to Africa movement, black pride, nonviolence, or the rise of Islam. Organize a formal debate. Videotape the results and discuss the strengths and weaknesses of each participant's arguments.

Black Sentiments

Originator: Leatrice Pearson, teacher, Lenoir, North Carolina.

Age/Grade Level or Audience: Middle school, high school, and college drama and literature classes; drama and literary societies.

Description: Use quotations as springboards to oral interpretation, skits, or dialogues.

Procedure: Consider the following examples:

- ◆ So de white man throw down de load and tell de nigger man tuh pick it up. He pick it up because he have to, but he don't tote it. He hand it to his women-folks. De nigger woman is de mule uh de world so fur as she can see. (Zora Neale Hurston, *Their Eyes Were Watching God*)
- ◆ Power concedes nothing without demand. It never did and never will. People might not get all that they work for in this world, but they must certainly work for all they get. (Frederick Douglass)
- ◆ So Baby's eight children had six fathers ... what she called nastiness of life was the shock she received upon learning that nobody stopped playing checkers just because the pieces included her children. (Toni Morrison, *Beloved*)
- ◆ Racism seems ageless, like the passion of those who war against it. (Gordon Parks)
- ◆ A cynical young person is almost the saddest sight to see, because it means that he or she has gone from knowing nothing to believing nothing. (Maya Angelou)
- ◆ Black people are the only segment in American society that is defined by its weakest elements. Every other segment is defined by its highest achievement. (Jewell Jackson McCabe)
- ◆ Service is the rent that you pay for room on this earth. (Shirley Chisholm)
- ◆ Never take a step backward or you never stop running. (W. E. B. Du Bois)
- ◆ The better we feel about ourselves, the fewer times we have to knock somebody down in order to stand on top of their bodies and feel tall. (Odetta)

Budget: $

Sources:

Carter, Stephen L., *Reflections of an Affirmative Action Baby,* BasicBooks, 1991.

Edelman, Marian Wright, *The Measure of Our Success: A Letter to My Children and Yours,* Beacon Press, 1992.

Kozol, Jonathan, *Savage Inequalities: Children in America's Schools,* Harper Perennial, 1992.

Steele, Shelby, *The Contest of Our Character: A New Vision of Race in America,* St. Martin's, 1990.

Terkel, Studs, *Race: How Blacks and Whites Think and Feel about the American Obsession,* New Press/Norton, 1992.

Alternative Applications: Organize an extemporaneous speaking contest as a part of Black History Month. Use the citations above as prompts for three-minute impromptu responses. Assign points to contestants based on these criteria:

- ◆ coverage of theme
- ◆ concrete examples
- ◆ organization
- ◆ stage presence and eye contact
- ◆ solid conclusion based on evidence presented

The Demands of Frederick Douglass

Originator: Leatrice Pearson, teacher, Lenoir, North Carolina.

Age/Grade Level or Audience: High school and college debate teams; community forums; civic clubs; newspaper editors.

Description: Discuss the merits of Frederick Douglass's speech in Washington, D.C., April, 1883.

Procedure: Read aloud Douglass's call to action:

If we find, we shall have to seek. If we succeed in the race of life, it must be by our own energies and our own exertions. Others may clear the road, but we must go forward or be left behind.... What Abraham Lincoln said in respect of the United States is as true of the colored people as of the relations of those states. They cannot remain half slave and half free. You must give them all or take from them all. Until this half-and-half condition is ended, there will be just ground of complaint.

Debate with a small group whether African-Americans have reached the state of progress and acceptance to which Frederick Douglass addressed his remarks.

Budget: $

Sources:
Concise Dictionary of American Literary Biography, Volume 1: *Colonization to the American Renaissance, 1640-1865,* Gale, 1988.
Estell, Kenneth, ed., *The African-American Almanac,* 6th ed., Gale, 1993.
Ravitch, Diane, *The American Reader: Words That Moved a Nation,* HarperCollins, 1990.

Alternative Applications: Assign small groups to discuss or debate other of Douglass's statements and their applicability to current racial tensions. For example:

◆ Go where you may, search where you will, roam through all the monarchies and despotisms of the Old World, travel through South America, search out every abuse, and when you have found the last, lay your facts by the side of the everyday practices of this nation, and you will say with me that for revolting barbarity and shameless hypocrisy, America reigns without a rival. (Independence Day Speech, Rochester, New York, 1852)

◆ Slavery has been fruitful in giving itself names. It has been called "the peculiar institution," "the social system," and the "impediment," as it was called by the General Conference of the Methodist Episcopal Church. It has been called by a great many names, and it will call itself by yet another name; and you and I and all of us had better wait and see what new form this old monster will assume, in what new skin this old snake will come forth. (Speech to the American Anti-Slavery Society, Boston, Massachusetts, May 10, 1865)

◆ We hold it to be self-evident that no class or color should be the exclusive rulers of this country. If there is such a ruling class, there must of course be a subject class, and when this condition is once established this Government of the people, by the people and for the people, will have perished from the earth. (Speech at the National Convention of Colored Men, Louisville, Kentucky, September 24, 1883)

Dramatizing the Black Experience

Age/Grade Level or Audience: Middle school, high school, and college drama classes; community and church theater groups.

Description: Rewrite famous scripts of dramatic, comic, musical, and historical plays and films from the black point of view.

Procedure: Have students view videotapes or read the scripts of stage and Hollywood classics, such as these:

You Can't Take It with You	*1776*
The Music Man	*Jesus Christ Superstar*
I Remember Mama	*Cat on a Hot Tin Roof*
Les Miserables	*A Streetcar Named Desire*
The King and I	*Oklahoma!*
Citizen Kane	*Fiddler on the Roof*
Harvey	*South Pacific*
Camelot	*Romeo and Juliet*
A Midsummer Night's Dream	*The Sound of Music*
Spartacus	*Ben Hur*
Cyrano	*Romeo and Juliet*
Lassie	*It's a Wonderful Life*

Organize a group of volunteer scriptwriters to reset and recast the production to feature black people, themes, and settings. Put on skits or a full production of the script. Advertise the shift in point of view through posters, radio and television spots, and handbills. Videotape the performance.

Budget: $$

Sources:

Tapes from video rental services.

Asante, Molefi K., *Historical and Cultural Atlas of African Americans*, Macmillan, 1991.

Low, W. Augustus, and Virgil A. Clift, eds., *Encyclopedia of Black America*, McGraw Hill, 1981.

Wilson, Charles Reagan, and William Ferris, eds., *Encyclopedia of Southern Culture*, University of North Carolina Press, 1989.

Alternative Applications: Have students brainstorm ways of increasing black roles in television and movie production, news gathering and reporting, sportscasting, and newspaper and magazine production. For example:

- ◆ create black history pages for children's magazines such as *Cricket, Cobblestone, National Geographic World, Ranger Rick,* and *Hopscotch*
- ◆ deliver television and radio editorials and political commentary from the black perspective
- ◆ comment on high school sports events for local radio and television stations
- ◆ encourage debating societies that feature questions about black welfare and culture
- ◆ establish black reading theaters
- ◆ organize Toastmasters clubs in black areas

Experiencing the Underground Railroad

Age/Grade Level or Audience: Middle school, high school, and college language and drama classes; religious schools.

Description: Present a pantomime of slaves escaping to the North.

Procedure: Explain to the group that a network of 3,200 people formed the Underground Railroad, which, from 1830 to 1860, led 2,500 slaves per year toward safety. Many died along the way from hunger, cold, wounds, falls, or drowning; some were recaptured and returned to slavery. Many more built new lives for themselves in free states or Canada. For the pantomime, let students select a role to dramatize, for example, bystander, farmer, doctor, minister, leader, parent, aged slave, child, patroller, slave catcher, sheriff, Quaker or Mennonite abolitionist, station master, conductor, or plantation owner. Enact the following scenes:

- ◆ intolerable slave conditions, such as the separation of families, hard labor, dangerous jobs, disease, and inadequate clothing, food, and shelter
- ◆ planning an escape
- ◆ gathering information from knowledgeable and trustworthy sources
- ◆ storing food and supplies for the journey
- ◆ making a getaway
- ◆ moving through forests and swamps or over rivers
- ◆ hopping trains or wagons
- ◆ locating roots, nuts, berries, grain, fruit, and mushrooms for food
- ◆ quietly snaring animals and birds
- ◆ staying warm, dry, and well
- ◆ treating wounds, illness, or crying infants
- ◆ hiding while sleeping
- ◆ getting directions and following the North Star
- ◆ avoiding patrollers, dogs, and slave catchers
- ◆ wearing a disguise
- ◆ locating a conductor and station house
- ◆ acquiring a fake pass or papers of manumission
- ◆ establishing a new home
- ◆ learning to read
- ◆ finding work
- ◆ reuniting with lost relatives and friends

Budget: $

Sources:

Cheek, William F., *Black Resistance before the Civil War,* Glencoe Press, 1970.

Evitts, William J., *Captive Bodies, Free Spirits: The Story of Southern Slavery,* Messner, 1985.

Himes, Chester, *The Third Generation*, Thunder's Mouth Press, 1989.

Stowe, Harriet Beecher, *Uncle Tom's Cabin*, 1852, reprinted, Norton, 1993.

Alternative Applications: Have students compose dialogue to accompany emotional moments such as these:

◆ parting from old friends and family
◆ trusting an agent of the Underground Railroad
◆ risking whippings and brandings for trying to escape
◆ reaching a safe house
◆ hearing dogs approach
◆ fighting off snakes, insects, alligators, and other animals
◆ getting lost
◆ reaching a free state
◆ searching for missing family members

First Day at School

Age/Grade Level or Audience: Elementary and middle school cross-curricular workshops.

Description: Reenact classes for newly freed slaves.

Procedure: Have students divide into groups to create lessons they would teach former slaves of all ages and backgrounds. Suggest that they concentrate on the most essential information first, for example:

◆ printing and writing
◆ numbers
◆ simple addition and subtraction of sums of money
◆ multiplication tables
◆ a bare outline of American history and constitutional rights
◆ anatomy and health
◆ days of the week and months of the year
◆ maps of the United States and world

Remind students to show sensitivity to the former slaves' heritage from Africa or the Caribbean. Videotape the teaching of each lesson.

Budget: $

Sources:

First grade textbooks; lessons from magazines such as *Instructor*.

Evitts, William J., *Captive Bodies, Free Spirits: The Story of Southern Slavery*, Messner, 1985.

Morrison, Toni, *Beloved,* Knopf, 1987.

Alternative Applications: Create a big book primer of basic lessons to use in post-slavery schools. Illustrate with large, simple line drawings, such as pictures of currency, calendar pages, anatomical drawings, the solar system, and maps.

Haiti Seeks Help

Age/Grade Level or Audience: High school and college debate teams.

Description: Debate the question of political asylum and/or humanitarian aid for Haitian refugees.

Procedure: Determine whether the U.S. position barring Haitians from seeking political asylum is racist. Weigh the alternatives to sending boatloads of political exiles back to their native island and the consequences of jail, torture, or death with accepting them into U.S. society and subjecting taxpayers to a massive influx of people requiring welfare, medical assistance, jobs, and education.

Budget: $

Sources:
Newsbank, Infotrac, *Time, Newsweek, U.S. News and World Report,* and other compendia of world events.

Alternative Applications: Hold an informal consortium to contrast the U.S. policy toward Haitians seeking asylum with these groups:

◆ Cuban, Vietnamese, Cambodian, and Laotian boat people escaping communism
◆ Russians escaping anti-Semitic communist leaders
◆ immigrant victims of AIDS
◆ Jews fleeing Hitler's death camps
◆ Muslims avoiding Serbian concentration camps
◆ Kurds escaping Iraqi persecution
◆ starving Somalis sailing toward famine relief

Joseph Cinque vs. the Slave Trade

Age/Grade Level or Audience: High school and college drama, creative writing, and speech classes.

Description: Write a speech by Joseph Cinque, the kidnapped African from Sierra Leone who escaped from Puerto Principe, Cuba, to the United States and successfully pled his case in court.

Procedure: Have students develop a logical argument for why Joseph Cinque deserved freedom. Stress the values U.S. judges would be most cognizant of, for example, the universal right to personal freedom as epitomized by the concept of *habeas corpus*. Include consideration of precedent or class action suits as well as humanitarian concerns. Include information derived from the Dred Scott decision.

Budget: $

Sources:
Biographies of John Quincy Adams and Martin Van Buren.
Estell, Kenneth, ed., *The African-American Almanac,* 6th ed., Gale, 1993.
Franklin, John Hope, *From Slavery to Freedom: A History of American Negroes,* 1979.
Hornsby, Alton, Jr., *Chronology of African-American History: Significant Events and People from 1619 to the Present,* Gale, 1991.
Hunt, Bernice Kohn, *The Amistad Mutiny,* McCall, 1971.

Alternative Applications: Invite a panel of volunteers to rebut Cinque's speech with the proslavery point of view and an equally impelling case against his return to Africa. Stress differing perspectives, including economic, legal, and historical.

Market Day

Age/Grade Level or Audience: Kindergarten and elementary social studies classes; church schools; scout troops.

Description: Have students simulate market day in an African community.

Procedure: Provide pictures of life in Africa, featuring weekly outdoor market days, where coffee, tea, fruit, vegetables, grains, and meats are sold alongside woven goods, baskets, carvings, leather belts, bags, sandals, musical instruments. Have students make booths of their own and sell simulated products, such as baskets, jewelry, whistles made from sticks, belts cut from cardboard, religious items molded of clay, and musical instruments made from found materials. Include professional letter writers and entertainers, for instance, puppeteers and storytellers, snake charmers, dancers, acrobats, and magicians. Create a sense of verisimilitude by providing stacks of imitation African currency. Videotape a day at the African market.

Budget: $$

Sources:
Films *Out of Africa* (1985), *Gorillas in the Mist* (1988), *Mister Johnson* (1991), *Sarafina!* (1992), and *The Power of One*.
Abebe, Daniel, *Ethiopia in Pictures*, Lerner Publications, 1988.
Lerner Geography Department Staff, *Kenya in Pictures*, Lerner Publications, 1988.
Lerner Geography Department Staff, *Madagascar in Pictures*, Lerner Publications, 1988.
Lerner Geography Department Staff, *Zaire in Pictures*, Lerner Publications, 1992.
Murray, Jocelyn, ed., *Cultural Atlas of Africa*, Facts on File, 1989.

Alternative Applications: Have students draw a mural of an African market day. Provide contrast by showing visitors from North and South America, Europe, Asia, Australia, and other African cultures who come to trade for foreign goods. Include food vendors, varied currencies, native transportation, and dogs and children playing in the street. Depict the arrival of an important chief or shaman.

Mule Bone

Age/Grade Level or Audience: College drama classes; literary societies.

Description: Research critical responses to *Mule Bone*, a Broadway hit by Zora Neale Hurston and Langston Hughes.

Procedure: Analyze critiques of *Mule Bone*, which opened on Broadway in 1991, more than sixty years after it was written. Determine how Zora Neale Hurston and Langston Hughes depict black dialect and slang and why the work failed to find an audience during the Harlem Renaissance, when it was first published.

Budget: $

Sources:
Hughes, Langston, and Arna Bontemps, eds., *The Harlem Renaissance Remembered*, Dodd, 1972.
"People," *U.S. News and World Report*, February 25, 1991, p. 18.

Alternative Applications: Organize a reading of important scenes from *Mule Bone*. Select a panel to discuss the significance of the play to black drama and the Harlem Renaissance. Note in particular the authors' compassion for oppressed people, particularly women and children.

LIVE | Oral Interpretation

Originator: Leatrice Pearson, teacher, Lenoir, North Carolina.

Age/Grade Level or Audience: Middle school, high school, and college drama classes; community and church theater groups.

Description: Organize a reading theater.

Procedure: Have participants select poems, essays, short stories, song and hymn lyrics, and excerpts from novels and biographies to read aloud, taking turns with parts. Have students concentrate on intonation, gesture, and cadence. Some titles worthy of excerpting for oral interpretation include these:

- ◆ William Armstrong's *Sounder*
- ◆ Maya Angelou's *I Know Why the Caged Bird Sings* or *Now Sheba Sings the Song*
- ◆ Ernest T. Gaines's *The Autobiography of Miss Jane Pittman*
- ◆ James Weldon Johnson's *The Creation*
- ◆ Charlie Smalls's *The Wiz*
- ◆ Ossie Davis's *Purlie Victorious*
- ◆ Richard Wright's *Black Boy*, "Almos' a Man," or *Native Son*
- ◆ Langston Hughes's *Don't You Want to Be Free*
- ◆ James Baldwin's *The Fire Next Time*
- ◆ Alice Walker's *The Color Purple*
- ◆ Zora Neale Hurston's *Mule Bone*
- ◆ Alex Haley's *Queen*
- ◆ Ralph Ellison's *Invisible Man*
- ◆ Jean Toomer's *Cane*
- ◆ Toni Morrison's *The Bluest Eye, Beloved,* or *Jazz*
- ◆ Ann Petry's *Tituba*
- ◆ Margaret Walker's *Jubilee*

Budget: $

Sources:

Chapman, Abraham, ed., *Black Voices: An Anthology of Afro-American Literature*, St. Martin's Press, 1970.

Williams, Mance, *Black Theater in the 1960s and 1970s: A Historical Critical Analysis of the Movement*, Greenwood Press, 1985.

Wilson, Charles Reagan, and William Ferris, eds., *Encyclopedia of Southern Culture*, University of North Carolina Press, 1989.

Alternative Applications: Add drama to oral interpretation by organizing tableaus, such as these:

◆ the arrest of the father in *Sounder*

◆ Maya Angelou's application for a job as streetcar conductor in *I Know Why the Caged Bird Sings*

◆ Richard Wright's baptism in *Black Boy*

◆ Sethe's attendance at Baby Suggs's religious meetings in *Beloved*

◆ Tituba's interaction with teenage girls in *Tituba*

◆ the meeting between Celie and her grown children in *The Color Purple*

Playing the Part

Originator: Leatrice Pearson, teacher, Lenoir, North Carolina.

Age/Grade Level or Audience: Middle school, high school, and college drama classes.

Description: Act out skits or plays about the black experience.

Procedure: Have students select a significant scene from *A Raisin in the Sun;* dialogue from *The Learning Tree, The Creation, And Still I Rise, Tituba of Salem Village, Beloved, The Bluest Eye, Jazz, I Know Why the Caged Bird Sings, The Autobiography of Miss Jane Pittman,* or *Sounder;* or an original drama to present to a school or church assembly, community arts festival, or local theater. Videotape the performance.

Budget: $$$

Sources:
Various issues of the magazine *Plays.*
Angelou, Maya, *And Still I Rise,* Random House, 1978.
Armstrong, William Howard, *Sounder,* ABC-Clio, 1987.
Gaines, Ernest, *The Autobiography of Miss Jane Pittman,* Dial, 1971.
Hansberry, Lorraine, *A Raisin in the Sun: A Drama in Three Acts,* Random House, 1959.
Johnson, James Weldon, *The Creation,* Little, Brown, 1993.
Morrison, Toni, *Beloved,* Knopf, 1987.
Morrison, *The Bluest Eye,* Holt, 1969.
Morrison, *Jazz,* Knopf, 1992.
Parks, Gordon, *The Learning Tree,* Harper, 1963.
Petry, Ann, *Tituba of Salem Village,* Crowell, 1964.

Alternative Applications: Have students trade roles, with nonwhites playing black parts and vice versa. Then lead a discussion of student perceptions of the change. Conclude with readings from Studs Terkel's *Race,* Stephen L. Carter's *Reflections of an Affirmative Action Baby,* or Dinesh D'Souza's *Illiberal Education: The Politics of Race and Sex on Campus.*

◼️ Quoting Black Voices

Age/Grade Level or Audience: Middle school, high school, and college drama, speech, journalism, and English classes; toastmasters clubs.

Description: Hold an annual declamation contest in which contestants present readings from great black writers.

Procedure: Publicize a recitation contest through schools, churches, libraries, civic clubs, and the news media. Organize a panel to score the performances of entrants on three levels: children, teens, and adults. Require participants to select pieces from a standard list. Some suggested pieces include the following:

- ◆ William Wells Brown's *Clotel*
- ◆ Richard Wright's "Between the World and Me"
- ◆ excerpts from James Baldwin's *The Fire Next Time*
- ◆ Martin Luther King Jr.'s "I Have a Dream" speech
- ◆ W. E. B. DuBois's speech to the 1919 Pan-African Conference in Paris
- ◆ Dudley Randall's "Booker T. and W. E. B. DuBois"
- ◆ excerpts from Toni Morrison's *The Bluest Eye*
- ◆ Margaret Burroughs's "What Should I Tell My Children Who Are Black"
- ◆ Arna Bontemps's "Golgotha Is a Mountain"
- ◆ excerpts from Ann Petry's *The Street*
- ◆ Frederick Douglass's *What to the Slaves Is the Fourth of July?*
- ◆ excerpts from Martin Luther King, Jr.'s "Letter from Birmingham Jail"
- ◆ Maya Angelou's *Sheba Sings the Song*
- ◆ Sojourner Truth's address to the New York legislature
- ◆ Paul Laurence Dunbar's "When de C'on Pone's Hot"
- ◆ Claude McKay's "America"
- ◆ Countee Cullen's "Yet Do I Marvel"
- ◆ Barbara Jordan's speech to the 1992 National Democratic Convention
- ◆ Langston Hughes's "The Negro Speaks of Rivers" and "Epilogue"
- ◆ excerpts from Julius Lester's *To Be a Slave*

Budget: $$

Sources:

Bontemps, Arna, *American Negro Poetry,* Hill & Wang, 1963, revised, 1974.

Chapman, Abraham, ed., *Black Voices: An Anthology of Afro-American Literature,* St. Martin's Press, 1970.

Kunjufu, Jawanza, *Lessons from History: A Celebration of Blackness,* African American Images, 1987.

Lester, Julius, *To Be a Slave,* Dial, 1969, reprinted.

Ravitch, Diane, *The American Reader: Words That Moved a Nation,* HarperCollins, 1990.

Alternative Applications: Videotape a series of public recitations by influential black speakers to use as classroom aids and models. Have students study the presentations to learn speaking techniques, audience awareness, eye contact, gesture, tone, and emphasis. Consider demonstrations by Ron Brown, Bill Cosby, Barbara Jordan, Coretta Scott King, Jesse Jackson, Faye Wattleton, Thurgood Marshall, Spike Lee, Colin Powell, and Maya Angelou.

Speaker's Bureau

Age/Grade Level or Audience: All ages.

Description: Create a card file or database of speakers.

Procedure: Organize a school list or library or museum database of speakers and experts on specific subjects. Include these possibilities:

- ◆ people who have traveled to or worked in Africa
- ◆ specialists in black religions, particularly Santeria or Islam
- ◆ retired military personnel
- ◆ health experts on sickle cell anemia
- ◆ drug awareness experts
- ◆ dramatists and actors who can given readings from black literature
- ◆ members of black fraternal organizations
- ◆ civil rights leaders
- ◆ politicians who display an interest in promoting racial harmony
- ◆ union organizers and business leaders
- ◆ judges and police officers
- ◆ social workers and counselors
- ◆ musicians, puppeteers, gymnasts, athletes, storytellers, dancers, artists, weavers, cooks, clothing and furniture designers, architects, and other professionals and performers

Keep this list up to date by adding and deleting information, clipping articles from local media sources, and collecting programs, outlines, speeches, and other useful material. Advertise the speaker's bureau in surrounding areas. Videotape presentations for later showings.

Budget: $$$

Sources:
Library lists, volunteer organizations, teachers, League of Women Voters, Business and Professional Women's League, chamber of commerce, job counselors, military recruiters, ministerial councils, fraternal organizations, and citizens who know the community well.

Alternative Applications: Collect speeches and sermons delivered by local experts on black culture, black history, Africa, the Caribbean, or race relations. Maintain a vertical file or database of speeches at a school or county library for use by researchers, students, or teachers.

Talk to Me

Age/Grade Level or Audience: High school and college speech and writing classes; adult radio audiences.

Description: Organize a Black History Month talk show.

Procedure: Create a format for a radio talk show. Include segments such as these:

- ◆ African-American news of the day
- ◆ news from black people around the world
- ◆ black history briefs, for example, "Twenty-Five, Fifty, and a Hundred Years Ago Today"
- ◆ a variety of black music, from rap, gospel, and rock to reggae, soul, jazz, and calypso
- ◆ a topic of the day, such as ways to counter violent street gangs, health and safety problems in the black community, support for black leaders, and assistance for elderly, sick, and handicapped people living in poverty
- ◆ call-in commentary

Set up a mock run-through by having participants write the script and volunteers call in questions and comments. Tape four weekly segments to run throughout Black History Month. Vary the types of voices during a single program to include youthful, older, male, and female speakers.

Budget: $$

Sources:

Current news sources such as *USA Today, Africa Watch, Time, U.S. News and World Report, Newsweek, Ebony, Jet,* and *Emerge* and Infotrac and Newsbank.

Estell, Kenneth, ed., *The African-American Almanac,* 6th ed., Gale, 1993.

Hornsby, Alton, Jr., *Chronology of African-American History: Significant Events and People from 1619 to the Present,* Gale, 1991.

Low, W. Augustus, and Virgil A. Clift, eds., *Encyclopedia of Black America,* McGraw Hill, 1981.

Alternative Applications: Find fifteen to thirty minutes of air time on local or campus radio broadcasts for a black history program. Spice your format with guest spots, which can be taped or presented live. Include a variety of commentators, particularly fashion designers, film makers, athletes, entertainers, judges, entrepreneurs, and activists, as well as news about black people in Africa, the Caribbean, and other parts of the world. If your area responds well to the format, encourage a local station to adopt the program as a regular weekly feature.

This Ol' Hat

Age/Grade Level or Audience: Elementary and middle school students.

Description: Present an informal skit titled "This Ol' Hat."

Procedure: Pass one of a series of hats to the first participant, who will put it on and describe a significant black person who might have worn it. Have each participant compose a three- or four-sentence explanation of why the hat is significant, then perform or read it aloud. For example:

◆ This ol' hat protected my granddaddy's head along the Mississippi Delta, where he hoed cotton from sunup to sundown. When he died, the hat passed on to my father, then to me. I wore it the day that freedom came to the slaves on the plantation and threw it into the air as church bells rang. All my relatives cried, "Jubilee! Freedom!"

◆ I wore this hat as I led runaways along a dark path to the river bank and waited for clouds to part so I could follow the Big Dipper. I held tight to my hat as the wind and snow blew, but I didn't let go of the hand I grasped. When Lincoln proclaimed all slaves free, I retired my hat.

◆ I wore this hat on the day that Rosa Parks refused to take a back seat to anybody. Proudly, I joined the groups that lined the streets of Montgomery to express their unity in the bus boycott. I removed my hat in honor of Dr. Martin Luther King, a brave and good man who did his best to stop violence.

◆ On the day that I was captured and bound by a neck chain, I was wearing this skullcap, which stayed with me across the Atlantic to the auction block at Annapolis, Maryland. During the crossing, I saw my brother leap to his death among hungry sharks and heard my aunt cry as her sickly infant was ripped from her arms and flung into the waves. I will pass my hat to my son in hopes that he might return to Africa and reunite with his grandparents.

◆ I wore this sun hat on the day that Dr. Mae Jemison became the first black woman to blast off into space. As I tilted my head to watch the rocket climb on its way to outer space, I wondered if this voyage would be the one to bring back vital information on pollution or propose an answer to the energy crisis. Whatever its scientific worth, I was sure that it represented great strides for black women.

◆ I wore this hat on the day that Marian Anderson sang in the Washington mall. My hat reminded me to hold up my head to acknowledge a world-famous singer who refused to be humiliated by the Daughters of the American Revolution. As a woman among great women, I felt privileged to be in the company of Mrs. Eleanor Roosevelt, a First Lady with the courage to face down bigotry.

◆ My hat is battered from the months I slogged through the jungles of Vietnam, fighting a war that many Americans called unjust. Despite my own feelings against violence, I followed my country's orders and brought my hat safely home to my family. I wore my hat to the dedication of Maya Lin's Vietnam Memorial in Washington, D.C., then passed my hat to my daughter, who served in the nursing corps in the Persian Gulf War.

◆ My sun hat shaded my eyes the day that Hitler snubbed the efforts of black athletes at the 1936 Olympics. When the athletes returned to the U.S. in victory, I removed my hat out of respect for Jesse Owens and Ralph Metcalfe. I tossed it high in the air the day that Hitler was defeated. In the scramble, I recovered my hat and wore it down Pennsylvania Avenue in the victory parade for returning troops.

Videotape this presentation, then show it at a PTA supper, retirement home, scout or 4-H banquet, or church assembly.

Budget: $$

Sources:

Asante, Molefi K., *Historical and Cultural Atlas of African Americans,* Macmillan, 1991.

Estell, Kenneth, ed., *The African-American Almanac,* 6th ed., Gale, 1993.

Hornsby, Alston, Jr., *Chronology of African-American History: Significant Events and People from 1619 to the Present,* Gale, 1991.

Alternative Applications: Have students select an inanimate object to epitomize a particular moment in black history, for instance, a belt, shoe, scarf, cup, saddle, sack, photo, newspaper clipping, runaway poster, chain, bottle, or stone. Organize a small group to compose a scenario depicting the importance of the object. Produce by desktop publishing a series of dramatic moments for classes to read or act out.

Thomas Jefferson and Slavery

Age/Grade Level or Audience: High school and college speech, history, and writing classes.

Description: Debate the antislavery paragraph removed from the Declaration of Independence in 1776.

370

Procedure: Read aloud the following paragraph that Thomas Jefferson intended for his declaration to England's King George III:

He [King George III] has waged cruel war against human nature itself, violating its most sacred rights to life and liberty in the persons of a distant people who never offended him, captivating and carrying them into slavery in another hemisphere, or to incur miserable death in their transportation thither. This piratical warfare, the opprobrium of infidel powers, is the warfare of the Christian King of Great Britain. Determined to keep open a market where men should be bought and sold, he has prostituted his negative for suppressing every legislative attempt to prohibit or restrain this execrable commerce.

Lead a discussion of how the inclusion of this paragraph would have changed U.S. history.

Budget: $

Sources:
Concise Dictionary of American Literary Biography, Volume 1: *Colonization to the American Renaissance, 1640-1865,* Gale, 1988.
Estell, Kenneth, ed., *The African-American Almanac,* 6th ed., Gale, 1993.

Alternative Applications: Organize a small group to rewrite this paragraph in more modern English so that it reflects current attitudes toward human rights. Compare the finished product to other statements concerning individual liberties published by the United Nations, the American Civil Liberties Union, and Amnesty International.

Sports

African-American Sports Maze

Age/Grade Level or Audience: High school students.

Description: Answer questions about famous black athletes.

Procedure: Distribute game and question sheets to each student. Beginning at START, have students draw a line either vertically, horizontally, or diagonally to the block that contains the answer to each question, and proceed to the end block.

Budget: $

Sources:
Bigelow, Barbara Carlisle, ed., *Contemporary Black Biography,* Gale, various volumes.
Connors, Martin, Diane L. Dupuis, and Brad Morgan, *The Olympics Factbook,* Visible Ink Press, 1992.
Estell, Kenneth, ed., *The African-American Almanac,* 6th ed., Gale, 1993.
Trager, James, *The People's Chronology,* Henry Holt, 1992.

Alternative Applications: Extend the game by having students name the achievement of the names that were unused. For example, Cinque, the slave from Sierra Leone who refused enslavement and in 1842 was returned to Africa.

Question Sheet
1. The first black American to compete in the Olympic Games (George Poage)
2. The black athlete who won four gold medals at the 1936 Berlin Olympics (Jesse Owens)
3. Black Olympic runner who was crippled until the age of nine   (Wilma Rudolph)
4. Female athlete who set a world record for the heptathlon in the 1988 Seoul Olympics (Jackie Joyner-Kersee)
5. Boxer originally named Cassius Clay (Muhammad Ali)

6. Middleweight boxer who won a gold medal in 1952 (Floyd Patterson)
7. Female runner who set an Olympic record in the 100-meter dash in 1984 in the Los Angeles games (Evelyn Ashford)
8. Sprinter who raised a fist in Mexico City in 1968 during the playing of the national anthem (John Carlos)
9. Heavyweight boxer who defeated Muhammad Ali in 1971 (Joe Frazier)
10. Track and football star who later headed the surgery department at Howard University (Charles Drew)
11. First black to manage a major league baseball team (Frank Robinson)
12. Black golfer who joined the top professionals in 1968 (Lee Elder)
13. First black NBA player (Nathaniel Clifton)
14. Boxer who won the middleweight title five times (Ray Robinson)
15. Batter who broke Babe Ruth's home run record in 1974 (Hank Aaron)
16. First black Heisman Trophy winner (Ernie Davis)
17. Star of the Milwaukee Bucks who became a sportscaster (Oscar Robertson)
18. 1968 Olympic 400-meter runner who works as a trainer in Cameroon, Africa (Lee Evans)
19. First track and field star to jump seven feet (Charles Dumas)
20. First American black to play major league baseball (Jackie Robinson)

Puzzle Matrix

START	George Poage	Jesse Owens	Carol Lewis	Guion Bluford
Carl Lewis	Smokey Robinson	Wilma Rudolph	Jackie Joyner-Kersee	Ed Bradley
Malcolm X	Diahann Carroll	Bernard Shaw	Muhammad Ali	Floyd Patterson
Tony Dorsett	Jamaica Kincaid	Clara Hale	William Warfield	Evelyn Ashford
Rosey Grier	Toussaint L'Ouverture	Patrice Lamumba	Bryant Gumbel	John Carlos
Lewis Latimer	Billy Dee Williams	Maya Angelou	Lee Elder	Joe Frazier
Hank Aaron	Ray Robinson	Nathaniel Clifton	Frank Robinson	Charles Drew
Ernie Davis	LeVar Burton	Kevin Hooks	Andrew Young	Edmonia Lewis
Oscar Robertson	Lee Evans	Charles Dumas	Jackie Robinson	FINISH

Answer Sheet

START ANSWERS	George Poage (1)	Jesse Owens (2)		
		Wilma Rudolph (3)	Jackie Joyner-Kersee (4)	
			Muhammad Ali (5)	Floyd Patterson (6)
				Evelyn Ashford (7)
				John Carlos (8)
	Ray Robinson (14)	Nathaniel Clifton (13)	Lee Elder (12)	Joe Frazier (9)
Hank Aaron (15)			Frank Robinson (11)	Charles Drew (10)
Ernie Davis (16)				
Oscar Robertson (17)	Lee Evans (18)	Charles Dumas (19)	Jackie Robinson (20)	FINISH

The Black Olympian

Age/Grade Level or Audience: Elementary, middle school, high school, and college physical education and health classes; community and church theater groups; scout troops.

Description: Study African-American contributions to current Olympic teams.

Procedure: Have participants read current newspapers and magazines for information about important Olympic contenders, particularly these:

- ◆ **baseball:** Calvin Murray
- ◆ **basketball:** Teresa Edwards, David Robinson, Magic Johnson, Patrick Ewing, Charles Barkley, Cynthia Cooper, Daedra Charles, Karl Malone, Pam McGee, Lynette Woodard, Cheryl Miller, Clyde Drexler, Clarissa Davis, Medina Dixon, and Michael Jordan
- ◆ **boxing:** Eric Griffin, Montell Griffin, Danell Nicholson, Tim Austin, and Chris Byrd

- ◆ **coaching:** Bob Kersee, Chris Martin, and Joe Byrd
- ◆ **figure skating:** Debi Thomas
- ◆ **gymnastics:** Dominique Dawes, Betty Okino
- ◆ **hurdling:** Edwin Moses
- ◆ **ice hockey:** Val James, Grant Fuhr, Tony McKegney, Ray Neufeld, Eldon Reddick
- ◆ **rowing:** Anita DeFrantz
- ◆ **soccer:** Edison Nascimento
- ◆ **swimming:** Bob Murray, Rick White, Charles Chapman
- ◆ **track:** Jackie Joyner-Kersee, Gwen Torrence, Merlene Ottey, Carl Lewis, Carol Lewis, Cornelius Johnson, Dennis Mitchell, Danny Everett, Alice Coachman, John Tillman, Gail Devers, Juliet Cuthbert, Kevin Young, Linford Christie, Frankie Fredericks, Kirk Baptiste, Thomas Jefferson, Florence Griffith Joyner, Ben Johnson, Derek Redmond, Mark Witherspoon, Daley Thompson, Quincy Watts, Steve Lewis, Bob Beamon, Wilma Rudolph, Charles Simpkins, Carlette Guidry, Evelyn Ashford, Esther Jones, Leroy Burrell, Dennis Mitchell, Mike Marsh, Joe Greene, and Mike Powell
- ◆ **volleyball:** Kim and Elaine Oden
- ◆ **weightlifter:** Marc Henry
- ◆ **wrestling:** Travis West, Rodney Smith, Kenny Monday, and Chris Campbell
- ◆ **Olympic Committee:** Anita DeFrantz and LeRoy Walker, president of the U.S. Olympic Committee.

Create a bulletin board of candid shots of Olympian contenders in action. Indicate the countries they represent.

Budget: $$

Sources:

Infotrac, Facts on File, Newsbank, and other on-line sources; *Sports Illustrated, Jet, Essence, Time, U.S. News and World Report, Ebony, People, Newsweek,* and other news magazines; sports pages of national and local newspapers, particularly *USA Today;* almanacs; the video "Olympic Track and Field, 1988."

Connors, Martin, Diane L. Dupuis, and Brad Morgan, *The Olympics Factbook,* Visible Ink Press, 1992.

"New USOC Head," *Jet,* October 26, 1992, p. 46.

Terry, Ted, *American Black History: Reference Manual,* Myles Publishing, 1991.

Alternative Applications: Have students design a monument to black Olympic stars. Suggest appropriate inscriptions.

The Harlem Globetrotters

Age/Grade Level or Audience: All ages.

Description: Have a local team imitate the style of the Harlem Globetrotters.

Procedure: Invite a team to study films, videos, and newspaper descriptions of the Harlem Globetrotters' unique comic style of basketball. Then have players volunteer to imitate the world famous team's warm-up and playing. Accompany the event with their theme song, "Sweet Georgia Brown."

Budget: $

Sources:
The film *The Harlem Globetrotters* (1951).
Estell, Kenneth, ed., *The African-American Almanac*, 6th ed., Gale, 1993.

Alternative Applications: Show videos of past performances of the Harlem Globetrotters. Have students comment on their combination of wit, agility, humor, and skill. Discuss why the Harlem Globetrotters have been called "American Clown Prince Ambassadors."

Hero to Hero

Age/Grade Level or Audience: Middle school and high school writing and journalism classes.

Description: Compare two famous black athletes.

Procedure: Have students select two athletes from different eras or fields of endeavor and write a comparison of their careers. For example, consider these pairings:

- ◆ Jesse Owens and Rosey Grier
- ◆ Carl Lewis and Joe Louis
- ◆ Arthur Ashe and Wilma Rudolph
- ◆ Debi Thomas and Kareem Abdul Jabbar
- ◆ Jackie Joyner-Kersee and Althea Gibson

Budget: $

Sources:
Infotrac, Facts on File, Newsbank, and other on-line library sources; *Sports Illustrated, Jet, Essence, Time, U.S. News and World Report, Ebony, People, Newsweek,* and other news magazines; sports pages of local and national newspapers, particularly *USA Today;* almanacs; the video "Olympic Track and Field, 1988."
Smith, Jessie Carney, ed., *Notable Black American Women*, Gale, 1992.
Terry, Ted, *American Black History: Reference Manual*, Myles Publishing, 1991.

Alternative Applications: Discuss the growth of one sport through the contributions of black athletes. For example, place the following boxers in chronological order and explain how each made strides for the black athletes following him: George Dixon, Muhammed Ali, Ezzard Charles, Floyd Patterson, Joe Frazier, Henry Armstrong, Joe Louis, Sugar Ray Robinson, Thomas Hearns, Mike Tyson, Riddick Bowe, Evander Holyfield.

The Professional Black Athlete

Age/Grade Level or Audience: Elementary, middle school, high school, and college physical education and health classes; community and church theater groups; scout troops.

Description: Study African-American contributions to American sports.

Procedure: Have participants read reference books, newspapers, and magazines for information about important sports figures, particularly these:

- ◆ **baseball:** Moses Fleetwood Walker, Jackie Robinson, Hank Aaron, Lyle Stone, Reggie Jackson, Satchel Paige, Willie Mays, Rickey Henderson
- ◆ **basketball:** Wilmeth Sidat-Singh, Magic Johnson, Michael Jordan, Kareem Abdul, Jabbar, Isiah Thomas, Cheryl Miller
- ◆ **boxing:** George Dixon, Muhammed Ali, Ezzard Charles, Floyd Patterson, Joe Frazier, Henry Armstrong, Joe Louis, Sugar Ray Robinson, Thomas Hearns, Riddick Bowe, Evander Holyfield
- ◆ **football:** Paul Robeson, Fritz Pollard, Joe Lillard, Kenny Washington, Woody Strode, Bill Willis, Marion Motley, Tony Dorsett, Jim Brown, Walter Payton, O. J. Simpson, Joe Green, Doug Williams
- ◆ **golf:** Charlie Sifford, Lee Elder, Althea Gibson, Calvin Peete
- ◆ **horse racing:** Jimmy Lee and William Sims
- ◆ **lacrosse:** Tina Sloan
- ◆ **sailing:** Art Price, Marty Stephan, William Pinkney, Teddy Seymour
- ◆ **tennis:** Arthur Ashe, Zina Garrison, Althea Gibson, MaliVal Washington, Chanda Rubin
- ◆ **track:** Charles Dumas
- ◆ **coaching and management:** Cito Gaston, Dennis Green, Peter C. B. Bynoe, Hal McRae, Lenny Wilkens, Wes Unseld, Frank Robinson

Organize a game of Twenty Questions in which students pose as famous sports figures. Have class members guess their identities.

Budget: $$

Sources:
Infotrac, Facts on File, Current Biography, Newsbank, and other on-line library sources; *Sports Illustrated, Jet, Essence, Time, U.S. News and World Report, People, Newsweek,* and other news magazines; sports pages of local and national newspapers, particularly *USA Today;* and almanacs.
Ebony, August 1992.
NCAA Basketball's Finest, Triumph Books, 1992.
NCAA Football's Finest, Triumph Books, 1992.

Alternative Applications: Have students create an oversized mobile featuring branches for each sport, with individual pendants marked with athletes' names from that sport hung from its branches.

Sports Clinic

Age/Grade Level or Audience: Elementary, middle school, and high school athletic teams and gym classes.

Description: Locate black athletes to staff a sports clinic.

Procedure: Invite black athletes to instruct students in the fundamentals of gymnastics, football, soccer, wrestling, swimming, tennis, and other sports. Provide the workshop free to assist indigent, elderly, and handicapped community members in improving their skills. Extend sports clinics to include cheerleaders, majorettes, and marching band members.

Budget: $$$

Sources:
Consult local school, college, and university athletic departments for suggested personnel to staff sports workshops.

Alternate Applications: Hold similar clinics to assist artists, particularly guitarists, pianists, drummers, singers, painters, muralists, potters, sculptors, carvers, and weavers.

Sports Debate

Age/Grade Level or Audience: High school and college black studies, journalism, gym, debate, and speech classes.

Description: Debate the actions of Tommie Smith and John Carlos at the 1968 Olympics.

Procedure: Decide whether Tommie Smith and John Carlos were justified in raising the Black Power salute at the Mexico City Olympics or whether their actions constituted an insult to their nation as a whole. As you debate the issue, consider the following points:

- ◆ Oppressed peoples have a right to demonstrate their disenfranchisement.
- ◆ Athletes and entertainers bear the burden of representing not only their talents but also the needs and demands of their race.
- ◆ No athlete representing the United States has a right to embarrass the whole country by displaying militant or unsporting behavior before the world.

Budget: $$

Sources:

Connors, Martin, Diane L. Dupuis, and Brad Morgan, *The Olympics Factbook*, Visible Ink Press, 1992.

Alternative Applications: Direct this assignment toward a journalism class and use it as an example of point/counterpoint editorial writing.

 ## Sports on Film

Age/Grade Level or Audience: All ages.

Description: Celebrate the success of Wilma Rudolph, Olympic gold medalist who overcame prejudice and polio to become an unprecedented track success.

Procedure: Show the biographical film Wilma starring Cicely Tyson and Denzel Washington. Invite a local black athlete to introduce or comment on the values demonstrated by Rudolph as well as the personal strengths and family and community support that buoyed her to victory. Contrast and compare her with other athletes, such as Dick Gregory, Earvin "Magic" Johnson, Arthur Ashe, Michael Jordan, Muhammad Ali, Kareem Abdul Jabbar, and Carl Lewis. Extend the range with film offerings such as these:

- ◆ *Clay vs. Liston*
- ◆ *Harlem Globetrotters: Six Decades of Magic*
- ◆ *The History of Great Black Baseball Players*
- ◆ *Jackie Robinson*
- ◆ *Jesse Owens Returns to Berlin*
- ◆ *Magic Johnson: Put Magic in Your Game*

- ◆ *Michael Jordan's Playground*
- ◆ *Michael Jordan: Come Fly with Me*
- ◆ *Muhammad Ali*
- ◆ *Muhammad Ali vs. Zora*
- ◆ *Ringside with Mike Tyson*
- ◆ *Sugar Ray Leonard*
- ◆ *Sugar Ray Robinson Pound for Pound*

Budget: $$

Sources:

The film *Wilma* (1977).

Connors, Martin, and Julia C. Furtaw, *Videohound's Golden Movie Retriever 1993,*
 Visible Ink Press, 1992.

Alternative Applications: Organize a writing contest open in three categories, for children, teens, and adults, using Rudolph's perseverance as a theme. Have entrants apply her example to problems such as gang warfare, AIDS, random violence, poverty, homelessness, and despair.

Storytelling

An Aesop Recitation

Age/Grade Level or Audience: Elementary, middle school, and high school literature, speech, and Latin classes.

Description: Create an illustrated display of homilies from Aesop's fables.

Procedure: Introduce the background of Aesop (c. 620-c. 560 B.C.), black Lydian slave who served a Greek owner and earned a reputation as a teller of witty, illustrative fables, most of which featured animal characters. Published by Demetrius Phalereus two-and-one-half centuries after Aesop's death, the fables, succinct and ironic, end in pointed aphorisms, such as:

- The greedy who demand more lose all.
- Danger often comes from where we least expect.
- To change place is not to change one's nature.
- There is always someone worse off than you.
- The lamb follows the wolf in sheep's clothing.
- Appearances are often deceiving.
- Don't count your chickens before they are hatched.
- No act of kindness, no matter how small, is ever wasted.
- Slow and steady wins the race.
- Familiarity breeds contempt.
- A crust eaten in peace is better than banquets consumed in fear.
- It is not fine feathers that make fine birds.
- In union we have strength.
- Who shall bell the cat?
- Be content with your life; one cannot be first in everything.
- People often grudge others what they cannot enjoy themselves.
- Self-conceit often leads to self-destruction.
- Any excuse serves the tyrant.

◆ Prepare today for tomorrow's needs.

◆ Put a shoulder to the wheel.

◆ The gods help those who help themselves.

◆ We often give the enemy the means to destroy us.

◆ We often see others' vices while ignoring our own.

◆ One person's meat is another's poison.

◆ Necessity is our best weapon.

◆ The smaller the mind, the greater the conceit.

◆ He who pleads with the most pitiful voice does not always suffer the greatest injury.

◆ He who laughs last laughs best.

◆ He who deserts old friends for new deserves to lose both.

◆ One good deed deserves another.

Budget: $

Sources:

Aesop, *Aesop's Fables*, Contemporary Books, 1988.
Aesop, *Aesop's Four-Footed Fables*, Star Rover, 1985.
Snodgrass, Mary Ellen, *Greek Classics Notes*, Cliff's Notes, 1988.

Alternative Applications: Have students work in pairs to create their own beast fables ending with a wise saying. Collect these classroom beast fables and publish them in a single collection, add to a database, or display in poster form on a hall bulletin board or civic display in celebration of Black History Month.

African Story Swap

Age/Grade Level or Audience: All ages.

Description: Hold an informal storytelling session.

Procedure: Arrange a story swap featuring African folk tales, such as *Mufaro's Beautiful Daughters, Fortune Tellers, Who's in Rabbit's House,* or *Why Mosquitoes Buzz in People's Ears.* Have volunteers act out key parts as the storyteller narrates the plot. Offer a prize to encourage participation, such as a book, record, or tape of stories by Jackie Torrence or Chinua Achebe.

Budget: $$

Sources:

Aardema, Verna, *Who's in Rabbit's House*, Dial Press, 1977.
Aardema, *Why Mosquitoes Buzz in People's Ears: A West African Tale*, Dial Press, 1975.

Achebe, Chinua, *Girls at War,* Heinemann, 1973.

Achebe, *The Sacrificial Egg, and Other Stories,* Etudo (Onitsha, Nigeria), 1962.

Alexander, Lloyd, *The Fortune-Tellers,* Dutton Children's Books, 1992.

Bauer, Caroline Feller, *Handbook for Storytellers,* American Library Association, 1977.

Courlander, Harold, *A Treasury of Afro-American Folklore: The Oral Literature, Traditions, Recollections, Legends, Tales, Songs, Religious Beliefs, Customs, Sayings, and Humor of Peoples of African Descent in the Americas,* Crown Publishers, 1976.

Dance, Daryl Cumber, *Shuckin' and Jivin': Folklore from Contemporary Black Americans,* Indiana University Press, 1978.

Spalding, Henry D., comp. and ed., *Encyclopedia of Black Folklore and Humor,* J. David Publishers, 1990.

Alternative Applications: Explore different kinds of folk tales. For example, examine the trickster motif, which is common in beast fables. A useful source is the collection of six posters, tales, and whole language activities packaged by Gerald McDermott as *Adventures in Folklore: Trickster Tales* (Jenson Publications). Other subgroups of folktales include stories about heaven and hell, ghost and haunt stories, tales of conjuring or magic potions and spells, stories of bondage and emancipation, stories of sexual escapades, self-denigration and ethnic jokes, tales about Mr. Charlie or the white overseer, the exploits of Stagolee, beast fables, parables, nature lore, and superstitions. Organize a discussion group to determine why black storytellers prize verbal prowess. Comment on the difference between economic or physical power and psychological power.

Encouraging the Storyteller

Age/Grade Level or Audience: Teenage and adult volunteers.

Description: Form a volunteer group to serve as migrant griots.

Procedure: Organize a local griot group to visit libraries, schools, storytelling festivals, malls, retirement homes, and centers for the handicapped. Conduct workshops demonstrating method and delivery styles. Provide the following information about the importance of the storyteller in society:

- ◆ Storytelling is the oldest literary art.
- ◆ It demonstrates the uniqueness of the griot's outlook.
- ◆ It has influenced every nation as a form of expression.
- ◆ Traditional tales grow and develop as outgrowths of the griot's creativity.
- ◆ Imaginative stories demonstrate the power of ideas.
- ◆ Characters can be animals and inanimate objects as well as people.
- ◆ Human themes remain constant from country to country.
- ◆ People naturally love stories.
- ◆ Oral stories pass naturally to the written page.

◆ The inspiration of stories often leads to other forms of expression: singing, dancing, drawing, making shadow pictures, creating string art, writing, pantomiming, acting, joke-telling, reading, conversing, debating, and worship.

◆ In whatever form they exist, they emphasize an important truth: that people everywhere have much in common.

Budget: $

Sources:

Bauer, Caroline Feller, *Handbook for Storytellers,* American Library Association, 1977.

Courlander, Harold, *A Treasury of Afro-American Folklore: The Oral Literature, Traditions, Recollections, Legends, Tales, Songs, Religious Beliefs, Customs, Sayings, and Humor of Peoples of African Descent in the Americas,* Crown Publishers, 1976.

Ki-Zerbo, Joseph, "Oral Tradition as a Historical Source," *UNESCO Courier,* April 1990, pp. 43-46.

McDermott, Gerald, *Anansi the Spider: A Tale from the Ashanti,* Puffin Books, 1977.

Alternative Applications: Have storytellers invite listeners to develop their own oral skills by embellishing or retelling stories in different settings. For example, try these alterations:

◆ Reset "Zomo the Rabbit" in a country with a different climate and terrain from its native West Africa.

◆ Tell the story of "Tim O'Toole and the Wee Folk" from a Southern black point of view.

◆ Create a trickster story about an African animal, such as a crocodile, gnu, dik-dik, ostrich, cobra, or hippopotamus.

Griot for a Day

Age/Grade Level or Audience: Elementary, middle school, and high school literature, language, drama, and speech classes.

Description: Assume the role of griot.

Procedure: Have students compile a family history dating back as far as they can put together. Have them relate their family's story in the style of the African griot, who is the repository of African genealogical lore. Use tape recorder or camcorder to record their performances.

Budget: $

Sources:

Interviews with elderly family members or family historians; written histories; genealogies; church records; letters; diaries; family Bibles; photo albums and scrap books; and other sources of family data.

"Our Family, Our Town: Essays on Family and Local History Sources in the National Archives," available through the National Archives and Records Administration, Washington, DC 20408.

Ki-Zerbo, Joseph, "Oral Tradition as a Historical Source," *UNESCO Courier,* April 1990, pp. 43-46.

Alternative Applications: Appoint a person to serve as family griot. Encourage the griot to refine and add to the history by performing at family gatherings, such as holiday feasts, reunions, neighborhood parties, or church festivals. Select a family photographer to record the events in snapshots, group portraits, or on videotape.

Rabbit Ears

Age/Grade Level or Audience: Kindergarten and elementary classes; library story hours; local storytelling festival; literary societies.

Description: Hold a Rabbit Ears festival.

Procedure: Open a storytelling festival with videotapes of African folk tales such as *Rabbit Ears: Anansi,* featuring actor Denzel Washington as narrator, or *Rabbit Ears: Koi and the Kola Nuts,* featuring storyteller and actress Whoopi Goldberg. Discuss the roles of the trickster hare, tortoise, chevrotain, and spider by comparing their functions and significance. Compare native American folk tales, such as *Spider Woman's Granddaughter* and *The Way to Rainy Mountain,* to Joel Chandler Harris's Uncle Remus tales, which derived from African slaves.

Budget: $$

Sources:

The video *Rabbit Ears: Koi and the Kola Nuts;* recordings by Jackie Torrance, Janie Hunter, Anita Timbers, and Benjamin Stanley; and cassettes such as "Why Mosquitoes Buzz in People's Ears," "Zulu and Other African Folktales from Behind the Back of the Mountain," "Black Fairy Tales," "The Dancing Granny and Other African Stories," available from Caedmon, HarperAudio, 10 East 53rd St., New York, NY 10022-5299; telephone: (212)207-7000.

Alternative Applications: Conduct a summer reading program featuring African folk tales, myths, riddles, proverbs, dramas, and tongue twisters. Provide a variety of hands-on activities, such as puppet shows, coloring contests, sidewalk chalk art, and taped retellings in the children's words. Offer prizes of books, tapes, and records by storytellers such as Jackie Torrance and Chinua Achebe.

Round-robin African Adventure

Age/Grade Level or Audience: Kindergarten, elementary, and middle school language classes; church schools; scout troops.

Description: Create an African adventure story.

Procedure: Begin a story by introducing a black protagonist, an African setting, and conflict. For example:

- ◆ On a hot summer morning, Dan rode over the wavy savannah and along the Niger River into the village. On the back of Jako, his faithful gray donkey, Dano was going to buy supplies for the grain harvesters. When he slid down from Jako and reached for the leather coin bag that the chief had tied to his belt, he discovered that the money was missing....
- ◆ Miriam stood at the top of the bluff and looked far out over the Serengeti toward a great black cloud. "Could be a herd of wildebeest," she mused. Waiting to see them gallop past, she sat in the tall grass and absentmindedly wove a grass crown spiked with blue tickweed and daisies. Suddenly, a black locust plopped on her lap, followed by three on her head and a fifth on her ear. Before she could jump up, the air filled with swarming locusts....

Have students take turns explaining what the protagonist does next. As the story passes from one participant to the other, ask questions about the purpose of the character's actions and the likely outcomes. Stop the story before the conclusion and assign each student to end the adventure on paper. Read aloud the varied responses.

Budget: $

Sources:

Baker, Augusta, *Storytelling: Art and Technique,* 2nd ed., R. R. Bowker, 1987.

Ki-Zerbo, Joseph, "Oral Tradition as a Historical Source," *UNESCO Courier,* April 1990, pp. 43-46.

Lester, Julian, *How Many Spots Does a Leopard Have? And Other Tales,* Scholastic, Inc., 1989.

MacDonald, Margaret Read, *Twenty Tellable Tales: Audience Participation Folktales for the Beginning Storyteller,* H. W. Wilson, 1986.

Alternative Applications: Circulate a group of story beginnings featuring African-American characters. Have students respond to what has been written on each. As the stories grow, continue passing them around until everyone has had a part in the telling. Select a group to illustrate some of the stories. Place typed copies alongside the artwork in a class scrapbook or add to a database.

Tell-It-Yourself

Age/Grade Level or Audience: Kindergarten and elementary classes; library story hours; local storytelling festivals; literary societies.

Description: Encourage children to make up their own versions of famous stories.

Procedure: Conclude a storytelling session with a prompt that leaves room for children to tell or write their own version of a similar story. For example, finish a telling of Br'er Rabbit stories with these openers:

- ◆ One day, Br'er Rabbit was just cranking the bucket up to the top of the well when he looked over his shoulder and saw…
- ◆ On a snowy January morning, Br'er Fox and Br'er Bear got so hungry they…
- ◆ During the spring, all of the Kenyan animals, big and small, got together in the grassland to…
- ◆ Even though the sun was shining and the grass green, Baby Zebra was worried because…
- ◆ Around the Yoruba village, there was a lot of talk about the elephant's child because…

Let children take turns audiotaping their conclusions to a story. Type up the finished tales for them to illustrate and bind into a storybook for later story hours, or present copies to parents.

Budget: $

Sources:
Baker, Augusta, *Storytelling: Art and Technique,* 2nd ed., R. R. Bowker, 1987.
Ki-Zerbo, Joseph, "Oral Tradition as a Historical Source," *UNESCO Courier,* April 1990, pp. 43-46.
MacDonald, Margaret Read, *Twenty Tellable Tales: Audience Participation Folktales for the Beginning Storyteller,* H. W. Wilson, 1986.

Alternative Applications: Have students retell or draw European favorites, such as "Goldilocks and the Three Bears," "Little Red Riding Hood," "Pinocchio," "Rapunzel," "Rumplestiltskin," "Snow White," "The Littlest Mermaid," and "The Three Billy Goats Gruff" from an African point of view.

Uncle Remus

Age/Grade Level or Audience: Kindergarten and elementary classes; religious schools.

Description: Hold a daily reading of an Uncle Remus story.

Procedure: Play recordings of Uncle Remus stories. Ask volunteers to explain how the weaker animal is able to evade the stronger. Organize groups of students to illustrate or act out key moments in each drama.

Budget: $$

Sources:

Harris, Joel Chandler, *Uncle Remus: His Songs and Sayings,* 1881, reprinted, 1982.

Harris, *The Tar-Baby, and Other Rhymes of Uncle Remus,* 1904, reprinted, Cherokee Publishing, 1984.

Harris, *Uncle Remus and Brer Rabbit,* 1907.

Parks, Van Dyke, *Jump Again! More Adventures of Br'er Rabbit,* Harcourt Brace Jovanovich, 1987.

Walt Disney's Uncle Remus Stories, Western Publishing, 1985.

Alternative Applications Screen a copy of the film or video *Song of the South* or show the Walt Disney Productions sound filmstrip "Uncle Remus and the Tarbaby Story." Have students learn the songs "Laughing Place" and "Zippity Doo Dah." Ask volunteers to add gestures and mimicry as the class sings the songs.

Using the Storyboard

Age/Grade Level or Audience: Kindergarten and elementary classes; church school classes; Cub and Brownie Scouts.

Description: Arrange storyboard pictures into a workable order, then form a group to compose a single story to fit the pictures.

Procedure: Have students draw pictures of African life, then post their creations in any order on a storyboard. With the group leader's help, have volunteers suggest ways of ordering the stories to comprise a single plot or several variations of a plot. Tape stories or place on a database.

Budget: $

Sources:
"Botswana," *National Geographic,* December 1990.
"Ivory Coast," *National Geographic,* July 1982.
"Malawi," *National Geographic,* September 1989.
"Mali," *National Geographic,* October 1990.
"Senegambia," *National Geographic,* August 1985.
"Serengeti," *National Geographic,* May 1986.
"Zaire," *National Geographic,* November 1991.

Alternative Applications: Have the class dictate a completed story into a tape recorder. Select one person to point to each picture as the story is played back or record the pictures in order on videotape. Use art software, such as *MacDraw* or MacPaint, and desktop publishing to produce finished copies for distribution and free reading. Use this program as the focal point of a church school, banquet, or PTA parent night program.

Writing

Black History Essay Contest

Originator: Atlanta-Fulton Public Library, Atlanta, Georgia.

Age/Grade Level or Audience: All ages.

Description: Establish a theme competition held annually in mid-February.

Procedure: Submit a 1,000-word theme on a particular topic, which changes annually. Winners of first and second place awards in middle school, high school, young adult, and adult categories appear at a televised ceremony in early March.

Budget: $

Sources:
Asante, Molefi K., *Historical and Cultural Atlas of African Americans,* Macmillan, 1991.
Estell, Kenneth, ed., *The African-American Almanac,* 6th ed., Gale, 1993.
Snodgrass, Mary Ellen, *Contests for Students,* Gale, 1991.

Alternative Applications: Organize your own essay contest as a part of a civic, school, library, museum, or church celebration of Black History Month. Some possible topics include:

- Black Women and the Civil Rights Movement
- The Future of Race Relations in America
- Why We Can't Wait
- The Dangers of Racial Stereotyping
- Returning to Our Roots
- Booker T. Washington's advice: "Cast down your bucket where you are"
- The example of Rosa McCauley Parks
- Black Youth and Violence

Black Mystery

Age/Grade Level or Audience: Middle school and high school creative writing classes; writers' clubs.

Description: Brainstorm a mystery around black themes.

Procedure: Join with a small group and outline the plot of a mystery mininovel set in a black community and featuring a black detective. Divide the writing of chapters evenly among the group. Pass the work from one to the other and add events that lead to a solution to the crime. Publish the finished black mystery in mimeographed form.

Budget: $$

Sources:
Bauer, Caroline Feller, *Handbook for Storytellers,* American Library Association, 1977. Lester, Meera, *Writing for the Ethnic Markets,* Writer's Connection, 1991.

Alternative Applications: Give a public reading of the finished mystery or have a group act out the story or perform the dialogue in the style of a reading theater. Submit the finished work to a publisher such as Highsmith or Mysterious Press, or to a mystery magazine, particularly *Inside Detective, P.I. Magazine,* or *Detective Files.* Consult *Writer's Market* for complete details about manuscript submissions.

Campaign Push

Age/Grade Level or Audience: Teenagers and adults.

Description: Support the campaigns of nonwhite candidates.

Procedure: Organize a volunteer group to assist the political campaigns of nonwhite candidates, particularly those entering politics for the first time. Consider the following strategies:

- ◆ Compose short radio and television spots emphasizing community issues.
- ◆ Create handouts, leaflets, and brochures relating facts about the candidates' backgrounds and qualifications for public office.
- ◆ Distribute material in a variety of neighborhoods, particularly where the candidate has the least name recognition.

◆ Organize a satellite group to create get-out-the-vote literature to encourage first-time voters, working people, the homebound, and the elderly to go to the polls to protect their interests by selecting worthy candidates.

◆ List an assortment of catchy phrases to use on banners, bumper stickers, lapel pins, and give-aways, such as key rings, balloons, shopping bags, mugs, and fans.

Budget: $$$$

Sources:

Consult the League of Women Voters or party headquarters for models used by other candidates.

Alternative Applications: Organize a letters-to-the-editor campaign to keep positive statements about the candidates before readers' eyes throughout the election preseason. Keep the tone upbeat and hopeful that your candidates will make a difference in the quality of people's lives.

The *Clothilde*

Originator: George Schroeder, genealogist and reference librarian, Mobile, Alabama.

Age/Grade Level or Audience: Middle school, high school, and college writing and drama classes; thespian societies; civic pageants.

Description: Compose a play about the *Clothilde,* the last slave ship to reach America.

Procedure: Assign participants to create their own roles in a play about the last slave ship. Characters might include boat-builder Timothy Meaher, Captain William Fowler, boatswain, first mate, overseer, slave dealer, cook, slaves, auctioneers, and buyers. Dramatize the following events:

◆ the end of slave trade in 1807
◆ the launching of the *Clothilde* in 1859
◆ the arrival of Africans kidnapped from the Guinea coast
◆ apprehension of the illegal delivery in the Mississippi Sound
◆ Captain William Fowler's escape up the Mobile River
◆ the unloading of the human cargo
◆ the burning of the *Clothilde*
◆ the freeing of the Guinea slaves
◆ the creation of the Plateau community
◆ the life of the last surviving passenger, Cudjoe Lewis

Budget: $

Sources:

George Schroeder, Local History and Genealogy Department, Mobile Public Library, 701 Government St., Mobile, AL 36602; telephone: (205)434-7093.

Cantor, George, *Historic Landmarks of Black America,* Gale, 1991.

Evitts, William J., *Captive Bodies, Free Spirits: The Story of Southern Slavery,* Messner, 1985.

Walvin, James, *Slavery and the Slave Trade: A Short Illustrated History,* University Press of Mississippi, 1983.

Alternative Applications: Write memoirs of individual passengers aboard the *Clothilde*, particularly the captain, crew, overseer, and the slaves themselves. Compose letters to relatives in Africa or friends who were previously enslaved. Note the political and social situation of the *Clothilde's* passengers.

 Denouncing Slavery

Age/Grade Level or Audience: High school and college writing and journalism classes.

Description: Rewrite the Germantown Mennonite Resolution Against Slavery of 1688.

Procedure: Study the logic, spelling, grammar, and phrasing of the first formal abolitionist protest in colonial America. Rewrite strategic sentences in modern English by removing sexist and racist language and archaic spelling and diction. Focus on human rights. Consider these original statements:

◆ Is there any that would be done or handled at this manner?
◆ Yea, rather it is worse for them, which say they are Christians; for we hear that the most part of such negers are brought hither against their will and consent, and that many of them are stolen.
◆ There is a saying, that we should do to all men like as we will be done ourselves; making no difference of what generation, descent, or colour they are.
◆ This makes an ill report in all those countries of Europe, where they hear of (it), that the Quakers do here handel men as they handel there the cattle.
◆ Pray, what thing in the world can be done worse towards us, than if men should rob and steal us away, and sell us for slaves to strange countries; separating husbands from their wives and children.

Budget: $

Sources:

Commager, Henry, *Fifty Basic Civil War Documents,* Van Nostrand Reinhold, 1965, reprinted, R. E. Krieger, 1982.

Estell, Kenneth, ed., *The African-American Almanac,* 6th ed., Gale, 1993.

Alternative Applications: Discuss in small groups additional points in the Germantown Mennonite Resolution, particularly these:

◆ Here is liberty of conscience, which is right and reasonable; here ought to be likewise liberty of the boyd, except of evil-doers, which is another case.

◆ How fearful and faint-hearted are many at sea, when they see a strange vessel, being afraid it should be a Turk, and they should be taken, and sold for slaves into Turkey.

◆ Have these poor negers not as much right to fight for their freedom, as you have to keep them slaves?

◆ Now consider well this thing, if it is good or bad.

Emblems of Africa

Age/Grade Level or Audience: Elementary and middle school writing classes; religious school; scout troops.

Description: Write emblem poems.

Procedure: Have students write an emblem poem about Africa. Have them begin by writing vertically on the page a short word connected with Africa, such as Benin, Nile, Congo, or Shaka. Then have them write a line of verse for each letter. For example:

> **A**long way from where I live,
> **F**ar from my town, my school,
> **R**ises the outline of a great black nation.
> **I** can't see Africa from here,
> **C**an't hear its music or taste its sweet fruits.
> **A**frica seems so far away.

Budget: $

Sources:

Courlander, Harold, *A Treasury of Afro-American Folklore: The Oral Literature, Traditions, Recollections, Legends, Tales, Songs, Religious Beliefs, Customs, Sayings, and Humor of Peoples of African Descent in the Americas,* Crown Publishers, 1976.

Ellis, Veronica Freeman, *Afro-Bets First Book about Africa: An Introduction for Young Readers,* Just Us Books, 1989.

Isadora, Rachel, *Over the Green Hills,* Greenwillow Books, 1992.

Alternative Applications: Other types of shaped verse may appeal to stronger writers or students learning to use a computer. For example, have students type on a word processor a poem shaped like a coconut, mamba, ostrich, ankh, or banana, or have them fill in the shape of Africa with simple written images, such as broad sands, mighty rivers, crinkly ferns, waterfalls, black skin, and smiling faces.

A Friend in Africa

Age/Grade Level or Audience: Elementary, middle school, and high school classes; church groups; scout troups; 4-H clubs: civic clubs; foreign language clubs; travel clubs.

Description: Start an African pen pal society.

Procedure: Petition African embassies for names of people willing to be pen pals. Match backgrounds with local writers eager to start a correspondence. Exchange photos, maps, and information about school events, government, local landmarks, wildlife, food, activities, and holidays.

Budget: $$

Sources:
Make your request for pen pals to one of these sources:

Mohamed Bashir Sani
Nigerian Embassy
2201 M St. N.W.
Washington, DC
(202)822-1500, ext. 541

Mary Wright-Singer
70 Maple St.
Bellingham, MA 02019

Angela Harkless
Discover! Africana! Club!: Newsletters
of the Africana Heritage Club
P.O. Box 800
Highsmith
Fort Atkinson, WI 53538-0800

Alternative Applications: Use pen pals as an extension of a French class by pairing writers with French-speaking Africans and Caribbean natives from Martinique, St. Bart's, and Guadaloupe.

A Letter of Application

Age/Grade Level or Audience: Middle school and high school writing classes.

Description: Compose a letter of application to a self-help organization aiding black people.

Procedure: Have students apply to the Catholic World Mission, Peace Corps, Red Cross, World Health Oganization (WHO), UNICEF, *Medecins sans Frontieres,* or other relief agencies helping black people in Africa, the Caribbean, or pockets of poverty in American cities or counties. Suggest that each letter state the following information:

- ◆ Why the candidate chose that place
- ◆ What social or other problems the applicant hopes to alleviate or eradicate, such as hunger, insufficient knowledge of farming or sanitation, poor health standards, or need of industrialization, religion, or education
- ◆ Proof that the applicant is dependable
- ◆ What talents or skills the applicant plans to utilize
- ◆ Examples of projects, responsibilities, or other demonstrations of capability that establish the applicant's sincerity and preparation

Budget: $

Sources:
Descriptions of major social agencies, their aims and purposes, and their organization's style and outreach.
Furtaw, Julia C., *Black Americans Information Directory, 1992-93,* 2nd ed., Gale, 1991.

Alternative Applications: Suggest that applicants make a list of preparations, equipment, materials, and supplies necessary for a one-year stay in the chosen location. For example, for a sojourn in Kenya, list innoculations, dehydrated foods, bottled water, bush clothing, shoes, camping gear, foodstuffs, first aid kit, and short-wave radio.

Letter-Writing Campaign

Age/Grade Level or Audience: Middle school, high school and college language, history, and African-American studies classes.

Description: Organize a letter-writing campaign to encourage businesses, newspapers, television stations, and the entertainment media to include blacks more equally in product design and advertising campaigns, particularly in areas heavily populated by African-Americans.

Procedure: Have students divide into small groups and select an area of American life in which blacks are underrepresented, such as fashion ads, toys, greeting cards, luxury items, and makeup. Help participants develop positive statements which stress that black Americans are also consumers and that a fair representation of all races benefits both the buyer and the seller. Have students propose specific items to be altered or deleted, such as Mother's Day cards that depict only white families or toys and games designed for white children. Conclude with a leaflet campaign directed at a particular group, such as the citizens of a metropolitan area that offers no transportation to nonwhite residences or bankers who refuse loans to working class people.

Budget: $$

Sources:
Business registries, local companies, newspapers, and radio and television networks.

Poetry Workshop

Originator: James C. Morris, poet.

Age/Grade Level or Audience: All ages.

Description: Organize a community, library, or school poetry workshop.

Procedure: Organize a poetry workshop to encourage beginning writers of all ages. Divide participants into groups loosely based on expertise rather than age. Use models of major poets as springboards for discussion. For example, discuss as a group the emotive, lyrical power of James C. Morris's "Chanson Petite":

> Oh, America!
> Oh, *my* America!
> How much longer
> Do I have to
> Remain stronger?
> Surely, America,
> You must know
> Endurance carries
> Elastic band
> Across the mental land
> That can only stretch and stretch ...
> And stretch just *so!*

How far yet, how far
Do I have to go?
Oh, America!
Oh, *my* America!

After students have developed their own style, subjects, and voice, select the best of their output for publication in a workshop chapbook, newsletter, bulletin board display, literary magazine, or public reading. Offer prizes, such as anthologies of poetry, essays, short fiction, and drama by black authors.

Budget: $$

Sources:

Bontemps, Arna, *American Negro Poetry,* Hill & Wang, 1963, revised, 1974.

Chapman, Abraham, ed., *Black Voices: An Anthology of Afro-American Literature,* St. Martin's Press, 1970.

Giovanni, Nikki, *My House,* Morrow, 1972.

Ravitch, Diane, *The American Reader: Words That Moved a Nation,* HarperCollins, 1990.

Stetson, Erlene, *Black Sister: Poetry by Black American Women, 1746-1980,* Indiana University Press, 1981.

Alternative Applications: Extend the writing workshop to other forms of expression, such as rap, songs, essays, letters, short stories, dialogues, biography, memoir, and history. Divide participants into groups to edit, rewrite, and produce works via desktop publishing.

Slave Days

Age/Grade Level or Audience: Middle school, high school, and college writing classes.

Description: Keep a journal from the point of view of a slave.

Procedure: Have participants record daily life and labors of either a fictional composite character or a real person, such as Frederick Douglass, Nat Turner, Sojourner Truth, Tituba, or Harriet Tubman.

Budget: $

Sources:

Films and videos such as *The Autobiography of Miss Jane Pittman* (1974) and *Roots* (1977); histories of the antebellum South.

Estell, Kenneth, ed., *The African-American Almanac,* 6th ed., Gale, 1993.

Lester, Julius, *To Be a Slave,* Dial, 1969.

Rhodes, Elisha Hunt, *All for the Union: The Civil War Diary and Letters of Elisha Hunt Rhodes,* Vintage Books, 1992.

Walvin, James, *Slavery and the Slave Trade: A Short Illustrated History,* University Press of Mississippi, 1983.

Alternative Applications: Have students write dialogue for two or more characters in these situations:

- ◆ conversation on market day
- ◆ the end of a work day
- ◆ celebration of a wedding or birth
- ◆ religious ceremonies
- ◆ arrival of a new slave
- ◆ plot to run away
- ◆ revolt against harsh conditions
- ◆ manumission or nationwide emancipation

Words and Snapshots

Age/Grade Level or Audience: Middle school and high school classes.

Description: Create a storyboard to describe black people in your community.

Procedure: Have students assemble a group of candid snapshots to discuss and group the photos by mood. Have participants work as a group to compose an essay describing the different categories, such as monuments, signs, buildings, families, recreation, entertainment, worship, markets, neighbors, and race relations.

Budget: $$$

Sources:

Local camera clubs, newspaper photos, and library clipping files.

Bauer, Caroline Feller, *Handbook for Storytellers,* American Library Association, 1977.

Alternative Applications: Create oversized bulletin board displays of photos and essays by copying the words of each composition onto poster paper and surrounding with a frame of photos.

Writing Epitaphs

Age/Grade Level or Audience: Elementary and middle school writing classes.

Description: Compose epitaphs for notable black people.

Procedure: Organize a writing workshop in which students work in pairs. Have them read a variety of source material, then draw on events in the lives of famous black people and compose suitable epitaphs to adorn a statue, plaque, or tombstone. Some worthy choices are Medgar Evers, Toussaint L'Ouverture, Garret Augustus Morgan, Sojourner Truth, Tituba, Nat Turner, Ernest Just, Madame C. J. Walker, Emmett Till, Charles Drew, or Ethel Waters. Have students print their inscriptions on poster paper. Mount their work in a display entitled "Honor Roll of History."

Budget: $$

Sources:

Estell, Kenneth, ed., *The African-American Almanac,* 6th ed., Gale, 1993.

Hornsby, Alton, Jr., *Chronology of African-American History: Significant Events and People from 1619 to the Present,* Gale, 1991.

Low, W. Augustus, and Virgil A. Clift, eds., *Encyclopedia of Black America,* McGraw-Hill, 1981.

Smith, Jessie Carney, ed., *Notable Black American Women,* Gale, 1992.

Alternative Applications: Read aloud the epitaphs and have students guess about whom each was written. Award the student who correctly answers the most with a prize, such as a book mark.

Writing Genre

Age/Grade Level or Audience: Elementary, middle school, high school, and college creative writing and literature classes.

Description: Create a resource notebook of literary genres.

Procedure: Instruct students on different forms of written language, for example, aphorism, slogan, riddle, letter, personal essay, descriptive essay, didactic essay, persuasive argument, haiku, sonnet, ballad, limerick, character sketch, vignette, tableau, dialogue, skit, short story, myth, legend, beast fable, satire, editorial, critique, oral or written history, memoir, and others. As they master the characteristics of each, have them apply their knowledge to an African-American subject, issue, or setting. For example:

- ◆ riddles about African animals
- ◆ a beast fable involving dissimilar African animals, such as a hyena and an ostrich or a dik-dik and a mamba
- ◆ a short story about a black family
- ◆ a persuasive argument encouraging employers to hire black laborers and managers
- ◆ a personal essay about a favorite black athlete or entertainer
- ◆ a critique of a film about the black point of view
- ◆ a history of a local event involving black people, for instance, a building project
- ◆ an editorial calling for government aid to black migrant workers
- ◆ a descriptive essay about an imaginary journey during slave times
- ◆ a series of aphorisms explaining why racism hurts everyone
- ◆ a haiku describing the goals of Kwanzaa
- ◆ slogans to encourage black voters to involve themselves in local political campaigns or community issues, such as representation on the city council
- ◆ a legend about a black cowboy, potter, sculptor, or pioneer
- ◆ a myth explaining why the leopard has spots, the cobra has fangs, or the zebra has stripes
- ◆ a dialogue between slave and master set in colonial times
- ◆ a skit advertising a product or service offered by a black-owned company
- ◆ a fan letter to a historical figure, such as Jackie Robinson, Jesse Owens, Josephine Baker, Judith Jamison, Ethel Waters, Hattie McDaniel, or Lionel Hampton
- ◆ a travelogue describing the marketplace in St. Bart's, Ocho Rios Falls in Jamaica, Aruba's World War II relics, skin diving in the Virgin Islands, or sailing around the Antigua harbor
- ◆ an oral history of how the hymn "Amazing Grace" came to be written

Collect the best of genre examples and produce a handbook or database for future reference.

Budget: $$

Sources:

Bauer, Caroline Feller, *Handbook for Storytellers,* American Library Association, 1977.
Frommer, Arthur, "Caribbean, No Charge," *Travel-Holiday,* June 1992, p. 18.
Snodgrass, Mary Ellen, *The Great American English Handbook,* Perma-Bound Books, 1987.

Alternative Applications: Create a series of posters on black themes that illustrate rhetorical devices, for example, metaphor, extended metaphor, apostrophe, simile, parallelism, alliteration, caesura, enjambment, personification, synecdoche, metonomy, masculine and feminine rhyme, euphony, cacophony, rhythm, onomatopoeia, and sense impressions.

Appendix

Books

African American Writers. New York: Scribner's, 1991.

Alexander, Lloyd. *The Fortune-Tellers*. New York: Dutton, 1992.

Anderson, David A. *Kwanzaa: An Everyday Resource and Instructional Guide*. Fort Atkinson, WI: Highsmith, 1992.

Asante, Molefi K. *Historical and Cultural Atlas of African Americans*. New York: Macmillan, 1992.

Benberry, Cuesta. *Always There: The African-American Presence in American Quilts*. Louisville, KY: Museum of History and Science, 1992.

Benjamin, Medea. *Bridging the Global Gap: A Handbook to Linking Citizens of the First and Third Worlds*. Arlington, VA: Seven Locks Press, 1989.

Benjamin. *Peace Corps and More: 114 Ways to Work, Study, and Travel in the Third World*. Arlington, VA: Seven Locks Press, 1991.

Bennett, Claudette E. *The Black Population in the United States: March 1991*. Washington, DC: U.S. Department of Commerce, Bureau of the Census, 1992.

Brelin, Christa, ed. *Who's Who Among Black Americans, 1992-1993*. Detroit: Gale Research, 1992.

Brown, Stewart, ed. *Caribbean Poetry Now*. London: Edward Arnold, 1992.

Carty, Winthrop P., and Elizabeth Lee. *The Rhino Man and Other Uncommon Environmentalists*. Arlington, VA: Seven Locks Press, 1992.

Cat, Christopher, and Countee Cullen. *The Lost Zoo*. Fort Atkinson, WI: Highsmith, 1990.

Champlin, Connie, and Nancy Renfro. *Storytelling with Puppets*. Chicago, IL: American Library Association, 1985.

Chijoke, F. A. *Ancient Africa*. New York: Africana Publishing, 1971.

Chocolate, Deborah M. Newton. *My First Kwanzaa*. New York: Scholastic: 1992.

Copage, Eric V. *Kwanzaa: An African American Celebration of Culture and Cooking*. Fort Atkinson, WI: Highsmith, 1991.

Davis, Ossie. *Just Like Martin*. New York: Simon & Schuster, 1992.

Dennis, Denise. *Black History for Beginners*. Fort Atkinson, WI: Highsmith, 1992.

Essed, Philomena. *Everyday Racism: Reports from Women of Two Cultures*. Fort Atkinson, WI: Highsmith, 1990.

Estell, Kenneth, ed. *The African-American Almanac*, 6th ed. Detroit, MI: Gale Research, 1993.

Finn, Julio. *The Bluesman: The Music Heritage of Black Men and Women in the Americas*. Fort Atkinson, WI: Highsmith, 1992.

Fodor's Kenya, Tanzania, Seychelles. New York: Fodor's Travel Publications, 1990.

Foster, Sandra Jean, and Ajamu Thabiti. *American Fruits with African Roots*. Fort Atkinson, WI: Highsmith, 1991.

Franklin, Barbara Hackman. *Statistical Abstract of the United States 1992*. Washington, DC: U.S. Department of Commerce, Bureau of the Census, 1992.

Furtaw, Julia C., ed. *Black Americans Information Directory, 1992-1993*. Detroit: Gale Research, 1991.

Gomez, Aurelia. *Crafts of Many Cultures*. New York: Scholastic, 1992.

Greenfield, Eloise. *Africa Dream*. New York: HarperCollins, 1989.

Halliburton, Warren J. *African Industries*. New York: Crestwood, 1993.

Halliburton. *African Landscapes*. New York: Crestwood, 1993.

Halliburton. *African Wildlife*. New York: Crestwood, 1992.

Halliburton. *Africa's Struggle for Independence*. New York: Crestwood, 1992.

Halliburton. *Africa's Struggle to Survive*. New York: Crestwood, 1993.

Halliburton. *Celebrations of African Heritage*. New York: Crestwood, 1992.

Halliburton. *City and Village Life*. New York: Crestwood, 1993.

Hamilton, Virginia. *Drylongso*. New York: Harcourt Brace Jovanovich, 1992.

Haskins, James. *Black Dance in America*. New York: Harper Trophy, 1990.

Haskins. *Black Music in America*. New York: Harper, 1987.

Haskins. *Black Theatre in America*. New York: Harper, 1982.

Haskins. *The Sixties Reader*. New York: Penguin, 1988.

Hedgepath, Chester M., Jr. *African and American Writers and Artists*. Chicago, IL: American Library Association, 1991.

Hornburger, Jane M. *African Countries and Cultures: A Concise Illustrated Dictionary*. New York: David McKay, 1981.

Hornsby, Alton, Jr. *Chronology of African-American History: Significant Events and People from 1619 to the Present*. Detroit: Gale Research, 1991.

Horton, Carrel Peterson, and Jessie Carney Smith. *Statistical Record of Black America*. Detroit: Gale Research, 1991.

Howard, Elizabeth F. *America as Story: Historical Fiction for Secondary Schools*. Chicago, IL: American Library Association, 1988.

Hunter-Gault, Charlayne. *In My Place*. New York: Farrar, Straus & Giroux, 1992.

Hutchinson, Earl Ofari. *Black Fatherhood*. Fort Atkinson, WI: Highsmith, 1992.

Johnson, James Weldon, and J. Rosamond Johnson. *The Books of American Negro Spirituals*. New York: Da Capo, 1954.

Kersey, Tanya-Monique, with Bruce Hawkins. *Black State of the Arts: A Guide to Developing a Successful Career as a Black Performing Artist*. Fort Atkinson, WI: Highsmith, 1991.

Kunjufu, Jawanza. *Black Economics: Solutions for Economics and Community Empowerment*. Fort Atkinson, WI: Highsmith, 1992.

Kurlander, Gabrielle, and Jacqueline Salit. *Independent Black Leadership in America*. Fort Atkinson, WI: Highsmith, 1990.

Lanker, Brian. *I Dream a World: Portraits of Black Women Who Changed America*. New York: Stewart, Tabori and Chang, 1989.

Lankford, Mary D. *Hopscotch around the World*. New York: Morrow Junior Books, 1992.

Lester, Meera. *Writing for the Ethnic Markets*. Fort Atkinson, WI: Highsmith, 1991.

Martin, Tony. *The Pan-African Connection: From Slavery to Garvey and Beyond*. Fort Atkinson, WI: Highsmith, 1984.

Metcalf, Doris Hunter. *African Americans: Their Impact on U.S. History*. Carthage, IL: Good Apple, 1992.

Metzger, Linda, et al. *Black Writers: A Selection of Sketches from Contemporary Authors*. Detroit: Gale Research, 1989.

Milligan, Dr. Rosie. *Negroes, Colored People, Blacks, African Americans in America*. Fort Atkinson, WI: Highsmith, 1992.

Minorities—A Changing Role in American Society. Wylie, TX: Information Plus, 1992.

Murray, Jocelyn, ed. *Cultural Atlas of Africa*. New York: Facts on File, 1989.

Nelson, Johnnie Renee. *Positive Passage: Everyday Kwanzaa Poems*. Fort Atkinson, WI: Highsmith, 1992.

Nelson. *A Quest for Kwanzaa*. Fort Atkinson, WI: Highsmith, 1989.

Newton, David E. *Gun Control: An Issue for the Nineties*. Hillside, NJ: Enslow, 1992.

Polette, Nancy. *Exploring Themes with Aesop's Fables and Picture Books*. O'Fallon, MO: Book Lures, 1992.

Popkin, Michael. *Modern Black Writers*. New York: Ungar, 1978.

Ringgold, Faith. *Aunt Harriet's Underground Railroad in the Sky*. New York: Crown, 1992.

Rosenberg, Donna, ed. *World Literature*. Lincolnwood, IL: National Textbook Co., 1992.

Saitoti, Tepilit Ole. *Maasai*. New York: Abradale Press, 1980.

Sandoz, Ellis. *Political Sermons of the American Founding Era*. Indianapolis: Liberty Press, 1991.

Smith, Jessie Carney, ed. *Notable Black American Women*. Detroit: Gale Research, 1991.

Steptoe, John. *All the Colors of the Race*. New York: Morrow, 1982.

Steptoe. *Mufaro's Beautiful Daughters*. New York: Morrow, 1987.

Taylor, Charles, ed. *Guide to Multicultural Resources*. Fort Atkinson, WI: Highsmith, 1990.

Taylor. *Handbook of Minority Student Services*. Fort Atkinson, WI: Highsmith, 1986.

Taylor. *How to Sponsor a Minority Cultural Retreat*. Fort Atkinson, WI: Highsmith, 1989.

Tischler, Alice. *Fifteen Black American Composers: A Bibliography of Their Works*. Warren, MI: Harmonie Park Press, 1981.

Washington, James M., ed. *A Testament of Hope: The Essential Writings and Speeches of Martin Luther King, Jr*. Fort Atkinson, WI: Highsmith, 1986.

Williams, Helen E. *Books by African-American Authors and Illustrators for Children and Young Adults*. Chicago, IL: American Library Association, 1991.

Williams, Dr. Richard. *They Stole It But You Must Return It*. Fort Atkinson, WI: Highsmith, 1992.

Wilson, Charles Reagan, and William Ferris, eds. *Encyclopedia of Southern Culture*. Chapel Hill: University of North Carolina Press, 1989.

Articles

"Believers and Achievers: A Salute to Black Americans," *Instructor*, February 1984, 66-68.

Birdsong, Donna, "Kudos to Culture," *Instructor*, February 1989, 70-71.

"Black History Month—Let Your Database Set the Stage," *Instructor*, February 12, 1991, 109-110.

Chilcoat, George W., "The History Student and the American Slave Experience: The Dime Novel as Method," *Western Journal of Black Studies*, Fall, 1987, 193-197.

Chilcoat, "The Melodrama and the American Slave Experience," *Social Studies*, November-December 1989, 235-239.

Collins, Jo, "Out of Africa," *Learning*, February 1989, 66-67.

Dobb, Edwin, "Thrice Blessed," *Reader's Digest*, December 1992, 65-71.

"Flaps, Tubes, Peekaboos," *New York Times Fashion*, November 22, 1992, 23.

Fleming, Maria, ed., "Poetic Heritage," *Instructor*, February 1991, 50-54.

Gomez, Aurelia, "Multicultural Crafts," *Instructor,* November/December 1992, 56-59.

Murray, Wendy, "The Holiday Dilemma," *Instructor,* November/December 1992, 50-53.

N'Namdi, Carmen A., "A Play in Three Acts: Boley, A Town You Could Bank On," *Learning,* February 1991, 54-56.

O'Neill, Molly, "Southern Thanksgiving," *New York Times Magazine,* November 22, 1992, 75-76.

Ordovensky, Pat, "Slave Graves Could Reveal a Way of Life," *USA Today,* November 10, 1992, 1D-2D.

Rader, Dotson, "I Knew What I Wanted To Be," *Parade,* November 1, 1992, 4-6.

Roth, Ilene, and Leah Roth, "Movers and Shapers," *Learning,* February 1991, 42, 53.

"A Strong Seed Planted: The Civil Rights Movement in St. Louis, 1954-1968," *OAH Magazine of History,* Summer 1989, 26-35.

"Thank You, Africa," *Learning,* February 1991, 31.

"Three Cheers for the Red, White, and Blue!" *Instructor,* February 1983, 27-32, 37-38, 40-42, 44.

Publishers

African American Images
Kimberly Vann, Editor
9204 Commercial Ave., Suite 308-SC
Chicago, IL 60617
(312)375-9682

African World Press
Kassahun Checole, President
P.O. Box 1892
Trenton, NJ 08607
(609)695-3766

American Demographics
Brad Edmondson, Editor
P.O. Box 68
Ithaca, NY 14851-0068
(607)273-6343

American Library Association
Publishing Services

50 East Huron St.
Chicago, IL 60611
(800)545-2433

Black Classic Press
W. Paul Coates, Director
P.O. Box 13414
Baltimore, MD 21203
(301)728-4595

Crestwood House
866 Third Ave.
New York, NY 10022
(800)223-1244

Da Capo Press, Inc.
233 Spring Street
New York, NY 10013

Empak Publishing Co.
Richard L. Greene, Editor
520 North Michigan Ave.,
Suite 1004, Dept. A
Chicago, IL 60611

Fire!! Press
Thomas H. Wirth, Publisher
241 Hillside Rd.
Elizabeth, NJ 07208
(201)964-8476

Gale Research Inc.
835 Penobscot Bldg.
Detroit, MI 48226
(800)347-GALE
Fax (800)961-6083

Lerner Publications
Carolrhoda Books, Inc.
241 First Ave. N.
Minneapolis, MN 55401

New Day Press, Inc.
Ebraska Ceasor, President
Karamu House
2355 East 89th St.
Cleveland, OH 44106
(216)795-7070

Rourke
P.O. Box 3328
Vero Beach, FL 32964
(407)465-4575
Fax (407)465-3132

Seven Locks Press
P.O. Box 68
Arlington, VA 22210
(800)354-5348

Twenty-First Century Books
115 West 18th St.
New York, NY 10011
(800)488-5233

University of California, Los Angeles
Center for Afro-American Studies
Claudia Mitchell-Kernan, Academic Editor
3111 Campbell Hall
Los Angeles, CA 90024
(213)825-3528

Films and Videos

"Africa before the Europeans, 100-1500," Landmark Films Inc.

"Africa: Caravans of Gold/Kins and Cities," Knowledge Unlimited

"African-American Art: Past and Present," Knowledge Unlimited

"The African American Holiday of Kwanzaa," Highsmith

"Africa: Different But Equal/Mastering a Continent," Knowledge Unlimited

"Africa: The Bible and the Gun/The Magnificent African Cake," Knowledge Unlimited

"Africa: The Rise of Nationalism/The Legacy," Knowledge Unlimited

"Booker T. Washington: The Life and the Legacy," Knowledge Unlimited

"Boy," Landmark Films Inc.

"The Civil War," Knowledge Unlimited

"Egypt," Knowledge Unlimited

"Frederick Douglass: An American Life," Knowledge Unlimited

"Gifted Hands: The Ben Carson Story," Highsmith

"The Klan: A Legacy of Hate in America," Knowledge Unlimited

"Martin Luther King Commemorative Collection," Knowledge Unlimited

"Martin Luther King: 'I Have a Dream,'" Knowledge Unlimited

"Men of Bronze," Knowledge Unlimited

"Mysteries of the Pyramids," Knowledge Unlimited

"Myths of the Pharaohs," Knowledge Unlimited

"Race and Prejudice in America Today," Highsmith

"Separate But Equal," Knowledge Unlimited

"Sharpton and Fulani in Babylon," Highsmith

"Skin," Landmark Films Inc.

"Tutankhamen: The Immortal Pharaoh," Knowledge Unlimited

"We Shall Overcome: A History of the Civil Rights Movement," Highsmith

"William H. Johnson: Art and Life of an African American Artist," Knowledge Unlimited

"Zora Is My Name!" Knowledge Unlimited

Video Distributors

Charles Clark Co., Inc.
170 Keyland Ct.
Bohemia, NY 11716
(800)247-7009

Schlessinger Video Productions
P.O. Box 1110
Dept. M-29
Bala Cynwyd, Pennsylvania 19004
(800)843-3620

Music Distributors

American Audio Prose Library
P.O. Box 842

1015 East Broadway, No. 284
Columbia, MO 65205
(314)443-0361

Anthology Record and Tape Corporation
P.O. Box 593
Radio City Station
New York, NY 10019
(212)586-6845

Smith/Folkways Recordings
Office of Folklife Programs
955 l'Enfant Plaza, Suite 2600
Washington, DC 20560
(202)287-3262
Fax (202)287-3699

Dance Ensembles

American Heritage Center for African
  Dance and Music
Melvin Deal, Director
4018 Minnesota Ave., N.E.
Washington, DC 20019
(202)399-5252

Harambee Dance Ensemble
Akili Denianke, Director
3026 57th Ave.
Oakland, CA 94605
(415)532-8558

Hedzoleh African Dance Troupe
Malzern Akyea, Artistic Director
2630 Smithfield Dr.
Madison, WI 53701
(606)274-9769

Umoja Dance Company
Cheryl West, Director
35 Harvey Ave.
Charleston, SC 29405
(803)744-5834

Theater Companies

Avante Theater Company
John R. Giugliano, Artistic Director

Manaheim and Pulaski
Philadelphia, PA 19144
(215)848-9099

Black Theater Troupe
333 East Portland St.
Phoenix, AZ 85004
(602)258-8128

Jomandi Productions
Gloria Lockhart, Managing Director
1444 Mayson St, N.E.
Atlanta, GA 30308
(404)876-6346

Software Packagers

Africa; African American History
Zenger Software
10200 Jefferson Blvd., Room C9
P.O. Box 802
Culver City, CA 90232-0802

Bank Street School Filer
Sunburst Communications
101 Castleton St.
Pleasantville, NY 10570
(800)628-8897

Children's Writing and Publishing Center
The Learning Company
6493 Kaiser Dr.
Cremora, CA 94555
(800)852-2255

Poet's Journal
Hartley Courseware
133 Bridge St.
Dimondale, Mississippi
(800)247-1380

Read, Write, and Publish!
William K. Bradford
310 School St.
Acton, MA 01720
(800)421-2009

Special Writer Coach
Tom Snyder Productions

80 Coolidge Hill Rd.
Watertown, MA 02172
(800)342-0236

Scholastic Process Writer
Scholastic Inc.
P.O. Box 7502
Jefferson City, MO 65102
(800)541-5513

Write On!
Humanities Softward
408 Columbia St.
P.O. Box 950
Hood River, OR 97031
(800)245-6737

Computer Networks

IRIS Network for Teachers
P.O. Box 29424
Richmond, VA 23242-0424
(703)243-6622

Supplies

Afram Press
(newsletter, cards, calendar, magazine)
181 Northampton Dr.
Wilmington, NJ 08046
(609)871-0639

American Demographics
(books, software, databases, cassettes, slides)
P.O. Box 68
Ithaca, NY 14851
(800)828-1133
Fax (607)273-3196

Calaloux Publications
(reprints, brochures, videos, documentaries, books)
22 Belair Rd.
Wellesley, MA 02181
(617)237-2230

Dover Publications
(coloring books, origami, hiergolyphics dictionary,
books, stencils, crafts)
31 East Second St.

Mineola, NY 11501
(516)294-7000

Essence By Mail
(historical calendars, Kwanzaa cards, videos)
Hanover, PA 17333-0286
(800)882-8055

Highsmith
(posters, books, Kwanzaa kits, notecards, games,
videos, cassettes)
Charles Taylor, Executive Director
P.O. Box 800
Fort Atkinson, WI 53538-0800
(800)558-2110

Just Us Books, Inc.
(books, learning materials, merchandise, cassettes,
posters)
Wade and Cheryl Willis Hudson, Editors
301 Main St.
Orange, NJ 07050
(201)672-7701

Knowledge Unlimited
(filmstrips, videos, posters, books)
Box 52
Madison, WI 53701-0052
(800)356-2303
Fax (608)831-1570

Landmark Films Inc.
(films, videos)
3450 Slade Run Dr.
Falls Church, VA 22042
(800)342-4336

Rand McNally
(atlases, videos, map games, software)
P.O. Box 1697
Skokie, IL 60076
(800)234-0679

Rosen Publishing Group
(books, videos)
29 East 21st St.
New York, NY 10010
(800)237-9932

Social Studies School Service
(laserdiscs, videos, posters, softward, reproducibles,
work texts, games)
10200 Jefferson Blvd., Room SD0

P.O. Box 8802
Culver City, CA 90232-0802
(800)421-4246
Fax (310)839-2249

Universal Black Writer Press
P.O. Box 5
Radio City Station
New York, NY 10101-0005
(718)774-4379

Resource Centers

African-American Institute
833 United Nations Plaza
New York, NY 10017
(212)949-5666

Afro-American Cultural Center
Wanda Montgomery, Director
401 North Myers St.
Charlotte, NC 20202
(704)374-1565

Association for the Study of Afro-American Life and
   History
1401 14th St., N.W.
Washington, DC 20005

Black Music Archives
Dr. Dominique-Rene de Lerma, Director
1130 S. Michigan Ave., No. 3204
Chicago, IL 60605-2322

Black Resource Guide, Inc.
Robert B. Johnson, President
501 Oneida Place, N.W.
Washington, DC 20011
(202)291-4373

Carib House
Rupert Singh, Owner
11305 Goleta St.
Los Angeles, CA 91342
(818)890-1056

Charles L. Blockson
Afro-American Collection
Temple University
Sullivan Hall
Philadelphia, PA 19122
(215)787-663

Great Plains Black Museum
Bertha Calloway, Director
2213 Lake St.
Omaha, NB 68110
(402)345-2212

Jacaranda Designs Limited (Kenya)
2701 East Warren Ave.
Denver, CO 80210
(303)756-1618

Motown Museum of African American History
Marian J. Moore, Executive Director
301 Frederick Douglass St.
Detroit, MI 48202
(313)833-9800

Museum of African-American Life and Culture
Dr. Harry Robinson, Director
P.O. Box 26153
Dallas, TX 75226
(214)565-9026

Museum of Afro-American History
Monica A. Fairbairn, Director
46 Joy St.
Boston, MA 02114
(617)742-1854

National Archives Trust Fund
Aids for Genealogical Research, NEPS Dept. 735
P.O. Box 100793
Atlanta, GA 30384

Praxis Publications
Dr. Charles Taylor
P.O. Box 9869
Madison, WI 53715

Shrine of the Black Madonna Bookstore and Culture
   Center
13535 Livernois Ave.
Detroit, MI 48238
(313)491-0777

Upper Midwest Women's History Center for Teachers
Janet M. Donaldson, Director of Publications
Central Community Center
6300 Walker St.
St. Louis Park, MN 55416
(612)925-3632

Entry Index

A

Action and Words 349
Advice from Marian Wright Edelman 279
An Aesop Recitation 383
Africa in the News 179
African-American Entrepreneurs 69
African-American Plaza 1
An African-American Profile 241
African-American Sculpture 2
African-Americans in the Media 180
African-American Sports Maze 373
An African-American Theme Park 242
African and Caribbean Fruits and Spices 291
African and World Events 135
African Animal Fair 15
African Archaeology 2
African Art and Architecture 4
African Authors 215
African Butterflies and Moths 292
African Cards 16
African Culture in the Sea Islands 329
African Dance Styles 95
African Dessert-a-thon 79
African Habitats 293
African Healers 294
African Heroes 180
An African Holiday 113
African Homes 5
African Leaders 41
African Lentils 82
African Meditation Methods 280
African Money 71
An African Museum 243
African Musical Instruments 251
African Music American Style 252
African Ornaments 17
African Peoples 114

African Rhythm Band 254
African Riches 115
African Story Swap 384
An African Travel Guide 117
An African Window Garden 295
Africa's Great Rivers 118
Africa's Liberation 351
Afrocentrism 197
Alex Haley's Genealogy 107
All Aboard! 136
All-Occasion Cards 18
All That Glitters 296
"Amazing Grace" and the Slave Trade 281
Animal Express 297
Animal Movies 18
Antiphonal Chant 255
Antislavery in England and the U.S. 137
Apartheid 198
Apartheid and the World 138
At Home in Africa 352
Atlanta-Bound 139
The Atlantic Triangle 119

B

Backing Police Efforts 181
Band Music 257
Banner Bolster 321
Baobab: The Tree of Life 298
Batiking 19
Bean Bag Toss 120
Benjamin Franklin and Slavery 353
Bessie Smith 42
"Between the World and Me" 216
Bio-Flash 43
Black Art 6
Black Autobiography and Biography 44
Black Award Winners 46
Black Book Fair 219

Black Builders 7
Black Cartoonists 182
Black Dance Troupes 96
Black Educational Institutions 121
Black English 199
Black Evangelism 282
Black Excellence 330
The Black Experience 331
The Black Flavor of New Orleans 123
Black Hall of Fame 47
Black Heritage Trivia 140
Black History Bingo 144
Black History Book Collection 220
Black History Calendar 145
Black History Desk Calendar 20
Black History Essay Contest 393
Black History Glossary 200
Black History in Miniature 146
Black History Month Newspaper 183
Black History Stamps 49
Black History Time Capsule 147
A Black History Time Line 147
Black Holidays 153
Black Indians 154
Black Landmark Ad Campaign 71
Black Landmarks 8
Black Language Roundup 202
Black Media 183
The Black Middle Class 73
Black Military Parade 155
Black Moses 283
Black Music Videos 258
Black Muslims 284
Black Mystery 394
The Black Olympian 375
Black on White 220
Black Philosophies 354
Black Pride Day 333
Black Sentiments 355
Black Social Doctrine 334
Black Study Group 221
Black Towns 335
Black Women in the Third World 336
Bookmarks 20
Books for Summer 224
Box Zoo 21
Brainstorming 300
Business Incubator 74

C

Camp Africa 22
Campaign Push 394

Caribana 97
A Caribbean Garden 10
Caribbean Idyll 124
Census Comparisons 244
Choral Music 259
The Civil War 157
Clasped Hands 23
The *Clothilde* 395
Colonialism 158
Comparing Wisdom 225
The Constitution and Black America 159
Cooking for Kwanzaa 86
Corn Rows 322
Counting in Swahili 245
Courts and Racial Justice 160
Crafts Clinic 24
Crocheting a Bit of Africa 25
Crocodile Trains 25

D

Dance Workshop 98
Deadly Organisms 301
The Demands of Frederick Douglass 356
Denouncing Slavery 396
Derek Walcott 227
Design America 26
Designer Mural 10
Doll Displays 27
The Door to Awareness 28
"D.P." 226
Dramatizing the Black Experience 357
The Drifting Continents 126
Dueling Pianos 260

E

Each One Teach One 161
Early Humans in Africa 304
The Economics of Slavery 75
Editorials from the Black Perspective 185
Editorials of J.C. Harris and H.W. Grady 186
Elephant Lore 305
The Emancipation Proclamation 162
Emblems of Africa 397
Encouraging the Storyteller 385
Everybody Limbo! 98
Expatriates 205
Experiencing the Underground Railroad 359
Explorers of Africa 163
Extra! Extra! 187

F

The Family Tree 108

Famine in Ethiopia and Somalia 337
Feminist Writers 228
Filming Ancient Africa 164
First Day at School 360
Food Clinic 87
Frederick Douglass 49
Freedom Fighters 51
Freedom's Journal 229
Freedom Stamps 29
A Friend in Africa 398
A Future in the Media 188

G

George Washington Carver, Inventor 306
George Washington's Will 165
Gertrude Johnson Williams Award 231
Getting the Public's Attention 76
Gourdheads 30
Graphing Racial Data 246
Griot for a Day 386
Guest Columnist 189
Gullah 205

H

Haiti Seeks Help 361
A Handful of Puppets 322
Harlem: Black America's Home Town 167
The Harlem Globetrotters 376
Hats Off to the Abolitionists 52
Health Tips 308
Herbs, Tonics, Teas, and Cures 309
Heritage Jubilee 30
Hero to Hero 377
Hieroglyphics 206
A History of African-American Music 261
Honoring the Past 190
Human Relations Report Card 338

I

In the Rice Fields 311
Interpretive Dance 99
Invent-O-Rama 312

J

Jamaican Specialties 88
Jivin' to the Oldies 100
Jointed Dolls 31
Joplin Expo 262
Joseph Cinque vs. the Slave Trade 361
Josephine Baker 101
Jump Rope Rhymes 207

K

Kite Flags 323
The Ku Klux Klan 168
Kwanzaa Flash Cards 209

L

Language Pairs 210
The Latest in Books by Black Authors 231
Lead Story Roundup 191
Learning the Colors of Africa 127
A Letter of Application 399
Letter-Writing Campaign 399
Liberia 127
Library Scavenger Hunt 170
Life along the Nile 128
Life in a Kenyan Village 129
Lyndon Johnson and the Black Panthers 232

M

Maasai Pendants 32
Maasai Seasons 339
Market Day 362
Martin Luther King, Jr. 53
Matthew Henson 171
Melville and Slavery 233
The Migrant Scene 248
Militant Verse 235
Moorish Architecture 11
The Moors 130
Motown 263
Mr. Johnson 340
Mule Bone 363
Music Workshop 265

N

Native African Biographies 55
Native Fashions 325
New Games for Old 33
New Names for Old 211

O

Oral Interpretation 364
Origami Animals 34
Out of Africa 341

P

The Palm Tree 314
Patois 265
Peoples of Africa 341
Photo History 109
Photo Map 12

Photo Tableaux of History 12
Pieces of Africa 34
Playing the Part 365
Poetry Workshop 400
Porgy and Bess 266
The Professional Black Athlete 378
Proud Stitches 326
Puppet Show 35
Puzzle Me Africa 130

Q

Quakers and the Underground Railroad 286
Quilted History 110
Quoting Black Voices 366

R

Rabbit Ears 387
Race and Controversy 192
Rap Wrap-Up 267
Reading the Black Female Writer 237
Read, Read, Read 235
Religions of Africa 287
Religious Themes in Negro Spirituals 288
Report Writing 172
Rhythm of Resistance 268
The Rights of the Child 342
Role-Playing History 57
Rosa Parks 58
Round-robin African Adventure 388

S

Safari 131
Sally Hemings 59
Schematic Drawings 249
1776 269
Shaka, the Zulu King 60
Sharing Words from Different Worlds 212
The Shotgun House 14
Sickle Cell Anemia 315
Sign Troupe 102
Simon Says 132
Sing-along 270
Slave Days 401
Slavery and Negro Spirituals 271
Slavery and the Caribbean 174
Slavery Diorama 175
Songs of Protest 272
Soul Food 90
Speaker's Bureau 367
Sports Clinic 379
Sports Debate 379

Sports on Film 380
Stained Glass Animals 36
Star of the Week 62
Stayin' Alive 343
Steinbeck on American Racism 239
"Stop the Drugs" Campaign 345
Studying the Bones 346
Sweets to the Sweet 37

T

T-shirt Factory 39
Talk to Me 368
Tapping to Stardom 103
Tell-It-Yourself 389
Things Fall Apart 289
This Ol' Hat 369
Thomas Jefferson and Slavery 370
'Toon Time 38
Translating Lyrics 214
A Tribute to Judith Jamison 104
Two-Feet, Four-Feet, Wings, Fins, Tail 317

U

Uncle Remus 390
Using the Storyboard 390

V

Volunteers without Borders 193
Voting Patterns 347

W

We Shall Overcome 273
What If? 177
What's My Line? 63
Who Does the Work? 347
Who's Writing News 194
William Lloyd Garrison 64
Words and Snapshots 402
Words to Live By 65
Work Songs 274
World Races 133
Writing Epitaphs 403
Writing Genre 403

Y

You Are There 194

Z

Zoo's Who 317

Bulletin Boards

Advice from Marian Wright Edelman 279
African and World Events 135
Black Educational Institutions 121
Black History Calendar 145
Black Holidays 153
Clasped Hands 23
Courts and Racial Justice 160
Hats Off to the Abolitionists 52
Health Tips 308
The Latest in Books by Black Authors 231
Learning the Colors of Africa 127
Songs of Protest 272

Contests

Black Award Winners 46
Black Hall of Fame 47
Black History Essay Contest 393
Design America 26
Dueling Pianos 260
Gertrude Johnson Williams Award 231
Library Scavenger Hunt 170
Poetry Workshop 400
Quoting Black Voices 366
'Toon Time 38

Displays

African-American Plaza 1
Black Book Fair 219
Black History Book Collection 220
Black History in Miniature 146
Black History Stamps 49
Black History Time Capsule 147
Black Pride Day 333
Corn Rows 322
Doll Displays 27
Getting the Public's Attention 76
Herbs, Tonics, Teas, and Cures 309
Human Relations Report Card 338
Invent-O-Rama 312
Liberia 127
Life in a Kenyan Village 129
Slavery Diorama 175

Games

African-American Sports Maze 373
Bio-Flash 43
Black Heritage Trivia 140
Black History Bingo 144
Jump Rope Rhymes 207
New Games for Old 33
Safari 131
Simon Says 132
What If? 177
What's My Line? 63

Age/Grade Level Index

Preschool (ages 3-4)

At Home in Africa 352
Learning the Colors of Africa 127
Simon Says 132

Elementary (ages 5-10)

Action and Words 349
An Aesop Recitation 383
Africa in the News 179
African Animal Fair 15
African Cards 16
African Dance Styles 95
African Habitats 293
African Heroes 180
An African Holiday 113
African Homes 5
African Leaders 41
African Musical Instruments 251
African Ornaments 17
African Peoples 114
African Rhythm Band 254
African Riches 115
An African Travel Guide 117
An African Window Garden 295
Africa's Great Rivers 118
Animal Express 297
Animal Movies 18
Antiphonal Chant 255
At Home in Africa 352
The Atlantic Triangle 119
Baobab: The Tree of Life 298
Batiking 19
Bean Bag Toss 120

Bio-Flash 43
Black Builders 7
Black Dance Troupes 96
Black Hall of Fame 47
Black History Desk Calendar 20
Black Indians 154
Black Military Parade 155
Black Moses 283
The Black Olympian 375
Bookmarks 20
Box Zoo 21
Brainstorming 300
Camp Africa 22
A Caribbean Garden 10
Caribbean Idyll 124
Clasped Hands 23
Cooking for Kwanzaa 86
Counting in Swahili 245
Crocheting a Bit of Africa 25
Crocodile Trains 25
The Door to Awareness 28
The Drifting Continents 126
Elephant Lore 305
The Emancipation Proclamation 162
Emblems of Africa 397
Everybody Limbo! 98
Extra! Extra! 187
Filming Ancient Africa 164
First Day at School 360
Freedom Fighters 51
Freedom Stamps 29
A Friend in Africa 398
George Washington's Will 165
Gourdheads 30
Griot for a Day 386
A Handful of Puppets 322
Hats Off to the Abolitionists 52
Hieroglyphics 206

Invent-O-Rama 312
Jump Rope Rhymes 207
Kite Flags 323
Kwanzaa Flash Cards 209
Language Pairs 210
Lead Story Roundup 191
Liberia 127
Library Scavenger Hunt 170
Life along the Nile 128
Life in a Kenyan Village 129
Maasai Pendants 32
Market Day 362
Matthew Henson 171
The Moors 130
Native African Biographies 55
New Games for Old 33
Origami Animals 34
Patois 265
Pieces of Africa 34
The Professional Black Athlete 378
Puppet Show 35
Puzzle Me Africa 130
Rabbit Ears 387
Role-Playing History 57
Round-robin African Adventure 388
Safari 131
Shaka, the Zulu King 60
Sharing Words from Different Worlds 212
Simon Says 132
Slavery and Negro Spirituals 271
Sports Clinic 379
Stained Glass Animals 36
Sweets to the Sweet 37
Tell-It-Yourself 389
This Ol' Hat 369
Two-Feet, Four-Feet, Wings, Fins, Tail 317
Uncle Remus 390
Using the Storyboard 390
What If? 177
Who's Writing News 194
World Races 133
Writing Epitaphs 403
Writing Genre 403
Zoo's Who 317

Middle School (ages 11-13)

An Aesop Recitation 383
Africa in the News 179
African-American Entrepreneurs 69

African-American Sculpture 2
African-Americans in the Media 180
African and Caribbean Fruits and Spices 291
African Archaeology 2
African Art and Architecture 4
African Authors 215
African Butterflies and Moths 292
African Cards 16
African Culture in the Sea Islands 329
African Dance Styles 95
African Habitats 293
African Healers 294
African Heroes 180
An African Holiday 113
African Leaders 41
African Money 71
An African Museum 243
African Musical Instruments 251
African Peoples 114
An African Travel Guide 117
Africa's Great Rivers 118
All That Glitters 296
"Amazing Grace" and the Slave Trade 281
Animal Express 297
Animal Movies 18
Antiphonal Chant 255
Antislavery in England and the U.S. 137
Apartheid and the World 138
The Atlantic Triangle 119
Banner Bolster 321
Benjamin Franklin and Slavery 353
Bessie Smith 42
"Between the World and Me" 216
Bio-Flash 43
Black Art 6
Black Award Winners 46
Black Builders 7
Black Dance Troupes 96
Black English 199
Black Evangelism 282
The Black Experience 331
Black Hall of Fame 47
Black History Calendar 145
Black History Desk Calendar 20
Black History Glossary 200
Black History Month Newspaper 183
A Black History Time Line 147
Black Indians 154
Black Landmark Ad Campaign 71
Black Landmarks 8
Black Language Roundup 202
Black Military Parade 155

Black Moses 283
Black Mystery 394
The Black Olympian 375
Black on White 220
Black Sentiments 355
Black Towns 335
Brainstorming 300
Camp Africa 22
Caribbean Idyll 124
Census Comparisons 244
Clasped Hands 23
The *Clothilde* 395
Comparing Wisdom 225
The Constitution and Black America 159
Crocheting a Bit of Africa 25
Deadly Organisms 301
Derek Walcott 227
The Door to Awareness 28
"D.P." 226
Dramatizing the Black Experience 357
The Drifting Continents 126
Early Humans in Africa 304
Elephant Lore 305
The Emancipation Proclamation 162
Emblems of Africa 397
Experiencing the Underground Railroad 359
Explorers of Africa 163
Extra! Extra! 187
The Family Tree 108
Filming Ancient Africa 164
First Day at School 360
Frederick Douglass 49
Freedom Fighters 51
Freedom's Journal 229
Freedom Stamps 29
A Friend in Africa 398
George Washington Carver, Inventor 306
George Washington's Will 165
Gourdheads 30
Graphing Racial Data 246
Griot for a Day 386
Harlem: Black America's Home Town 167
Hats Off to the Abolitionists 52
Hero to Hero 377
Hieroglyphics 206
A History of African-American Music 261
In the Rice Fields 311
Invent-O-Rama 312
Jointed Dolls 31
Kite Flags 323
Language Pairs 210
Lead Story Roundup 191

A Letter of Application 399
Letter-Writing Campaign 399
Liberia 127
Library Scavenger Hunt 170
Life along the Nile 128
Maasai Seasons 339
Martin Luther King, Jr. 53
Matthew Henson 171
The Migrant Scene 248
Militant Verse 235
The Moors 130
Motown 263
Native African Biographies 55
Native Fashions 325
New Games for Old 33
New Names for Old 211
Oral Interpretation 364
Origami Animals 34
The Palm Tree 314
Patois 265
Peoples of Africa 341
Pieces of Africa 34
Playing the Part 365
Porgy and Bess 266
The Professional Black Athlete 378
Puzzle Me Africa 130
Quoting Black Voices 366
Religions of Africa 287
Rhythm of Resistance 268
Role-Playing History 57
Rosa Parks 58
Round-robin African Adventure 388
Safari 131
Schematic Drawings 249
Sharing Words from Different Worlds 212
Slave Days 401
Slavery and Negro Spirituals 271
Slavery and the Caribbean 174
Sports Clinic 379
Stained Glass Animals 36
Star of the Week 62
Steinbeck on American Racism 239
This Ol' Hat 369
Translating Lyrics 214
Voting Patterns 347
What If? 177
What's My Line? 63
Who Does the Work? 347
Who's Writing News 194
William Lloyd Garrison 64
Words and Snapshots 402
Work Songs 274

World Races 133
Writing Epitaphs 403
Writing Genre 403
Zoo's Who 317

High School (ages 14-18)

An Aesop Recitation 383
Africa in the News 179
African-American Entrepreneurs 69
An African-American Profile 241
African-American Sculpture 2
African-Americans in the Media 180
African-American Sports Maze 373
An African-American Theme Park 242
African and Caribbean Fruits and Spices 291
African Archaeology 2
African Art and Architecture 4
African Authors 215
African Butterflies and Moths 292
African Culture in the Sea Islands 329
African Habitats 293
African Healers 294
African Heroes 180
An African Holiday 113
African Leaders 41
African Money 71
An African Museum 243
African Music American Style 252
Africa's Liberation 351
Alex Haley's Genealogy 107
All That Glitters 296
"Amazing Grace" and the Slave Trade 281
Animal Express 297
Antislavery in England and the U.S. 137
Apartheid 198
Apartheid and the World 138
Band Music 257
Banner Bolster 321
Benjamin Franklin and Slavery 353
Bessie Smith 42
"Between the World and Me" 216
Black Art 6
Black Autobiography and Biography 44
Black Award Winners 46
Black Cartoonists 182
Black Dance Troupes 96
Black Educational Institutions 121
Black English 199
Black Evangelism 282

The Black Experience 331
Black Hall of Fame 47
Black History Glossary 200
Black History Month Newspaper 183
A Black History Time Line 147
Black Indians 154
Black Landmark Ad Campaign 71
Black Landmarks 8
Black Language Roundup 202
Black Media 183
Black Military Parade 155
Black Muslims 284
Black Mystery 394
The Black Olympian 375
Black on White 220
Black Philosophies 354
Black Sentiments 355
Black Social Doctrine 334
Black Towns 335
Black Women in the Third World 336
Brainstorming 300
Campaign Push 394
Caribbean Idyll 124
Census Comparisons 244
Choral Music 259
Clasped Hands 23
The Clothilde 395
Colonialism 158
Comparing Wisdom 225
The Constitution and Black America 159
Crocheting a Bit of Africa 25
Deadly Organisms 301
The Demands of Frederick Douglass 356
Denouncing Slavery 396
Derek Walcott 227
The Door to Awareness 28
"D.P." 226
Dramatizing the Black Experience 357
The Drifting Continents 126
Early Humans in Africa 304
The Economics of Slavery 75
Editorials from the Black Perspective 185
Editorials of J.C. Harris and H.W. Grady 186
The Emancipation Proclamation 162
Encouraging the Storyteller 385
Expatriates 205
Experiencing the Underground Railroad 359
Explorers of Africa 163
Extra! Extra! 187
Famine in Ethiopia and Somalia 337
Feminist Writers 228
Frederick Douglass 49

Freedom Fighters 51
Freedom's Journal 229
Freedom Stamps 29
A Friend in Africa 398
A Future in the Media 188
George Washington Carver, Inventor 306
George Washington's Will 165
Gourdheads 30
Graphing Racial Data 246
Griot for a Day 386
Gullah 205
Haiti Seeks Help 361
Harlem: Black America's Home Town 167
Hero to Hero 377
A History of African-American Music 261
In the Rice Fields 311
Jointed Dolls 31
Joseph Cinque vs. the Slave Trade 361
Kite Flags 323
The Ku Klux Klan 168
Language Pairs 210
Lead Story Roundup 191
A Letter of Application 399
Letter-Writing Campaign 399
Lyndon Johnson and the Black Panthers 232
Maasai Seasons 339
Martin Luther King, Jr. 53
Melville and Slavery 233
The Migrant Scene 248
Militant Verse 235
The Moors 130
Motown 263
Native Fashions 325
New Games for Old 33
New Names for Old 211
Oral Interpretation 364
Origami Animals 34
Out of Africa 341
The Palm Tree 314
Patois 265
Peoples of Africa 341
Pieces of Africa 34
Playing the Part 365
Porgy and Bess 266
The Professional Black Athlete 378
Proud Stitches 326
Quoting Black Voices 366
Rap Wrap-Up 267
Religions of Africa 287
Religious Themes in Negro Spirituals 288
Report Writing 172
Rhythm of Resistance 268

The Rights of the Child 342
Role-Playing History 57
Rosa Parks 58
Sally Hemings 59
Schematic Drawings 249
1776 269
Sickle Cell Anemia 315
Slave Days 401
Slavery and Negro Spirituals 271
Slavery and the Caribbean 174
Slavery Diorama 175
Soul Food 90
Sports Clinic 379
Sports Debate 379
Stained Glass Animals 36
Star of the Week 62
Stayin' Alive 343
Steinbeck on American Racism 239
Talk to Me 368
Things Fall Apart 289
Thomas Jefferson and Slavery 370
Translating Lyrics 214
A Tribute to Judith Jamison 104
Voting Patterns 347
What If? 177
What's My Line? 63
Who Does the Work? 347
William Lloyd Garrison 64
Words and Snapshots 402
Work Songs 274
Writing Genre 403
You Are There 194

Adult (ages 18 and above)

Action and Words 349
African-American Entrepreneurs 69
African-American Plaza 1
An African-American Profile 241
African-American Sculpture 2
African-Americans in the Media 180
African and Caribbean Fruits and Spices 291
African Art and Architecture 4
African Authors 215
African Butterflies and Moths 292
African Culture in the Sea Islands 329
African Habitats 293
African Healers 294
An African Museum 243
African Music American Style 252

Africa's Liberation 351
Alex Haley's Genealogy 107
All That Glitters 296
Animal Express 297
Antiphonal Chant 255
Antislavery in England and the U.S. 137
Apartheid 198
Apartheid and the World 138
Backing Police Efforts 181
Band Music 257
Banner Bolster 321
Benjamin Franklin and Slavery 353
Bessie Smith 42
"Between the World and Me" 216
Black Art 6
Black Autobiography and Biography 44
Black Cartoonists 182
Black Dance Troupes 96
Black Educational Institutions 121
Black English 199
Black Evangelism 282
The Black Experience 331
Black History Month Newspaper 183
A Black History Time Line 147
Black Indians 154
Black Landmarks 8
Black Language Roundup 202
Black Media 183
The Black Middle Class 73
Black Muslims 284
Black Mystery 394
The Black Olympian 375
Black on White 220
Black Philosophies 354
Black Sentiments 355
Black Social Doctrine 334
Black Study Group 221
Black Towns 335
Black Women in the Third World 336
Brainstorming 300
Business Incubator 74
Campaign Push 394
Caribbean Idyll 124
Choral Music 259
The *Clothilde* 395
Colonialism 158
Comparing Wisdom 225
Deadly Organisms 301
The Demands of Frederick Douglass 356
Denouncing Slavery 396
Derek Walcott 227
The Door to Awareness 28

Dramatizing the Black Experience 357
Each One Teach One 161
Early Humans in Africa 304
The Economics of Slavery 75
Editorials from the Black Perspective 185
Editorials of J.C. Harris and H.W. Grady 186
Encouraging the Storyteller 385
Expatriates 205
Experiencing the Underground Railroad 359
Explorers of Africa 163
Extra! Extra! 187
Famine in Ethiopia and Somalia 337
Feminist Writers 228
Frederick Douglass 49
Freedom Fighters 51
Freedom's Journal 229
A Friend in Africa 398
A Future in the Media 188
George Washington Carver, Inventor 306
Graphing Racial Data 246
Gullah 205
Haiti Seeks Help 361
Harlem: Black America's Home Town 167
A History of African-American Music 261
In the Rice Fields 311
Joseph Cinque vs. the Slave Trade 361
Josephine Baker 101
The Ku Klux Klan 168
Letter-Writing Campaign 399
Lyndon Johnson and the Black Panthers 232
Maasai Seasons 339
Martin Luther King, Jr. 53
Melville and Slavery 233
The Migrant Scene 248
Militant Verse 235
Moorish Architecture 11
The Moors 130
Motown 263
Mule Bone 363
Native Fashions 325
Oral Interpretation 364
Out of Africa 341
The Palm Tree 314
Patois 265
Peoples of Africa 341
Photo Tableaux of History 12
Playing the Part 365
The Professional Black Athlete 378
Proud Stitches 326
Quakers and the Underground Railroad 286
Quoting Black Voices 366
Rabbit Ears 387

Race and Controversy 192
Reading the Black Female Writer 237
Religions of Africa 287
Religious Themes in Negro Spirituals 288
Report Writing 172
Rhythm of Resistance 268
The Rights of the Child 342
Role-Playing History 57
Sally Hemings 59
1776 269
Sickle Cell Anemia 315
Slave Days 401
Slavery and Negro Spirituals 271
Slavery and the Caribbean 174
Slavery Diorama 175
Soul Food 90
Sports Debate 379
Star of the Week 62
Stayin' Alive 343
Steinbeck on American Racism 239
Talk to Me 368
Tapping to Stardom 103
Tell-It-Yourself 389
Things Fall Apart 289
Thomas Jefferson and Slavery 370
Translating Lyrics 214
A Tribute to Judith Jamison 104
Voting Patterns 347
Who Does the Work? 347
Work Songs 274
Writing Genre 403
You Are There 194

Elderly

An African Window Garden 295
Clasped Hands 23
Crocheting a Bit of Africa 25
Freedom Stamps 29
Gourdheads 30
Origami Animals 34
Pieces of Africa 34
Stained Glass Animals 36
Sweets to the Sweet 37

All Ages

Advice from Marian Wright Edelman 279

African and World Events 135
African Dessert-a-thon 79
African Lentils 82
African Meditation Methods 280
African Story Swap 384
Afrocentrism 197
All Aboard! 136
All-Occasion Cards 18
Atlanta-Bound 139
Black Book Fair 219
Black Excellence 330
The Black Flavor of New Orleans 123
Black Heritage Trivia 140
Black History Bingo 144
Black History Book Collection 220
Black History Essay Contest 393
Black History in Miniature 146
Black History Stamps 49
Black History Time Capsule 147
Black Holidays 153
Black Music Videos 258
Black Pride Day 333
Books for Summer 224
Caribana 97
The Civil War 157
Corn Rows 322
Courts and Racial Justice 160
Crafts Clinic 24
Dance Workshop 98
Design America 26
Designer Mural 10
Doll Displays 27
Dueling Pianos 260
Food Clinic 87
Gertrude Johnson Williams Award 231
Getting the Public's Attention 76
Guest Columnist 189
The Harlem Globetrotters 376
Health Tips 308
Herbs, Tonics, Teas, and Cures 309
Heritage Jubilee 30
Honoring the Past 190
Human Relations Report Card 338
Interpretive Dance 99
Jamaican Specialties 88
Jivin' to the Oldies 100
Joplin Expo 262
The Latest in Books by Black Authors 231
Mr. Johnson 340
Music Workshop 265
Photo History 109
Photo Map 12

Poetry Workshop 400
Quilted History 110
Read, Read, Read 235
The Shotgun House 14
Sign Troupe 102
Sing-along 270
Songs of Protest 272
Speaker's Bureau 367

Sports on Film 380
"Stop the Drugs" Campaign 345
Studying the Bones 346
'Toon Time 38
T-shirt Factory 39
Volunteers without Borders 193
We Shall Overcome 273
Words to Live By 65

Budget Index

$ (under $25)

Action and Words 349
Advice from Marian Wright Edelman 279
An Aesop Recitation 383
Africa in the News 179
African-American Entrepreneurs 69
African-Americans in the Media 180
African-American Sports Maze 373
An African-American Theme Park 242
African and Caribbean Fruits and Spices 291
African and World Events 135
African Archaeology 2
African Cards 16
African Habitats 293
African Healers 294
An African Holiday 113
African Leaders 41
African Meditation Methods 280
African Money 71
An African Travel Guide 117
Africa's Great Rivers 118
Africa's Liberation 351
All That Glitters 296
"Amazing Grace" and the Slave Trade 281
Antiphonal Chant 255
Antislavery in England and the U.S. 137
Apartheid 198
Apartheid and the World 138
The Atlantic Triangle 119
Benjamin Franklin and Slavery 353
Bessie Smith 42
"Between the World and Me" 216
Bio-Flash 43
Black Award Winners 46
Black Cartoonists 182
Black Dance Troupes 96

Black Educational Institutions 121
Black English 199
Black Evangelism 282
The Black Experience 331
Black History Bingo 144
Black History Essay Contest
Black History Glossary 200
Black Indians 154
Black Language Roundup 202
Black Media 183
The Black Middle Class 73
Black Military Parade 155
Black Moses 283
Black Muslims 284
Black Philosophies 354
Black Sentiments 355
Black Social Doctrine 334
Black Towns 335
A Caribbean Garden 10
Caribbean Idyll 124
Census Comparisons 244
The *Clothilde* 395
Colonialism 158
Comparing Wisdom 225
The Constitution and Black America 159
Counting in Swahili 245
Courts and Racial Justice 160
Deadly Organisms 301
The Demands of Frederick Douglass 356
Denouncing Slavery 396
Derek Walcott 227
"D.P." 226
The Drifting Continents 126
The Economics of Slavery 75
Editorials from the Black Perspective 185
Editorials of J.C. Harris and H.W. Grady 186
The Emancipation Proclamation 162
Emblems of Africa 397

Encouraging the Storyteller 385
Expatriates 205
Experiencing the Underground Railroad 359
Explorers of Africa 163
Extra! Extra! 187
Famine in Ethiopia and Somalia 337
First Day at School 360
Frederick Douglass 49
Freedom Fighters 51
Freedom's Journal 229
A Future in the Media 188
George Washington's Will 165
Gertrude Johnson Williams Award 231
Griot for a Day 386
Guest Columnist 189
Haiti Seeks Help 361
Harlem: Black America's Home Town 167
The Harlem Globetrotters 376
Hero to Hero 377
In the Rice Fields 311
Invent-O-Rama 312
Joseph Cinque vs. the Slave Trade 361
Josephine Baker 101
Jump Rope Rhymes 207
Kwanzaa Flash Cards 209
Language Pairs 210
The Latest in Books by Black Authors 231
Lead Story Roundup 191
A Letter of Application 399
Lyndon Johnson and the Black Panthers 232
Maasai Seasons 339
Martin Luther King, Jr. 53
Matthew Henson 171
The Migrant Scene 248
Militant Verse 235
Motown 263
Mr. Johnson 340
Mule Bone 363
Native African Biographies 55
New Names for Old 211
Oral Interpretation 364
The Palm Tree 314
Puzzle Me Africa 130
Quakers and the Underground Railroad 286
Report Writing 172
The Rights of the Child 342
Role-Playing History 57
Rosa Parks 58
Round-robin African Adventure 388
Safari 131
Sally Hemings 59
Shaka, the Zulu King 60

Sharing Words from Different Worlds 212
Sickle Cell Anemia 315
Simon Says 132
Slave Days 401
Slavery and the Caribbean 174
Songs of Protest 272
Star of the Week 62
Stayin' Alive 343
Steinbeck on American Racism 239
Studying the Bones 346
Tell-It-Yourself 389
Things Fall Apart 289
Thomas Jefferson and Slavery 370
A Tribute to Judith Jamison 104
Using the Storyboard 390
Volunteers without Borders 193
Voting Patterns 347
What If? 177
What's My Line? 63
Who Does the Work? 347
William Lloyd Garrison 64
Words to Live By 65
Work Songs 274
World Races 133

$$ ($25–$50)

An African-American Profile 241
African-American Sculpture 2
African Art and Architecture 4
African Authors 215
African Butterflies and Moths 292
African Culture in the Sea Islands 329
African Dance Styles 95
African Heroes 180
African Homes 5
African Lentils 82
An African Museum 243
African Musical Instruments 251
African Music American Style 252
African Peoples 114
African Riches 115
African Story Swap 384
Alex Haley's Genealogy 107
Animal Express 297
Animal Movies 18
At Home in Africa 352
Backing Police Efforts 181
Banner Bolster 321

Baobab: The Tree of Life 298
Black Autobiography and Biography 44
Black Builders 7
Black Excellence 330
Black Hall of Fame 47
Black Heritage Trivia 140
Black History Calendar 145
Black History Desk Calendar 20
Black History Month Newspaper 183
Black History Stamps 49
A Black History Time Line 147
Black Holidays 153
Black Landmark Ad Campaign 71
Black Mystery 394
The Black Olympian 375
Black on White 220
Bookmarks 20
The Civil War 157
Clasped Hands 23
Cooking for Kwanzaa 86
Corn Rows 322
Crocodile Trains 25
Doll Displays 27
The Door to Awareness 28
Dramatizing the Black Experience 357
Dueling Pianos 260
Early Humans in Africa 304
Elephant Lore 305
Everybody Limbo! 98
The Family Tree 108
Feminist Writers 228
Filming Ancient Africa 164
Freedom Stamps 29
A Friend in Africa 398
George Washington Carver, Inventor 306
Graphing Racial Data 246
Gullah 205
Hats Off to the Abolitionists 52
Health Tips 308
Herbs, Tonics, Teas, and Cures 309
Hieroglyphics 206
Honoring the Past 190
Interpretive Dance 99
Jointed Dolls 31
Joplin Expo 262
Kite Flags 323
The Ku Klux Klan 168
Learning the Colors of Africa 127
Letter-Writing Campaign 399
Liberia 127
Library Scavenger Hunt 170
Life along the Nile 128

Life in a Kenyan Village 129
Maasai Pendants 32
Market Day 362
Melville and Slavery 233
The Moors 130
New Games for Old 33
Origami Animals 34
Out of Africa 341
Patois 265
Peoples of Africa 341
Poetry Workshop 400
Porgy and Bess 266
The Professional Black Athlete 378
Puppet Show 35
Quoting Black Voices 366
Rabbit Ears 387
Race and Controversy 192
Rap Wrap-Up 267
Reading the Black Female Writer 237
Religions of Africa 287
Religious Themes in Negro Spirituals 288
Rhythm of Resistance 268
Schematic Drawings 249
1776 269
The Shotgun House 14
Sing-along 270
Slavery and Negro Spirituals 271
Slavery Diorama 175
Sports Debate 379
Sports on Film 380
Stained Glass Animals 36
Sweets to the Sweet 37
Talk to Me 368
Tapping to Stardom 103
This Ol' Hat 369
Translating Lyrics 214
Two-Feet, Four-Feet, Wings, Fins, Tail 317
Uncle Remus 390
We Shall Overcome 273
Writing Epitaphs 403
Writing Genre 403
You Are There 194
Zoo's Who 317

$$$ ($50-$75)

African Animal Fair 15
African Dessert-a-thon 79
African Ornaments 17
African Rhythm Band 254

An African Window Garden 295
Afrocentrism 197
All Aboard! 136
All-Occasion Cards 18
Band Music 257
Batiking 19
Bean Bag Toss 120
Black Art 6
Black Book Fair 219
The Black Flavor of New Orleans 123
Black History Book Collection 220
Black History in Miniature 146
Black History Time Capsule 147
Black Landmarks 8
Black Music Videos 258
Black Study Group 221
Black Women in the Third World 336
Books for Summer 224
Box Zoo 21
Brainstorming 300
Business Incubator 74
Camp Africa 22
Caribana 97
Choral Music 259
Crafts Clinic 24
Crocheting a Bit of Africa 25
Dance Workshop 98
Design America 26
Designer Mural 10
Each One Teach One 161
Food Clinic 87
Getting the Public's Attention 76
Gourdheads 30
A Handful of Puppets 322
Heritage Jubilee 30
A History of African-American Music 261
Human Relations Report Card 338

Jamaican Specialties 88
Jivin' to the Oldies 100
Moorish Architecture 11
Music Workshop 265
Photo History 109
Photo Map 12
Pieces of Africa 34
Playing the Part 365
Proud Stitches 326
Sign Troupe 102
Soul Food 90
Speaker's Bureau 367
Sports Clinic 379
"Stop the Drugs" Campaign 345
'Toon Time 38
T-shirt Factory 39
Who's Writing News 194
Words and Snapshots 402

$$$$ ($75-$100)

Atlanta-Bound 139
Black Pride Day 333
Campaign Push 394
Native Fashions 325
Photo Tableaux of History 12
Quilted History 110
Read, Read, Read 235

$$$$$ (more than $100)

African-American Plaza 1